Uncommon Wealths in Postcolonial Fiction

# Cross/Cultures

READINGS IN POST/COLONIAL
LITERATURES AND CULTURES IN ENGLISH

*Edited by*

Gordon Collier
Geoffrey Davis
Bénédicte Ledent

*Co-founding editor*

†Hena Maes-Jelinek

VOLUME 201

The titles published in this series are listed at *brill.com/cc*

# Uncommon Wealths in Postcolonial Fiction

*Edited by*

Helga Ramsey-Kurz
Melissa Kennedy

BRILL
RODOPI

LEIDEN | BOSTON

Cover illustration: Anna Steinhäusler, "1 : 1" (2014>), Limoges porcelain with white glazing and brown engobe, height 10 cm × width 12 cm × depth 15 cm. Photo © the artist.

Library of Congress Control Number: 2017957965

Typeface for the Latin, Greek, and Cyrillic scripts: "Brill". See and download: brill.com/brill-typeface.

ISSN 0924-1426
ISBN 978-90-04-35260-5 (hardback)
ISBN 978-90-04-35958-1 (e-book)



This book is printed on acid-free paper and produced in a sustainable manner.

# Table of Contents

# Acknowledgements

MOST OF THE ESSAYS IN THIS COLLECTION started as papers presented at the 2014 Triennial Conference of the European Association for Commonwealth Literature and Language Studies (EACLALS) at the University of Innsbruck, 14–18 April, 2014. Thanks to EACLALS for endorsing the theme "Uncommon Wealths: Riches and Realities" for this conference, and to its members for the many creative and inspiring contributions proving the urgency and potential of engaging in a critical discussion of issues of wealth in the field of postcolonial studies. Thanks also to Professor Judith Eisler for facilitating an exhibition of artwork by students of the Class for Painting and Animation Film at the University of Applied Arts, Vienna, thus giving visual stimulus to our exchanges at Innsbruck.

The cover image of this book, "1 : 1," by the painter and ceramics artist Anna Steinhäusler, features one of the pieces displayed at the exhibition. As its title indicates, the object, a Limoges porcelain cup, unites two cultures, African and European, without merging them. The contrasting characteristics attributed to these cultures are made visible in the material, its texture, and its ornamentation – rough and smooth; matte and shiny; bright and muted; 'traditional' and 'refined'. The European and African halves of the ceramic drinking vessel cannot be regarded in the isolation of their original cultural context. A distinctive difference is maintained, but synergistically and equally, suggesting the promise of an open, global society capable of seeing differences as enrichment and a source of stability and vitality. For the artist, the whole process of creating a cup, side by side with expert artisans, intensifies the sense of dedication, renews respect for everyday yet high-quality objects, and prompts reflection on one's own values and those of society as a whole. "What I consume becomes part of me."

The editors wish to thank the contributors for their efforts and patience during the editing process, the peer-reviewers for their constructive feedback, and Gordon Collier for his unmatched editorial advice, encouragement, wit, and hours of legwork.

# Introduction

## *Uncommon Wealths in Postcolonial Fiction*

Helga Ramsey-Kurz and Melissa Kennedy

The historical fact of empire is the incontrovertible *raison d'être* of postcolonial studies. Less commonly acknowledged by the discipline, however, is the capitalist drive for profit that lies at the heart of empire. The lack of attention to wealth is surprising, given that the enormous gains yielded by the colonial enterprise were, and still are, far from invisible. In assembling essays by postcolonial literary critics who address the concept of wealth depicted in fiction, this collection fleshes out a terrain of great potential. The task of 'following the money' which takes place in these essays not only illuminates the history of wealth, in colonial extraction of labour and resources, accumulation, and circulation, but also maps the transformation from colonial to neocolonial and neoliberal forms of capitalism in which modern-day divisions of 'haves' and 'have-nots' clearly follow those of the colonial period. Even so, postcolonial scholars have eschewed inquiry into what, in their view, is a typically Western and intrinsically capitalistic ambition, highlighting instead unique, culture-specific structures of social value and modes of exchange. In keeping with their commitment to challenging received (Western) accounts of success and progress, critics have focused on the damage caused by colonization. This has directed attention away from the winners of the European race for overseas territories, and the wealth these contained, to its victims: the colonized as well as their offspring, generations still afflicted by a legacy of long-term exploitation, dispossession, and subjugation. The project of giving voice and visibility to the casualties of capitalism has moved subalternity and abjection as intrinsically postcolonial configurations of poverty to the centre of postcolonial discourse and practically eclipsed the beneficiaries of imperialist expansion. Despite its rootedness in Marxist critique, postcolonial discourse has thus omitted to document and study affluence not only as an expected but also as an *actual* and lasting outcome of colonial domination.

To be sure, as the gap between rich and poor is seen to be widening, in both the richest nations of the world, such as the USA and, say, Germany and in the developing world, including China, India, Nigeria, and South Africa,[1] postcolonial analysis may for the first time be aligned with the mainstream rather than with the marginalized. Yet its emphasis on local resistances to and negotiations of imperialism's ideologies has held back inquiry into the global pervasiveness of capitalism and the appropriation of capitalist social relations into pre-existing cultural practices and social hierarchies. In tacitly upholding received assumptions of a capitalist West (or North) hoarding enormous riches in its metropolises, the discipline resists engaging with the presence of moneyed elites in all parts of the world and analysing their local and transregional, national and international influence. A focus on wealth and the wealthy further reveals the validity of reintroducing the concept of class into the discourse of exploitation and thus correcting the impression of its obsolescence that postcolonial critique's concentration on the *cultural* specificity of socio-economic inequality has produced.

The ground for such shifts of focus in postcolonial analysis has been well prepared by such emphatic critics of neoliberalism as Noam Chomsky, Mike Davis, Nancy Fraser, Stuart Hall, David Harvey, Doreen Massey, Ellen Meiksins Wood, Michael Rustin, Saskia Sassen, and Joseph Stiglitz.[2] It is not surprising that most of these critics are based in the USA and that many of them have a special interest in global cities as sites of capital accumulation. The very concreteness of wealth concentration in urban spaces enables a way of thinking about affluence

[1] See, for example, Thomas Piketty, *Capital in the Twenty-first Century*, tr. Arthur Goldhammer (*Le capital au XXI siècle*, 2013; Cambridge MA: Harvard UP/Belknap Press, 2014).

[2] See Noam Chomsky, from *Profit over People: Neoliberalism and Global Order* (New York: Seven Stories, 1999) to *Requiem for the American Dream: The Principles of Concentrated Wealth and Power*, ed. Peter Hutchinson et al. (New York: Seven Stories, 2017); *Evil Paradises: Dreamworlds of Neoliberalism*, ed. Mike Davis & Daniel Bertrand Monk (New York: New Press, 2008); Nancy Fraser, *Scales of Justice: Reimagining Political Space in a Globalizing World* (New York: Columbia UP, 2009); Stuart Hall, "The Neo-Liberal Revolution," *Cultural Studies* 25.6 (2011): 705–28; Stuart Hall, Doreen Massey & Michael Rustin, *After Neoliberalism?: The Kilburn Manifesto* (London: Lawrence & Wishart, 2015); David Harvey, *The Enigma of Capital and the Crises of Capitalism* (London: Profile, 2010); Ellen Meiksins Wood, *Empire of Capital* (New York: Verso, 2003); Saskia Sassen, *Expulsions: Brutality and Complexity in the Global Economy* (Cambridge MA: Harvard UP/Belknap Press, 2014); Joseph Stiglitz, *The Great Divide: Unequal Societies and What We Can Do About Them* (New York: W.W. Norton, 2015) and *Freefall: America, Free Markets, and the Sinking of the World Economy* (New York: W.W. Norton, 2010).

that resists the routine mystification of extreme prosperity by the media. This is reflected in the work of the geographers Iain Hay and Jonathan Beaverstock, authors of the 2016 *Handbook on Wealth and the Super-Rich*.[3] Already in 2004, four years prior to the global financial crisis, Beaverstock warned that social and economic polarization had become so acute that scholarship on serious affluence could no longer be delayed. "It seems we currently know more about the poor than the groups who most benefit from global processes of capital accumulation," he wrote, adding that "there is now a pressing need for studies that explore how global networks work to the advantage of the very wealthy."[4] In so doing, he identified the need for a discussion of economic inequality that addresses excessive riches and enormous wealth, as well as poverty, as matters of grave concern. However, such concern has still not fully crystallized, despite the steady proliferation of media reports on the growing share of national wealth held by the richest one percent; on the increasing number of billionaires from developing countries added to the Forbes Rich list; or on the escalating bonuses of executives in multinational companies, including banks and financial institutions bailed out by the tax-payer in 2008. In a global economy dependent on people's longing for prosperity, wealth accumulation – however extreme – seems to remain a goal virtually impossible to contest.

All the more subversive are literary texts seeking to do just that. While postcolonial critical discourse has neglected to document and study affluence and its role in colonial and neocolonial domination, much postcolonial fiction closely describes, almost always critically, the mechanics of money-making, labour, and exchange that produce and maintain hierarchies of wealth and its corollary, immiseration. In the process, such fiction also reflects on the deceptive conspicuousness of material wealth, which belies the actual intangibility of riches and the great lengths to which the rich go to conceal and protect their possessions. Symptomatically, the (in)visibility of wealth and the resultant difficulty of imaginatively representing it are a preoccupation of many of the writers of fiction analysed in this collection. They highlight the great contradiction of our times – that the wealth that epitomizes, motivates, and, indeed, drives neoliberal capitalism is, in its substance, evanescent: multi-national, multi-billion-dollar deals are signed behind closed doors, financial trade occurs through silent, instantaneous electronic transfers, and the lack of banking transparency

---

[3] Iain Hay & Jonathan V. Beaverstock, *Handbook on Wealth and the Super-Rich* (New York: Edward Elgar, 2016).

[4] Jonathan V. Beaverstock, Philip Hubbard & John Rennie Short, "Getting Away With It?: Exposing the Geographies of the Super-Rich," *Geoforum* 35 (2004): 406.

lends anonymity to off-shore account-holders and owners of shell companies. Essays in this collection work to shed light on processes of deliberate obfuscation of wealth as well as on the social conventions dictating how the rich in different cultures flaunt, spend, and distribute their fortunes. Such analysis is crucial for unveiling the structures of power and underlying ideologies that sustain capitalism's hegemony and engender widespread belief in its achievements and benefits. The focus is also timely, given the recent explosion of visual representations, both mainstream Western and postcolonial, of capital and its owners, offering insights into contemporary neoliberal uses and abuses of money.[5]

Postcolonial fiction has here been ahead of critical scholarship in trying to give visibility to wealth and the wealthy. More often than not, it has done so by explicitly framing the poor as possessing acute vision and perfect understanding of the superiority displayed by the rich whom their gaze captures. Probably one of the most chilling examples is Salman Rushdie's clown Shalimar stalking the wealthy and powerful Max Ophuls, waiting for the right moment to assassinate him. There is something wrong, other characters in the novel find, with Shalimar's "watchful stare" – "it was like being watched by a vulture or carrion crow. It was like being watched by Death himself."[6] What Rushdie's novel allows the reader to (mis)take for a poor man's resentment exacerbated by political fanaticism (Shalimar works for various jihadi organizations) is rendered as pure frustration of the dispossessed at social injustice in Mohsin Hamid's satirical 'self-help' novel *How to Get Filthy Rich in Rising Asia* (2013). Hamid has his narrator "watch the stares that follow a luxury SUV as it muscles its way down a narrow road" and reflect on

> a rising tide of frustration and anger and violence, born partly of the greater familiarity the poor today have with the rich, their faces pressed to that clear window on wealth afforded by ubiquitous television.[7]

Hamid thus claims, or perhaps warns of, the danger of wealth made visible – a notion also expressed by the United Nations President Jim Yong Kim, who, in a speech he gave in 2014, claimed that television, the internet, and mobile tech-

---

[5] See, for example, post-Crash journalism, such as Chrystia Freeland's *Plutocrats: The Rise of the New Global Super-Rich* (London: Penguin, 2012); multiple television documentaries on billionaire life-styles, such as the BBC's *The Super-Rich and Us*, dir. Jacques Peretti (London, 2015), and films, including *The Wolf of Wall Street*, dir. Martin Scorsese (Hollywood: Paramount Pictures, 2013).

[6] Salman Rushdie, *Shalimar the Clown* (2006; London: Penguin Vintage, 2015): 250.

[7] Mohsin Hamid, *How to Get Filthy Rich in Rising Asia* (London: Hamish Hamilton, 2013): 205–206.

nology have brought new levels of global awareness to the poor: "What's new in today's world is that the best-kept secret from the poor, namely, how the rich live, is now out." Like Hamid, Kim equates "awareness" with social unrest and "political turbulence [...] rooted in this one new feature of today's world."[8]

The similarity of the points made by Hamid and Kim testifies to the close proximity between fictional and non-fictional appraisals of wealth inequality and, as several contributors in this collection show, it is this proximity that lends particular relevance, if not urgency, to the study of literary configurations of wealth. The title *Uncommon Wealths* under which the studies assembled here have been conducted offers itself to multiple interpretations. First, it quite literally registers the ongoing economic priority in ensuring the common wealth of empire in the postcolonial Commonwealth of Nations, to which fifty-two former British colonies belong. The title further gestures at the unconventional or non-Western, the unusual, even fictitious. At the same time, the attribute 'uncommon' may be understood as connoting privately or exclusively owned wealth, in contrast to a shared common good. The plural form of 'wealth' ('wealths') stresses the diversity of the approaches gathered in this volume, which has been put together in the awareness that a conversation about wealth must begin not by striving for consensus, but by allowing quite different vantage points to prepare the ground for a wider recognition of phenomena of wealth and its unevenness across commonwealth spaces (alternatively labelled core and periphery, First- and Third-World, developed and developing countries, the West and the Rest, the North and the Global South).

Still, the individual essays are similarly positioned in a search for real possibilities for future change and the ambition to bring to the social sciences the specific insights encoded in postcolonial literature by way of aesthetic transformation and critical reconstruction of historical realities. They agree that finding such alternatives entails conceptualizations of wealth beyond the dominant materialistic notion, to also embrace the common, the shared, and the affective. At the same time, the contributions to the present volume are aware of fiction's curious affinities with other forms of speculation, including those of investment for material profit. The distinctly postcolonial sensitivity to exploitation as well as to the social, political, and economic processes productive of global and local wealth inequalities lends cohesion to a body of critical texts otherwise marked

---

[8] "Speech by World Bank Group President Jim Yong Kim at Council on Foreign Relations: 'Count on Us'," 1 April 2014, http://www.worldbank.org/en/news/speech/2014/04/01/speech-world-bank-group-president-jim-yong-kim-council-on-foreign-relations (accessed 26 October 2016). See also Alex Wanjala's quotation from this speech in his essay in this collection (114).

by the wealth of research interests established in postcolonial literary criticism today. *Uncommon Wealths in Postcolonial Fiction* covers a broad range of these, from indigenous to immigrant writing, from questions of race, ethnicity, and gender to questions of ecological justice and cultural heritage, from dominant discourses of growth to alternative models of degrowth.

The first group of essays, placed under the heading 'Aesthetics of Wealth', consciously steer away from orthodox postcolonial readings of poverty and make a point of concentrating on literary renderings of wealth for wealth's sake. Concerned with nuances of textualities, they open investigation into the potentialities of aesthetics, showing how literature evacuates dominant ideas of wealth (or, for that matter, of labour as a form of wealth-creation) from material reality to the realm of fiction, infusing them with new meaning by aesthetic transformation. Fiction thereby becomes a site of speculation that is profoundly enabling, in that it clarifies in writing as yet unvoiced intuitions about (well) being. The beginning is made by NEIL LAZARUS, who, in his essay "Into Our Labours," performs exemplary close readings of passages from Lao She's *Rickshaw,* Anita Desai's *The Village by the Sea*, Yang Jiang's *A Cadre School Life: Six Chapters*, Seamus Heaney's "Digging," Maxim Gorky's *My Universities*, and Knut Hamsun's *Hunger* to extract a social phenomenology of work crystallizing at two epochal moments in the history of world literature: that of the 'worlding' of modernity, with its experiences of modernization, commodity production, and wage labour, and the more contemporary moment of the experience of globalization. Paying special attention to representations of mental labour and to literary texts as commodities, the essay examines how rhetorical richness facilitates an aesthetic mediation between socially separated forms of work. From Lazarus' panoramic opening, the chapters by HELGA RAMSEY–KURZ and SANDHYA SHETTY shift to the workings of individual texts and their recuperation of past wealths. Ramsey–Kurz revisits Michael Ondaatje's novel *In the Skin of a Lion* and exposes the enduring blindness of critics to the complex portrayals Ondaatje offers of Toronto's economic elites. Drawing on Nancy Fraser's work on cultural and social injustice, she demonstrates how these portrayals and the politics of seeing underlying them invite a reading of Ondaatje's novel as a critique of economic inequality which literature is unable to remedy. Somewhat more optimistically, Shetty's essay "Spartan Luxury" examines how Amit Chaudhuri's novel *A Strange and Sublime Address* revokes the genteel, unhurried Calcutta of the 1970s and, with the richness of everyday life in the city's "small houses, unlovely and unremarkable" at the time, creates an artful, even dissident materiality, thereby enabling an imaginary withdrawal from the deeply troubling transformations Calcutta has since undergone from the impact of global neoliberalism.

The second group of essays, 'Historical Wealth and Material Injustice', focuses on historical processes of impoverishment and enrichment and their documentation in literature. Their authors are interested in the 'greater truth' literary fiction tells about wealth by way of contesting official historiography. In comprehending wealth as, in the first place, a motivation for and product of exploitation and indexing literary representations of wealth accordingly, they assign to them a place in the postcolonial archive of colonial injustices. In so doing, they exemplify the productiveness of bringing socio-economic discourse to bear on postcolonial readings of literature. "Writing Congo" by HELEN TIFFIN argues that the Congo has been an area of uncommon material wealth, such that the abuse of the Congolese under King Leopold's notorious fiefdom is being continued today by the multinational corporations that extract Congolese materials by inhumane labour practices for the manufacture of electronic devices. This explains why, in the Western imaginary, the Congo remains a source of 'uncommonwealth', frequently written, or significantly influenced, by outsiders. Thus, from Joseph Conrad's *Heart of Darkness* to survivor narratives set against the 1994 Rwandan genocide, persisting tropes and images continue to circulate in Western literature as well as to re-project into traditionally oral cultures, influencing African/Congolese self-perceptions and potentially also the events that shape these. CHERYL STOBIE and ALEX WANJALA address contemporary phenomena of social inequality in their readings of Zakes Mda's *Black Diamond* (2009) and Lebogang Matseke's debut novel, *Queen B.E.E.* (2015), and Stanley Gazemba's *The Stone Hills of Maragoli*, respectively: the recent emergence of well-educated, professional black suburbanites, popularly known as 'black diamonds', enabled by the South African government's policy of Black Economic Empowerment (BEE), on the one hand, and the persistence of extreme poverty in rural Kenya in the face of official assertions of the country's booming economy, on the other. Both essays consider the stances to work, equity, and freedom adopted in the novels treated and assess the extent to which their authors posit a fairer future for their countries. DAVID WATERMAN's chapter on "Neoliberalism, Water Scarcity, and Common Wealth" concentrates above all on the ruthless individualism to which the narrator-protagonist of Mohsin Hamid's *How to Get Filthy Rich in Rising Asia* ironically appeals and the cancellation of any social conscience which it ultimately implies. The essay exposes the futility of what the protagonist constantly seeks to justify as self-help when a neoliberal economy comes to be faced with large-scale ecological disasters, such as a drastic shortage of drinking water.

Apart from registering the sociological impact of capitalism on its victims, the essays assembled under the rubric 'Indigenous Common Wealths' encourage recognition of the empowering capacity of Indigenous knowledges and economic practices as alternatives to capitalist epistemology. Taking seriously the universal validity of Indigenous models of wealth creation and distribution as expressed also in Aboriginal fictions, the essays dare to take a moral (rather than a moralizing) position in favour of Indigenous ethical authority as one capable of forging vital new ways of conceiving of wealth and its relevance to individual and collective wellbeing. Thus, SNEJA GUNEW posits a moral imperative to explore the uncommon wealth of those who have been excluded from globalization, and argues for an Indigenous cosmopolitanism in order to enable the aboriginal inhabitants of global empires to assert their rights and thereby decolonize their own history. Turning to the work of the Australian Aboriginal writers Kim Scott (*That Deadman Dance*) and Alexis Wright (*Carpentaria*), and the Canadian Cree writer Tomson Highway (*Kiss of the Fur Queen*), she demonstrates how literary texts are already contributing to this project. SHEILA COLLINGWOOD–WHITTICK's essay effectively backs Gunew's claim of a moral imperative by examining the despoliation of Australia's natural environment as a recurrent leitmotif in both Indigenous and non-Indigenous Australian literature and the representation of 'country' as the matrix of Aboriginal wealth and well-being in both fictional and autobiographical texts by authors such as Kim Scott, Alexis Wright, and Sally Morgan. GEOFF RODOREDA continues the reflection on land and land ownership and also locates the need for a conceptual change. To this end, his essay "Weal/th in the Land" departs from the long-standing *terra nullius* debate and considers the ways in which both Indigenous and non-Indigenous writers, notably Kate Grenville and Kim Scott, as well as geographers, historians, and archaeologists, are (re)writing histories of Indigenous land-use and re-interpreting what the journals of colonial-era explorers say about Aboriginal conceptions of the land as a common *weal* rather than as *wealth*. Adopting the views of Serge Latouche and Maurizio Pallante, who refute the viability of the growth-based capitalist system introduced to the 'New World' by European colonization, PAOLA DELLA VALLE analyses degrowth concepts in Māori cultural practices and business models, particularly through novels by and about Māori: Patricia Grace's *Potiki* and *Dogside Story*, Noel Hilliard's *Maori Girl*, *Power of Joy*, *Maori Woman*, and *The Glory and the Dream*, and Roderick Finlayson's *Brown Man's Burden* and *Our Life in This Land*.

The essays in the final section, 'The Location of Wealth in Culture', move away from the classic postcolonial theme of land ownership to discuss trajectories leading to completely different forms of possession frequently overlooked or buried in cultural norms. While arguing for recognition of the extent to which contemporary Western culture is – often literally – indebted to capitalism's structures and implicit ideology, they highlight above all positive new structures of belonging to family, nation, and culture contained in the affective topographies mapped by the authors and artists they study. Retracing the uncommon lines of affiliation and alienation drawn by these writers, they arrive at novel ways of seeing that literally and metaphorically locate wealth. Examining three recent representations of transcultural adoption, JOHN MCLEOD reflects on the centrality of wealth and its lack to both family-making and -breaking: Martin Sixsmith's *The Lost Child of Philomena Lee* (2009), Stephen Frears's film adaptation *Philomena*, and Caryl Phillips's recent novel *The Lost Child* (2015). McLeod's analyses focus on the works' exposure of the contradictory terms in which the identities of birth-mothers and their children are costed in the adoption process and the devastating consequences this has on their later lives. Routes and roots of a different kind are central to FRANCESCO CATTANI's essay on the 'Grand Tours' staged by the black-British writers and artists Caryl Phillips, Bernardine Evaristo, Keith Piper, and Yinka Shonibare, in the novels *The European Tribe* and *Soul Tourists*, and in the installations *A Fictional Tourist in Europe* and *Gallantry and Criminal Conversation*, respectively. It demonstrates how all four texts choreograph a collision between colour and whiteness, between those who have 'always belonged' and those who have 'newly arrived', questioning homogenizing accounts of what makes up European heritage and its common cultural wealth. EVA-MARIA MÜLLER's text also dwells on continental Europe, yet expands its geographical scope by comparing the oral storytelling legend of Frau Hitt, one of the most prominent and storied peaks in Austria's Tyrol region, with the nineteenth-century Romantic imaginary of the Alps captured in the British Alpine Club co-founder Leslie Stephen's 1871 *Playground of Europe*, in Angie Abdou's *The Canterbury Trail* (2011), and in Elfriede Jelinek's *In den Alpen* (2002). Müller submits that these contemporary texts work against the imperialist imagery surrounding mountain travel by exposing the overcrowding of alpine regions, unearthing the violent history that emptied mountains of local communities, and demonstrating that mountain regions with extensive tourism have become emptied of life through their participation in the money-making industry. "How to Be Rich, Popular, and Have It All" by MELISSA KENNEDY, finally, examines upward mobility from poverty to wealth as portrayed in several post-crisis novels. The fictions stress the difficulty of identifying the mechanics of wealth creation and, concomitantly, the reluctance to give up on the unlikely dream that ambition, hard work, and intelligence will lead to economic improvement. Kennedy identifies this imaginative lacuna not only in postcolonial fiction but also as embedded in media genres and cultural expression in the developed, Western world, a world that, despite the 2008 crisis, has so far failed to shape a new narrative of success that is not capitalist and materialistically aspirational in nature.

## Works Cited

Beaverstock, Jonathan V., Philip Hubbard & John Rennie Short. "Getting Away With It?: Exposing the Geographies of the Super-Rich," *Geoforum* 35 (2004): 402–407.

Chomsky, Noam. *Profit over People: Neoliberalism and Global Order* (New York: Seven Stories, 1999).

Chomsky, Noam. *Requiem for the American Dream: The Principles of Concentrated Wealth and Power*, ed. Peter Hutchinson et al. (New York: Seven Stories, 2017).

Davis, Mike, & Daniel Bertrand Monk, ed. *Evil Paradises: Dreamworlds of Neoliberalism* (New York: New Press, 2008).

Fraser, Nancy. *Scales of Justice: Reimagining Political Space in a Globalizing World* (New York: Columbia UP, 2009).

Freeland, Chrystia. *Plutocrats: The Rise of the New Global Super-Rich* (London: Penguin, 2012).

Hall, Stuart. "The Neo-Liberal Revolution," *Cultural Studies* 25.6 (2011): 705–28.

Hall, Stuart, Doreen Massey & Michael Rustin. *After Neoliberalism?: The Kilburn Manifesto* (London: Lawrence & Wishart, 2015).

Hamid, Mohsin. *How to Get Filthy Rich in Rising Asia* (London: Hamish Hamilton, 2013).

Harvey, David. *The Enigma of Capital and the Crises of Capitalism* (London: Profile, 2010).

Hay, Iain, & Jonathan V. Beaverstock. *Handbook on Wealth and the Super-Rich* (New York: Edward Elgar, 2016).

Meiksins Wood, Ellen. *Empire of Capital* (New York: Verso, 2003).

Peretti, Jacques. *The Super-Rich and Us* (London: BBC, 2015)

Piketty, Thomas. *Capital in the Twenty-first Century*, tr. Arthur Goldhammer (*Le capital au XXI siècle*, 2013; Cambridge MA: Harvard UP/Belknap Press, 2014).

Rushdie, Salman. *Shalimar the Clown* (2006; London: Penguin Vintage, 2015).

Sassen, Saskia. *Expulsions: Brutality and Complexity in the Global Economy* (Cambridge MA: Harvard UP/Belknap Press, 2014).

Scorsese, Martin. *The Wolf of Wall Street* (Hollywood: Paramount Pictures, USA 2013; 180 min.).

Stiglitz, Joseph. *Freefall: America, Free Markets, and the Sinking of the World Economy* (New York: W.W. Norton, 2010).

Stiglitz, Joseph. *The Great Divide: Unequal Societies and What We Can Do About Them* (New York: W.W. Norton, 2015).

Yong Kim, Jim. "Speech by World Bank Group President at Council on Foreign Relations: 'Count on Us'" (1 April 2014), http://www.worldbank.org/en/news/speech/

2014/04/01/speech-world-bank-group-president-jim-yong-kim-council-on-foreign-relations (accessed 26 October 2016).

❄

# I ❄

# Aesthetics of Wealth

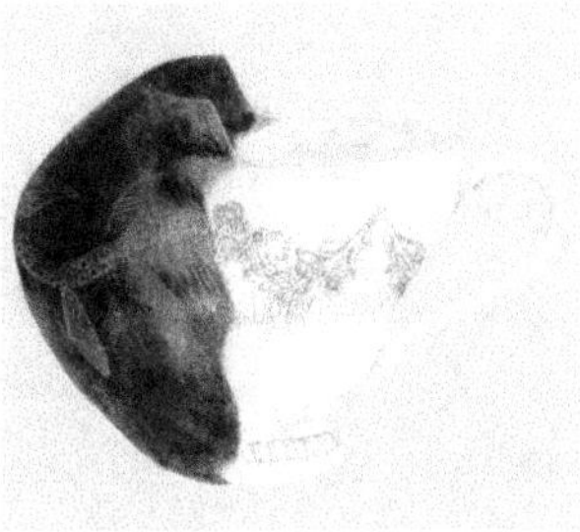

# Into Our Labours

## *Work and Literary Form in World Literature*

NEIL LAZARUS

FREDRIC JAMESON BEGINS the long concluding chapter of his book *Postmodernism or, The Cultural Logic of Late Capitalism* by observing that many critics of his celebrated 1984 essay on postmodernism seem to him "to [have] confuse[d] taste […] analysis, and evaluation" – "three things," he says, that he "would have thought we had some interest in keeping separate."[1] The definitions that he then proposes of these three separable forms of critical practice are very suggestive, and would certainly repay careful consideration. But it is his conceptualization of the second of them – analysis –that bears directly on what I want to explore in this essay. There is some circularity in Jameson's formulation, unfortunately: he writes that he takes analysis "to be that peculiar and rigorous conjuncture of formal and historical analysis that constitutes the specific task of literary and cultural study." The word 'analysis' appears both as what is being defined and in the definition itself. But this momentary clumsiness need not detain us unduly: what is being suggested is that the *differentia specifica* of 'literary and cultural study' consist in the conjoining of 'formal and historical' inquiry; and it follows from this that one of our central objectives as literary critics – perhaps our single central objective – ought to be to "investigat[e] […] the historical conditions of possibility of specific forms" (297). Historical analysis; formal analysis: Jameson believes that these 'perspectives' are not merely to be fused or brought into simultaneous alliance but are, rather, 'inseparable'. (With beguiling indirection, he adds that these 'twin perspectives' were 'often thought to be irreconcilable or incommensurable in the past': he knows, of course, that they are just as often and as tendentiously thought to be irreconcilable or incommensurable *today*; I take it that his

[1] Fredric Jameson, *Postmodernism or, The Cultural Logic of Late Capitalism* (Durham NC: Duke UP, 1995): 298. Further page references (after *Postmodernism*) are in the main text.

indirection here is tactical, predicated on the suspicion that to state this truth without varnish would be to risk offending readers whose formalist commitments remain altogether – and, indeed, militantly – free of any historicist sensibility.)

So, what exactly would literary scholarship that plausibly conjoined historical and formal analysis look like? In the renewed discussion of 'world literature' today, the work of Roberto Schwarz has rightly been seen as exemplary in just this respect. In *A Master on the Periphery of Capitalism*, his study of Machado de Assis's 1880 novel *The Posthumous Memoirs of Brás Cubas*, Schwarz argues that the work's "Babel of literary mannerisms," the heterogeneity and bewildering multiplicity of its juxtapositions of narrative form and style, is to be read neither as inconsistency nor as baroque exhibition, but as a figuration of the contradictoriness of the Brazilian social order in the later-nineteenth century, "slave-owning and bourgeois at the same time."[2] The sheer *volubility* of Machado's prose is itself the point here. Schwarz draws our attention to "the profusion and crucial nature of the relationships implied in the rhythm of Machado's prose, and the extraordinary contrasts between the voices orchestrated in its truly complex music" (16) in order to suggest that what might seem at first – and especially to a metropolitan reader – excess or superfluity is in fact "intensified realism" (73), more 'realistic', actually, than the Romantic, nationalist endeavours of such contemporaries of Machado's as José de Alencar.

In *A Master on the Periphery of Capitalism*, Schwarz describes his own methodology as an extension to the cultural field of the arguments that had been advanced by the members of a group of scholars of his teachers' generation at the University of São Paulo, who "used to meet to study *Capital* with a view to understanding Brazil":

> This group had reached the daring conclusion that the classic marks of Brazilian backwardness should be studied not as an archaic leftover but as an integral part of the way modern society reproduces itself, or in other words, as evidence of a perverse form of progress. For the historian of culture and the critic of the arts in countries like ours, ex-colonies, this thesis has an enormous power to stimulate and deprovincialize, for it allows us to inscribe on the present-day international situation, in polemical form, much of what seemed to distance us from it and confine us to irrelevance. (3)

---

[2] Roberto Schwarz, *A Master on the Periphery of Capitalism: Machado de Assis*, tr. John Gledson (*Um Mestre na Periferia do Capitalismo: Machado de Assis*, 1990; Durham NC: Duke UP, 2001): 17, 3. Further page references are in the main text.

Hence Schwarz's argument that the aesthetic of *The Posthumous Memoirs of Brás Cubas* is not simply *uneven* – "fractured" (158), its constituent elements uneasily juxtaposed, concatenated, imposed one upon the other – but also *combinatory*, its elements telescoped and accordionized. This marks the difference between Machado and his contemporaries, and also between the early Machado and Machado from the *Memoirs* onwards:

> When Machado in his first phase retreated from the so-called contemporary terrain and practically excluded the new and critical discourse of individual freedoms and the right to self-fulfillment from his novels, he was fleeing from the false position in which liberal ideology and the conspicuous virtues of progress found themselves in the Brazilian context. Once this position of discernment is established, it will permit him, from the *Memoirs* on, to reintroduce the presumptions of modernity, only now explicitly marked by belittlement and dislocation, as was demanded by the circumstances. (158)

The volubility of the *Memoirs* bespeaks neither marginalization nor restriction, nor the pseudo-universality of a dominant discourse that imagines itself to be unisonant, but, rather, the accordionized combination of all aspects of Brazilian sociality: the work's volubility "squeezes" these contradictory aspects, Schwarz writes,

> stretches them, and explores them in every direction, in any way it pleases. In other words, we have a firework display of a caricatured universal culture, a kind of down-market universality, in the best Brazilian tradition, in which Brás Cubas's caprice takes as its province the total experience of humanity and makes itself absolute. *It is no longer a passing tendency, psychological or stylistic, but a rigorous principle, placed above everything else, and that therefore is exposed, and can be appreciated all along the line.* This universalization establishes the axis that gives ideological power to the *Memoirs*. (18; italics in original)

No wonder, then, that a novel of the 1880s can appear to a present-day reader as anticipating the dislocated and absurd worlds of Eastern and Central Europe conjured up in the writing of the early decades of the twentieth century by such authors as Kafka and Musil.

Closer to home, we find another critic whose thinking about literary form in historical perspective is particularly noteworthy. In his essay "Notes on English Prose 1780–1950," Raymond Williams writes of Dickens, for instance, that "the most important thing to say about [him] [...] is not that he is writing in a new way, but that he is experiencing in a new way, and that this is the substance of his language."[3] In Dickens's work, he continues,

> the scale and nature of the change break through the composed forms and set out in new ways. [...] We can then see more clearly what Dickens is doing: altering, transforming a whole way of writing, rather than putting an old style at a new experience. It is not the method of the more formal novelists, including the sounds of measured or occasional speech in a solid frame of analysis and settled exposition. Rather, it is a speaking, persuading, directing voice, of a new kind, which has taken over the narrative, the exposition, the analysis, in a single operation. Here, there, everywhere: the restless production of a seemingly chaotic detail; the hurrying, pressing, miscellaneous clauses, with here a gap to push through, there a restless pushing at repeated obstacles, everywhere a crowding of objects, forcing attention; the prose, in fact, of a new order of experience; the prose of the city. It is not only disturbance; it is also a new kind of settlement. (93–94)

Jameson's own work might also be cited in these terms, for he, too, has been concerned very significantly with the relations between capitalist modernity and literary form. Recall, if you will, his repeated statement of the centrality of combined and uneven development for any understanding of modernism. The terms of his meta-commentary here are well known:

> Modernism must [...] be seen as uniquely corresponding to an uneven moment of social development, or to what Ernst Bloch called the 'simultaneity of the nonsimultaneous,' the 'synchronicity of the non-synchronous'.[4]

Less often cited are his many profound readings of individual modernist writers, works, and situations that collectively underpin and light up the general formulations.[5]

In the concluding chapter of *Postmodernism*, in a section entitled "Notes Toward a Theory of the Modern," Jameson calls for "a comparative sociology of modernism and its cultures." Such a sociology, he says –

---

[3] Raymond Williams, *Writing in Society* (London: Verso, 1991): 91. Further page references (after *Writing*) are in the main text.

[4] Jameson, *Postmodernism*, 315.

[5] In just one of these, from "Secondary Elaborations," Jameson writes of modernist literary production in its historical context, and presents its peculiar power as a function not of its radical modernity but, on the contrary, of its relative backwardness. Here, modernism "gives off a message that has little to do with the content of the individual works: it is the aesthetic as sheer autonomy, as the satisfactions of handicraft transfigured" (*Postmodernism*, 307).

> which like Weber's remained committed to measuring the extraordinary impact of capitalism on hitherto traditional cultures, the social and psychic damage done to now irrevocable older forms of human life and perception – would alone offer an adequate framework for rethinking 'modernism' today, provided it worked both sides of the street and dug its tunnel from both directions; one must, in other words, not only deduce modernism from modernization, but also scan the sedimented traces of modernization within the aesthetic work itself. (304)

This formulation might be taken to ground the research that I have been engaged in recently, and that follows on from the collectively written WReC (Warwick Research Collective) volume, *Combined and Uneven Development* (2015).[6] The overarching ambition of this work is to contribute to the formulation of a new comparativist approach in literary studies today. In a new project, I have begun to explore the social phenomenology of work as it finds literary representation in different locations across the world system from the mid-nineteenth century to the present. The transformation of the nature of work, and the identification of the effects of this transformation on social consciousness, has obviously been a central feature of writing across the range of the past 150 years, from Gaskell, Flaubert, and Melville to Panait Istrati, Mulk Raj Anand, and Agnes Smedley, and on to Bessie Head, Lawrence Joseph, and Aravind Adiga. By examining how work in its multiple and changing modes is formally registered in literary works, my intention is to take further the argument advanced in the WReC volume, that 'world literature' is literature that registers the human experience of capitalist modernity.

A specifically literary contribution to the cultural history of work, the new project, which I have provisionally entitled *Into Our Labours*, will examine the literary encoding of two aspects of the 'worlding' of modernity. These two aspects are interlinked – indeed, they are both part of the same world-historical process – but they are perhaps analytically distinguishable. First is an 'inaugural' moment linked to the experience of modernization, commodity-production, and wage labour. Much celebrated literary writing has lingered significantly on the moment when commodification achieves sufficient density to become the organizing principle of society and to insinuate itself into the fabric of everyday life, becoming visible as the uncanny colonizer of consciousness and the puzzling substrate of 'common sense'. We might plausibly label this body of work 'modernist', it seems to me, but only if we stop thinking of it as being

6 WReC (Warwick Research Collective), *Combined and Uneven Development: Towards a New Theory of World-Literature* (Liverpool: Liverpool UP, 2015).

geographically or historically discrete in these terms: there is no reason to start with, or to stop at, Baudelaire, Döblin, Hamsun, or Scott Fitzgerald, for instance; such other writers as Wang Anyi, Ayi Kwei Armah, Abdul Rahman Munif, and Arundhati Roy will enable us to make the arguments we need to make just as well, and in some respects even better. The second moment is then that governed by the experience of capitalist development in its consolidation, regularization, and global dispersal. Again, there is a lot of celebrated writing that has been concerned to find formal means by which to capture and question the experiences corresponding to this development: I am thinking here not only of the work of such contemporary writers as Thomas Pynchon, Rana Dasgupta, Monica Ali, Jamaica Kincaid, Victor Pelevin, Carlos Fuentes, Pepetela, Yuri Andrukhovych, and Roberto Bolaño but of their many nineteenth- and early-twentieth-century precursors, among them Zola, Mallarmé, Conrad, Upton Sinclair, and Pío Baroja.

In alignment with Schwarz's enigmatic definition of form as "the abstract of social relations,"[7] my ambition is to seek to determine the relation between changing modes of work and transformations in the forms, genres, and aesthetic strategies of the literary writing that seeks to describe, represent or bear witness to these changes. The *literary* registration of the vast historical process of 'development' or 'modernization' sometimes makes itself known to us through a crisis of representation, as the forms of space- and time-consciousness demanded by life in contexts in which the commodity has become the dominant social form are counterposed with inherited ways of seeing and knowing, now under acute pressure, if not already obsolete. The divide between 'old' and 'new', between urban and land-based forms of consciousness is acutely registered in Lao She's *Rickshaw*, for instance. The narrator tells us that when 'Camel' Hsiang Tzu (Xiangzi) first arrives in Shanghai, "he was a country boy and not like the city folks who hear the wind and expect the rain."[8] Very quickly, however, Hsiang Tzu's sensibilities are remoulded in accordance with the rigours of life in the city. What Lao She deplores as 'individualism' is nothing other than the social logic corresponding to capitalist urbanism:

> Rumors, truths – Hsiang Tzu seemed to have forgotten the farmer's life he once led. He didn't much care if the fighting ruined the crops and didn't pay much attention to the presence or absence of spring rain. All he was concerned about was his rickshaw; his rickshaw could produce

---

[7] Roberto Schwarz, *Misplaced Ideas: Essays on Brazilian Culture*, ed. John Gledson (London: Verso, 1992): 53.

[8] Lao She, *Rickshaw*, tr. Jean M. James (1937; Honolulu: U of Hawai'i P, 1979): 12.

> wheat cakes and everything else he ate. It was an all-powerful field which followed obediently after him, a piece of animated, precious earth.
>
> The price of food went up due to drought and news of warfare; this much Hsiang Tzu knew. But like the city folk, he could only grumble about the high cost of food. There was nothing he could do about it at all. So food was expensive; did anyone know how to make it cheaper? This kind of attitude made him concerned only about himself; he put all other disasters and calamities out of his head.[9]

Hsiang Tzu's every thought and action register his own thoroughgoing objectification through labour. Everything he sees he reckons as exchange value, in terms of what it costs or how much it might realize; everything he does he calculates as investment or expenditure. His 'needs' are merely those that enable his social reproduction as labour power. He eats only what he has to eat to keep himself strong enough to pull his rickshaw; he sleeps just enough to enable him to recover from the day's exertions; he has no friends, and he keeps his dealings with the other rickshaw men with whom he comes into contact to an instrumental minimum; he dislikes drinking, does not gamble, has no interest in women or in conversation – indeed, he regards language with mistrust, as a wasteful indulgence. Lao She makes it clear that Hsiang Tzu's gruff inarticulacy is to be understood as the effect of a form of systematic repression that is simultaneously social and psychological.

In many literary works, the fact of combined unevenness is gestured at through barometric indications of invisible forces acting from a distance on the local and familiar. Consider, for instance, the opening pages of Anita Desai's *The Village by the Sea*, a novel whose carefully layered representation of Bloch's "simultaneity of the nonsimultaneous" has seldom been given the attention it deserves. The novel's own blurb, for instance, introduces its *mise-en-scène* thus: "Untouched by the twentieth century, the small fishing village near Bombay was still ruled by the age-old seasonal rhythms."[10] Perhaps a paragraph or two of the work, read out of context, might seem to support this construction:

> At the edge of the village was a big pond. Here buffaloes stood knee-deep, drinking or bathing. Lotuses bloomed – crimson ones with crimson leaves and green stalks. Ducks paddled between the large, flat, round leaves, and china-white egrets stood in the shallows, fishing. On the farther bank women were washing clothes and shouting and laughing as they beat the clothes on flat stones and sent up showers of water. They

---

[9] Lao She, *Rickshaw*, 12–13.

[10] Anita Desai, *The Village by the Sea* (1982; Harmondsworth: Penguin, 1985).

> were dressed in bright pink and orange and lime-green saris which they had tucked up at their waists so that they could wade into the water and stand in the mud. They seemed to be enjoying this part of their house-work.[11]

Reading on, however, we discover that, far from being somehow "untouched" by the twentieth century, Desai's village by the sea is everywhere structured by the play of modernity. Its peripherality is a mark, not of its being *outside* modern development, but of its specific location *within* it. The paragraphs immediately following the above describe boys and girls in khaki uniforms attending schools that had presumably been established during the colonial era; provide evidence of the capitalization of both fishing and agriculture in the village – the fish caught are trucked to Bombay to be sold, as are the crops that have been grown – and of the 'slow violence' of environmental despoliation consequent upon overproduction; provide evidence, also, that wealthy people in Bombay are buying and refurbishing homes in the village to live in during their holidays (so that the village is progressively being drawn into a new service and leisure economy); and give us news that a government-owned cement factory is going to be built near the village, and that wage-labourers are going to be recruited to work in it. When Hari and Lila lament their poverty, and discuss the limited options open to them, they refer to all of these realities, construing them as existentially simultaneous – which for them, of course, they are: local, regional, national, trans-national; colonial, post-colonial; capitalist, pre-capitalist, non-capitalist. Rather than the 'big-picture' sociological view from outside, the characters can only see impersonal, external forces that dominate them, with a few tiny windows of opportunity created in the interstices of these from time to time.

The representation of *work* in Desai's novel is interesting, not least because, in a gesture characteristic of the dominant ideology of the aesthetic, the novel represents work either by not representing it directly at all or by representing it through reference to consciousness. There is a concern to register the existence and the actuality of a sexual division of labour. Where Hari is concerned, work is described as being hard, dangerous, physically demanding; what this poor young man does, with diminishing returns, on his tiny plot of land, his livelihood actively jeopardized by capitalist modernization, is brought into explicit *qualitative* counterpoint with factory work, wage labour. Hari's friend Ramu tells him: "The Government is going to build a great factory here":[12]

---

[11] Desai, *The Village by the Sea*, 12.

[12] *The Village by the Sea*, 13.

> Hari thought about it all morning while he worked quietly in the field behind their hut. All the time that he hoed and dug out stones and pulled up roots, preparing the single small field for a winter crop of vegetables, the same words kept ringing in his ears – 'A job. A factory. Many jobs. Many factories….' He was soon sweating in the sun as he bent and pulled and tugged and dug. Once he cut his big toe quite painfully on a sharp stone. Once, as he approached a sturdy ixora bush that had to be cut, he saw a black snake slither under it and hide so that he had to leave it alone. But all the time he thought of the factory and a job. […]
>
> He stopped to study his hands. They were worker's hands – square and brown and callused. It was true he had done nothing with them but dig and sow and break coconuts from the trees and drag nets in the sea, but he could teach them to work machines. He felt sure he could. Was he sure? No, perhaps not quite sure.[13]

We note here both the abstracting quality of the language used to describe Hari's work – the hoeing and digging and pulling are relatively unanchored as real activities – and also the studied emphasis on the joylessness of the work, the physical demands it makes and its stultifying repetitiveness – hoeing and digging and pulling and pulling and tugging and digging.

Desai's approach is different with Lila. Here, a sentence that reads "It was time to start work" is followed by several intricate paragraphs that do not describe her working but, rather, set up a lexical economy which functions to place Lila and her village – or, better, Lila-in-her-village – relative to both history ('development') and nature:

> It was time to start work.
>
> She climbed over the dunes that were spangled with the mauve flowers of seaside ipomea into the coconut grove and passed the white bungalow that was locked and shuttered. It belonged to rich people in Bombay who came only rarely for their holidays. Its name was written on a piece of tin and tacked to the trunk of a coconut tree: *Mon Repos*. What did that mean? Lila had never found out and she wondered about it every time she walked past it, up the path that led through the coconut grove.
>
> The morning light was still soft as it filtered through the web of palm-leaves, and swirls of blue wood-smoke rose from fires in hidden huts and mingled with it. Dew still lay on the rough grass and made the spider webs glitter. These webs were small and thickly matted and stretched across the grass, each with a hole in the centre to trap passing insects.

---

[13] *The Village by the Sea*, 14.

> Butterflies flew up out of the tussocks and bushes of wild flowers – large zebra-striped ones with a faint tinge of blue to their wings, showy black ones with scarlet-tipped wings, and little sulphur-yellow ones that fluttered about in twos and threes.
>
> Then there were all the birds flying out of the shadowy, soft-needled casuarina trees and the thick jungle of pandanus, singing and calling and whistling louder than at any other time of the day. Flute-voiced drongoes swooped and cut through the air like dazzling knives that reflected the sun and glinted blue-black, and pert little magpie robins frisked and flirted their tails as they hopped on the dewy grass, snatching at insects before they tumbled into the spider's traps. Pairs of crested bul-buls sang from the branches. A single crow-pheasant, invisible, called out 'coop-coop-coop' in its deep, bogey-man voice from under a bush, and a pigeon's voice cooed and gurgled on and on. It was the voice of the village Thul as much as the roar of the waves and the wind in the palms. It seemed to tell Lila to be calm and happy and all would be well and all would be just as it was before.
>
> But when Lila came to the log that bridged the swampy creek and led to their hut on the other bank, she looked at the hut and knew that nothing was as it had been before, and nothing was well either.[14]

The reader notes how the focalization shifts repeatedly from Lila to an external (and explicitly metropolitan) consciousness. It is the latter, obviously, that knows what to do with "Mon Repos," but also that can work with "spangled" and "ipomea" and that has a familiarity with zebras and their stripes. Reported and free indirect speech are both used, as well as the external narration that, among other things, represents "the voice of the village Thul" to us. The opening paragraph of the passage is marked not only by its relative density but also by the studied use of adjectives that seem to have an almost Adamic quality: mauve flowers, white bungalow, rich people. This is Lila's consciousness, presumably. In the subsequent paragraphs, the extension of the colour palette and its complexification (notably through the use of hyphenation) suggests the merging of Lila's consciousness with that of another observer, and secures the sympathetic identification of ourselves as readers with Lila: blue wood-smoke, zebra-striped and sulphur-yellow butterflies, showy black butterflies with scarlet-tipped wings, flute-voiced drongoes, etc. Nature and village Thul are on one side; work and hardship are on the other: "she looked at the hut and knew that nothing was as it had been before, and nothing was well either."

Jameson suggests that research into world literature should involve

---

[14] *The Village by the Sea*, 8–9.

> the comparison, not of [...] individual texts, which are formally and culturally very different from each other, but of the concrete situations from which such texts spring and to which they constitute distinct responses.[15]

I derive my new project's title from John Berger's trilogy of works, *Into Their Labours*, which deal with the experience of the residual Alpine peasantry across the twentieth century. In the moving "Historical Afterword" to *Pig Earth*, the first volume, Berger attempts to formulate something like a metaphysics of peasant life: he does so, he explains, because he believes that peasant culture is quite literally threatened with extinction by modern capitalist development, and that what is at issue in this obliteration is much more than the – as it were – contingent eclipse of a social class whose time has come and gone. *Into Their Labours* represents his attempt "to examine the meaning and consequence of [the] threat of historical elimination" facing the peasantry worldwide.[16] Spinning off from Berger's work, my own project is, then, intended as an examination of the ways in which social labour overall has been transformed over the course of the past two centuries, and more specifically of the ways in which these developments have been represented in literature.

My interest, partly, is in the relationship between mental and manual labour – for example, in Yang Jiang's *A Cadre School Life: Six Chapters*, a memoir first published in the early 1980s. A notable academic, author, and translator, Yang, together with her husband Qian Zhongshu (also a distinguished scholar and novelist, author of the remarkable *Fortress Besieged*[17]), was 'sent down', during the Cultural Revolution, at the age of sixty, to the cadre school of the Chinese Academy of Social Sciences, to work on a communal farm. The general instruction, following Mao Zedong's 'May 7 Directive' of 1966, was for Chinese intellectuals to be taught to 'unclass' themselves through political study, manual labour, and the progressive unlearning of 'bourgeois' habits and forms of thought. Yang's memoir is exceptional for its modesty, forbearance, and generosity, even in its recording of the hardship of the life that its author was forced to endure in her two years 'down under'. At one point Yang describes the staging, one evening in her camp,

> of performances and skits on the theme of manual labour. Among the sketches was a short play about a member of a certain regiment who

[15] Fredric Jameson, "Third-World Literature in the Era of Multinational Capitalism," *Social Text* 15 (1986): 86–87, fn. 5.

[16] John Berger, *Pig Earth* (New York: Pantheon, 1979): 213.

[17] Qian Zhongshu, *Fortress Besieged*, tr. Nathan K. Mao & Jeanne Kelly (1947; London: Penguin, 2006).

> risked life and limb to keep the fire in a brick kiln going even though the roof was about to cave in. Someone said it was based on a true story. Another regiment put on a performance that was simply called 'Well-digging'. The whole regiment crowded on to the stage and moved around in a large circle as though they were pushing a well drill while they chanted a work song in chorus. There was no script and no other action apart from the circling movement and rhythmic chanting. Everyone moved and worked as one, drilling on without stopping until they reached the right depth. 'Hey-ho, hey-ho!' – the choral reverberation reminded me of a once-popular film theme song, 'The Song of the Volga Boatmen'. Listening to the performers, I could nearly see the boatmen on the riverbank pulling their boats along, step by step, struggling forward exhausted and leaning all of their weight against the ropes. Although the well-digging piece was a little monotonous it was more realistic and moving than the heroics in the kiln with its message 'to fear neither hardship not death'. At the end of the evening everyone went away full of praise for the well-digging performance; after all, people said, it didn't require any rehearsal: all they had to do was climb on the stage and do it.
>
> Suddenly someone blurted out,
>
> 'Just a minute. There must be something ideologically wrong with it… It must be… that is, if intellectuals are so impressed by it, it must mean…'
>
> Everyone understood the point he was trying to make and laughed knowingly. This was followed by an uncomfortable silence. We quickly changed the subject.[18]

There is a good deal that might be said about this passage. Yang and her camp-mates recoil from the heavy-handed moralism of the sketch about the brick-kiln, which, in its explicit didacticism, undertakes to tell them how to think, preferring a piece in which aesthetic mediation has been stripped away almost completely, such that what is enacted comes close to not being a representation at all but, rather, the thing that it represents – in this case, the work of well-digging – itself. The sketch presents itself as mute, but it provokes considerable discussion. It is 'realistic', of course – what else could it be, since (if I might put it in such arch terms) it is what it nearly is? – but it is also artistically 'moving'. It *is* work; it *shows* work; and between the being and the showing, a gap comes into view that the members of the audience – by virtue, arguably, of their very experience as writers and teachers – are immediately able to recognize as reflecting on the relationship between work and culture, or between manual and

[18] Yang Jiang, *A Cadre School Life: Six Chapters*, tr. Geremie Barmé, with Bennett Lee (1982; New York & London: Readers International, 1984): 29–30.

mental forms of labour. Yang and her colleagues home in on this enigmatic quality of the sketch, finding it intellectually pleasing or 'good to think'. But because they are acutely conscious of the fact that they have been 'sent down' precisely to unlearn their intellectualism – and we must assume that some of them, at least, are open to this re-education; Yang herself certainly seems to be – they are plunged into doubt about the reliability or political correctness of their interpretation of the performance. "If intellectuals are so impressed by it," as one of them says, "it must mean...." Where thought in accordance with the party line is concerned, it seems that an impasse has been reached: on the one hand, the aesthetic representation of manual labour fails if it succeeds; on the other, it does not, of course, succeed if it fails. The brick-kiln piece is dismissed as a bad play; but the well-digging piece seems to become 'good' only to the degree that its ostensible blankness is given the opportunity to signify something – that is, in interpretation; and interpreting plays and thinking about what they mean is the work of intellectuals, and as such inseparable from social privilege. Yang and her colleagues find themselves trapped in the vicious circle of an anti-intellectualist intellectualism. Opposed, on the one side, to 'bourgeois' culture, which romanticizes work or else ignores it altogether, they do not quite trust, either, a sketch that reflects on work *as* work, for they understand that what gives this latter sketch its meaning and value is nothing other than its estrangement from work *as culture* – and this estrangement, or mediatedness, always already bespeaks the social division of labour that they have been 'sent down' to unlearn. The situation might be stated in Adornian terms: where the relation between mental and manual labour is concerned, "the split between them is itself the truth."[19]

Yang seems to be open to the re-education mandated by the Maoist directive, an openness that manifests itself in her memoir. In a chapter explicitly addressed to the subject of labour, Yang describes the work that she and the colleagues in her regiment undertake in digging their own well, soon after their arrival at the camp. She focuses at first on the arduousness of their toil, the sheer physical exertion involved in "shovelling out dry earth" to a considerable depth. But then, when the mud below the dry earth is reached, the lexicon of Yang's account switches decisively from an objective to a subjective register, for she perceives mud not merely in material terms – as wet earth – but in cultural-value terms, as *disgusting*. A footnote in the English translation of *A Cadre School Life* explains that "Urban Chinese regard walking barefoot as distasteful

[19] Max Horkheimer & Theodor W. Adorno, *Dialectic of Enlightenment: Philosophical Fragments*, ed. Gunzelin Schmid Noerr, tr. Edmund Jephcott (1987; Stanford CA: Stanford UP, 2002): 107–108.

and mud with absolute revulsion."[20] "The distaste one has for mud –," Yang writes,

> with its usual mixture of phlegm, mucus, urine and faeces – vanished once we had taken off our shoes and socks and started walking around in the warm and yielding ooze. It was slippery and wet, but it did not seem at all 'dirty'. You felt the way you did about a loved one with a contagious disease, holding hands and kissing without concern for becoming ill yourself. The thought suddenly struck me: is this what they mean about 'changing your attitude' toward physical labour?[21]

The passage describes an ideological movement: from an urban, metropolitan, intellectualist outlook to a different outlook, better informed about other ways of seeing and doing things and also more respectful towards these other ways. This movement is captured, even in English translation, in the shift from the formal pronomial construction with which Yang begins the passage ("the distaste one has for mud"), which simply takes for granted that the privileged speaker's way of seeing things is the only way possible, through the familial "you" of the middle sentence, to the socially more inclusive discursivity of the final sentence, in which self and society, consciousness and authority, appear to occupy the same universe without mutual antipathy: "The thought suddenly struck me: is this what they mean about 'changing your attitude' toward physical labour."

As she watches the dramatic enactment of well-digging, cited earlier, Yang recalls the "Song of the Volga Boatmen," which she remembers as the theme song from an old film. She could be referring here to Cecil B. DeMille's *The Volga Boatmen*, first released in 1926, and which she might have seen either in China or during the three years that she spent at Oxford University in the UK in the mid-1930s. *The Volga Boatmen*, however, was a silent film, and it is more likely that Yang is thinking of Sun Yu's *The Big Road* (*Dàlù*), a 1934 film dramatizing the ordeal of a group of workers who are endeavouring to build a highway for the Chinese resistance to use in their struggle against the invading Japanese forces. Like *The Volga Boatmen, The Big Road* was also made as a silent film, with music and sound effects added in distribution to enhance its appeal and popularity.[22] Commissioned to write the theme song, Nie Er used the "Song of the Volga Boatmen" as his model for the track that came to be incorporated into

---

20 Yang Jiang, *A Cadre School Life: Six Chapters*, 33.

21 *A Cadre School Life: Six Chapters*, 33.

22 See Sue Tuohy, "Metropolitan Sounds: Music in Chinese Films of the 1930s," in *Cinema and Urban Culture in Shanghai, 1922–1943*, ed. Yingjin Zhang (Stanford CA: Stanford UP, 1999): 200–21.

the film.[23] The "Song of the Volga Boatmen" has its own interesting history. An old shanty sung by barge-haulers (*burlaks*) on the Volga River, its lyrics were first collected by Mily Balkirev and published in 1866 in a book of Russian folk-songs contributing to a Herderian project of cultural nationalism. The song is said to have inspired Ilya Repin's renowned 1873 oil-painting *Barge Haulers on the Volga*, the first of Repin's great protesting depictions of the hardship of peasant life in Tsarist Russia.

Certainly, the shanty has generally been spoken of in the context of a progressive politics, in which clear-eyed documentation of social relations has gone hand in hand with protest at the exploitation of the labouring classes. The song became very popular throughout Europe in the early years of the twentieth century, initially through recitals by the great opera singer Feodor Chaliapin, who toured very widely in these years, and whose appearances at La Scala and in programmes mounted and arranged in London and Paris by Sergei Diaghilev helped to put the great Russian operas of the nineteenth century, by such composers as Mussorgsky, Tchaikovsky, Borodin, and Rimsky–Korsakov, on the world's stage. "The Volga Boatmen" has remained a standard repertoire piece ever since Chaliapin's performances of it. Transliterated into English, it was performed to great effect by Paul Robeson; and at the request of the League of Nations, the Spanish composer Manuel de Falla wrote and released an arrangement of the song in 1922 (*Canto de los remeros del Volga* [*del cancionero musical ruso*]), the proceeds from which were donated to providing relief for the millions of Russian refugees who had been displaced from their homes during World War I.

Chaliapin was born and raised in the city of Kazan, at the confluence of the Volga and Kazanka Rivers. In 1917 his then close friend Maxim Gorky helped him to publish his autobiography, which appeared as a series of articles in the Russian journal *Letopis*. Gorky himself had moved to Kazan as a young man in 1884. In the third volume of his own autobiography, *My Universities*, published in 1923, he would write of the desolate years that he spent in the Tatar capital – years in which the only university he actually attended was the university of life, and in the course of which he worked in a series of demeaning and dispiriting jobs, struggling to eke out an existence and barely managing to survive. In a remarkable sequence in *My Universities*, Gorky describes his recruitment as a *burlak* one night. A barge has run aground on the rocks below Kazan, and

---

[23] In the year following, incidentally, and shortly before his premature death in Japan at the age of twenty-three, Nie Er also composed his "March for the Volunteers," which subsequently became the national anthem of the People's Republic.

additional hands are needed immediately to retrieve and stow the goods with which the barge is laden before it sinks or breaks up. Gorky's account is both exceptional and, at the same time, exemplary of one important way in which progressive writers tend to represent work and working people. Gorky frames the event as "The music of toiling men drew me down to the Volga. Even now it has an intoxicating effect and I remember very clearly that day when I first became aware of the heroic poetry of everyday life":

> A gang of stevedores took me on to help unload the cargo. It was September, the wind was blowing upstream and made the waves angrily dance on the grey river as it savagely tore at their crests, whipping up a cold spray. The fifty men who made up the gang gloomily huddled under tarpaulins and old mats on the deck of an empty barge that a little tug had in tow, panting away as it scattered red sheaves of sparks into the driving rain. [...]
>
> The stevedores bunched together into a black mass on the dark deck and growled like bears. The foreman finished his prayers first and screeched: 'Get some lamps! Come on, let's have some work out of you! Come on, lads, God help us!'
>
> And those ponderous lazy men, drenched by the rain, began to show how they could work. Just as though they were going into battle they rushed onto the deck and down into the holds of the grounded barge, whooping, roaring and cracking jokes. Sacks of rice, boxes of raisins, hides, furs from Astrakhan, flew past me like feather cushions. Stocky figures tore by, urging each other on with their howling, whistling and violent swearing. It was hard to believe that these were the same morose, sluggish men who only a few minutes before had been gloomily complaining about life, rain and the cold – now they were working away gaily and quickly, and with great skill. The rain became heavier and colder, the wind rose and tugged at their shirts, blowing them up over their heads and baring their stomachs. In that damp murkiness, dark figures worked by the dim light of six lamps and their feet made a dull, thudding sound on the decks. They worked as though they had been starved of it and as though they had been waiting a long time for the sheer pleasure of throwing sacks weighing 160 pounds or more to each other, and tearing around with bales on their backs. [...]
>
> I joined in, grabbed some sacks, dragged them down and threw them to someone. Then I ran back for more and it seemed that I too was caught up with everything and whirling around in a mad dance. Those men could go on working furiously and gaily without getting tired, without sparing themselves, for months, for years, and they would have

> no trouble in seizing belfries and minarets in the town and taking them wherever they wanted to!
>
> I spent that night in a state of ecstasy that I had never experienced before. My soul was brightened by the desire to spend my whole life in that half-insane rapture of work. Waves danced around the sides of the barges, rain lashed the decks, and the wind whistled over the river. In the greyish haze of the dawn, half-wet naked figures ran swiftly and incessantly, shouting, laughing and revelling in their own strength and labour.[24]

Here is an account of the humanity-engendering, world-making power of incorporated labour. Gorky does not show us one man working and ask us to multiply this image fifty times in our heads, one for each labourer. Rather, he presents us with an image of a transcendental, collective subject of labour. The work that Gorky's Volga boatmen perform is not merely skilful or dedicated or swift, though it is that, too. It is, rather, creative, erotic, demoniacal; rapturous, ecstatic, furious, gay, mad. It is both entranced and entrancing. Gorky describes this work as the "heroic poetry of everyday life": in his representation of it, it seems to escape prose and the prosaic, the routine and the quotidian. Such work can evidently move mountains, seize belfries and minarets, make and break cultures and social worlds.

The relation between language and labour in this passage bears thinking about. Notably, Gorky's description of the work of the boatmen is rhetorically rich. "Waves danced around the sides of the barges, rain lashed the decks, and the wind whistled over the river": allusive, insistently metaphorical, self-consciously 'writerly', the language here seems to want to do justice to the transfiguring quality of the work it is describing by itself exceeding the boundaries of naturalistic denotation. It is as though the writer believed that it was only by lending enchantment or heightened resonance to his own language that the enchanting character of the labour that he is attempting to describe could be represented properly: as though an elective affinity of sorts existed between this kind of physical labour and this kind of thought or writing.

Gorky's practice might, then, be distinguished from an influential variant of left-wing anti-intellectualist idealism that, because it impatiently wants to bring before us the spectre of an apocalyptic moment in which the existing social division of labour will collapse, and word become deed, has little time for the idea that mental labour might have its own medium, its own formal properties

---

24 Maxim Gorky, *My Universities*, tr. Ronald Wilks (*Мои университеты*, 1923; Harmondsworth: Penguin, 1979): 32–34.

– that language might (try to) *register* manual labour, but that it cannot be folded into it. In his 1957 essay "Myth Today," Roland Barthes famously counterposed two modes of language – a first, valorized mode, representative of "man as producer," and said to be in evidence "wherever man speaks in order to transform reality [...] wherever he links his language to the making of things"; and a second, degraded form, observable, by negative implication, wherever language undertakes to "preserve [reality] [...] as an image."[25] The binary opposition that Barthes constructs in his essay, between a transformative language, on the one hand, and a merely reflective one, on the other, is too reductive, it seems to me. His model for transformative language is revolution, which he defines as a "cathartic act meant to reveal the political load of the world: it *makes* the world; and its language, all of it, is functionally absorbed in this making."[26] But Gorky's prose directs us, rather, to the idea that language might lodge a claim to adequacy in its representation of reality – and especially of new realities – not by seeking to dissolve itself in any extra- or non-linguistically-conceived "making," but by struggling to be true to reality – and especially to new realities – in accordance with its own specific character and attributes.

The gap between mental and manual labour clearly looms as a problem for politically progressive writers – a source of guilt, among other things, as well as of the anti-intellectualist intellectualism to which I referred in my discussion of Yang Jiang's *A Cadre School Life*. In the work of some of these writers, however, writing (and mental labour generally) is often brought into focus *as work*, with its own – specific and irreducible – modes and materialities. Literature in this idiom is, of course, often realist or naturalist in register, but it is by no means always or exclusively so. Acutely conscious of the gap or discrepancy between manual and mental labour, writers often deploy the language of craft or artisanal production metaphorically or ironically in description of their work, signalling their recognition of the immateriality of the social use-values that it produces, but allowing them to hold fast to the idea that their work is not for this reason *useless*. Thus, Seamus Heaney in his great poem "Digging" from his 1966 volume evocatively and slyly entitled *Death of a Naturalist*:

> Between my finger and my thumb
> The squat pen rests; snug as a gun.
>
> Under my window, a clean rasping sound
> When the spade sinks into gravelly ground:
> My father, digging. I look down

---

25 Roland Barthes, *Mythologies*, tr. Annette Lavers (1957; New York: Hill & Wang, 1984): 18.

26 Barthes, *Mythologies*, 18 (italics in the original).

Till his straining rump among the flowerbeds
Bends low, comes up twenty years away
Stooping in rhythm through potato drills
Where he was digging.

The coarse boot nestled on the lug, the shaft
Against the inside knee was levered firmly.
He rooted out tall tops, buried the bright edge deep
To scatter new potatoes that we picked,
Loving their cool hardness in our hands.

By God, the old man could handle a spade.
Just like his old man.

My grandfather cut more turf in a day
Than any other man on Toner's bog.
Once I carried him milk in a bottle
Corked sloppily with paper. He straightened up
To drink it, then fell to right away
Nicking and slicing neatly, heaving sods
Over his shoulder, going down and down
For the good turf. Digging.

The cold smell of potato mould, the squelch and slap
Of soggy peat, the curt cuts of an edge
Through living roots awaken in my head.
But I've no spade to follow men like them.

Between my finger and my thumb
The squat pen rests.
I'll dig with it.[27]

Heaney figures working the land as the means of cultural transmission across the generations: the poet himself, his father before him, and his grandfather before his father in turn: social production and cultural and familial reproduction have been threaded together in this process. However, the poet is unable to assume his bespoken position as the heir to this tradition. "I've no spade to follow men like them," he says: does he lack the skill, the aptitude, or, more likely, has he been trained to other things? But the desire looms nevertheless to bring what he *has l*earned, to bend what he *now* does, to the task of cultural reproduction that it was once thought he might shoulder simply by virtue of being his father's son, but that, it is assumed, he has abandoned, because he has chosen a

---

[27] Seamus Heaney, "Digging," in *Death of a Naturalist* (1966; London: Faber & Faber, 1988): 13–14.

different path or because a different path has been chosen for him. What if writing also can be understood as digging – as a digging in another medium? And we then see that the poet's language in this poem is self-consciously straining to put into words, feelings, sensations, emotions – the "cool hardness of potatoes," the "squelch and slap of soggy peat" – that had presumably always been perceived and experienced and understood, but perhaps never before articulated, by those men who had lived by the fruits of their labour, cutting turf and heaving sods.

Here is Camara Laye, writing from Paris in 1953, and recollecting his childhood in the town of Kouroussa, in what was then the French colony of Guinée. He is describing the annual harvest, when people from all the nearby villages would come together to help gather the rice crop:

> On the day of the harvest, the head of each family went at dawn to cut the first swath in his field. [...] Once the signal had been given, the reapers set out. [...] When they had reached the first field, the men lined up at the edge, naked to the loins, their sickles ready. My uncle Lansana or some other farmer – for the harvest threw people together and everyone helped everyone else – would signal that the work was to begin. Immediately, the black torsos would bend over the great golden field, and the sickles begin to cut. Now it was not only the morning breeze with made the field tremble, but also the men working.
>
> The movement of the sickles as they rose and fell was astonishingly rapid and regular. [...] [I]f I happened to stop work for a moment and look at that long, long line of reapers, I was always impressed and carried away by the infinite love and kindliness of their eyes, as they glanced here and there. Yet, though their glances were also distant and preoccupied, though they seemed miles from their task, they never slighted it. Hands and sickles moved without interruption.
>
> And, what actually *were* they looking at? At one another? A likely idea! Perhaps at the distant trees or the still more distant sky. And again, perhaps not. Perhaps they were looking at nothing. Perhaps there was nothing to look at, and this only made them seem distant and preoccupied. The long line of reapers hurled itself at the field and hewed it down. Wasn't that enough? Wasn't it enough that the rice bowed before these black bodies? They sang and they reaped. Singing in chorus, they reaped, voices and gestures in harmony. They were together! – united by the same task, the same song. It was as if the same soul bound them.[28]

---

[28] Camara Laye, *The Dark Child*, tr. James Kirkup & Ernest Jones (*L'Enfant noir*, 1954; New York: Farrar, Straus & Giroux, 1984): 56–61.

Every literary representation of labour is, of course, unforgoably a representation. What is evoked here is perhaps less the work being done than the writer's attitude towards what he is describing. Here the work itself is abstracted in and by its description: we see sickles and hands and fields, but impressionistically rather than naturalistically. This is *aesthetic* production. Movement, fluidity, grace, strength, the flowing of bodies and the trembling of the field; colour and song – the black bodies and the golden crop, the harmony of the song repeated, at a much deeper level, in the unity and togetherness of the community, bound together, as the writer puts it, by the same great soul. The passage also, and simultaneously, describes the writer's own externality to these proceedings. Again, as with Heaney, a different road has been marked out for him: Heaney takes milk to his grandfather; Camara Laye takes water to his uncle. Like Heaney, he has been placed on the path of education which will take him away from the community whose integrity he therefore seeks to recall – indeed, remember – with such passionate longing. He recalls how upset he was to be told by his elders that he could not participate in the harvest, but only watch it. Following a road that would lead him from Kouroussa to Conakry and on to Paris, his migration across the social division of labour – manual to mental work – marked also by a migration across the international division of labour, colony to metropole, he feels his separation from his family, peers, community as a wound, that perhaps his writing can help to heal, bringing him back to them, and bringing them something of value from where he has been.

The social value of mental labour is fiercely debated and disputed across the range of the literary corpus. The attempt is often made to defend such labour – on the one hand, against the instrumentalist charge that, since it is 'unproductive' (of exchange-values), it is without warrant; on the other, against the ultraleftist and anti-intellectualist charge that it is decadent or indulgent, something like playing the fiddle while Rome burns. Hence, for example, the urgent discussions between Baako and Ocran in Ayi Kwei Armah's *Fragments*, and between Omovo and Okocha in Ben Okri's *Dangerous Love*, which turn on the question of how writers and artists can justify themselves in social contexts in which the most fundamental of material needs – for food, for shelter, for 'freedom' from physical extermination, even – often remain unmet. A different line of vision unfolds in Knut Hamsun's *Hunger*, which explores in horrifying detail the effects of the commodification of thought and writing –of literature and the creative process – in the new world of capitalist class relations. The protagonist of this 1890 novel is a vulnerable young man from the countryside who comes to Christiania (Oslo) and struggles to make a name for himself as a writer. Make a name for himself? In fact, his economic situation is so desperate that his struggle is, rather, to earn enough from his writing just to stay alive. In one typical passage, we encounter him waking up very early one morning, his mind bursting with ideas. His alertness is half-delirium. He is starving – he hasn't eaten anything at all for days and hasn't had a proper meal for weeks. He takes up a pencil and starts to write. What is then striking is that his ideas begin to take for him the form of saleable goods, whose true measure is monetary. His hope is only to be able to sell what he writes, to turn his ideas into money, to be exchanged in turn for food:

> All at once, one or two remarkable sentences occurred to me, good for a short story or a sketch, windfalls in language as good as I had ever come on. I lay saying the words over to myself and decided they were excellent. Soon several other sentences joined the two; instantly I was wide awake, stood up, and took paper and pencil from the table at the foot of my bed. It was like a vein opening, one word followed the other, arranged themselves in right order, created situations; scene piled on scene, actions and conversations welled up in my brain, and a strange sense of pleasure took hold of me. I wrote as if possessed, and filled one page after the other without a moment's pause. Thoughts poured in so abruptly, and kept on coming in such a stream, that I lost a number of them from not being able to write them down fast enough, even though I worked with all my energy. They continued to press themselves on me; I was deep into the subject, and every word I set down came from somewhere else… I became giddy with contentment, gladness swelled up in me, I felt myself to be magnificent. I weighed the piece in my hand and assessed it on the spot with a rough guess as five kroner. No one would ever haggle about five kroner for this. On the contrary. In view of the quality, one could call it pure thievery to get the piece for ten. The last thing I had in mind was to do such a remarkable work free; my experience was that one did not find stories of that sort lying about on the street! I decided definitely on ten kroner.[29]

## WORKS CITED

Barthes, Roland. *Mythologies*, tr. Annette Lavers (*Mythologies* 1957; New York: Hill & Wang, 1984).

Berger, John. *Pig Earth* (New York: Pantheon, 1979).

Desai, Anita. *The Village by the Sea* (1982; Harmondsworth: Penguin, 1985).

[29] Knut Hamsun, *Hunger*, tr. Robert Bly (*Sult*, 1890; London: Picador, 1974): 48.

Gorky, Maxim. *My Universities*, tr. Ronald Wilks (*Мои университеты*, 1923; tr. Harmondsworth: Penguin, 1979).

Heaney, Seamus. *Death of a Naturalist* (1966; London: Faber & Faber, 1988).

Hamsun, Knut. *Hunger*, tr. Robert Bly (*Sult*, 1890; London: Picador, 1974).

Horkheimer, Max, & Theodor W. Adorno. *Dialectic of Enlightenment: Philosophical Fragments*, ed. Gunzelin Schmid Noerr, tr. Edmund Jephcott (*Gesammelte Schriften: Dialektik der Aufklärung und Schriften 1940–1950*, 1987; Stanford CA: Stanford UP, 2002).

Jameson, Fredric. *Postmodernism or, The Cultural Logic of Late Capitalism* (Durham NC: Duke UP, 1995).

Jameson, Fredric. "Third-World Literature in the Era of Multinational Capitalism," *Social Text* 15 (1986): 65–88.

Laye, Camara. *The Dark Child*, tr. James Kirkup and Ernest Jones (*L'Enfant noir*, 1954; New York: Farrar, Straus & Giroux, 1984).

Qian Zhongshu. *Fortress Besieged*, tr. Nathan K. Mao & Jeanne Kelly (1947; Harmondsworth: Penguin, 2006).

Schwarz, Roberto. *A Master on the Periphery of Capitalism: Machado de Assis*, tr. John Gledson (*Um Mestre na Periferia do Capitalismo: Machado de Assis*, 1990; Durham NC: Duke UP, 2001).

Schwarz, Roberto. *Misplaced Ideas: Essays on Brazilian Culture*, ed. John Gledson (London: Verso, 1992).

Lao She. *Rickshaw*, tr. Jean M. James (1937; Honolulu: U of Hawai'i P, 1979).

Tuohy, Sue. "Metropolitan Sounds: Music in Chinese Films of the 1930s," in *Cinema and Urban Culture in Shanghai, 1922–1943*, ed. Yingjin Zhang (Stanford CA: Stanford UP, 1999).

Williams, Raymond. *Writing in Society* (London & New York: Verso, 1991).

WReC (Warwick Research Collective). *Combined and Uneven Development: Towards a New Theory of World-Literature* (Liverpool: Liverpool UP, 2015).

Yang Jiang. *A Cadre School Life: Six Chapters*, tr. Geremie Barmé, with Bennett Lee (1982; New York: Readers International, 1984).

❄

## Hidden in the Chaotic Tumble of Events

### *Toronto's Rich in Michael Ondaatje's* In the Skin of a Lion

Helga Ramsey–Kurz

"Lights," Michael Ondaatje has his protagonist Patrick Lewis command at the end of *In the Skin of a Lion* (1987), thus taking the reader straight back to the very beginning of his novel when Patrick is travelling eastward from York, Toronto to Marmara, Ontario.[1] In the four hours this 200-km car journey used to take in the 1930s, Patrick recounts the story that makes up the main part of the novel. His listener is Hana, daughter of his late partner Alice Gull, a nun turned actress after miraculously surviving a 40-metre fall from the Bloor Street Viaduct back in 1918. Alice was also a fervent supporter of the loggers' union in whose battles "up north" Hana's father Cato, a labourer and political activist from Finland, was murdered in 1921. Patrick's narration shines light on Cato's death, as well as more generally on the lives of the many other European immigrants who came to Toronto in the early-twentieth century to find work in the building boom that cemented the city's ascent to a wealthy cosmopolitan metropolis. Up until the end of the novel the direction and purpose of Patrick's narrative remain obscure, not least because of the manner in which it keeps steering towards his main antagonists and away from them, as if hesitant to be contaminated by their enormous wealth and the dubious ways in which they obtained it.

Although instantly nominated for the Governor General's Award for English Language Fiction, Ondaatje's story of Canadian-born Patrick Lewis – underdog, self-appointed researcher, and working-class rebel siding with foreign labourers – did not earn unconditional critical acclaim at the outset. *In the Skin of a Lion* was faulted in particular for its intricate design, which critics took as proof of Ondaatje's overtly bourgeois aestheticism and a concomitant tendency to

---

[1] Michael Ondaatje, *In the Skin of a Lion* (1987; New York: Random House, 1997): 244. Further page references are in the main text.

subordinate, if not sacrifice, political content to artistic form.[2] This perception had changed significantly by the 1990s. Charges that Ondaatje's novel only pretended to advance a political message without actually having one were dropped, particularly when critical interest shifted from the novel's form to its depiction of the multiculturalism nascent in Toronto in the first decades of last century.[3] The subsequent reappraisal of *In the Skin of a Lion* as historiographic metafiction[4] by an immigrant about immigrants was indicative of a new appreciation of cultural difference and diversity. In recognizing this change of focus, literary studies were attuned to a changing conception of identity-politics that, spurred on by the increasingly mainstream discourse on globalization, transnationalism, and diaspora, was convinced that the antidote to marginalization and discrimination was systematic validation of cultural otherness. Somewhat ironically, though, critics, with this aim in mind, overlooked the doubt Ondaatje himself expresses, through his story of Patrick Lewis, about the usefulness of cultural recognition in restoring justice to devalued groups – especially if

---

[2] See esp. Frank Davey, *Post-National Arguments: The Politics of the Anglophone-Canadian Novel since 1967* (Toronto: U of Toronto P, 1993), as well as Katherine Acheson, "Anne Wilkinson in Michael Ondaatje's *In the Skin of a Lion*: Writing and Reading Class," *Canadian Literature* 145 (1995): 107–19, Julie Beddoes, "Which Side Is It On? Form, Class, and Politics in *In the Skin of a Lion*," *Essays on Canadian Writing* 53 (1994): 204–15, and Christian Bök, "The Secular Opiate: Marxism as an Ersatz Religion in Three Canadian Texts," *Canadian Literature* 147 (1995): 11–22. For an excellent appraisal of these and the tendency they share "to read the text [*In the Skin of a Lion*] against itself" (445), see Robert David Stacey, "A Political Aesthetic: Michael Ondaatje's *In the Skin of a Lion* as 'Covert Pastoral'," *Contemporary Literature* 49.3 (Fall, 2008): 439–69.

[3] See, for example, Carol L. Beran, "Ex-Centricity: Michael Ondaatje's *In the Skin of a Lion* and Hugh MacLennan's *Barometer Rising*," *Studies in Canadian Literature/Études en Littérature Canadienne* 18.1 (1993): 71–78; Winfried Siemerling, "Oral History and the Writing of the Other in Ondaatje's *In the Skin of a Lion*," *Comparative Cultural Studies and Michael Ondaatje's Writing*, ed. & introd. Steven Tötösy de Zepetnek (West Lafayette IN: Purdue UP, 2005): 92–103; Minoli Salgado, "Nonlinear Dynamics and the Diasporic Imagination," in *Diaspora and Multiculturalism: Common Traditions and New Developments*, ed. & intro. Monika Fludernik (Cross/Cultures 66; Amsterdam & New York: Rodopi, 2003): 183–98; Susan Spearey, "Mapping and Masking: The Migrant Experience in Michael Ondaatje's *In the Skin of a Lion*," *Journal of Commonwealth Literature* 29.2 (June 1994): 45–60; Wolfgang Werth, "Immigration and Acculturation in Michael Ondaatje's *In the Skin of a Lion*," in *Wandering Selves: Essays on Migration and Multiculturalism*, ed. Michael Porsche & Christian Berkemeier (Essen: Blaue Eule, 2001): 125–33.

[4] See Linda Hutcheon, *The Canadian Postmodern: A Study of Contemporary Canadian Fiction* (*Wynford Project*) (Oxford: Oxford UP, 2012): esp. 93–104, and Gordon Bölling, "Metafiction in Michael Ondaatje's Historical Novel *In the Skin of a Lion*," *Symbolism: An International Journal of Critical Aesthetics* 3 (2003): 215–53, and

these groups exist in as fiercely capitalistic an environment as the city space he charts in his novel.

This essay spotlights Ondaatje's cautious expression of doubt – hesitations which can now be more openly explored in the contemporary environment of sustained critiques of capitalism. To this end, I shall draw on the ideas about justice advanced by the American critical theorist Nancy Fraser in response to the growing popularity of the cultural-recognition theories of the 1990s. Fraser attributes this popularity to the neoliberal climate of the 1980s and outlines how the resultant cult of individualism gave rise to a new political imaginary centred on notions of difference, cultural domination, and recognition. Jarring with previous universalist and essentialist ideas of equality and justice, justice was now conceived of as an intrinsically *cultural* category "rooted in social patterns of representation, interpretation, and communication."[5] This led to a situation in which the struggle for recognition of one's cultural distinctiveness became "the paradigmatic form of political conflict." As Fraser explains,

> Demands for "recognition of difference" fuel struggles of groups mobilised under the banners of nationality, ethnicity, "race," gender, and sexuality. In these "postsocialist" conflicts, group identity supplants class interest as the chief medium of political mobilisation. Cultural domination supplants exploitation as the fundamental injustice. And cultural recognition displaces socioeconomic redistribution as the remedy for injustice and the goal of political struggle.[6]

Convinced that cultural recognition has been overestimated by political theorists such as Charles Taylor, John Rawls, and Axel Honneth as an operation constitutive of justice, Fraser seeks to recuperate the socio-economic dimension such critics have allowed to fade from their analyses. Her main objection to the idea that injustices, both cultural *and* social, can be remedied by upwardly revaluing the culture of maligned groups or group members is that cultural discrimination and economic injustice, although closely related, ought not to be collapsed into one but require separate theorization as well as different prophylaxes and remedies. As Fraser concedes, culture and political economy

---

[5] Nancy Fraser, *Justice Interruptus: Critical Reflections on the "Postsocialist" Condition* (New York: Routledge, 1997): 14.

[6] Fraser, *Justice Interruptus*, 11.

> are always imbricated with each other, and virtually every struggle against injustice, when properly understood, implies demands for both redistribution and recognition.[7]

Nevertheless, to respond adequately to these demands and take concrete measures, analytical distinctions are indispensable. Indeed, Fraser is convinced that without such distinctions the more recent cultural politics of difference are impossible to reconcile with the social politics of equality they claim to serve.

The precision with which Fraser teases apart different notions of justice[8] provides a formidable corrective to current debates on social-economic difference, and in particular to the obliqueness such debates tend to acquire when conducted as a postcolonial exploration of abjection. The failure of literary and cultural theorists to canvass the larger picture of poverty becomes most clearly manifest in their inability, or reluctance, to consider poverty's opposite: prosperity and great wealth. Arguably, this is also a glaring problem in postcolonial critical discourse, where constant attention to devalued groups and the cultural expression of their disadvantage has, to a large extent, led scholars to neglect identification of those agents directly responsible for the injustices they criticize. Typically, therefore, socio-economic elites have received practically no scholarly consideration other than by way of a generalized Marxist critique as (neo-)colonial exploiters. Nor has the nature of their economic advantage been subjected to any thorough critical inquiry. In its rigorous chronicling of poverty and abjection, postcolonial criticism has omitted to develop a proper understanding of scenarios and processes of enrichment and their beneficiaries. This lacuna in postcolonial critical debate has hindered rather than aided its declared aim to contest mechanisms of subjugation. While busy recuperating the forgotten pasts of subalterns, it has failed to summon resistance to the systematic mystification of wealth and the wealthy, as if blind to the fact that it is on precisely such mystification that the great promise of enrichment as the mainstay of all capitalist systems hinges.

The political relevance of *In the Skin of a Lion*, so vehemently disputed by its fiercest critics, resides precisely in the way in which it plays with the promise of economic betterment and at the same time undermines it by consistently gesturing at the close proximity of wealth and the wealthy without ever proffering a turn of events that allows its main characters to benefit from the affluence

---

7 Fraser, *Justice Interruptus*, 12–13.

8 In so doing, she goes well beyond a retrieval of the socialist notion of distributive injustice, elaborating on justice claims, and, perhaps even more pertinently, on agency of redistribution. See, for instance, "Abnormal Justice," *Critical Inquiry* 34.3 (Spring 2008): 393–422.

around them. Critics' often single-minded concentration on Ondaatje's special depiction of these characters as Toronto's first immigrants, living in complete non-recognition and with no hope of fulfilling a Canadian version of the American Dream, seems to have distracted them from the careful demystification of Toronto's moneyed elites in *In the Skin of a Lion*. In the very gradual process of this demystification, the rich keep emerging from the background of the novel into the limelight, only to withdraw swiftly into invisibility again so that the hopelessness pervading the immigrants' characterization solidifies, acquiring sad probability and foreclosing any chance of a change for the better.

Only at the end of the novel is it clear that this is the function of two characters not part of the community of immigrants: the millionaire and theatre tycoon Ambrose Small and the engineer Rowland Harris, known for overseeing the construction of such landmarks as the Bloor Street Viaduct and the R.C. Harris Water Purification Plant on the shore of Lake Ontario. Patrick's story keeps gravitating towards these two, a fictive figure, on the one hand, an historical celebrity, on the other, in a narrative dynamic energized by the protagonist's desperate desire for justice. One of the novel's main tragedies is that this desire is never fulfilled – above all because of the essential intangibility of the rich, the implications of which begin to dawn on Patrick only towards the close of the novel. As the following shall demonstrate, this intangibility crucially defines the politics of seeing that Michael Ondaatje lays out in *In the Skin of a Lion* by juxtaposing the deceptive visibility (or, indeed, hyper-visibility) of the rich with the immigrants' unnoticed, unrecognized existence in apparent darkness.

Intricate effects of light and darkness qualify both the rich and the poor in the novel, impairing as well as aiding perception and showing how characters not only crave recognition but also dread and shun it. Just as they may experience darkness as both safe and treacherous, they respond to full illumination as liberating and oppressive, revealing and blinding alike. This significantly complicates and destabilizes the popular associations, to which the novel alludes, of poverty with obscurity and of wealth with fame or to what Robert Van Krieken calls accumulated "attention capital."[9] Just as the visibility of the rich proves more changeable than meets the eye, the invisibility in which the immigrants seem trapped does not mean an existence in total darkness but one typically qualified by glimmers of light and even by occasional bursts into full brightness and colour. Images of them gravitating towards light inform Patrick's childhood memories as when he recalls the foreign loggers he would pass with his father.

---

9 See, for example, Robert Van Krieken, "The economics of attention," in Van Krieken, *Celebrity Society* (London: Routledge, 2012): 53–61.

Every day he would see them working in the dark of the forest. One evening, though, he catches sight of them lost in a secret dance on ice, skating noiselessly against the night, their faces illuminated by the sheaves of burning cattails in their hands. When, as an adult, he moves to Toronto, his loneliness causes him to think of himself as an immigrant doomed to live unseen even in surroundings as colourful as the abattoirs at the tannery where he works for some time, wading with other dyers waist-deep in in reds and ochres and greens – a spectacular sight, seen only, however, by other dyers.

Patrick knows he is luckier than those recruited to work night-shifts on Prince Edward Bridge or in tunnels underground. There, invisibility becomes a profoundly daunting physical reality, as potentially life-threatening as for the desperately braying mules and pit-horses lowered into the heat and mud and noise of a tunnel built under Lake Ontario. Patrick remembers the frightened creatures –

> the teeth of the animals distinct, that screaming, the feet bound so they wouldn't slash out and break themselves, lowered forty feet down and remaining there until they died or the tunnel reached the selected mark under the lake. And when would that be? The brain of the mule no more and no less knowledgeable than the body of a man who dug into a clay wall in front of him. (108)

The recognition of sameness across national, linguistic, and even biological differences is repeatedly asserted in *In the Skin of a Lion* as a seeing in darkness, a momentary illumination of an injustice otherwise well concealed. It marks a horizontal identification, a sense of being together in one place, of sharing an outsider position. On occasion, such experiences of empathetic understanding may prompt an act of opposition or protest, which, however, more often than not proves ineffectual. This is the case when Patrick, entranced by a puppet show, suddenly rushes from the darkness of the auditorium onto the brightly lit stage to rescue a human figure mercilessly assaulted by an army of small puppets. Only later does he learn that his attempt to help was a calculated intervention in the play he was watching, part of a script and a choreography of whose existence he had had no idea. For all the light into which he had stormed, his reaction to the violence played out on the stage was as much of a wasted effort as the frenzied fluttering of the moths he used to observe as a child as they gravitated impetuously towards light. As a gesture of solidarity, it remains as inconsequential as the spontaneous march onto the Bloor Street Viaduct with which workers, on the night before the official opening of the bridge, seek to commemorate their dead comrades "with their own flickering lights [...] like a wave of civilization, a net of summer insects over the valley" (27).

Historical records suggest that even in the early-twentieth century there must have been more light in Toronto than Michael Ondaatje allows into most of his novel's settings (especially more *electric* light than seen by his characters, who are constantly shown handling candles and petroleum or naphtha lamps).[10] If the predominance of darkness creates the impression that the immigrants exist on their own in the city they are building, it always also suggests that there is another space outside their world, a much brighter space inaccessible to the workers, a retreat for the rich, who even at night can afford to remain oblivious to the darkness beyond their own haunts as they saunter through ballrooms illuminated by chandeliers, gardens irradiated by false stars and moons, property ablaze with searchlights, beach cottages and country estates lit up by oil lamps.

Despite the limelight in which they move, the rich mostly constitute an indistinct crowd, a body of well-dressed shapes drifting faceless over dance floors to indistinct music. Only at rare moments does this presence of wealth crystallize into the entry of either Ambrose Small or Rowland Harris. The two men are placed at either end of Patrick's gradual development from searcher to researcher, from labourer to anarchist, from immigrant to prisoner, and, finally, to free man. Alike in many respects, Small and Harris are still positioned far apart within the text, like pillars between which Patrick's story spans, bridge-like, bringing together subjects from different walks of life, lifting them, for the brief episode of a crossing, out of rigid class divisions. This comparison seems warranted not only by Ondaatje's use of the construction of Prince Edward Bridge as a backdrop to his novel[11] but also by the place Small and Harris occupy within the new urban space charted in *In the Skin of a Lion*. The stories of their rise from nothing to enormous wealth and fame – myth in Small's case; concrete historical reality in Harris's – are part and parcel of Toronto's ascent to a metropolis.

---

[10] Chris Bateman, "A Brief History of the First Electricity Company in Toronto" (7 September 2013), http://www.blogto.com/city/2013/09/a_brief_history_of_the_first_electricity_company_in_toronto/ (accessed 5 June 2016).

[11] Accordingly, Murnaghan notes the contrast Ondaatje draws between the "calculating mental labour of the engineers, planners, and politicians who saw the bridge as a monument to their investment in the development of modernity, and the gross masculinity that accompanied that project" and the participation of skilled labourers in the construction of the bridge who, due to their physical investment in the structure, saw the building in much different terms. Ann Marie F. Murnaghan, "The City, the Country, and Toronto's Bloor Viaduct, 1897–1919," *Urban History Review/Revue d'histoire urbaine* 42.1 (Fall 2013): 49.

The ambition to surpass the presumed limits of the materially possible drives their personal ascent, and in their success breeds stories of achievement in excess, biographies which the city claims as its own in a desire to earn at least some credit for the wealth of its most successful inhabitants. Thus, Ambrose Small is appropriated into Toronto's lore, turned into a legend, transformed into myth, and preserved as such long after both he and a million dollars from his bank account have vanished without a trace. Even in his unexplained absence he retains a place in Toronto's imaginary as "the jackal of Toronto's business world," "manipulator of deals and property," owner of Toronto's Grand Opera House and of theatres "all over the province – in St. Catharines, Kingston, Arkona, Petrolia, Peterborough, and Paris, Ontario – until he held the whole web of theatre traffic in his outstretched arms" (57). The tales of his affluent life – his appalling parties with showgirls and live peacocks, his obsession with greyhounds, and his alibi-serving marriage to a prohibitionist – proliferate, especially after he has vanished. In effect, they take his place and, as if to compensate for his much-noted absence, become ever more fantastic, to the point where people preposterously claim to have sighted him or even to be him. Reiterated by the press, these stories add to a feeling of "open season" and fuel a frenetic treasure-hunt in the course of which the millionaire's body is turned "into a rare coin, a piece of financial property" fought over by a whole army of searchers who invest in "the project" "as if it were an oil field or a gold mine" (59). For a while, Patrick Lewis is one them, and, for a moment, the most successful of them all.

At first glance, the historical figure of "Rowland Harris, Commissioner of Public Works" forms a clear contrast to the mythic persona of Ambrose Small. His presence in Ondaatje's Toronto is solidly physical, not only by dint of the stark visibility of the many buildings he has supervised. Accordingly, he enters the narrative in pronouncedly material terms, "having himself driven," on one of his long work-days, to the very edge of the Bloor Street Viaduct in his limousine "to sit for a while" before removing himself from the car, lighting a cigar, and walking onto the bridge (29). Despite his physicality, Harris remains just as detached from ordinary people as Small. Aloofness marks all his dealings with others, by whom he expects to be revered as "Commissioner Harris," designer of "one of the city's grandest buildings" (29), provider of many jobs over decades, and patron of subcontractors from across the province, including "Richie Cut Stone Company, Raymond Concrete, Heather & Little Roofing and Sheet metal, [...] Architectural Bronze and Iron Works, [...] Canadian Metal Window and Steel Works [...]" (109). He thinks of himself as "a man who underst[ands] the continuity of the city" (109) and likes to quote Baudelaire to his critics to remind them that the "form of a city changes faster than the heart of a mortal" (110). Unlike Small's popularity, which rests on such mundane pursuits as gambling and sponsoring the province's theatre world, the commissioner's eminence is built on more reputable performances earning him admiration as far as New York State, where, rumour has it, people looking north across Lake Ontario can still discern the aura of his fabulous "water palace." At this key locale, the ultimate symbol of his wealth and success, Harris meets Patrick, who, having become a political activist by this point in the novel, arrives to blow up the commissioner's beloved 'fortress'.

Visible to everyone even in darkness, yet not tangible, Harris's and Small's superior status is seriously compromised on those two separate nights on which Patrick Lewis succeeds in passing the barriers into their well-protected quarters and, in coming physically close enough to command their attention, casts sudden doubt on the presumed impregnability of their wealth. In facing and speaking to them, Patrick breaks out of the object-status to which Harris and Small like to consign their dependents. So unexpected is Patrick's invasion that Small feels he must resort to murderous action. In an attempt to extract himself from the visibility into which Patrick has pulled him, he pours petrol over his persecutor and sets him ablaze. Patrick escapes badly injured and feeling that – rather than having found and met Small, a feat accomplished by none of the other men employed to track the fugitive millionaire down – he has been defeated by the theatre tycoon's elusiveness. Small's cold indifference to Patrick as a fellow human is duplicated in a brief and literally fleeting but no less dramatic encounter between Harris and Alice Gull at the beginning of the novel, when Harris is forced to watch how a gust of night wind sweeps Alice off the Bloor Street Viaduct. Harris is dismayed in the same way that Small is at Patrick's intrusion into his private space. Indeed, he is shocked at the life his bridge has just claimed – not, however, for the sake of the young nun, but for his own reputation and that of his bridge. The reader catches him thinking that the bridge "was his first child and it had already become a murderer" (31). Next to this grand, elegant, and, for its creator, even animate bridge, nuns, immigrants, and workers are insignificant to Harris, mere members of the masses whose civilizing progress he is spearheading with his superior understanding of the possibilities of improvement that modernity offers.

Harris's hubris brings to mind the robber barons of later-nineteenth- and early-twentieth-century America, such as Andrew Carnegie, fervent subscriber to Herbert Spencer's idea of the rich as the "socially elect."[12] Carnegie passionately disputed claims that the new super-rich brought forth by industrial capitalism were a tyrannical "aristocracy of the dollar." Rather, he viewed them as an "aristocracy of intellect,"[13] devoted to "all that is highest and best in literature and the arts" and in the interest of the entire human race.[14] Convinced (like Harris) of the inherent nobility of men of money, Carnegie saw nothing wrong with the extreme luxuries the millionaires of his time were enjoying while ever larger numbers of people in America and Great Britain had to live in dire poverty. "Much better this great irregularity," he famously argues in "The Gospel of Wealth," "than universal squalor."[15] Harris employs similar self-serving reasoning to legitimize his ambition to build "a palace for water," an edifice in neo-Byzantine style, with the best ornamental iron, herringbone tiles from Siena, rose-coloured marble, Art-Deco clocks and pump signals, unfloored high windows, and a brass elevator (110). Already before he has drawn up any plans for it, this palace possesses greater reality for Harris than do any of his employees. In fact, he "could *smell* the place before it was there, knew every image of it as well as his arms" (109; emphasis in the original).

It seems to take a female to see through Rowland Harris and Ambrose Small and see their wealth for what it is – not, as Harris likes to think, a singular achievement, but the manifestation of a stereotypical life, endlessly re-enacted by members of a class for whom Alice Gull only has the collectivizing label "the rich." As if to mimic their typical obliviousness to the poor, Alice declares herself blind to their specific characteristics. She insists that they are all the same to her, even Small and Harris, who in her view are no different from other members of their class, in that they revel in the luxury of an otherness that, in its utter unoriginality, is able only to keep reproducing hackneyed phrases and mannerisms. "The rich," she tells Patrick,

> are always laughing. They keep saying the same things on their boats and lawns: *Isn't it grand! We're having a good time!* And when the rich are

[12] Spencer, quoted in John Kampfner, *The Rich: From Slaves to Super-Yachts: A 2,000-Year History* (New York: Little, Brown, 2014): 242. In a non-postcolonial but equally late-capitalist context, Patrick's originally working-class perspective and mission to wrest justice from the likes of such icons of wealth as Harris recall Coalhouse Walker's mission of reparation against J.P. Morgan and other exemplars of cultured, robber-baron prosperity in E.L. Doctorow's novel *Ragtime* (1975) (Doctorow stated that he deliberately steered clear of using Andrew Carnegie as the *bête noire*). Thanks to Gordon Collier for drawing this connection to my attention.

[13] Kampfner, *The Rich*, 241.

[14] *The Rich*, 242.

[15] *The Rich*, 242.

> getting drunk and maudlin about humanity you have to listen for hours. But they keep you in the tunnels and stockyards. They do not toil or spin. Remember that... understand what they will always refuse to let go of. There are a hundred fences and lawns between the rich and you. (132)

For a long time, Patrick's response to the class divisions Alice tries to make him see is to identify with the immigrants around him. He willingly immerses himself in their lives, blends into the exotic *tableau vivant* their community supplies, ignoring the obvious limits to his understanding of his friends, whose languages he does not speak and to whose homelands he has never been. Believing himself to be "a searcher [...] a watcher, a corrector" (157), he starts paying visits to the Riverdale Library, where he basks in the "oceans of light" pouring through the leaded windows of the reading room and combs through newspapers and journals, only to discover that the lives and works of those who actually laid the material foundations of modern Toronto have never been recorded. Their absence from the city's archives, hence also from public memory, becomes an obsession from which Patrick cannot tear himself free despite Alice's warnings that his efforts will change nothing.

Not until Alice's unexpected death does Patrick take notice of her persistent calls for more effective action, a precondition of which, in her view, is a seeing directed not at the past but at the present. It is a bitter irony that she herself should be killed walking through the crowds along the Danforth, not seeing that she has accidentally picked up a bag carrying a clock bomb: "A simple mistake" (239) made by one of her anarchist friends. Reaching Alice just before the bomb detonates, but too late to save her, Patrick is forced to watch her die,

> an idea, a cause in her eye about wealth and power, forever and ever. And at the end as she turned round to him on the street hearing her name yelled, surprised at Patrick being near, there was nothing completed or attained. And he could think of nothing but the eyes looking for him above the terrible wound suddenly appearing as she turned. (165)

The sight of vision leaving Alice's eyes catapults Patrick out of his languor – an attitude, Alice would argue, only the self-sufficient could afford, and a quality, the novel offers by way of important self-reflexive commentary, sadly characteristic of art's responses to history, its often failed endeavours to bring order to "the chaotic tumble of events":

> Official histories, news stories surround us daily, but the events of art reach us too late, travel languorously like messages in a bottle.
>
> *Only the best art can order the chaotic tumble of events. Only the best can realign chaos to suggest both the chaos and order it will become.*

> Within two years of 1066 work began on the Bayeux Tapestry, Constantine the African brought Greek medicine to the western world. The chaos and tumble of events. The first sentence of every novel should be: "Trust me, this will take time but there is order here, very faint, very human." Meander if you want to get to town. (146, italics in the original)

Faced with the immediacy of history, Patrick abandons his compassionate chronicling of the lost lives of immigrants. Finally understanding what Alice meant when she warned him that compassion only blurs one's vision of the truth because it "forgives too much" (123–24), he is able to take on her class struggle and shift his focus from compassionate reconstruction to dispassionate destruction. To see the truth, Alice had explained to him, one must not look into the past but at the present, not at one's own kind but at the o/Other: "You must name the enemy [...]," he remembers Alice imploring him, "and destroy their power. Start with their luxuries – their select clubs, their summer mansions" (124–25).

Naming the enemy, not the friend, naming the rich, not the poor, naming affluence, not abjection used to be impossible for Patrick, who, with his "passive sense of justice" (122), has been able to look only at the victims of exploitation, never at its perpetrators. Yet, consumed by blind fury at the futility of Alice's death, he is able to summon the energy to do as the actresses did in a play Alice once told him about: each seized their moment "when they assumed the skins of wild animals, when they took responsibility for their story" (157). In Patrick's moment, light, all of a sudden, "is only an idea"; in fact, everything is, so much so that

> he could put his hand under the wheel of a train to spite the driver. He could pick up a porcupine and thrash it against the fence not caring how many quills were flung into his hands and neck in retaliation. (166)

Thus transformed and ready to leap beyond the "terrible horizon in him" (157), he takes action and randomly picks one of those many fenced and belawned "playground[s] of the rich" (166) on an island in the Lake of Bays. He travels to the island, knowing that a regatta dinner will be held at the local Muskoka Hotel, waits until the guests move outside to watch the fireworks, then sets the hotel on fire, and blows up the marina on the lake-shore. There is a moment of mild triumph when for once he catches and holds the attention of the wealthy: "Every one on the blue evening lawn looked at the flames, dumbfounded." Some men even see him and point before he lights the fuse, waving back (168). Patrick feels "fully alive, feral, exhilarated" (172) as he dives into the lake and escapes to a nearby island. There he hides in the Garden of the Blind, an estate with plants chosen to allow visitors without sight to "move from fragrance to fragrance with precise antennae" (168). Under the guidance of a blind woman, he takes in the smells ablaze in the garden as well as subtler scents hidden in the leaves of herbs.

This intensely sensory experience foreshadows the new way of seeing that he will cultivate during his subsequent imprisonment, a seeing that attends not to what was or will be, but seeks to grasp solely what is. No longer an historian but, indeed, as he believes, "a member of the night [...] never emerging out of the shadows. Unhistorical" (172), Patrick applies himself to watching over the thief Caravaggio in the cell opposite his, warning him when he is attacked by other inmates, telling him what to do after they have cut his neck, and gazing at him reassuringly when, after his return from hospital, he keeps waking up in pain. Like the touch of the woman he met in the Garden of the Blind, Patrick's seeing has become dialogic and in this is opposed to that of Harris, who proudly deems himself a visionary for the fantastic designs appearing before his inner eye. While the engineer is busy forcing his private dreams into material reality, Patrick assists Caravaggio in extracting himself from the deadly reality of the prison. To this end, he devises a plan no less ingenious than Harris's, not least for the ironic reference it constitutes to Caravaggio's name: during a job recoating the prison ceiling, he paints his friend in the sky blue he has been using so that he may hang from the prison roof perfectly camouflaged and wait for a suitable moment to escape.

Caravaggio's fantastic vanishing act celebrates invisibility as a condition not imposed but consciously chosen and as such prepares the ground for Patrick's re-emergence from prison and clandestine entry into the world of the rich. Scenes at the regatta dinner as well as his encounter with Ambrose Small earlier in the novel are revoked as Caravaggio and Patrick gate-crash the summer costume ball at the Yacht Club on Toronto Island and hijack a sailing boat for Patrick to reach the intake pipe at the bottom of Lake Ontario and, through it, Rowland Harris's filtration plant. Traversing the grounds of the yacht club, Patrick once more observes the rich in what he earlier in the novel calls their "half-lit lives." Already then he would feel anger stirring in him at "those half-formed people who were born with money and who did nothing except keep it like a thermometer up their ass. The mean rich. The soft rich" (84). At this later point, too, he registers with distaste the useless, conspicuous consumption of the rich. His eye notes the false moons and stars lighting up the ballroom, champagne corks aimed at live monkeys, a silk canopy over an orchestra, cotton snowballs handed out for the guests to have a battle with. He watches Caravaggio, dressed as a pirate, adeptly conversing, jesting, and flirting with the rich. Having "traipsed through the gardens and furnishings of the wealthy for many years," Patrick's friend knows how to play the part of a rich man pretending to be a buccaneer while eating canapés, "patting women on the ass," and waltzing among the couples with his dog on his arm (222). The conspicuous materiality of affluence mirrors the ball guests' self-abandonment to merry thoughtlessness, and proves that their *gravitas* resides entirely in their possessions, or, as Caravaggio puts it: "The only thing that holds the rich to the earth is property [...] their bureaus, their marble tables, their jewellery" (223).

Echoes of the costume ball resound in the basement of the waterworks where Patrick, later that same evening, plants his explosives, calmly humming the tune of Ira Gershwin's "I Can't Get Started," a song lamenting the impossibility of buying love with fame, power, or wealth. When Patrick has finished, he seeks out Harris in his office. "I am Patrick Lewis," he announces, but leaves it to Harris to guess from the blasting-box under his arm what he wants. The reader already knows:

> He wants the heart of the place. He wants to [...] destroy meticulously, efficiently. This is not to be a gesture of an egg hurled against a train window. (227)

Though orchestrated in similar fashion, Patrick's confrontation with Harris stands in meaningful contrast to his encounter with the millionaire Ambrose Small years earlier. Patrick no longer expects anything from his interlocutor. While once so naive as to think that he can seek out a rich man and ask him for an act of kindness, he has nothing but revenge to long for now that Alice is dead. While driven by a will to live and ready to bolt when Small tried to kill him, he now is prepared to die and already insensate to the wounds he has inflicted on himself while breaking into the waterworks.

Yet *In the Skin of a Lion* will not militate against Toronto's history and allow Patrick to blow up what is still one of the city's most famous landmarks, the R.C. Harris Water Purification Plant. The possibility that the water-works could suffer devastation is too grand a scenario even for a fictional narrative to take on, too radical a departure from history to allow. Historical reality defeats fiction in *In the Skin of a Lion* and ensures that the rise of the workers remains a fantastic projection. Dropping the idea, Ondaatje's novel meanders on through the "chaotic tumble of events,"[16] towards the order it has promised, eventually selec-

---

[16] Clearly, there is more deliberation behind the deferral of the ending than Ondaatje concedes with his account of an ominous general reluctance to bring his novels to closure: "Quite often I don't want to complete the plot, I keep postponing it. People are about to die, and then they have a flash back, and I think, 'Wait a minute, I still want to say this about that person,' or 'Do you

ting another possibility of closure and suggestively offering a final glimpse of the figure of Ambrose Small in the throes of death: a "dark, half-naked shape," a person "imploded," "a Gothic child suddenly full of language which was aimed nowhere" (214). With the pitiable demise of Patrick's arch-enemy, the novel steers precariously close to confirming the popular fantasy of a restoration of justice that has the wealthy suffer, too – if not a loss of their riches, then at least an end in miserable loneliness. Extreme aestheticization conceals the vulgarity of this fantasy but does not annul its futility. The narrative must meander on and veer back to Patrick, who, by the end of a long night listening to Rowland Harris soliloquizing into "permanent darkness" (241), is suddenly overcome by fatigue and falls asleep. Standing over the limp and bloodied body of his would-be assassin, Harris is relieved and the reader, for once forced to view Patrick through Harris's eyes, relieved, too, at the admiration for Patrick by which the master-builder is suddenly overcome as he becomes aware of the visionary power that must have brought Patrick to the water-works. More than that, there is even a glimmer of understanding in Harris's subsequent comparison of Patrick with Gilgamesh:

> He saw the lions around him glorying in life… then he took his axe in his hand, he drew his sword from his belt, and he fell upon them like an arrow from the string. (242)

Yet, the "events of literature" tumbling into the chaotic story of Patrick's sadly ineffective struggle literally reach Harris too late for him to grasp that, in his immutable superiority, he, too, is responsible for Patrick's despair. The justice Patrick has envisaged must dwindle to a pathetic gesture of mercy on the part of Harris, who magnanimously refrains from having Patrick arrested and instead calls for a nurse to dress Patrick's wounds. In line with this gesture but also with his narrator's earlier assertion that "*only the best art can realign chaos to suggest both the chaos and order it will become*," Ondaatje, too, makes a concession and, by letting Clara Dickens re-enter Patrick's life, suggests that Patrick may finally be vindicated and inherit Ambrose Small's girlfriend. There is more bitter truth in this final twist than beautifully crafted sentiment allows us to discern at first glance as a rather cynical vision of redistribution casts its shadow over the

---

remember that time when …?' There's an element of not wanting to move into that final room where a character meets his fate. I can quite understand Orson Welles hating to finish a film. To lock it up. To be final about everything one has been thinking about and circling around." Michael Ondaatje and Catherine Bush, "An Interview by Catherine Bush," *Conjunctions* 15 (1990): 91–92, http://www.jstor.org/stable/24515127 (accessed 27 January 2016).

romantic reunion towards which Patrick travels after he has been given the final word in the novel and calls out "Lights!"

## WORKS CITED

Acheson, Katherine. "Anne Wilkinson in Michael Ondaatje's *In the Skin of a Lion*: Writing and Reading Class," *Canadian Literature* 145 (1995): 107–19.

Bateman, Chris. "A Brief History of the First Electricity Company in Toronto" (7 September 2013), http://www.blogto.com/city/2013/09/a_brief_history_of_the_first_electricity_company_in_toronto/ (accessed 5 June 2016).

Beddoes, Julie. "Which Side Is It On? Form, Class, and Politics in *In the Skin of a Lion*," *Essays on Canadian Writing* 53 (1994): 204–15.

Beran, Carol L. "Ex-Centricity: Michael Ondaatje's *In the Skin of a Lion* and Hugh MacLennan's *Barometer Rising*," *Studies in Canadian Literature/Études en Littérature Canadienne* 18.1 (1993): 71–78.

Bök, Christian. "The Secular Opiate: Marxism as an Ersatz Religion in Three Canadian Texts," *Canadian Literature* 147 (1995): 11–22.

Bölling, Gordon. "Metafiction in Michael Ondaatje's Historical Novel *In the Skin of a Lion*," *Symbolism: An International Journal of Critical Aesthetics* 3 (2003): 215–53.

Davey, Frank. *Post-National Arguments: The Politics of the Anglophone-Canadian Novel since 1967* (Toronto: U of Toronto P, 1993).

Doctorow, E.L. *Ragtime* (New York: Random House, 1975).

Fraser, Nancy. "Abnormal Justice," *Critical Inquiry* 34.3 (Spring 2008): 393–422.

Fraser, Nancy. *Justice Interruptus: Critical Reflections on the "Postsocialist" Condition* (New York: Routledge, 1997).

Hutcheon, Linda. *The Canadian Postmodern: A Study of Contemporary Canadian Fiction* (*Wynford Project*) (Oxford: Oxford UP, 2012).

Kampfner, John. *The Rich: From Slaves to Super-Yachts: A 2,000-Year History* (New York: Little, Brown, 2014).

Murnaghan, Ann Marie F. "The City, the Country, and Toronto's Bloor Viaduct, 1897–1919," *Urban History Review / Revue d'histoire urbaine* 42.1 (Fall 2013): 4–50.

Ondaatje, Michael. *In the Skin of a Lion* (1987; New York: Random House, 1997).

Ondaatje, Michael, & Catherine Bush. "An Interview by Catherine Bush," *Conjunctions* 15 (1990): 87–98, http://www.jstor.org/stable/24515127 (accessed 27 January 2016).

Salgado, Minoli. "Nonlinear Dynamics and the Diasporic Imagination," in *Diaspora and Multiculturalism: Common Traditions and New Developments*, ed. & intro. Monika Fludernik (Cross/Cultures 66; Amsterdam & New York: Rodopi, 2003): 183–98.

Siemerling, Winfried. "Oral History and the Writing of the Other in Ondaatje's *In the Skin of a Lion*," in *Comparative Cultural Studies and Michael Ondaatje's Writing*, ed. & intro. Steven Tötösy de Zepetnek (West Lafayette IN: Purdue UP, 2005): 92–103.

Spearey, Susan. "Mapping and Masking: The Migrant Experience in Michael Ondaatje's *In the Skin of a Lion*," *Journal of Commonwealth Literature* 29.2 (June 1994): 45–46.

Stacey, Robert David. "A Political Aesthetic: Michael Ondaatje's *In the Skin of a Lion* as 'Covert Pastoral'," *Contemporary Literature* 49.3 (Fall 2008): 439–69.

Van Krieken, Robert. "The economics of attention," in Van Krieken, *Celebrity Society* (London: Routledge, 2012): 53–61.

Werth, Wolfgang. "Immigration and Acculturation in Michael Ondaatje's *In the Skin of a Lion*," in *Wandering Selves: Essays on Migration and Multiculturalism*, ed. Michael Porsche & Christian Berkemeier (Essen: Blaue Eule, 2001): 125–33.

❄

# Spartan Luxury

## *A Poetics of Finitude and Fullness in* A Strange and Sublime Address

SANDHYA SHETTY

GENERALLY ACCEPTED as the year when no one could deny the 1970s were finally over, 1991 has come to be enshrined through countless citations as the *annus mirabilis* of postcolonial India's economic life. 1991 also saw the publication of Amit Chaudhuri's first work of fiction, *A Strange and Sublime Address*. Looking back at a certain genteel, unhurried Calcutta, the book painstakingly salvages a time and form of middle-class dwelling that today seems to belong to an uncomfortable and constrained decade now thankfully past.[1] The sagging fortunes and ambitions of the city's middle classes are focalized through Sandeep, a vacationing ten-year-old from Malabar Hill, Bombay. The novel's Bombay (busy corporate fathers in high-rise homes) casts a distant glow in relation to which Sandeep's uncle's Calcutta home radiates only the patina of overuse.[2] But far from decrying its dust, rust, and decrepitude, the novel makes a case for the richness of everyday life in Calcutta's "small houses, unlovely and unremarkable," presenting an unembarrassed registry of the worn-out things these scaled-back dwellings contain.[3] Illuminated by "ruinophilia"–

---

[1] Saikat Majumdar, "Dallying with Dailiness: Amit Chaudhuri's Flâneur Fictions," *Studies in the Novel* 39.4 (Winter 2007): 460. Majumdar notes: "[Chaudhuri's] novels [...] change as they enter the troubled, rapidly changing 1990s in India when drastic movements in economic structures [...] begin to cause shifts in [...] personal habits and lifestyles. In his third novel, *Freedom Song* [...] the strongly felt backdrop is [...] of Calcutta in the 1990s [...] caught between a decaying Marxism and an incoming globalization."

[2] For Chaudhuri's writings on Bombay, see *Clearing a Space: Reflections on India, Literature and Culture* (Oxford: Peter Lang, 2008): 170–81, 182–94.

[3] Amit Chaudhuri, *A Strange and Sublime Address*, in *Freedom Song: Three Novels* (1991; New York: Vintage International, 2000): 7. Further page references are in the main text.

an important element of the novel's "reflective nostalgia"[4] – this "far from affluent" (12) domestic object world exhibits a strange vibrancy as well as a vernacular urbanity and fullness uncoupled from the allure of the commodity fetishism and perky life-styles *de rigueur* since the 1990s. Certainly not an emporium of the world's riches, either in the way seventeenth-century Dutch homes once were or the showy twenty-first-century that the "South City" apartments of Kolkata now aspire to be, the modestly furnished *intérieures* of *A Strange and Sublime Address* nevertheless possess an artful, even dissident, materiality that speaks the "off-modern" register of urban India in the 1970s.[5]

In *Clearing A Space*, Chaudhuri observes,

> in the globalized world, there is no 'outside,' no escape from the global; every landscape or place is a showroom of a world transformed absolutely by capitalism. (178)

Yet, as others have noted, Chaudhuri's modernist project has been precisely to unfurl such an "outside" and to elongate its moment of "escape."[6] In fact, the plethora of object-centred images that presences households as "off-modern" timescapes in *A Strange and Sublime Address* also disrupts free-market globalization formally, countering the latter's collusion with narrativity by offering a poetics of dwelling that is artful and finite.[7] I am particularly interested in the images that intimate a "philosophy of economy"[8] practised without object-allergy yet sensitive to the finite, estranged nature of things. In the urban dwellings of *A Strange and Sublime Address*, where the day still abuts on chrematistic striving, the flow of life moves along the grain of used and off-kilter things with which people dwell and make do. Furthermore, in the case the novel presents of an old couple's home on the city's outskirts, we encounter domestic interiors and human–thing entanglements privy to what Chaudhuri carefully distin-

[4] Svetlana Boym, *Architecture of the Off-Modern* (New York: Architectural Press, 2008): 4, 26; *The Future of Nostalgia* (New York: Basic Books, 2001): 49–51.

[5] Simon Schama, *An Embarrassment of Riches* (Berkeley: U of California P, 1988); Mark Jackson, "'Live the Way the World Does!': Imagining the Modern in the Spatial Returns of Kolkata and Calcutta," *Space and Culture* 13.1 (February 2010): 38–41; Boym, *Architecture*, 35–37.

[6] See, for instance, Majumdar, "Dallying," 451; Patrycja Magdalena Austin, "Local Histories, Global Perspectives in Amit Chaudhuri's *A Strange and Sublime Address* and *Afternoon Raag*," *Postcolonial Text* 6.2 (2011): 1–11; Dirk Wiemann, *Genres of Modernity: Contemporary Indian Novels* (Amsterdam & New York: Rodopi, 2008).

[7] See Chaudhuri's important statements on writing in an age of plenty, "Notes on the Novel After Globalization," in *Clearing*, 207–13.

[8] Ricardo F. Crespo, *A Re-Assessment of Aristotle's Economic Thought* (New York: Routledge, 2014): 4.

guishes as “a strange composure” (62), divorced from consuming desire and the *otium* of surplus.[9] The nature, arrangement, and quantity of things contained or judged to be in excess in these 1970s domiciles, I argue, encode a “philosophy of economy” (not yet) subsumed under unsustainable but hegemonic scripts for wellbeing. In what follows, I explore the peculiar aesthetic and ethical economies embedded in the sparsely furnished rooms and ‘dated’ objects of middle-class home life in the Indian 1970s. Although revisiting that receded (and not innocent) decade in the company of *A Strange and Sublime Address* opens one potentially to many charges, including moribund sentimentality and impotence, it is my sense that the novel’s nostalgia for this time and place is, to mobilize Svetlana Boym’s terms, “reflective” rather than “restorative”: that is to say, it offers a perspective on the past as possibly a necessary, livable, even pleasurable future.[10]

Chaudhuri’s stylistic and thematic retrenchments, in particular his preference for tiny ingrown fictional spaces over the grand sweep of national history, have been well noted.[11] My essay builds on established critical assessments that focus on the importance of domestic spaces, but I advance a differently nuanced, new-materialist perspective on the novel’s interiors. This perspective doubles the frame, overlaying Chaudhuri’s modernist, Benjaminian presencing of the allochronic ruin within capital’s time–space with a critical description of the lived meshwork of human–object relations in which humans do not have the upper hand over the man-made world. I point out that the novel’s interleaving of the household’s bio-network (linking pigeons, lizards, flies, mosquitoes, idle men in the neighborhood, studious children, aunts, cousins, visiting relatives, road workers, and passing vendors) with a middling thing-world (of fans, a car, water droplets, saris, clocks, radios, pots and pans, brooms, a wooden clothes-horse, beds) turns the latter vibrant and visceral. The emergence into the reader’s perception of the strange primevality of man-made household stuff is, of course, intimately tied to another well-discussed dimension of the novel: its devotion to the poetics of *ostranenie* or defamiliarization.[12] Paired with “ruinophilia,” this luxurious unfolding of depreciated and ordinary

---

9 Thorstein Veblen, *The Theory of the Leisure Class* (New York: Macmillan, 1912): 95.

10 Boym, *The Future of Nostalgia*, 49.

11 See Majumdar, “Dallying,” 451; Patrycja Magdalena Austin, “Local Histories, Global Perspectives,” 3; Dirk Wiemann, *Genres of Modernity*; Sumana R. Ghosh, “Aalap,” in *The Novels of Amit Chaudhuri*, ed. Sheo Bhushan & Anu Shukla (Delhi: Sarup and Sons, 2004): 159–86.

12 Viktor Shklovsky’s “Art as Technique” (1916) is the most influential articulation of literary defamiliarization. See *Four Formalist Essays*, tr. & ed. Lee Lemon & Marion J. Reis (Lincoln: U of Nebraska P, 1965): 3–24.

things to the senses restores their worth, at the same time reinstating the temporality of use-less household stuff and 'inefficient' everyday acts nestled in non-teleological dimensions of now-time or "world-time."[13] The limited and used-up materiality of the Bengali *oikos* comes to be endowed with aesthetic value as its recesses and ephemera are coaxed into momentary visibility by defamiliarization and ruinophilia. But in current scholarship on *A Strange and Sublime Address*, the way literary defamiliarization estranges to beautiful effect the ordinary and banal has been better understood than the way it, in effect, discloses the depletion, recalcitrance, and disaffection of household matter or stuff. In short, from a new-materialist angle, the novel's high-modernist aesthetics does other important critical work, de-reifying materiality and exposing the finitude and brokenness of things, which make the world – certainly of the Indian 1970s – a place not exactly ready-to-hand. It is precisely the novel's emphasis on the estranged materiality of a past era and the temporality and life of its imperfect objects, stripped of the allure of the commodity by defamiliarizing presentation, that gives it critical purchase. The retrospective depiction of middle-class Calcutta households' sensitivity to finitude affords us a prospect that speaks both to the compulsory prodigality of contemporary economic life and to its potential futures. Arguably, the novel's mimesis of the scaled-back human–object entanglements of a recently bygone era ironizes the proliferation of hyper-commoditized high-rise real-estate developments post-1990s, prefigured in the diegesis by Sandeep's Malabar Hill eyrie.[14] Locating the novel within this expanded temporal perspective allows us to read its ruinophilic nostalgia in the interests of an alternative notional history of wellbeing asymptotic with unsustainable dream-futures peddled by growth-and-development discourses in globalization.

The beat-up object-world and austere spaces depicted in the down-to-earth dwellings of *A Strange and Sublime Address* should not, however, be confused with a simple, joyless economy that absolutely forswears all excess and artifice. Chhottomama's urban household and the residence of distant relatives on the outskirts of Calcutta are, in fact, marked by modes of dwelling that cultivate beauty and "fullness" at a distance from commodity allure, but not in renunciatory apartness from object enjoyment. Indeed, there is in these interiors another inlaid aesthetic related to bodily need (sustenance) and aspiration (the luxury of raiment and adornment) that raises these otherwise pinched 1970s

---

[13] William Blattner, "Temporality," in *A Companion to Heidegger*, ed. Hubert L. Dreyfus & Mark Vrathall (Oxford: Blackwell, 2005): 311–24.

[14] Mark Jackson, "'Live the Way the World Does'," 33, 44–48.

household spaces out of the realm of finitude. While the textual movement between excess and finitude, repletion and austerity is evident in both domestic spaces, the austere suburban home offers a more extended sense of vernacular registers of prosperity pegged to the basic ritual and physical unit of Indian dwelling (*griha*).[15] The coincidence of object-paucity with aesthetic surplus (*alankara*) and gastronomic fulfilment (*annapurna*) in this household space invokes what I call spartan luxury, a feature elaborated at length in the final section.[16] Suffice it to say here that an older dialect of household economics derived from Indic materialism, deftly worked into the text, limns an unselfconsciously complex dwelling somewhere "between conspicuous excess and extreme poverty."[17] (My amplification of this partially submerged feminine-polytheist matrix is not an attempt to indigenize, or ethnicize, much less Hindu-ize, wellbeing. Prompted by the literary text, I follow the pattern of its engagement with cultural–spiritual scenarios of wellbeing not shy of artifice, plenty, or gain.[18])

## Household Goods and Things

Notwithstanding its philosophical inclination toward the spartan, A *Strange and Sublime Address* remains enchanted by material things and dedicated to teaching its readers patient connoisseurship through repeated, unexpected, pleasure in the life of things – especially those in poor working order. Activities such as bathing, laundering, dressing (up), eating, going for a drive, listening to the radio, napping, reading, or chatting bring into play fans swinging "drunkenly from side to side" (9), "shabby, reposeful doors" (47), boa constrictor-like saris, a radio babbling like a local idiot (13), a disgruntled car, a shower-head bent like the neck of a "tired giraffe" (11), a ticking lizard, and so on. Untinged by Naipaul-

---

[15] See "Aalap," 168–72 for Chaudhuri's interest in the fullness of textuality, the things built with care in household space: ritual arts like Lakshmi *puja*, "epical" food preparation, *rangoli* (which turns floors into "manuscripts"). Cautious about the "bad faith" of bemoaning the lost plenitude of ordinary things post-1980, he notes the erasures continually breaching fullness.

[16] See *Clearing a Space* for references to Hinduism as "a rich man's, a trader's religion" (160). Cf. Vikram Chandra's take on the gendered polytheist auspices of money-making in "Shakti," *Love and Longing in Bombay* (New York: Back Bay, 1998): 33–74.

[17] Chaudhuri, "Hollywood and Bollywood," in *Clearing a Space*, 179.

[18] This linkage of Hindu concepts and the question of material well-being accords with Chaudhuri's urgings in *Clearing a Space*, 107–12, 160–64 that having "passed out of its old locations in religion" and emerged as "something we may call 'culture' the spiritual is *not* antithetical to secular modernity." The self-conscious staking of a claim on behalf of secular modernity in the narrative of 'spiritual India' defends alternative *cultural* locations of "the spiritual" against Hindutva ideological appropriations.

esque disappointment, an affectionate literary attentiveness uplifts this 'Third-World' thing-world of (mostly) mechanically inept objects in Chhotomama's old household, renovating them only perceptually, letting their used, imperfect lives be (*Gelassenheit*).[19] Mass-produced family belongings – car, fan, radio, shower – thus come alive as drunken, geriatric, idiotic, or tired under Sandeep's defamiliarizing gaze, the unselfconscious connoisseurship of his eye catching the sentience of household possessions – their hybrid "quasi-subject quasi-object" character.[20] Like old retainers, they continue honourably, and frequently insubordinately, to serve in their approaching desuetude, impressing us with the tragicomedy of humans' everyday entanglements with stuff and insinuating as well a sensible home economics able to contest the unsustainable glamour of superabundance.

The aesthetic usefulness of defamiliarization in unveiling an alternative ontology of household objects in *A Strange and Sublime Address* has been well understood; its more radical potential for broaching a sensible economics of consumption less so. Maurizia Boscagli's insistence that "the aesthetic, as practice and mode of perception because of its plasticity is an apt sphere in which to articulate and study hybrid materiality" is well taken.[21] Her polemical point about turning the new-materialist account of matter's vibrancy back in the direction of both aesthetics and historical–materialist critique is also, I believe, on the mark.[22] *A Strange and Sublime Address* works as a literary proving ground for both propositions. The child Sandeep apprehends the calculable material world catachrestically, inefficiently, blurring the line between the organic and inorganic and thus de-reifying household goods and things; the Bengali domicile consequently becomes an alternative experience of everyday materialities with huge implications for post-1990s middle-class imaginaries of economic growth and wellbeing, which today keeps the "inflationary direction of in-

---

19 See Lucas Introna, "Ethics and the Speaking of Things," *Theory, Culture & Society* 26.4 (July 2009): 37–42.

20 Bruno Latour, *We Have Never Been Modern*, tr. Catherine Porter (*Nous n'avons jamais été modernes: Essai d'anthropologie symétrique*, 1991; Boston MA: Harvester Wheatsheaf, 1993): 51.

21 See Maurizia Boscagli, *Stuff Theory: Everyday Objects, Radical Materialisms* (London: Bloomsbury, 2014): 4–13.

22 Boscagli, *Stuff Theory*, 22–32. For new-materialist approaches, see also Diana Coole & Samantha Frost, "Introduction" to *New Materialisms: Ontology, Agency and Politics*, ed. Coole & Frost (Durham NC: Duke UP, 2010): 1–46, Jane Bennett, *Vibrant Matter: A Political Ecology of Things* (Chicago: U of Chicago P, 2010), Bruno Latour, *We Have Never Been Modern*, and Ian Hodder, "The Entanglements of Humans and Things: A Long Term View," *New Literary History* 45.1 (Winter 2014): 19–36. Further page references are in the main text.

creased human–thing entanglement [moving] forward relentlessly" (31). To be sure, in turning the 1970s' "fetid industrialization" (34) and depleted middle-class households into artful matter, Chaudhuri's literary gaze invites the charge of elevating the stagnant smallness of the interregnum between independence and neoliberal globalization; however, today, slightly over two decades later, things appear in a rather different light. Read as a record of human–object entanglements in a certain time and place, *A Strange and Sublime Address* can serve contemporary rethinking of the idea that the fate of matter is to be ceaselessly transformable, collectible, consumable, and disposable.

The headache of dependency, even entrapment, produced by human entanglement in the "lives and temporalities of things,"[23] is most vividly caught in the farcically incorrigible objects with which Chhotomama's household makes do: a clock that insists on running fast and a car that insists on not moving at all. Car and clock, of course, are clichés of capitalist modernity's ultra-efficient organization of time, matter, and space – central elements in the "vast apparatus of humans and things that has to be mobilized on a global scale" to keep capital's world running (21).[24] As properties of a household on the global peripheries, the off-kilter clock and the superannuated family Ambassador remind us that this apparatus chronically operates at half-cock. The "everyday expectation of stability and order" is unguaranteed. Unpredictable cuts in electricity and water supply along with ancient fans, old beds, pigeon-shit-spattered ledges, and the ubiquitous dust on floors that Chhaya must sweep and repress with a wet rag create a different experience of materiality in the Vivekananda Road house, man-made objects becoming complexly estranged from humans, even faintly minatory. More than any of Chhotomama's possessions, the Ambassador, the first "Made in India" automobile, emerges as the tragicomic signifier of postcolonial bourgeois modernity's premature dotage. Object of the novel's ruinophilia, the derelict Ambassador, "monument [...] of the bourgeoisie as ruin"[25] par excellence, ironizes Nehruvian and post-Nehruvian 'development' visions as always already and so much stuff and debris.[26]

---

[23] Hodder, "The Entanglements of Humans and Things," 20.

[24] While true of the global North, these formulations require modulation with respect to "human–object entanglements" in the South.

[25] Walter Benjamin, "Paris, the Capital of the Nineteenth Century (Exposé of 1935)," in Benjamin, *The Arcades Project*, tr. Rolf Tiedemann (*Passagen-Werk*, 1982; Cambridge MA: Harvard UP, 1999): 13.

[26] See Hormazd Sorabjee, "An Epitaph for India's Appalling Car," *BBC Newsmagazine* (8 July 2014). The history of the Ambassador's production shadows the history of the rise, decline, and fall of the centrally planned Indian economy before the 1990s. By the early 1990s, the Ambassador was

Yet, under the defamiliarizing gaze of the narrator in *A Strange and Sublime Address*, the Ambassador as a member of Chhotomama's menagerie, along with drying python-like saris and a gecko residing behind the clothes-horse in the bedroom, possesses a "lively immanence"[27] as well. In this form, the decaying car emerges as the unamenable stuff of human headaches rather than ease. Arresting the forward momentum of the narrative of the day, and hence the household's economic life, the dysfunctional car registers Hodder's point that things are always drawing us into their care, making difficult everyday work even harder (21). As Chhotomama's wife, Mamima feels keenly enough the pinch of domestic austerity, but it is the unmoving car that brings home to her and us the melancholy of "entrap[ment] in the needs and demands of things and their limits and instabilities" (21). Here is one instance of the old Ambassador making a terrible scene, revving up idlers while Chhotomama at the steering wheel tries to appear nonchalant:

> A few idle men had gathered around the decrepit car.
>
> "Okay boys, start pushing," Chhotomama commanded.
>
> The idlers were quite unexpectedly altered into purposeful, energetic men, as if someone had turned a key in their backs. They took position, like a small battalion [...] At Chhotomama's words, the team strained forward, and the recalcitrant care, after some solid silent thought, decided to concede a few feet into the road. People had come out on the balconies [...] watching with sympathetic curiosity. Their eyes followed the car's reluctant progress [...] husbands and wives who had quarreled the previous night were reunited in their avid appreciation the spectacle.
>
> Sandeep and his cousins stared in embarrassed silence. As they watched [...] their necks craned with painful tension as the disgruntled car moved beyond view. There was an apprehensive hush, then a faint rumble, then excitement as they saw the car returning, this time facing the other side of the road.
>
> "Harder, boys, harder!" persuaded his uncle.
>
> He looked almost heroic and serene, in complete control of the troubled situation. (32–33)

We, of course, know that Chhotomama only *appears* in control over the car comically represented as matter with an unpredictable temper and defiant will.

---

symbolic of everything that had gone wrong with economic governance. In 2014, Calcutta-based Hindustan Motors, makers of the Ambassador, ended operations first begun in 1958. The death knell was rung in the 1980s, when the Maruti 800 entered the market; thereafter, foreign car companies, permitted to enter the Indian market in the 1990s, dealt the final blow.

[27] Diana Coole & Samantha Frost, "Introduction" to *New Materialisms*, 8–9.

With Mamima, we understand the hollowness of her husband's heroism as well as the unreliability not only of the family car but of modern things in general, especially in the world euphemistically dubbed 'developing'. Her frustration, even daily shame, frames the novella's otherwise comic presentation of the car as the unreliable vehicle that sustains and fails the domestic economy of this postcolonial middle-class household. Like Chhotomama's business, the car just won't get going.

Mamima's exasperation signifies what undergirds complaints about the technical-object world in Third-World modernity: not all things are ready-to-hand, capable as such of securing us and/to our world; nonetheless, her express discontent does not, as one might expect, re-ignite dashed ownership aspirations. She does not hope for a new replacement. When Sandeep asks her over lunch, "Mamima, what did you pray for today?," she replies, "separating some tiny and particularly persistent bones from the fish": "Oh, I prayed the car would start in the mornings." Her son, "a high-pitched inflection of disappointment in his voice," cries out, "Didn't you pray for a new car" (37). A moment in home-economics instruction, if ever there was one, Mamima's deflection of the need for a new car embodies the kind of nice conscientious judgment (cleverly signified by her delicate separation of the edible from the inedible) required by *oikonomia* if life is to be sustained: a new car would be excessive; if old stuff can continue to be *sufficiently* efficient, that would be satisfactory. Aristotelian *oikonomia* triumphs over chrematistics in this scene of middle-class urban dwelling on the postcolonial margins of global commodity culture in an era of economic stagnation. Accommodating the limits of her time and place, Mamima's decision on economy can also spark imaginings of an alternative relationship to materiality and consumption in ours.

The frail, obsolescent Ambassador and Mamima's decision against a new car open important lines of thinking about the "inflationary direction" of humans' everyday entanglements with the object-world as well as the entrapping agency of used and use-less things that compel reconsideration of the nature of human being itself. The novella's interest in the old car as ruin usefully evolves into a depiction of it that enables us to "rethink commodity as matter that is alive [vibrant] and not as simply bearing in its form the ever-same fetish-logic of consumer capital."[28] When her husband's suddenly energized *lumpen* helpers return to assure her that "the car's alright!" – all malingering having come to end – Mamima smiles, but thinks

[28] Boscagli, *Stuff Theory*, 24.

> that this kind of thing occurred too frequently in the mornings, and the derelict, geriatric car changed into a difficult, obstinate animal. It was one of those beasts that the people of Calcutta had been unable to domesticate– better, perhaps, to go back to the horse and the horse carriage. On bad days like this when the fans stopped turning because of a power cut, when the telephones went dead because of a cable-fault, when the taps became dry [...] and, finally, when the car engine curtly refused to start, it seems a better idea to return to a primitive unpretentious means of subsistence – to buy a horse and a plough, to dig a well ... to plant one's own trees and grow one's own fruit and vegetables. Calcutta, in spite of its fetid industrialization was really part of [...] the Bengal of the bullock cart and the earthen lamp. It has pretended to be otherwise, but now it had grown old and was returning to that original darkness: in time [...] earthen lamps would burn again in the houses. (34)

The car's recalcitrance opens a window onto a past prospect: the "terracotta landscape" of Bengal now littered with the debris of "fetid industrialization" (34). Mamima's nostalgia is temporally complex, but before parsing its tense, let us note the significance of animation and animal imagery that the car's mechanical decrepitude invokes and which in turn occasions her spiralling litany of the entire urban household's trouble with things. No longer self-sufficient in provisioning its needs, the modern *oikonomia* is too networked to complex mechanical prostheses – cars, taps, fans – whose functionality is forever breaking down, making materiality seem not only dead and dry but also unattractively alive. Hence, things appear curtly unresponsive, "obstinate" (34), "disgruntled" (33). As entanglements and dysfunctionality increase, animation and agency burgeon; objects become quasi-subjects.[29] In Mamima's words, the car is a "beast" that cannot be domesticated for household use. Like the city itself, in Mamima's musings, this beast of an Ambassador "grown old" breaks free, reverting to primitive thinghood. Its animation and animality are precisely aspects of its becoming thing, of the regression and/or liberation of the commodity as ruin into the primevality ("original darkness") of matter.

The primevality of time, indexed in Mamima's exasperated recall of "original darkness" (34), returns us to Chaudhuri's broad critical-modernist orientation. I would argue that *A Strange and Sublime Address* expressly wants to make a case for nostalgia and against its "inadmissibility" within globalization's hallmark marketing of being at-home anywhere in the world.[30] And it is Mamima's re-

---

[29] Cf. Martin Heidegger, "The Thing" ("Das Ding," 1950), in *Poetry, Language, Thought*, tr. & intro. Albert Hofstader (New York: HarperCollins, 2001): 161–85.

[30] Chaudhuri, "Notes on the Novel after Globalization," in *Clearing*, 204.

cognition of the "long-term increase in [modernity's] entanglement with things" that marks the place in the text where the stakes of nostalgia as critique are explicitly raised. The passage triggered by the obduracy of man-made stuff leverages nostalgia as partner in the "ethical consideration of the paths we should consider taking as a species" (34). The first thing to note about the passage in question is that Mamima's frustrated recall of a terracotta Bengal possesses a strange, vague temporality. This ambiguity of temporal reference should preclude a reading of the putatively recalled past as some ascertainable, premodern historical moment. Rather, positioned as an allochronic site with polemical potential, we might tease out the sense of the tense in the last sentence quoted: "in time [...] earthen lamps would burn again in the houses" (34). "Would," I submit, puts the future in a new and different light – the light, specifically, of earthen lamps of the past. This future which will slowly "return" back to a past can only be seen as regressive nostalgia if "the earthen lamp," horse carriages and such are read literally. What they really signify is the *idea* of a different, "sustainable," and "dignified" scale of human–object entanglements.[31] Mamima's outburst at the sight of the wilful geriatric car points us, potentially, to the form of an alternative kind of being in the world, reminding us of how humans historically *have been* human not apart from things, but with a healthy sense of their finitude. The novella's turn to "original" simplicity, then, is neither sentimental nor anti-modern. If nostalgia there is, then let us read it as ironic and temporally complex – as "enamored of distance, not of the referent itself [bullock cart Bengal in this case]."[32]

## Vernacular Materialisms: *Alankara*, Austerity, *Annapurna*

An excursion, detailed in chapter eight, takes Sandeep from the interior of the Vivekananda Road house to the home of relatives on the city's outskirts. In his extended rendition of this outing, Chaudhuri works with something similar to the Aristotelian distinction between *oikonomia* ("natural" home economics) and 'chrematistics' (bad, artificial economy of money, marked by infinite desire), alluded to above. But rather than offering a philosophy of economy that reifies the distinction (in favour of *oikonomia* over chrematistics), his scenic description offers a way of ethically closing the gap between these two opposed economies (restricted and unrestricted). Crucial to this deconstruction are certain Indic concepts of enjoyment and wellbeing: *annapurna* (repletion), *shringara*

[31] See Wiemann's insightful discussion of this passage in *Genres*, 223–24.

[32] Quoted in Svetlana Boym, *The Future of Nostalgia*, 50.

(facial adornment), *alankara* (architectural, bodily, or poetic artifice). These reinscribe the bare materiality of the suburban household as poetic dwelling consistent with need *and* desire, tending toward sparseness *and* luxury, austerity *and* ornamentation.[33] As the text travels between three points – which I designate as *alankara* (artifice), austerity (culture of material sparseness), and *annapurna* (full of food) – it limits each by opening each onto the other, producing the ethos and ethics of what I have been calling 'spartan luxury'.

Post-2008, the term 'austerity' has come to signify curbs on fiscal irresponsibility and the grief of mostly Western nations – Greece's in particular. Some scholars, however, have made compelling arguments for rethinking 'austerity' as a "language of reasoned hangover" that everyone should learn, given economic disaster and looming environmental catastrophe.[34] Usually, ancient Sparta is cited as the only secular precedent for the cultivation of austerity *as a way of life* and political platform from which to attack luxury and the passion for wealth.[35] But austerity has an Indic provenance as well. Chaudhuri's literary depiction of the 1970s' suburban home in *A Strange and Sublime Address* invokes its normative, everyday presence. Although Indic austerity in the novel connotes vulnerability and scarcity, it is not a moralistic response to national or domestic giddiness, nor does it speak the idiom of modern economics. As depicted, lived austerity cohabits with fullness and a certain excess. If Sandeep's discovery of the object-world in Chhotomama's home conveys the aesthetic of ruin and sensitivity to finitude, his apprehension of austere materiality in the suburban home on Calcutta's outskirts mounts an unexpected redefinition of luxury, wealth, and wellbeing.

Driving to the old relatives' home in the "geriatric" Ambassador, Sandeep imagines the outskirts of Calcutta as a "remote and unrecognizable" (59) space–time, echoing Mamima's earlier musings on a terracotta Bengal:

> the city was no longer clearly demarcated from the folk-tale Bengal that surrounded it so thickly. Myths and ghosts and Bengal tigers roamed beyond an unclear boundary. (59)

---

[33] Vidya Dehejia, *The Body Adorned: The Sacred and the Profane* (New York: Columbia UP, 2009): 24, 71. This undoing of the Aristotelian distinction also resonates with Jacques Derrida's re-reading of *oikonomia* as "unlivable" – see *Given Time*, tr. Peggy Kamuf (Chicago: U of Chicago P, 1992), Also, Nadja Gernalzick, "From Classical Dichotomy to Differantial Contract," in *Metaphors of Economy*, ed. Nicole Brachter & Stefan Lerbrechter (Amsterdam & New York: Rodopi, 2005): 55–69.

[34] Derek Edyvane, *Civic Virtue and the Sovereignty of Evil* (New York: Routledge, 2013): 67–81.

[35] Edyvane, *Civic Virtue*, 72–73.

Initially, then, folktales and ghost stories mark the relatives' home as distant and different from the chrematistic city. The tacit and explicit Indic allusions also act to move us from the city into a dwelling-place characterized as a spatial and temporal beyond. In fact, the chapter detailing the visit spans two 'A's, as it were: *alankara* (adornment, ornamentation, self-devotion or ardour in relation to self) and *annapurna*. First, *alankara*: the "simple" visit to unassuming relatives begins in the Vivekananda Road house with complex preparations on the women's part: mother and aunt apply *kaajal*, *kumkum*, *bindi*, and lipstick, slip on gold bangles, wrap pressed, shimmering saris around their bodies, dab on perfumes. In Sandeep's estimation, all of this seems like "fuss," a little in excess of the occasion. These acts of make-up (*maquillage*) are, however, to be read not just or only as another instance of Sandeep's attentiveness (or as signifiers of Indian women's ideological performance of oppressive femininity). Rather, Chaudhuri is at pains to underline that the everyday – dressing up prior to a visit – is steeped in a certain vernacular aesthetic.[36] The narrator expands this moment's significance, marking "fuss" as "ritual" (social ritual, convention), not, he insists, as "fashion" (58) but as an event that invokes an "immemorial tradition of applying *shringara* ("*kaajal* and *kumkum*, and other ancient cosmetics like sandalwood paste and *mehndi*") and reveals "the craftsman-like way in which the women made themselves up ('making oneself up' – the same, after all, as creating oneself)" (58). A form of passionate self-devotion, something necessary and expected, yet in excess of what is necessary from the perspective of simplicity or need, the women's self-making is compared to the artisanal work of idol-making before a festival, which, too, constitutes a salient example of the art of *alankara*, which "adorned from simplicity to a complexity that was [...] feminine" (58). *Alankara*, then, is for women and the gods, but also for temple building and poetry.[37]

In the reading the text promotes, make-up and ornament move the body's surface to another state – a state of complexity and auspiciousness. Despite the restricted material and conceptual economy within which the narrative locates them, the simple old couple the women are preparing to visit would as hosts want (desire) or expect to see their female guests made-up, dressed: that is, ornamented as part of the social ritual of visiting. The women's 'extravagant' preparation for a simple meeting would entertain, please, provoke sensation and conversation: "the old lady would finger the texture of their saris and ask

---

[36] See Chaudhuri's conversation about Indian body ornamentation in *The Novels of Amit Chaudhuri*, ed. Sheo Bhushan & Anu Shukla, 172–78.

[37] Dehejia, *The Body Adorned*, 71–74.

questions" (58). The old man would be pleased by feminine "luxury" – he would indulge in the women's "extravagance" (58). Ornament is that which for a moment quietly uplifts "small, clear lives" (58) and, in so doing, implicates the restricted economy of the novel's suburban *oikonomia* in the excesses of *alankara* and *shringara* – forms of 'writing' (in the Derridean sense) that conceptually participate in the unrestricted economy of chrematistics as art and desire.

## The Austere Room

Having arrived at the relatives' home, Sandeep looks about him as the social gift-giving economy and other adult niceties unfold. It is precisely during his pivoting away from the 'luxury' of social decorum that the narrative seizes the opportunity to expatiate upon "the impression" (62) made by an unstylish, sparsely decorated room and to frame its austerity within a "culture and tradition of sparseness" (62). In contrast to the rituals of *alankara* that turn the simple into the complex and nothing into something, and in contrast to 'fuss', this household's physical space appears unfussy and modest. The not-big room, "despite its bareness," gives Sandeep the impression of "austerity rather than poverty" (62). It has a "cool, accommodating presence" and its emptiness suggests "composure" (63); although it encloses nothing, strangely, the room itself still seems to possess thingness. The text offers its own explicit reading of this interior space, guiding readers towards conceptualizing a "kind of being" (62) in an object-world asynchronous with "the expression of the commodity."[38] A thesis is established for us: "poverty" meant "displacement as well as lack" while "austerity" meant "being poor in a rooted way, within a tradition and culture of sparseness, which transformed even the lack, the paucity, into a kind of being" (62). The rootedness here is both physical and cultural – a kind of poetic dwelling not wholly intentional (not necessarily deliberately chosen or self-reflexive, though it might be) but certainly inhabited in an immanent way. Still, the object-paucity is not entirely random, either; nor is it bemoaned.

Chaudhuri's sentence straightforwardly takes on the task of defining "austerity" and "poverty" and in so doing re-semanticizes the loaded term "poverty" that has generated so many thousands of scripts of amelioration and abolition in development discourses. Poverty is not the opposite of riches, nor *is* it riches metaphorized to bear some idealist-spiritual tenor as wealth. Poverty *is* a material condition. The novel's thesis sets it beside material *austerity*, as its *différance*. Continuing to parse the concepts in play, it becomes clear that poverty is

---

[38] Mark Jackson, "'Live the Way the World Does'," 37.

*not lack* itself but *a* particular kind of "lack" (63) *within lack* generally; the particular "lack" (63) within lack that makes poverty *is the lack of rootedness* or place in a "culture of sparseness" (62). The association with place or dwelling is what gives lack weight and value, again, not by turning it into metaphorical wealth, but as an anti-metaphysical "kind of being" (62) or secular dwelling. Lack (paucity) is thus re-presented to the imagination as a mode of dwelling in/on an alternative way of being rooted in, or part of, an intentionally lived, not entirely random experience.

Dilating on Sandeep's impression of austerity, the narrator lists all the objects in the room rather than giving the kind of luxurious sweep of sensuous description of just one or two in his usual manner. A quick enumeration, reminiscent of a furniture-mover's perspective on a room, takes precedence over the slow aneconomic perceptual effort we have witnessed so far. But perhaps that is the very point made by the brisk listing: "The objects in the room were *numerous enough* to be noticed and *a few enough* to be counted and remembered" (63; emphasis added). Uncountable and countable: the objects fall between a big number and a small number. What number is this? We cannot say, but the operative word is "enough," a term that signals a limit, finitude. Although the listing of things in this object-world does not exactly give it "the expression of the commodity,"[39] it still signals a sort of accumulation that discloses an alternative worlding. Ramakrishna's sayings, *shatranjis*, the harmonium, and *tanpura* (62) gather to themselves a modest way of being that does not, however, lack a certain kind of ornamentation; musical instruments, the sayings of mystics, the mango tree outside and the money plant inside – all 'dress' this world up, decorate it. If we are tempted to read this scene of the Bengali household in Aristotelian terms of measured household management of finite needs, an art of limited ends, the presence of a *money plant* that Sandeep's eye picks out as one of the objects in the sparsely furnished room should give us pause. There is a reading of this passage that, while resonant with the Aristotelian approval of *oikonomia* as opposed to chrematistic desire, remains far from identical with it. The presence of the money plant signifies, if not excessive accumulation, then at least an expectation, a hope of money or good fortune, not a rejection of it. The question is whether the domestic space of this household as it appears can be read as proof of that expectation's having been met or approximated, or whether, given the paucity of material objects in it, this bare space can be read as expectant – still awaiting Laxmi's visit, Laxmi, the goddess of wealth, invoked in the *Rig-Veda* as the one "who is radiant with ornaments /

[39] Jackson, "'Live the Way the World Does'," 37.

And is the goddess of wealth."[40] She is also, significantly, one not pleased by asceticism or repression of desire. The goddess most frequently associated with the Hindu home (*griha*), Laxmi contradicts any tendency to reify the opposition between restricted household economy and unrestricted desire for *chrema*.

But the real point of Chaudhuri's clever passage describing the bare room on the city's outskirts, faintly reminiscent of Heidegger's thinking on a farmhouse and jug, comes at the very end.[41]

> The short stretches of empty space in between seemed to have been deliberately created by the congruence of the walls and the balance between light and shadows. Space gave the little room its strange composure and a cool, accommodating presence. (62–63)

Here the novel's economic subtext pinpoints the way austerity becomes definitive of this room and not just a term indicating what the room lacks by way of solid material objects; there are *enough* of those. Paradoxically, austerity is precisely a quality of "cool" (*šila*) or true presence (63). Indeed, the thingness of this room is the empty space (or void) itself, the emptiness or negative spaces that the walls enclose and that flows between the "few enough" (62) solid objects in it; this emptiness is not a byproduct of dearth; it seems, he says, to have been "*deliberately created* by the congruence of the walls and the balance between light and shadow" (63; emphasis added) and it is this artificial space – the artifice of it – that lends to the room true "presence" (63) – the subtle *alankara*, as it were – that impresses itself on Sandeep's senses. The very notion of what constitutes thingness and things, what is essential, is here, as in Heidegger, redefined away from object-paucity and commodity presence to the walls and building itself, to what encloses nothing (a void) and thus elevates it to a certain "composure" and complexity. Far from being signifiers of poverty, object-paucity and empty space are themselves the "deliberately created" ornament or excess that grace a room ("within a tradition and culture of sparseness"). In underlining this, Sandeep's perceptual subtlety privileges material paucity, in effect negating the commodity expression of spatial materiality, training our eye to see object-paucity as the absence of dearth. From the standpoint of the commodity spectacle, the room would appear simply *too* bare, in keeping with *oikonomia*, bare of desire, un-desiring or unsuccessfully desiring: hence, undesirable. But Chaudhuri's Sandeep also *sees* the money plant, seizing therefore a key image that counters reductive readings of bareness and complicates the notion of "being poor" (62).

---

[40] Quoted in Vanamali, *Shakti: Realm of The Divine Mother* (Rochester VT: Bear, 2008): 197–98.

[41] Heidegger, *Poetry, Language, Thought*, 141–60 and 161–85.

## Being Poor/Being Full

Following Sandeep's quick accounting of things which ends with a paean to the negative space between things as the essential thing or presence, we are directed to focus on another animate object on the floor: "a moist, unctuous thing" (63–64). This "thing," it turns out, is an infant girl named Annapurna and with her we come to the second 'A' that book-ends this outing on the outskirts of the city and ends the chapter as well. Sandeep learns how to parse the word and meaning of 'Annapurna' incidentally – through an overheard conversation: *anna* means rice or food and *purna* means 'full' or 'complete'. I prefer to translate *purna* into the English 'replete' rather than 'complete', full as in satiated rather than finished or ended. Chaudhuri provides a somewhat blander definition of the Sanskrit word, translating it as "Provider of Food or Sustenance" (63), a phrasing, however, that resonates with the Aristotelian definition of the essential work of *oikonomia*. Sandeep plays with the baby Annapurna prior to dinner when its grandmother, "the old lady," "took pains to see that everyone ate well" (64). The episode closes with Sandeep asleep in the car on the way home with the sound of conversations recently heard echoing in his head: "What's its name?" asked someone and someone replied, "Annapurna," and a third voice said, "It's a lovely name" (65). We are prompted by the impersonal pronoun to broaden the reference and perhaps to ask: what is the name not just of the baby but of this experience that we, with Sandeep, have just witnessed in this small and simple home? What is the name of this alternative mode of dwelling that the text has been at pains to elaborate on the limits of the city (historical site of sumptuous display), as its supplement? I venture to suggest 'Annapurna' as the name of this kind of dwelling in the world – a bare, sparse, austere kind of being/habitation that is nevertheless full, filled, and replete. Annapurna as the Goddess of Food and Sustenance is also, let us recall, another version of Laxmi or Shri, the goddess of wealth.[42] Laxmi, we know, signifies affluence and good luck (always feminized); she marks an anti-ascetic strain in Indic philosophy and culture; as Shri, she signifies the material side of life and, as *grihalaxmi*, auspicious domestic space. In the Indic economy, plenitude through food is often recast as money, wealth. (Chaudhuri plays on this frequently throughout the text.) The association of food, eating, and prosperity is underlined by the goddess Laxmi, who, we might say, is only another version of plenitude or bounty: that is, of Annapurna, who signifies the repletion that lines the austere spare economy of the household.

[42] Indira Vishwanathan Peterson, *Design and Rhetoric in a Sanskrit Court Epic* (Albany: State U of New York P, 2003): 65.

In other words, Annapurna embodied in the female infant breaks the closed system of necessity or *oikonomia*, introducing repletion, expectation, ornament, fullness, and bounty into the household's restricted economy. As perhaps the money plant and appreciation of feminine *alankara* also indicate, there is, in this heterotopic site of the spartan household, always something more, a certain ornament or repletion that is not routed predictably through commodity consumption or capital accumulation. Might we say, then, that an alternative experience of chrematistics as *annapurna*, auspiciousness, good fortune, is made available in Chaudhuri's novella – a secular postcolonial chrematistics that provincializes the chrematistics of commodity capitalism, typically limned as eternal consumption without repletion? Can Annapurna bypass commoditized materiality and wellbeing without falling back on impossible renunciatory gestures? Can it point to austerity as an everyday practice that is not mere nothing – not an ascetic, unlivable, non-derivative simplicity wherein everything has only use-value and nothing is wasted? What is too much, too little, truly necessary to the household as space of responsibility, measure, beauty, and aspiration? What is useful surplus and what is dangerous surplus? Moving between simplicity and *alankara* (ornament and surplus), austerity (object-paucity), and Annapurna (repletion), *A Strange and Sublime Address* raises such questions, helping us imagine and articulate the paradox of unsustainable limits and livable luxuries.

## WORKS CITED


Benjamin, Walter. "Paris, Capital of the Nineteenth Century (Exposé of 1935)," in Benjamin, *The Arcades Project*, tr. Rolf Tiedemann (*Passagen-Werk*, 1982; Cambridge MA: Harvard UP, 1999): 3–13.

Bennett, Jane. *Vibrant Matter: A Political Ecology of Things* (Durham NC: Duke UP, 2010).

Blattner, William. "Temporality," in *A Companion to Heidegger*, ed. Hubert L. Dreyfus & Mark Vrathall (Oxford: Blackwell, 2005): 311–24.

Boym, Svetlana. *Architecture of the Off-Modern* (New York: Architectural Press, 2008).

Boym, Svetlana. *The Future of Nostalgia* (New York: Basic Books, 2001).

Boscagli, Maurizia. *Stuff Theory: Everyday Objects, Radical Materialism* (London: Bloomsbury, 2014).

Chandra, Vikram. "Shakti," in *Love and Longing in Bombay* (New York: Back Bay, 1998): 33–74.

Chaudhuri, Amit. *Clearing a Space: Reflections on India, Literature and Culture* (Oxford: Peter Lang, 2008).

Chaudhuri, Amit. *A Strange and Sublime Address*, in *Freedom Song: Three Novels* (New York: Vintage, 2000): 1–121.

Coole, Diana, & Samantha Frost, "Introduction" to *New Materialisms: Ontology, Agency and Politics*, ed. Coole & Frost (Durham NC: Duke UP, 2010): 1–46.

Crespo, F. Ricardo. *A Re-Assessment of Aristotle's Economic Thought* (London: Routledge, 2014).

Dehejia, Vidya. *The Body Adorned: Sacred and Profane in Indian Art* (New York: Columbia UP, 2009).

Derrida, Jacques. *Given Time: I Counterfeit Money*, tr. Peggy Kamuf (Chicago: U of Chicago P, 1992).

Edyvane, Derek. *Civic Virtue and the Sovereignty of Evil* (London: Routledge, 2013).

Gernalzick, Nadja. "From Classical Dichotomy to Differantial Contract: The Derridean Integration of Monetary Theory," in *Metaphors of Economy*, ed. Nicole Brachter & Stefan Lerbrechter (Amsterdam & New York: Rodopi, 2005): 55–69.

Ghosh, R. Sumana. "Aalap," in *The Novels of Amit Chaudhuri*, ed. Sheo Bhushan Shukla & Anu Shukla (Delhi: Sarup & Sons, 2004): 159–86.

Heidegger, Martin. "The Thing" ("Das Ding," 1950), in *Poetry, Language, Thought*, tr. & intro. Albert Hofstader (New York: HarperCollins, 2001).

Hodder, Ian. "The Entanglements of Humans and Things: A Long-Term View," *New Literary History* 45.1 (Winter 2014): 19–36.

Introna, Lucas. "Ethics and the Speaking of Things," *Theory, Culture, and Society* 26.4 (July 2009): 25–46.

Jackson, Mark. "'Live the Way the World Does': Imagining the Modern in the Spatial Returns of Kolkata and Calcutta," *Space and Culture* 13.1 (February 2010): 32–53.

Justin, Patrycja Magdalena. "Local Histories, Global Perspectives in Amit Chaudhuri's *A Strange and Sublime Address* and *Afternoon Raag*," *Postcolonial Text* 6.1 (2011): 1–11.

Latour, Bruno. *We Have Never Been Modern*, tr. Catherine Porter (*Nous n'avons jamais été modernes: Essai d'anthropologie symétrique*, 1991; Boston MA: Harvester Wheatsheaf, 1993).

Majumdar, Saikat. "Dallying with Dailiness: Amit Chaudhuri's Flâneur Fictions," *Studies in the Novel* 39.4 (Winter 2007): 448–64.

Peterson, Indira Viswanathan. *Design and Rhetoric in a Sanskrit Court Epic: The Kiratarjuniya of Bhairavi* (Albany: State U of New York P, 2003).

Schama, Simon. The *Embarrassment of Riches: An Interpretation of Dutch Culture in the Golden Age* (Berkeley: U of California P, 1988).

Shklovsky, Viktor. "Art as Technique" (1916), in *Four Formalist Essays*, tr. & ed. Lee T. Lemon & Marion J. Reis (Lincoln: U of Nebraska P, 1965): 3–24.

Sorabjee, Hormazd. "An Epitaph for India's Appalling National Car," *BBC Newsmagazine* 8 July 2014.

Vanamali. *Shakti: Real of the Divine Mother* (Rochester VT: Bear, 2008).

Veblen, Thorstein. *The Theory of the Leisure Class* (New York: Macmillan, 1912).

Wiemann, Dirk. *Genres of Modernity: Contemporary Indian Novels in English* (Amsterdam & New York: Rodopi, 2008).

❄

II ❄

# Historical Wealth and Material Injustice

# Writing Congo

HELEN TIFFIN

BROADLY DEFINED, the Congo region of Africa might be considered a territory of the European or Western imagination. The 'boundaries' drawn by European treaty in the nineteenth century were products of European politics and European greed.[1] They had nothing to do with any knowledge of the territory being carved up by Europe's rulers, nor with the Congolese peoples themselves. But the area had been, and would continue to be, a place of European imagination in another sense: a ground upon which Western writers, many of whom had never set foot on the African continent at all, conducted often heated debates about conditions there.

The Congo is also an area of uncommon material wealth, but again, mostly for outsiders.[2] During the era of King Leopold's notorious fiefdom, the vast wealth extracted was primarily through ivory and native vine rubber. During most of the twentieth century and until today, this 'uncommon' wealth has been in minerals. Synthetics and rubber plantations have overtaken the once immensely profitable Central African rubber trade, though ivory still remains a source of wealth, making its way, illegally, and in spite of international endangered species treaties, to China and, to a lesser degree, India. But it is now the uncommon wealth of minerals in the region, and the demand of the rest of the world for these, that has been primarily – not exclusively – responsible for the continuation of political turmoil, appalling labour conditions, and the overall impoverishment (with the exception of some native elites) of the peoples of the Congo region. The minerals now in demand include gold, copper, diamonds, and particularly coltan (tantalite), which, like gold, is an essential component of

[1] For a comprehensive and up to date history of the Congo area, see David Van Reybrouck, *Congo: The Epic History of a People* (London: Fourth Estate, 2014).

[2] For an in-depth study of Leopold's regime in the Congo, see Adam Hochschild, *King Leopold's Ghost: A Story of Greed, Terror and Heroism in Colonial Africa* (New York: Houghton Mifflin, 1998).

the gadgetry of our brave new world of global communications: computers, iPads, smart phones.

And just as ivory and rubber – the sources of the uncommon wealth of Leopold's (and subsequently Belgium's) administration – involved notorious labour practices, so today the means of extraction of minerals demanded by the world replicate that infamous history. Today the overlords are not Leopold's company officers but government armies, local warlords, anti-government militias; and while some of the wealth remains in the hands of these new bosses, much ends up in the pockets of Chinese and Western companies through illegally operating entrepreneurs. It continues because we are hungry for these Congolese materials (mined, of course, by 'cheap' labour) for our electronic devices – the 'our' now including the African countries themselves. 'Conflict' minerals are no longer exclusively sought after by the West.

The ruthless extraction of the Congo's natural resources under 'unnatural' labour conditions, from King Leopold's day to the present, has, however, generated a different kind of wealth, largely from the recipient world (particularly the West), and more recently from the Congo itself. In this essay, I concentrate on one particular branch of the plethora of writing *about* the Congo – writing in English. This account is restricted to extra-Congolese anglophone writing because, even though most areas within my broad definition of 'Congo' were colonized by francophone Belgium (and to a lesser degree France and Germany), writing in English has had a disproportionate purchase, historically, on the representation and even fate of the area. It is only very recently that Congolese writers have had the opportunity to tell their stories to outside audiences; but more often than not, these accounts have been in English and French. Congolese experiences have thus been 'translated' through foreign language (or languages), and international publishing houses have also intentionally (or unintentionally) acted as *generic* filters on Congolese narratives. One crucial example is offered by survivors of the 1994 Rwandan genocide whose accounts have frequently found an outlet through Western journalism and anglophone biographical – sometimes ghosted – writing.

As an area of the Western imagination, the Congo remains a source of 'uncommon wealth', frequently written, or significantly influenced, by outsiders whose accounts, or linguistic and generic overlays, can have potential influence on Congolese self-perception and even on events in the Congo itself. As the Nigerian writer Chinua Achebe argued in his essay on Joseph Conrad's novel *Heart of Darkness*, images of Africa generated by Western writers and re-projected through, for instance, colonial education systems can have powerful effects on African self-perceptions.[3] For, as Philip Gourevitch, in his collection of stories from Rwanda, notes, "we are, each of us, functions of how we imagine ourselves and how others imagine us";[4] and in his essay "An Image of Africa" Achebe argues that Conrad's portrait of the Congo is an unremittingly racist one. For those educated in Nigeria, as Achebe was, the impact of Conrad's racism not only identifies 'Africa' as a (continuing) 'area of darkness' in the Western imagination but projects it through Anglo-colonial education systems back to Africans themselves.

Published in 1901, *Heart of Darkness* exemplified significant tropes present in Western writing about Africa – an Africa with a stereotypical 'Congo' at its heart – in texts both before and after Conrad's iconic work. These tropes, in their various forms, are characteristic of writing by Westerners about the so-called 'dark continent'. They are the persisting 'images of Africa', to adopt Achebe's title. First, the image of the European, American, or just plain 'outsider' as bringing 'light' to African darkness. Second, Africans as unable to speak for themselves; hence, a 'voice' speaking for them always comes from the outside world. Third, the African or Congolese as inherently abject – always exploited, always incapable of self-help and in need of assistance, whether humanitarian, technological, or educational. All three tropes are, of course, intrinsically interwoven, and they are found in one form or other in some of the earliest English writings about Central Africa, those by explorers and adventurers.

Iconic in the history of the Western exploration of the continent is the famous moment of Henry Morgan Stanley's encounter with David Livingstone. Depicted not just in written form, but frequently illustrated, "Dr. Livingstone, I presume" has become one of the most frequently invoked phrases – whether seriously, ironically or comically – from the history of European exploration, and inevitably associated with Central Africa. Stanley, an inveterate liar and a particularly cruel expedition leader, meets the well-intentioned David Livingstone in a scene most usually depicted as a moment of illumination in what is otherwise an African 'darkness'. This moment of 'light', of civilization in the midst of apparent 'savagery', also indicates another of those persistent tropes of English (and Western) writing about Africa. While Stanley's phrase is recorded, the genuine inhabitants of the just 'discovered' African interior, though present, have no voice in the exchange.

---

[3] Chinua Achebe, "An Image of Africa: Racism in Conrad's *Heart of Darkness*" (1975), *Massachusetts Review* 18.4 (1977): 1783–94, repr. in *"Heart of Darkness": An Authoritative Text, Background and Sources, Criticism*, ed. Robert Kimbrough (New York: W.W. Norton, 1988): 251–61.

[4] Philip Gourevitch, *We Wish to Inform You That Tomorrow We Will be Killed with Our Families: Stories from Rwanda* (New York: Farrar, Straus & Giroux , 1998): 71.

Subsequent European encounters with the Congo, of greater duration and thus potentially more damaging than Stanley's cruel expedition, began with King Leopold's acquisition of the Congo in 1885. In that year, the Berlin Treaty ceded Leopold II of Belgium vast tracts of land in the Congo region, an area he began to exploit ruthlessly. His own personal fiefdom, from which he extracted materials for his personal fortune, soon made him one of Europe's most wealthy monarchs. Under the guise of a civilizing/crusading mission to the unenlightened heathen, Leopold's effective public-relations machine presented his asset-stripping and slave-labour practices as humanitarian endeavours. Claiming he was bringing to the Congo David Livingstone's ideals of 'Christianity and commerce' and evicting Arab slave traders, Leopold was able to introduce a veritable army of his company officials to oversee and enforce his plundering. In reality, his 'humanitarian enterprise' was one of forced labour, the kidnapping and rape of women to coerce Congolese men as labourers; the torture, murder, and terrorization of apparently non-compliant villagers; the mutilation of 'inefficient' workers; and the burning of homes. Most of Europe initially applauded Leopold's 'humanitarian' activities in the Congo; but, as the reality gradually emerged, through independent missionaries, travellers, journalists, and, later, poets and novelists, Leopold's methods – most notoriously the severing of hands and limbs for work infringements or from villagers unable to meet imposed quotas of vine rubber and ivory – Leopold was increasingly vilified. Protests in a number of European languages, but particularly English, resulted in an 'uncommon wealth' of writing. Some writers – Joseph Conrad, for instance – still favoured colonial projects but condemned Leopold's operations in the Congo. Together with J.D. Morel, a leader of the anti-Leopold campaign in London, a list of those on both sides of the Atlantic reads like a roll-call of prominent writers of the time: George Bernard Shaw, Ford Madox Ford, Roger Casement, Arthur Conan Doyle, Joseph Conrad, and Mark Twain, to name a few.[5] Leopold's name increasingly became synonymous with torture, and as Vachel Lindsay wrote after Leopold's death, the condemnation continued:

> Listen to the yell of Leopold's ghost
> Burning in Hell for his hand-maimed host.
> Hear how the demons chuckle and yell
> Cutting his hands off, down in Hell.[6]

---

[5] See Hochschild for more detail on important literary, political, and religious figures of the age who campaigned against Leopold's treatment of the Congolese and his ruthless exploitation of resources.

[6] Vachel Lindsay, "The Congo: A Study of the Negro Race" (1914), in Lindsay, *The Daniel Jazz and Other Poems* (London: G. Bell, 1920): 42, repr. in *American Poetry: The Twentieth Century*, vol. 1:

Two works written in protest at the time of Leopold's regime are particularly important: Mark Twain's *King Leopold's Soliloquy*, and Joseph Conrad's *Heart of Darkness*.

Mark Twain's short work is an illustrated diatribe against Leopold's crimes in the Congo. Twain, as the title suggests, couches his protest in the form of a dramatic monologue by Leopold himself. In this, he refers to some of the charges being made against him, and dismisses them as lies, jealousy, and foreign spite. Twain's "Leopold" justifies his presence in the Congo as fulfilling Livingstone's ideals: bringing Christianity and commerce for the benefit of the Congolese themselves. The fictional Leopold dismisses the plethora of protest writing against him –such as that in which Twain himself is engaged – as useless in thwarting his project; but he does admit he fears "the Kodak," realizing that photographs are harder to counter than drawings or writing. Reproducing some of these photos, and illustrating Leopold's self-justificatory monologue with drawings of the skeletal remains of the victims of the King's enterprise, Twain's text is vehemently angry and satirical, and constitutes an unremitting attack on its object.

As such, the work is, of course, pro-African (and pro-Congolese); and it satirizes the trope of European (i.e., in this case, Christian) 'light' being brought to African 'darkness'. But the three tropes so prevalent in English writing about Africa are still present in Twain's work, however much we are shown Leopold's perversion of them. Some passages are formatted as crosses, such as Leopold's own self-justifying words as well as a condemnation of his practices. African voices are absent, even as reportage, and there is, inevitably perhaps, the sustained abjection of African bodies – what some critics have termed the "necropoetics"[7] of Western writing about the Congo and Africa.

Joseph Conrad's *Heart of Darkness*, unlike Twain's comparatively ephemeral attack in the soliloquy, is still widely known and read, and has frequently been a set text in schools and universities. Twain's diatribe against Leopold is a deliberately unsubtle piece of propaganda. By contrast, Conrad's novel is subtle and complex, but like Twain's it condemns Leopold's regime. It does so through its unforgettable account of the dying Congolese semi-slaves in "the grove of death" (70); the casually murdered African encountered on the track by Marlow, Conrad's narrator, on his way to board the steamer; the greed and petty-minded

---

*Henry Adams to Dorothy Parker* (New York: Library of America, 2000): 276, quoted in *King Leopold's Ghost*, 266–67.

[7] See, for instance, Heike Härting, "Global Humanitarianism, Race, and the Spectacle of the African Corpse in Current Western Representations of the Rwandan Genocide," *Comparative Studies of South Asia, Africa and The Middle East*, 28.1 (2008): 61–77.

evils of "the company" (minor officials termed "pilgrims" by the narrator), because of their worship of ivory and because Leopold's cover for the exploitation of the Congo was the bringing of the "lesson" of Christianity to African "savages"; and the heads of Africans on the poles surrounding the compound of the nefarious apostle of European 'enlightenment', Mr. Kurtz. Conrad's condemnation of Leopold and Belgium is as stringent as Twain's. But the persistence of *Heart of Darkness* as a circulating text well into the twentieth and twenty-first centuries found it called down as racist by Chinua Achebe. I will return to a discussion of *Heart of Darkness* and Achebe's critique of it at the end of the essay; but there is no doubt that, once again, the three familiar tropes of English-language writing about Central Africa are nevertheless present.

The continuation of these tropes in twenty-first-century writing in English about the Congo is also evident in two genres prevalent in the late-1990s and early-2000s. These are accounts of the acts of genocide committed in Rwanda, and the so-called 'child-soldier narratives'. These accounts have been deliberately chosen, rather than, for instance, fictional works such as V.S. Naipaul's *A Bend in the River* or Barbara Kingsolver's *The Poisonwood Bible* (one a critique of the African administration of a supposedly Congolese state; the other a critique of Western missionizing). One might expect that, in contrast to fictional narratives, works like the child-soldier accounts and reports on the Rwandan genocide do not to repeat the Western tropologies outlined above. Child-soldier narratives and genocide accounts would indeed seem to be invoking distinctively African voices. In actual fact, however, they can be shown to filter these voices through Western editing, publishing, and even writing processes. Much of the writing in English about Rwanda interweaves reported direct speech from survivors, witness testimony, and autobiographical accounts with outside commentary. Child-soldier narratives are usually presented in the form of biography or autobiography, so that, to a far greater extent than in nineteenth- and early-twentieth-century texts, African voices can be heard, albeit with a degree of English circumscription. The events on which these accounts draw differ from those of Leopold's reign in the Congo, in that they deal with the impressment of children as labourers or child soldiers by Congolese politicians, non-government Congolese militias, and local warlords. Their experiences under these circumstances frequently include hard labour, rape, killing, and drug-taking. In the case of Rwanda, the acts of genocide recounted involve Hutus against Tutsis, with various inputs from nearby armies, exiled 'rebels', and proximate politicians.[8]

Although the events out of which these texts emerge are very different from European and American 'explorer' accounts of Central Africa or critiques of Leopold's (and, subsequently, Belgium's) regime in the Congo, they nevertheless evince familiar tropes. They have indeed provided readers with what can only be regarded as a "wealth" of writing in English. Child-soldier narratives frequently involve the child soldiers' return to – or discovery of – a lost innocence; in some cases, even, a return to 'voice' after traumatic experiences so damaging that they had reduced the child to speechlessness. Furthermore, as critics such as Alison Mackey and Eleni Coundouriotis have argued, child-soldier narratives, ending as they do with Western rescue of the child and his (usually) subsequent rehabilitation (often in European or American settings), present what Makau Mutua has termed the "savage, victim, saviour" metaphor of human-rights narrative, where Africa is

> the stage on which a confrontation between 'victims' and 'savages' takes place, inviting the intervention of morally superior outsiders, who undertake the salvage work at least partially so that they can be reassured of the superiority they already presumed for themselves.[9]

While critiques such as Mutua's may seem a little harsh, Africans continue to be *victims*, either of Chinese/African/Western greed for the Congo's 'uncommon wealth' or of Central African 'tribal' atavism; the latter frequently invoked in the popular press in relation to the Rwandan genocide as well. There is, then, a persistent repetition of the trope of European light brought to African darkness; the abject African body, the African as perpetual victim; and, at least up to a point, the 'voicelessness' of Africans themselves in the need for various forms of 'translation' into and through Western genres.

---

[8] While this drastically oversimplifies both situations and takes no immediate account of the foundational roles of Leopold, Belgium, France, and Germany in these conflicts, it focuses on the ways in which 'the Congo' has been depicted by writers in English across a variety of times and genres, rather than all accounts of the causes of those events. For more interviews with Rwandans on the 1994 genocide and its aftermath, see Jean Hatzfeld, *The Strategy Of Antelopes: Rwanda After the Genocide* (London: Profile, 2009).

[9] Makau Mutua, "Savages, Victims, and Saviors: The Metaphor of Human Rights," *Harvard International Law Journal* 42.1 (2001): 215. See also Alison Mackey, "Troubling Humanitarian Consumption: Reframing Relationality in African Child Soldier Narratives," *Research in African Literatures* 44.4 (2013): 99–122, and Eleni Coundouriotis, "The Child Soldier Narrative and the Problem of Arrested Historicization," *Journal of Human Rights* 9.2 (2010): 191–206.

I want now to consider a series of relatively recent events which demonstrate, in their post-genocide textual forms, the ways in which such persisting tropes and images not only circulate in the West but can also be re-projected into traditionally oral cultures; influencing African/Congolese self-perceptions and thus, potentially, the events themselves. The circumstances leading up to the 1994 Rwandan genocide, in this case the massacre of Tutsis by the Hutu majority, are familiar to most people: human overpopulation in a very small country; a history of previous tensions erupting in genocide between the two groups (as well as, apparently paradoxically, neighbourliness and intermarriage); but, most significant of all, the exacerbation and, some would claim, even the creation of a rift between the two groups during the period of colonial rule. The Belgians (and Germans) issued identity cards and constantly favoured one group over the other in terms of education, government positions, and general livelihood. Political turmoil in the country became increasingly ethnicity-based, while individual power-grabbing and the assassination of a Hutu President by, it would seem, Hutu extremists eager to provoke the genocide triggered the tragic massacre of 1994. Once again, Westerners in the Congo, from as far back as Stanley and Livingstone to the twenty-first century, have been implicated to a greater or lesser degree. Not the least of these were the 'carve-up' of Africa by the European powers in the late-nineteenth century, the cruel practices of Leopold's regime, and the divisive policies of the subsequent Belgian government.

In his account of the Rwandan genocide, entitled *We Wish to Inform You That Tomorrow We Will be Killed With Our Families*, Philip Gourevitch writes: "we are all of us functions of how we imagine ourselves and of how others imagine us,"[10] a point made in the 1970s by Achebe in relation to British texts, education, and popular Western perceptions of 'Africa' and 'Africans'. But, given that most of the Congo region was colonized by francophone powers, one might expect that the English texts – literary texts in particular – would have little refractive purchase in the Congo.[11] And yet Philip Gourevitch's account of the Tutsi massacres opens with a surprising post-genocide exchange between the author and a man he simply terms "the pygmy" in a Rwandan bar (pygmies, as he explains, belong neither to Hutu nor Tutsi groups, but are considered "primitives" by both – so low on the ethnic scale that they were used by Hutus to rape Tutsi women as an extra form of humiliation before they were killed).

[10] Gourevitch, *We Wish to Inform You*, 71.

[11] And, indeed, the Trinidadian writer V.S. Naipaul, in his A *Congo Diary* (Los Angeles: Sylvester & Orphanos, 1980), comments that he could find no one there who has read Joseph Conrad's *Heart of Darkness*.

Three drunken Rwandan soldiers are also in the bar, but it is the more sober "pygmy" to whom the narrator speaks:

> The soldiers were too drunk for conversation, but a civilian among their party [...] asked my name in stern robotic English, each syllable precise and abrupt. I told him, "Philip."
>
> "Ah." He clutched my hand. "Like in Charles Dickens."
>
> That's Pip, I said.
>
> "*Great Expectations*," he pronounced. He dropped my hand [...]. Then he said, "I am a pygmy from the jungle. But I learned English from an Anglican bishop."
>
> He didn't say his name. [...] "I have a principle" he announced. "I believe in the principle of *Homo sapiens*. You get me?"
>
> I took a guess. "You mean that all humanity is one?"
>
> "That is my theory," the pygmy said. "That is my principle. But I have a problem. I must marry a white woman."
>
> "Why not?" I said. Then, after a moment, I said, "but why, if we are all the same? Who cares what colour your wife is?"
>
> "She *must* be a white woman," the pygmy said. "Only a white woman can understand my universal principle of *Homo sapiens*. I must not marry a Negro."[12]

The pygmy has understood the difficulty of this and is frustrated by it. Gourevitch attempts to ease his frustration by saying that, even for white men, it is difficult to find a suitable partner.

> But the man replies, "I am talking about the African," he said, "the African is sick." [...]
>
> "There is a novel," he went on, "The book is *Wuthering Heights*. [...] This is my larger theory. It doesn't matter if you are white or yellow or green or a black African Negro. The concept is *Homo sapiens*. The European is at an advanced technological stage, and the African is at a stage of technology that is more primitive. But all humanity must unite together in the struggle against nature. This is the principle of *Wuthering Heights*. This is the mission of *Homo sapiens*.
>
> [...] "It is the only hope – all humanity one against nature."

But Gourevitch says: "'But humanity is part of nature, too'." "'Exactly,' the pygmy said. 'That is exactly the problem'."[13]

---

[12] Gourevitch, *We Wish to Inform You*, 56.

[13] *We Wish to Inform You*, 58.

These lengthy passages are worth quoting in full, because although they are puzzlingly cryptic, they are, as Gourevitch explains, inevitably underwritten, like all conversations post-1994 in Rwanda, by the slaughter which was the first mass killing in history to be designated as 'genocide' by the U.N. While the "pygmy's" reading of the English novels he mentions appears completely bizarre, as John Frow shows,

> texts are differently constituted and enter into different kinds of relationships with readers as they are positioned within different frameworks of understanding – an open ended chain of reception transforms the initial constellation as it moves the text, serially or laterally, into unforeseeable contexts. [...] the historicities of the text flow backwards and forwards from the uses to which they are put.[14]

And:

> Readers are formed by texts as much as texts are formed by readers. What matters is precisely the relationship between the two and although this relationship is formed moment to moment, it is nevertheless regulated by the regimes of reading that constitute texts, readers and the manner of their encounter as a historically specific reading assemblage.[15]

In terms of the reception and reproduction of English textual materials within a largely francophone Congo, neither limpid reflection nor Bhabhabian mimicry offers an appropriate model; nor do idiosyncratic, personal interpretations of texts. Instead, Frow notes, texts are "endlessly remade with different political consequences and effects."[16] Of course, within the Congo region, it is most likely to be francophone images that have the greater potency. Yet, as Gourevitch's conversations with "the pygmy" demonstrate, both Catholic and Protestant missionary education in the Congo also introduced English writing with its specific attitudes and perceptions.

Because the effect(s) of some texts persist over time, albeit being "remade with different political consequences and effects," it is worth turning back at this point to the era of English exploration of Central Africa. In writing the accounts of his journey, John Hanning Speke drew extensively on the Bible to formulate what has become known as the 'Hamitic hypothesis', from the story of Noah. The Hamitic myth was frequently used in the American South as a

---

[14] John Frow, "Texts as Usage," in *The Practice of Value: Essays on Literature and Cultural Studies* (Crawley: U of Western Australia Publishing, 2013): 42.

[15] Frow, "Texts as Usage,"40.

[16] "Texts as Usage," 41.

justification for slavery, and, as Hanning Speke proposed, "the true curly-head, flab-nosed, pouch-mouthed negro" was the ancestor of all the black races in Africa. But for the very Christian, late-twentieth-century population of Rwanda, as Gourevitch notes, "whether they accept or reject it, few Rwandans would deny that the Hamitic myth is one of the essential ideas by which they understand who they are in this world."[17] Although Biblical in origin and drawn on in the USA, the hypothesis was given a specific African location through Speke's work. It was that very hypothesis which was invoked prior to and during the Rwandan genocide:

> In November 1992, the Hutu Power ideologue, Leon Mugesera delivered a famous speech calling on Hutus to send Tutsis back to Ethiopia by way of the Nyabarongo River, a tributary of the Nile that winds through Rwanda. He did not need to elaborate. In April 1994, the river was choked with dead Tutsis, and tens of thousands of bodies were washed up on the shores of Lake Victoria.[18]

Joseph Conrad's *Heart of Darkness* is the anglophone text of the Congo par excellence. In it, the three central African tropes are emphasized. Africans are abjected, they remain voiceless, and Western 'light' is, potentially, brought to African darkness. As indicated above, *Heart of Darkness* was frequently a set text for upper-level schooling, and the novel was examined within a system which used literature and literary criticism as powerful tools of colonialist control. This was especially significant, as interpretation of imaginative works such as *Heart of Darkness* could be controlled through a central (Cambridge) examination system. And although *Heart of Darkness* is, as much as anything, a stringent condemnation of Leopold's treatment of Congolese peoples – perhaps the most famous protest, among many, against the labour conditions he imposed and the ruthless exploitation he condoned and encouraged – it was not this aspect of the novel that the British curriculum emphasized. Instead, students were obliged (in order to follow critical protocols and produce the 'correct' answer) to interpret Conrad's novel as being about a 'universal' darkness lurking in every human heart. Under its surface urbanity, civilization could all too easily crumble and 'civilized man' return atavistically to the condition of a 'brute'. This was the lesson to be learned from the fate of the European, Kurtz, in Conrad's novel. Once an apostle of civilization, Kurtz, transformed by contact with (African) savagery, has become a savage himself. "All Europe," we are told by

---

17 Gourevitch, *We Wish to Inform You*, 5.

18 Gourevitch, *We Wish to Inform You*, 53.

Conrad's narrator, had "gone into" the making of Kurtz, yet he was not immune to the erasure of his once cultured exterior. But, as Achebe would point out in relation to this reading of the novel, however apparently 'universal' this warning, civilization *as a quality* had already been located in Europe and Europeans, while savagery *as a quality* necessarily resided in Africa (and with Africans). And, as Achebe would also point out, the Africans in *Heart of Darkness* say virtually nothing except for two phrases couched in a primitive pidgin, "Catchim, eatim" and "Mr. Kurtz, he dead," both of which served only to confirm Western stereotypes of the 'darkness' of Africa and the inherent 'backwardness' and savagery of Africans themselves.

As post-colonial historicist readings increasingly displaced the former 'universal' interpretation, however, different parts of the text began to be noticed and emphasized, producing rather different readings. Even if readers are unaware of the author's own unequivocal condemnation of Leopold's enterprise in the Congo, Conrad's main narrator, Marlow, draws our attention to Belgian atrocities: to the "grove of death" where starved and overworked Congolese are dying; to the African casually executed and left on the track upriver; and to Marlow's contemptuous depiction of the mendacious company "pilgrims" – the greedy devotees of profit. Like Twain in his more overtly savage satire, Conrad deploys the language and metaphors of religion – specifically Christianity – to point to the hypocrisy of Leopold's "mission" to the Congo. Leopold's great lie to Europe about what he was actually doing in the Congo – Christianity and commerce – is here unmasked. And in direct contrast to this lie, Conrad's narrator Marlow declares that what he most abhors is a lie.

Marlow's own integrity is eventually, it seems, called into question when, on returning to Europe, he tells Kurtz's "intended" that the last words her insane and dying fiancée pronounced "were your name." Yet Marlow may not, after all, be lying. These famous final words of Kurtz, "the horror, the horror," may indeed be "the name" of Europe's perverted "intentions" in Africa, exposing as they do the chasm between Leopold's intentions in the Congo as much of Europe initially understood them and the real horror of his reign of terror.

Although Achebe no doubt recognized Conrad's critique of Leopoldian and later Belgian colonialism as present in the text, he charged Conrad's work with demonstrating an unambiguous racism. For Achebe, Africa – the Congo specifically – becomes, in *Heart of Darkness*, a "mere backdrop" for "the breakup of one petty European mind" (i.e. Kurtz's). Moreover, the Africans are virtually speechless, and once again Europe (however compromised by contact with Africa) can *appear* to be bringing light to an African darkness.

It is, however, possible to argue that while Conrad employs these persisting tropes he (like later twentieth- and twenty-first-century writers) simultaneously problematizes them. The African forest is indeed 'dark', but the whites have brought anything but 'light'. The grove of death may be attached to a white space, but it is redolent only of African deprivation, torture, and death. The white company officials (as in Conrad's companion novella *An Outpost of Progress*) are petty, cruel, and conniving. And in the portrait painted by Kurtz and left in the rest-house, Marlow sees a depiction of this classic image: a European woman dressed in white holding out a candle towards the darkness on the other side of the portrait. But she is blindfolded – like Europe, and like its "intentions" in Africa, she is unable to see what she is actually doing. And her light is, after all, only a candle.

While it is also possible to claim that the Africans in Conrad's text are abjected – the 'necropoetics' of the grove of death, the dead African on the track – there is nothing abject about the magnificently alive woman who apparently objects to the removal of Kurtz to the steamer. Nor is there a lack of agency in the attack that kills Marlow's helmsman, and whose blood spills onto Marlow's shoes. His remarks at this point are indeed 'racist', but the blood that spills over his own shoes offers a counter-significance, linking the dead helmsman – by blood – to Marlow himself.

The notion of 'voice' is an important one throughout the novel. As well as being the most successful (i.e. greediest) company agent, Kurtz is renowned for his voice, so resonant, so compelling, that it is the stuff of legend. To hear it constitutes an unforgettable experience; yet, in the form of a novel, voice cannot be actually heard, its qualities only reported. Moreover, even as reported, Kurtz himself is heard to utter very little in the entire novel – not a great deal more, in fact, than the Africans themselves. The narrative frames of *Heart of Darkness* also problematize the authority of voice, and the potential impact of that which is directly reported. And, in what is more an irony of literary and cultural history than Conradian intention, eight words from the novel have resonated in literary and other genres: not Kurtz's final speech, but that of the African who pronounces prophetically: "Mr. Kurtz, he dead." Whether deployed ironically or even comically, this particular, if anonymous, African voice has survived in anglophone cultural parlance for well over a century.

The Congo region, as a colony (or colonies) of Europe, but not, in fact, of England, has nevertheless provided the ground of an uncommon wealth of writing in English over a period of three centuries. And the uncommon material wealth of the Congo has, since the advent of Europeans, been its curse, bringing exploitation, destruction, death, war, and cultural annihilation. But this tragic history has, ironically, been the catalyst for a wealth of writing about the area, not only in French and more recently in local languages but also, and rather unexpectedly, in English, with some of the most illustrious writers of the nineteenth and twentieth centuries drawn to the Congo's continuing plight.

## Works Cited

Achebe, Chinua. "An Image of Africa: Racism in Conrad's *Heart of Darkness*" (1975), *Massachusetts Review* 18.4 (1977): 1783–94. Repr. in *"Heart of Darkness": An Authoritative Text, Background and Sources, Criticism*, ed. Robert Kimbrough (New York & London: W.W. Norton, 1988): 251–61.

Conrad, Joseph. "Heart of Darkness" (1902), in *Two Tales of the Congo: An Outpost of Progress; Heart of Darkness*, revised edition with copper engravings by Dolf Rieser (London: Folio Society, 1952).

Coundouriotis, Eleni. "The Child Soldier Narrative and the Problem of Arrested Historicization," *Journal of Human Rights* 9.2 (2010): 191–206.

Frow, John. "Texts as Usage," in *The Practice of Value: Essays on Literature and Cultural Studies* (Crawley: U of Western Australia Publishing, 2013): 23–45.

Gourevitch, Philip. *We Wish to Inform You That Tomorrow We Will be Killed with Our Families: Stories from Rwanda* (New York: Farrar, Straus & Giroux, 1998).

Härting, Heike. "Global Humanitarianism, Race, and the Spectacle of the African Corpse in Current Western Representations of the Rwandan Genocide," *Comparative Studies of South Asia, Africa and The Middle East* 28.1 (2008): 61–77.

Hatzfeld, Jean. *The Strategy of Antelopes: Rwanda After the Genocide* (London: Profile, 2009).

Hochschild, Adam. *King Leopold's Ghost: A Story of Greed, Terror and Heroism in Colonial Africa* (New York: Houghton Mifflin, 1998).

Lindsay, Vachel. "The Congo: A Study of the Negro Race" (1914), in Lindsay, *The Daniel Jazz and Other Poems* (London: G. Bell, 1920): 41-49, repr. in *American Poetry: The Twentieth Century*, vol. 1: *Henry Adams to Dorothy Parker* (New York: Library of America, 2000): 275–80.

Mackey, Alison. "Troubling Humanitarian Consumption: Reframing Relationality in African Child Soldier Narratives," *Research in African Literatures* 44.4 (2013): 99–122.

Mutua, Makau. "Savages, Victims, and Saviors: The Metaphor of Human Rights," *Harvard International Law Journal* 42.1 (2001): 201–45.

Naipaul, V.S. *A Congo Diary* (Los Angeles: Sylvester & Orphanos, 1980).

Twain, Mark. *King Leopold's Soliloquy: A Defense of His Congo Rule* (Boston MA: P.R. Warren, 1905).

Van Reybrouck, David. *Congo: The Epic History of a People* (London: Fourth Estate, 2014).

❄

# The Black Diamond and the Queen BEE

## *Representations of Wealth, Corruption and Women's Sexuality in Two South African Novels*

Cheryl Stobie

The elite echelons of the black nouveaux riches in South Africa, popularly known as 'black diamonds', constitute a fast-developing and influential market in the South African economy. This group of people can be studied with respect to growing disparities in wealth, both internationally and within South Africa's borders. Recent research by Oxfam about the world's richest people found that 85 individuals owned as much as the 3.5 billion people making up the poorest half of the planet's population.[1] Opinion polls in seven countries, including South Africa, found that most of the respondents felt that the wealthy are too influential.[2] A recent painting by Ayanda Mabulu, called *Spear Down My Throat* (*The Pornography of Power*), illustrates the current atmosphere of disillusionment regarding disparities of wealth in South Africa. In the picture, President Jacob Zuma is standing with his trousers around his ankles, orally raping a young girl representing South Africa. She is saddled, to indicate that she is a slave being tamed in order to be exploited by the economy, and is being violated from the rear by a hyena, representing mining and commercial conglomerates. The girl is also being milked like a cow, and this milk is running into a container stamped with the ruling African National Congress logo. The artist comments:

---

[1] "Oxfam Finds 85 Elites as Rich as 3.5-billion People," *Mail & Guardian* (21 January 2014), http://mg.co.za/article/2014-01-21-oxfam-finds-85-people-as-rich-as-half-the-global-population (accessed 31 March 2014).

[2] "Oxfam Finds 85 Elites."

> The elite are living lavishly at the expense of others, by lying to the people with their false promises. [...] We know that politicians serve people who control the economy."[3]

The provocative painting uses the imagery of patriarchal sexual abuse in the public domain of a circus tent to express abhorrence at the abuse of power in achieving wealth for the politically connected elite at the expense of the majority of the populace. The artist's aim is to contribute to positive change in society.

Important in this desirable shift to an emphasis on social justice is awareness of race, gender, and sexuality. The term 'black diamond' is contentious, as it highlights race right at a time when wealth is increasingly becoming deracialized in South Africa. It refers to members of the black middle class, who are well educated, professional, living in suburbs demarcated for whites under apartheid, and wealthy, partly because of the government policy of Black Economic Empowerment (BEE), which developed from the Employment Equity Act of 1998. As this group is growing and accruing more wealth, the gap between the most affluent and the poorest members of society is being exacerbated. A 2010 survey showed that 1,6% of the South African population earned 25% of personal income, while 85% of the population earned a mere 22% of total personal income.[4] Rebecca Haynes notes: "The bottom line is that a disproportionate amount of the rewards of democracy and economic transformation have accrued to the super rich."[5] This discrepancy has political ramifications. The politically connected beneficiaries of BEE have an interest in maintaining their connections with the regime that supports them (as did many whites under apartheid), while the disaffected "underpowered masses" tend to push for far-reaching, radical changes in the allocation of wealth.[6] At this lower end of the wealth pyramid, women are "constantly overrepresented amongst the poor."[7]

---

[3] "Pornography of Power," *Culture Review Magazine* (2015), http://www.culture-review.co.za/pornography-of-power (accessed 13 October 2015).

[4] Natale Labia, "Black Diamonds Sparkle – for Some," *Mail & Guardian* (15 November 2010), http://mg.co.za/article/2010-11-15-black-diamonds-sparkle-for-some (accessed 31 March 2014).

[5] Rebecca Haynes, "SA's Mysterious 'Middle Class'," *Mail & Guardian* (31 January 2014), http://mg.co.za/article/2014-01-31-00-sas-mysterious-middle-class (accessed 27 March 2014).

[6] Roger Tangri & Roger Southall, "The Politics of Black Economic Empowerment in South Africa," *Journal of Southern African Studies* 34.3 (2008): 699–718.

[7] Justin Visagie, *Race, Gender and Growth of the Affluent Middle Class in Post-Apartheid South Africa* (Economic Research Southern Africa Working Paper 395, 2013): 20, online (accessed 31 March 2014).

Further, even in the middle and upper classes, women lag financially behind their male counterparts.[8]

In a patriarchal, capitalist system like that of South Africa, where a structural asymmetry exists between women and men, one of the forms of capital that women possess is their sexuality, although exploiting women's sexuality as an asset is often the prerogative of men. For women themselves, though, their bodies and sexuality may be used as a means of commodification and economic exchange, such as in sex work, or they may be used as a creative expression of women's own desires. Such complex social negotiations, whether explicit or implicit, have long been foregrounded in works of literature.

As Robert Balfour points out,

> The novel [...] is a genre that because of its popularity as a form over the last three centuries offers an opportunity to understand the variety of means used to negotiate the disjunction between reality and systems of signs like language, currency, class, gender and race.[9]

Novels (and other cultural artefacts) represent the relationship between money and moral worth ambiguously, illuminating the effects of the power accrued through capitalism and the converse suffering and alienation caused by poverty and marginalization. Novels encode ideologies, anxieties, and fantasies. Balfour suggests that, like money, literature "has real power and yet is also preoccupied with representation and value."[10] Further, while texts are partial representations of reality, they also contribute to the production of reality, and require an active intellectual and emotional response on the part of the reader. Specific forms of writing create powerful effects through form as well as content. The myths about money re-worked by contemporary novelists may exhibit the tension between a desire for the rewarding of the worthy, on the one hand, and contempt for social regulatory processes such as the law, on the other.

This essay analyses two recent novels dealing with wealth, corruption, gender, and sexuality: Zakes Mda's *Black Diamond* (2009) and Lebogang Matseke's debut novel, *Queen B.E.E.* (2015). Each novel is discussed in turn in order to provide an overview of its concerns and highlight relevant thematic details about wealth, power, and sexuality, after which I contrast the two texts with regard to the gendered point of view chosen by Mda and Matseke, respectively,

---

8 Visagie, "Race, Gender and Growth," 20.

9 Robert J. Balfour, "Introduction: Culture, Capital and Representation," in *Culture, Capital and Representation*, ed. Robert J. Balfour (London: Palgrave Macmillan, 2010): 4.

10 Balfour, "Introduction," 4.

and how these affect their representation of human bodies and their choice of diction, as well as the attitudes to freedom and social justice they convey in their texts.

Zakes Mda, born in 1948, is an acclaimed and prize-winning writer of poetry, plays, novels, and a memoir. His work has been analysed in two books of criticism and numerous articles. Mda's novel *Black Diamond* illustrates a number of tensions in terms of representations of wealth, race, gender, and autonomy. The text was originally conceived as a film-script, but was subsequently revised into novel form. It still retains farcical and disturbing filmic elements as it satirically represents the effects of a culture of excessive consumerism, greed, nepotism, and corruption in the elite echelons of black diamonds. An employee of the South African government's Department of Arts and Culture, Sandile Memela, attacked Mda's novel for its open criticism of contemporary South Africa, calling it "reactionary, simple and predictable."[11] Considering the portrayal of one particular minor character of *Black Diamond*, it is not surprising that such a vehement response was prompted. Molotov Mbungane has

> morph[ed] from a poor kid growing up in [a] village [...] to a Marxist guerrilla to a political prisoner to a member of parliament and cabinet minister in the first Mandela government. In the last stages of that process he accumulated the political capital that he was able to convert to financial capital and equity in some of the biggest corporations in the land as soon as he left government service. It is the political capital that made him palatable to white business. Banks plied him with cash, until he became known as Comrade Deal-a-Minute because he put together consortia that acquired huge stakes in the mining industry. In less than five years he was the owner of some of the most lucrative diamond, gold and platinum mines.[12]

Married to an Afrikaner woman, Mbungane obtains further access to "the art of accumulation" (17). He receives a number of honorary doctorates after he becomes "an overnight dollar billionaire" (10). His ex-comrades mock him by calling him "Comrade Capitalist" (10) behind his back. This contrast between the public bestowal of honours for financial success and the covert dismissal of his success as a betrayal of (Marxist) ideals exposes not only the economically successful Mbungane but also the society in which he lives and thrives. Clearly this

[11] Maureen Isaacson, "In his Personal Capacity," *Sunday Independent* (29 November 2009), Books Section: 17.

[12] Zakes Mda, *Black Diamond* (Johannesburg: Penguin, 2009): 17. Further page references are in the main text.

society is complicit in his affluence, as it opportunistically honours him yet fails to admit that it does not consider this success honourable. Despite allusion to historical and continuing white privilege, the satirical focus of *Black Diamond* is more on the black bourgeoisie, who are shown to profit through their political connections rather than merit, a criticism that would be distasteful to the ruling political elite.

The plot-line of the novel concerns a white magistrate, Kristin Uys (pronounced like the Afrikaans word for 'ice'), who is hearing a case about a brothel run by the brothers Stevo and Shortie Visagie. After she sentences one of the brothers to an excessively long period in jail for contempt of court, she is threatened with violence and secures the services of the bodyguard Don Mateza, whose girlfriend Tumi constantly exhorts him to engage in "positive thinking!" and jump onto the black diamond bandwagon by accruing wealth. Don is painfully aware that he fails to be financially as successful as Tumi expects him to be. His feeling that he is a fraud is revealed as he reflects that unlike him "real Black Diamonds are not behind with instalments on a sports car they can't afford" and that they "don't live in their girlfriends' one-bedroomed apartments either!" (16) Tumi's materialism and pushiness, and Kristin's developing vulnerability and sexual allure, propel Don into initiating an affair with the latter. At the end of the novel he rescues Kristin from the released convict Stevo, who humiliates her and intends to kill her.

Gail Fincham, the only critic to my knowledge who has engaged in a sustained analysis of *Black Diamond*, acknowledges the authorial contempt for BEE policies but reproves Mda for refusing in this novel to allow for the possibility of collective performativity that characterizes his other novels. Fincham also criticizes the reliance on stereotypes and formulae in the novel, and the overly controlling voice of the omniscient narrator, which forecloses independent interpretation on the part of the reader.[13] She observes in passing that four of Mda's six novels, including *Black Diamond*, contain a male narrator who controls the voice of the most vital, transgressive female characters, and further suggests that the fit between his gender politics and the narrative strategies adopted in his novels needs to be further explored.[14]

My interest in *Black Diamond* has partly to do with its satirical depictions of the alienating, deadening effects of consumerism. More than this, however, I am interested in depictions of gender, power, and women's bodies as a form of

---

[13] Gail Fincham, *Dance of Life: The Novels of Zakes Mda in Post-Apartheid South Africa* (Cape Town: U of Cape Town P, 2011): 147–58.

[14] Fincham, *Dance of Life*, 161.

capital, seen especially in episodes involving dance. In Mda's novel, access to wealth is portrayed as shifting traditional power dynamics between men and women, causing significant anxiety. The relationship between Tumi and Don is shown to be unequal as she comments proudly: "'You don't *find* a guy like this; you create him for yourself'" (170). Her own wealth makes her feel superior to Don, so much so that she can see herself as having created and controlling him, especially as an object of sexual desire. Tumi's sexual voracity excites Don, but it also belittles him: "when it's her turn to be on top she rides him so roughly that he sobs like a child who is being spanked for engaging in some mischief" (116). Similarly, Kristin is shown to overstep the mark in using her power as a magistrate. As well as giving Stevo a disproportionately long sentence for disrespecting her in court, she visits him in prison, mocking him for being a pimp, "playing with little girls" (55). She demeans him by calling him a "scared little boy" and "a wiggly little worm" (55). Her mockery makes him cry. In both cases, women are revealed as infantilizing men and reducing them to unmanly tears, metaphorically emasculating them and revealing the stresses underpinning changes in society as shifts in the power-structure go hand in hand with a redistribution of wealth and increasing access by women to jobs formerly occupied by men.

A further strain, this time with regard to women's ability to express sexual desires and the scripts available to them in a society where sex is commodified, is evident in the representation of Kristin's attitude to sex work. She is on a personal crusade to stamp it out, as her then husband frequented sex workers and was caught visiting a professional dominatrix in a sleazy dive, leading to their divorce. At that stage she blamed herself for not being more accommodating towards his demands that she wear sexy clothes and dance erotically for him in private. In the present time-frame of the text, however, despite her crusade, Kristin reads Xaviera Hollander's *The Happy Hooker* as her cat lies between her legs. Further, in masochistic style, she de-stresses by humiliating herself by wearing stripper gear, dancing provocatively, and wielding a whip. Although she crusades against sex workers, much of her own behaviour is remarkably similar to theirs, as if her shame-filled desire is to emulate their blatant display of sexual power. Mda thus portrays the character as hypocritically enacting staples of pornography which are intended to titillate a male implied reader, and sets the character up for exposure of her shameful secret.

Given the brittle, satirical tone of the novel, it is perhaps not surprising that sex work is not investigated as a social reality, but merely used as an occasion for ribald laughter. The sex workers who attend the Visagie brothers' trial are seen by the narrator as jokes, and are referred to familiarly and condescendingly by him as "our prostitutes," with no heed given to the distinction in current progressive nomenclature made between 'sex workers', who enter the business willingly, and 'prostitutes', who are coerced into it. Other examples of polarizing language-use are the constant distancing references to Kristin as "the Magistrate," in contrast to Don, who is generally mentioned by name, and the frequent allusions to Kristin as variants on "bitch" and "ice queen." Although Stevo and Don occupy different positions on the crime continuum, Mda parallels them by having both express their disregard for female sexuality and freely call Kristin a "bitch."

In an episode where Kristin is first shown dancing her stripper dance, Don enters the room and observes her. The description is thus mediated, first, through the gaze of the implicitly male, satirical narrator, who repeatedly dismisses her dance as "pathetic," then through the gaze of Don, who, with unease, observes her "gyrating and moaning as if she is in sexual ecstasy" (158). This juxtaposing of dissimilar gazes produces an uneasy oscillation of viewpoint for the reader, revealing that what both perspectives have in common is the assumption of masculine entitlement in intruding on a private performance not intended for public consumption, foregrounding the ethical dubiousness of the two men's way of evaluating a performative female figure. This effect of incongruity is exacerbated when Kristin breaks down in tears and Don feels "something stir[ring] within him" as he notes her vulnerability: "He holds her tightly and she submits" (158). Don's reaction can be perceived as exploitative, and the narrator's word "submits" suggests stereotypes of feminine acquiescence in the face of masculine assertiveness.

As the relationship between Don and Kirstin develops further, in the next step towards consummation, he finds her skimpy skirt and fishnet stockings, and parodies her dance, leading her to re-live the humiliation she endured at the hands of her husband; however, the previous pattern of submission referred to above is employed, and she submits to Don's sexual overtures. Despite the crossing of conventional gender stereotypes in Mda's depiction of Don as a talented cook and passionate lover of cats, both conventionally associated with femininity, the ideal pattern of heterosexual pairing is shown as characterized by male action and female subjection. Even in the interest in cookery and cats shared by Don and Kirsten, he is more knowledgeable about food and more affectionate towards felines. Furthermore, he is her bodyguard and saviour-figure, despite her relative wealth and status. This pattern, in which a feisty woman is subdued by a hot-blooded male, is familiar from *The Heart of Redness* (2000), in the case of which the female protagonist conforms to the masculine fantasy of conceiving while a virgin. In *Black Diamond*, although Mda is subverting the weary literary trope of the 'black peril,'[15] he reiterates familiar gender conventions and heteronormativity. This is ironic, as he claims in his autobiography that he has "written extensively on women's issues" and that his "books have been labelled feminist."[16] In addition, in the Acknowledgements page at the start of the novel, Mda notes that he wrote almost half of it when he was "the Gladstone Professor of Human Rights at the Human Rights Institute, University of Connecticut."[17] In *Black Diamond*, women's bodies are commodified in precisely the way Mda critiques with reference to other forms of exploitation such as racism.

This callous commodification is most strikingly apparent in the final chapter of the book, where, as Fincham comments, "The writing [...] degenerates into a chilling combination of sadism and banality."[18] For maximum effect in draining the repeated image of the dance to the dregs, Kristin is yet again enacting her degrading ritual when she is disturbed by Stevo, set on humiliating and then murdering her. He slashes her arms and her bra, mocking her for her small breasts and making her cry. He assaults her and has his knife ready to slit her throat, saying, "'I am going to kill the fuck out of you'," the words making the typical masculinist connection between violence, sex, and death. At this moment Don and Shortie enter, Stevo shoots Don, and "The magistrate seizes the moment and kicks Stevo in the balls" (276). Kristin's name does not occur throughout this incident; instead, she is referred to as "the magistrate" five times, as she knocks Stevo out and sobs beside the wounded Don. The novel ends with her visiting Don in hospital, asking him when he will be coming back to her home, where his cat is, to which he replies, "'For now ... maybe. Me and Snowy ... we can no longer be kept'" (279). The implication at the end is that Don asserts his authority over Kristin, refusing to see himself in the long run as occupying the same status as a pet, reliant on her wealth and goodwill. The masculine viewpoint is reinforced at the end of the novel.

---

[15] The term 'black peril' was used initially to refer to social panics expressing racist fears of white women being raped by black men in South Africa. Charles Van Onselen's research details media accounts of such stories in the late-nineteenth and early-twentieth centuries, reflecting white anxieties during times of social and economic crisis. See Charles Van Onselen, "The Witches of Suburbia: Domestic Service on the Witwatersrand 1890–1914," *Studies in the Social and Economic History of the Witwatersrand 1886–1914*, vol. 2: *New Nineveh* (Johannesburg: Ravan, 1982): 45–60. The term was subsequently applied to a trope in South African literature, which became overworked.

[16] Zakes Mda, *Sometimes There Is a Void: Memoirs of an Outsider* (Johannesburg: Penguin, 2011): 530.

[17] Mda, *Black Diamond*, np.

[18] Fincham, *Dance of Life*, 156.

Lebogang Matseke was born in 1983, and her debut novel, *Queen B.E.E.* (2015), shares a number of similarities with Mda's *Black Diamond.* The setting for both is the economic heart of South Africa, Johannesburg; the legality of certain actions is questioned, and the role of the law in society is raised; many of the characters are black diamonds; and intimate relationships are central to the plot. Significant differences can be traced between the two texts, however, in terms of genre, tone, representations of wealth and corruption, and perspectives on gender issues, including the use of sexual pejoratives by characters. After delineating the plot and main thematic concerns of the novel, I shall offer a more in-depth analysis of the significance of the differences between the two novels.

Mda's novel *Black Diamond* illustrates the struggles of an individual aspirant black diamond, and the present-tense third-person narration privileges an androcentric viewpoint to express anxieties about gender, race, wealth, and worth, leading up to an inconclusive but unsettling ending. By contrast, *Queen B.E.E.* places the focus on a woman's perspective about gender, wealth, and merit, and the past-tense first-person narration explores issues such as domestic violence, corruption, friendship, the relationship between tradition and modernity, and improving one's own situation through decisive action, as well as assisting others to do the same. The closure of the narrative arc emphasizes success in handling adversity and realizing one's potential through intelligence, hard work, and support from others.

The central protagonist, Neo Dube (née Mokoena), is told by one of her friends, Refilwe, that she should rightfully be a "'Queen BEE in her thirties'," which Refilwe glosses as meaning a "'B.E.E. woman who has the potential to run things in Jo'burg […]. You're only a Queen if you own your own company and scare the B.E.E. boys'."[19] The term 'Queen BEE' is richly suggestive. In the insect world, the queen bee is the alpha member of the colony, as she is the sole reproductive female responsible for the success of the hive. Used metaphorically, the term references the position of royalty, and is applied to a woman who has a dominant place in a particular group or sphere. Psychological research published in 1974 identified the 'Queen Bee syndrome', which suggested that women in positions of authority undermine other women in order to promote their own relative wealth and privilege;[20] this concept has entered popular discourse, particularly representations of female–female relationships in film and

---

[19] Lebogang Matseke, *Queen B.E.E.* (Pietermaritzburg: Otterley Press, 2015): 12–13. Further page references are in the main text.

[20] Graham Staines, Carol Tavris & Toby E. Jayaratne, "The Queen Bee Syndrome," *Psychology Today* 7.8 (January 1974): 55–70.

novels. However, more recent studies maintain that this research relies on stereotypes and is not supported by empirical findings.[21] Similarly, in the novel both Neo's friend Refilwe and, by implication, the author herself refute this stereotyped understanding of the narcissistic successful woman who refuses to support other women outside the private domestic sphere, where their success in male-dominated domains breeds a competitiveness perceived as natural among men and as a failing only among women. In the first place, Refilwe makes it plain that to attain the status of Queen BEE in the South African capital of wealth, Johannesburg, a woman has to be in charge and also stand up to the "B.E.E. boys," the term implying the kind of supportive pack-mentality cultivated in all-male sports teams or old-boys' clubs, and the word "boys" suggesting immaturity. In the second place, Neo is shown to have a warmly supportive relationship not only with her group of three friends but also with her older role models; as Neo muses: "it seemed that the older Queen BEEs were watching and saw some form of poetic justice in one of their own children seeking vengeance" (52).

The plot of *Queen B.E.E.* details Neo's efforts to achieve freedom and redress after she suffers a brutal robbery, which she learns has been orchestrated by her abusive husband, Tshepo Dube, and his lover, Ntombi Dime. The robbery prompts Neo to rekindle her friendship with the successful young women she met during her student years, Refilwe, Thato, and Lucy Finkelstein. She was estranged from them over the course of her marriage because of her shame at the abuse she suffered at the hands of her husband and the degradation she endured even as the daughter of a man who was one of the founding figures of black business enterprise. Reconnecting with her friends allows Neo to break her sense of isolation and demoralization, as they assist her in photographing evidence of her husband's beatings and encourage her to seek a divorce in due course. They refer to the A-team and the First Wives Club in their efforts to inspire Neo to work with them to restore justice and recuperate her heritage.

Neo attends a party thrown by her husband's lover Ntombi. After an unsuccessful attempt to poison Neo, Ntombi arranges for a photograph of Neo and

---

21 See Christine Silva, Nancy M. Carter & Anna Beninger, "Good Intentions, Imperfect Execution? Women Get Fewer of the 'Hot Jobs' Needed to Advance," *Catalyst* (2012): 15–17, http://webmail.catalyst.org/system/files/Good_Intentions_Imperfect_Execution_Women_Get_Fewer_of_the_Hot_Jobs_Needed_to_Advance.pdf and Cristian L. Dezső, David Gaddis Ross & Jose N. Uribe, "Why Are There So Few Women Top Managers? A Large-Sample Empirical Study of the Antecedents of Female Participation in Top Management," *Social Science Research Network* 11.1 (2013), https://wwwo.gsb.columbia.edu/mygsb/faculty/research/pubfiles/5848/WomeninTMT.pdf (accessed 27 June 2015)

Lucy to appear in newspapers, with a caption suggesting that the two women are lovers. This innuendo leads to an outburst of vitriol by Tshepo:

> "Now what am I going to tell my friends, heh? That my stupid wife hangs around stupid lezzy girls, heh? That they shouldn't beat her up like they do to girls like that in the townships." (39)

These words, put in the mouth of a verbally, physically, and sexually abusive husband, articulate the patriarchal power which is at the root of the violence against Others – both women and homosexuals – that is so problematic in South African society, where black lesbians are subjected to the horror of 'corrective rape' with the aim of making them become heterosexual. It subsequently emerges that Lucy is indeed a lesbian, a discovery that the other three friends accept with equanimity. The novel endorses a progressive attitude towards lesbianism and alternative gender expression as displayed by Lucy – and the novel also places her in a wealthier and more hopeful situation than that suffered by J.M. Coetzee's lesbian character, Lucy, in *Disgrace* (1999).

Neo discovers that Tshepo has been using her father's name to enhance his own business opportunities, and that she may therefore be implicated in his dubious dealings. Significantly, the information is offered by the wife of a business associate of Tshepo's, in exchange for help in finding a divorce lawyer. Neo is further helped by an old university friend, Geoff Higgins, whose mother was killed by her abusive husband, and by a female *sangoma*, or traditional healer.

At a party, Tshepo, who is increasingly anxious about the success of his tender bid, hits Neo in public, then later beats her severely in private, with the expectation that his vicious attacks will be socially condoned, just as corruption in tenders often is in South Africa. The shocked reaction of a number of men, including Geoff, to Tshepo's public assault gives Neo courage to believe that some good men exist who are prepared to assist her. After Tshepo wrongly accuses Neo of having an affair with Geoff, she stands up to her husband, proudly declaring:

> "I am Neo Dimakatso Mokoena. I am the daughter of Miles Mokoena and I can be friends with anyone I want. If you have a problem with that then go! […] If you ever call me a slut or a whore or a bitch again I'll ruin you." (104)

Matters come to a tragic head at another party, when Tshepo's business associate fatally shoots Geoff for losing him all his money in the divorce. Neo reveals her bruises from Tshepo's beatings to the crowd, and exposes his plan to commit tender fraud. Supported by her friends and the *sangoma*, Neo divorces

Tshepo, who is jailed and dishonoured, while his lover is denounced for sleeping "with anyone with a large bank account" (124). Through the intervention of the *sangoma*, Neo takes up law practice again, specializing in divorce law to assist women in gaining their freedom. The novel ends with Neo hearing voices from within her body:

> It started off in my heart and reverberated in my rib cage – 'Queen BEE.' My mother's voice started, it was soon joined by the voices of my father and Geoff. 'Queen BEE,' they said simultaneously. It thrummed with my heartbeat and for the first time in a long time I smiled. (130)

Neo's representative embodiment of triumph over domestic violence and verbal abuse in the private sphere, and her exposure of corruption in the public sphere, occur as a result of support from various quarters, ranging from a female traditionalist, the *sangoma*, to young professionals; all sectors of society are needed to engage in combatting dominant patterns of violence, greed, and selfishness.

*Queen B.E.E.* is marked by various flaws typical of debut novels published by a new press: it contains clichés and inconsistencies, and suffers from poor editing. However, it has strong, interesting characters and a compelling plot. It also offers a fruitful comparison and contrast with Mda's *Black Diamond*, particularly with regard to the different gendered perspectives from which the new black moneyed elite is portrayed in the two novels, to the representation of bodies, to language use, including pejorative expressions directed at female and male characters, and to the treatment of such central themes as freedom, work, dignity, equity, and social justice.

With regard to the gendered perspective adopted by each novel, the point of view in *Black Diamond* is clearly masculine, that of Don Matera. This can be seen most clearly in the slippage of the following passage:

> Soweto is ringing in Tumi's and Don's heads. And when Soweto is ringing in your head you make love. No, you fuck. That is what you call it because making love sounds too clinical. Too neat and clean and proper. You wear your Rough Rider ultra ribbed latex and fuck like you are back at Matseke Secondary School. [...] You fuck like Tumi has sneaked into your bedroom for illicit sex when your mother is doing night duty [...], Like you must ravage each other very quickly, which becomes even more breathtaking, because Tumi has to rush home before [her father] discovers that the person sleeping in her bed is a rolled up blanket and beats her black and blue with his belt until her buttocks are sore [...].

> Yes, you will fuck like you have just discovered Tiger Balm [...] and have applied it to your penis to enhance both your pleasure. (43)

Initially there is an evocation of the consciousness of Tumi and Don, which then shifts to the singular "your head," implying a focus on one character. The reference to "you" wearing "your" Rough Rider condom makes it plain that Don is the centre of consciousness and his body is being described. In general, reading "you" in a text leads the reader to imagine that one is also being addressed, and as the passage progresses this usage interpellates the reader into identifying with Don's privileged masculine perspective, seeing Tumi as an object of sexual desire and the phallus as the prime agent of sexual pleasure.

Tumi's black-diamond women friends wryly note that their male counterparts are too intimidated by high-achieving women to marry them. Instead, such a male black diamond prefers his wife to behave as passive accessory decorated with conspicuously expensive clothes and reconciled to her husband's spending money on "pub-crawling or bonking schoolgirls" (80) in apartments he rents for them. It is clear that Don feels no compunction about the flings he has with women while he is in a relationship with Tumi, while Kristin feels guilty about her affair with Don, when he is still attached to Tumi, and urges him to return to her and clarify where he stands.

Women characters in *Black Diamond* are portrayed in terms of stereotypes of gender and race, as seen, for instance, in the widespread misogynist media treatment of the black South African celebrity Khanyi Mbau as a promiscuous gold-digger, compared to the more admiring reportage of the extravagance and sexual prowess of her male counterpart, Kenny Kunene. Tumi is represented as a typical female black diamond, in that she is shown to be highly sexed, controlling, and avaricious. As the owner of a modelling agency, she is complicit with the superficiality of the lucrative fashion world, unscrupulously exploiting the bodies of other women. Kristin Uys, whose first name suggests her Calvinist roots and can be connected to the colonizing enterprise of the missionaries in Africa in the nineteenth century, wields her legal powers as a magistrate irresponsibly and selfishly. Kristin's surname epitomizes her façade of frigid control. While in line with her religious convictions, this façade is to deflect from her history as model for a soft-porn magazine. Don's ministrations reconcile this virgin/whore dichotomy so prevalent in South African culture. Another character, the 'Coloured'[22] Aunt Magda, who was the Visagies' "maid" (130), is portrayed as sexually available to all, including Mr Visagie and his son Stevo: in an odd turn of phrase, as it refers to the rupturing of the female hymen, the reader

---

[22] The word is a South African term for a person of mixed racial heritage.

learns that "she broke his virginity when he was only slightly older than a tyke" (130). She discusses her murderous intentions towards Ma Visagie. This matriarch, who views herself as the alpha figure of her household, is represented in comic terms, as a shotgun-wielding working-class white criminal specializing in running a brothel. This characterization presents her as a foil of sorts to female black diamonds, as she stands for the fading but still exploitative power of white South Africans in the wake of the black diamonds' growing affluence.

The novel encodes both masculine entitlement and anxieties, and serves to re-inscribe the gendered status quo, as is also manifest in the uses to which Mda puts the genre of the novel as satire, which

> has usually been justified by those who practice it as a corrective of human vice and folly [...]. Its frequent claim (not always borne out in the practice) has been to ridicule the failing rather than the individual, and to limit its ridicule to corrigible faults, excluding those for which a person is not responsible.[23]

Mda's choice of Don as focalizer in *Black Diamond* is an attempt to elicit sympathy for this character and his aspiration to acquire wealth and prestige, while contrasting this with the ambitions of more corrupt characters, and endorsing his masculine power and insecurities while presenting his shortcomings as mere peccadilloes rather than objects of satire.

By contrast, the gendered perspective in *Queen B.E.E.* displays an African feminist sensibility through the eyes of the first-person narrator, Neo Dube, who by the age of twenty-six finds herself admitting to her friend Geoff that marriage to an opportunistic and abusive husband has drained her of her youthfulness and determination to change the world. The greed for unearned benefits in business displayed by Neo's husband, Tshepo Dube, is a correlative of his abuse of masculine privilege in the private sphere of his marriage, as he uses her father's name to gain tenders, mistreats her, and applies double standards, accusing her of unfaithfulness irrespective of the reputation as a womanizer he has earned for himself. Both male and female black diamonds are shown to be susceptible to the temptation to behave dishonourably, in concert with similarly corrupt white people, the previous captains of industry. However, in this novel there are also examples of decency in characters from all walks of life who assist Neo. Her first name is Sesotho ('gift' or 'talent'), and over the course of the novel she shifts from identifying as "Mrs Dube" to identifying herself as "Ms

---

[23] M.H. Abrams & Geoffrey Galt Harpham, *A Glossary of Literary Terms* (Boston MA: Wadsworth Cengage Learning, 9th ed, 2005): 320.

Mokoena." The surname Mokoena is Sesotho for members of the clan whose totem animal is the crocodile,[24] and Matseke's use of this name suggests Neo's strength and tenacity in moving from the position of a downtrodden wife to an independent woman who has reconnected with her family heritage, which helps her reclaim her talent of practising law. Unlike *Black Diamond*, *Queen B.E.E.* emphasizes the importance of staying rooted in family and tradition, while using the tools and possibilities of modernity for the common good. Neo is encouraged by Geoff and forms an unacknowledged love for him, but they do not have a sexual relationship, and her development is ultimately dependent on her own decisions and actions rather than on a transformation occasioned by a romantic liaison, as seen in the character of Kristin Uys.

Further differences between the two novels can be discerned in their representations of female bodies. Mda disturbingly reifies women, with the narrative dwelling on Kristin's small breasts, her appearance in a soft-porn magazine, and her dancing in stripper gear, and by his use of the perspective of the criminal Stevo to project fantasies of Kristin's losing control of her body, wetting her pants in fear of him.

Dance is a form that has the potential to offer female agency of expression beyond the limits of phallogocentrism. However, in *Black Diamond*, the representation of dance conforms to just as confining a patriarchal paradigm. The final dance scene repeats elements of the earlier scene in which Don observed Kristin dancing, a scene represented in the novel as a key instance of their developing intimacy and her subsequent submission in a sexual relationship with him. The dance scene begins with Kristin applying makeup "in the garish manner of prostitutes. She gets into her 'whore' costume with grace and deliberation as if it is something sacred" (270). For a number of reasons this dance scene is problematic from a feminist perspective. Kristin's repeated compliance with male expectations is a character trait Mda employs to justify her ultimate reification as her own doing. When Stevo forces Kristin to dance seductively while he insults, threatens, and slaps her, and slashes her clothes and body with a knife, a disturbing connection is drawn between dance, spectatorship, and violence that accords with extreme pornographic representations of women. Little attention is given to Kristin's feelings or reactions in this section of the scene. Although she triumphs in the end – after Don and Shortie rush in and Don is shot, Kristin kicks Stevo "in the balls" and knocks him out with a chair – this is presented in slapstick fashion, a manoeuvre that effectively diminishes

---

[24] "Surname Mokoena," *Namespedia* (2006–2015), http://www.namespedia.com/details/Mokoena (accessed 29 June 2015).

her success and puts it on the same level as the acts of violence Kristin suffers from the male characters, allowing no space for the reader to judge her behaviour as necessary self-defence, and serving to endorse violence as a response to violence. Androcentric norms of voyeurism, desire, aggression, and violence are normalized in the novel.

In *Queen B.E.E.*, the representation of women's bodies is more realistic and sympathetic towards suffering than in *Black Diamond*. Neo's 'leaky' body is also shown in a state of degradation, as she cries, wets herself, and vomits when maltreated by her husband. However, in her case, the reader is granted insight into her mind rather than invited to observe the narrated violence as the fulfilment of a male character's fantasy. Brutal actions leave bodily and psychological scars. Neo suffers bruises, experiences isolation and shame, and even harms herself by escaping into bingeing; however, the text shows actions that can be taken to improve matters, such as her agency in going to the gym to become fit, for her own sake, not to conform to a sexy feminine stereotype to attract men's attention. The novel illustrates the vulnerability of men as well as women to masculine violence. It goes beyond the ending of the female character's defeat proposed by Mda and allows the black diamond Neo to repair and eschew violence (as a means both of self-defence and of retribution).

Abuse is enacted not only physically but also verbally. Both forms of violence affect women's self-esteem, their image in the eyes of society at large, and consequently their value and earning potential. *Black Diamond* is replete with instances in which male characters refer to women as "bitch" or "whore." *The Shorter Oxford English Dictionary* defines the word "bitch" in its metaphorical usage as a Medieval English term "applied to a (lewd) woman."[25] The brackets mark a telling slippage between all women and "lewd" women, suggesting that all women may be considered liable to sexual slurs. As Dorothy Hage points out, there is no term for "normal sexual power in women,"[26] which is remarkable, given the high number of expressions available to reference women's sexual behaviour and Muriel R. Schultz's finding that words and phrases "describing women in sexually derogatory ways" by far exceed in number equivalent terms applicable to men.[27] While the words "bitch" and to a lesser extent "whore" are applied to the main female character Kristin in *Black Diamond*, when verbal

---

[25] *The Shorter Oxford English Dictionary on Historical Principles*, ed. William Little, H.W. Fowler & Jessie Coulson, rev. C.T. Onions, reset G.W.S. Friedrichsen (Oxford: Clarendon, 3rd ed. 1973), vol. 1: 196.

[26] Dorothy Hage, "There's Glory for You," *Aphra: The Feminist Literary Magazine* 3.3 (1972): 10.

[27] Muriel R. Schultz, "The Semantic Derogation of Woman," in *Language and Sex: Difference and Dominance*, ed. Barrie Thorne & Nancy Henley (Rowley MA: Newbury House, 1975): 72.

barbs are directed at male characters, the terms used are "motherfucker," "son of a bitch," and "bastard" (where in each case the slur reflects back to the mother figure).

A further dimension to the prevalence of sexual slurs in the novel is the use of qualifiers of race, as in "stone-cold white bitch" (155). When Don breaks up with Tumi she lashes out:

> "That's always the case with you bastards. [...] Once you become a Black Diamond black sisters are no longer good enough for you! Fucking a white woman is a bloody status symbol. Now you're a bloody CEO you think you are Molotov Mbungane all of a sudden." (247–48)

Tumi concludes by calling him "'*njandini*, you dog'" (248), which he takes as a supreme insult, although the term is devoid of the sexual innuendo that the word "bitch" contains. Don's friend berates him for leaving Tumi once he has "'tasted a white woman's cake,'" speculating that Don "'thinks a white woman's cake is the fastest way to becoming like Comrade Capitalist'" (258). Another friend asks, "'Did we fight the liberation struggle so that we can get between the thighs of white women?'" (258). In other words, sexual association across racial lines is heavily stigmatized. The novel normalizes gendered slurs, and betrays historical anxieties with regard to gender and race.

*Queen B.E.E.* also contains a number of uses of the word "bitch," although not as many as in *Black Diamond*, and in much more varied contexts. There is one *sotto voce* reference by Thato, a member of Neo's group of friends to another one who is annoying her, but in the past Thato has punched a young woman who called Neo a "rich bitch" (108). So the word can be used with care and jocularly within the in-group, but is considered an insult when applied by a member of the out-group. Neo herself cathartically refers to Tshepo's lover as "'That bitch. That witch'" (25). Neo remembers an instance when Tshepo spoke pleasantly to a woman, then afterwards referred to her as a bitch; this she belatedly sees as a warning signal of his attitude towards women. As the relationship between Neo and Tshepo deteriorates, he calls her a "'filthy bitch'" (80), a "'dirty whore'" (86), and a "'slut'" (104). This final insult leads to her threat to ruin him. After he is jailed, Tshepo phones Neo to ask her to bail him out, beginning with "'Neo, baby, I'm so sorry'," and when Neo refuses to pay his bail he shows his true colours and masculine assumption of superiority with the insult "'You're a stupid bitch. You're nothing without me!'" (123). Neo's success reveals that she does not rely on Tshepo for financial support or social status, in line with the title of the novel *I Ain't Yo Bitch*,[28] which refutes the ascription of this sexist jibe and its implied abjection. Similarly, *Queen B.E.E.* problematizes the use of gendered slurs such as "bitch," particularly as applied within the intimate sphere, and portrays them as oppressive and dehumanizing.

*Black Diamond* and *Queen B.E.E.* display very different attitudes to freedom, work, dignity, equity, and social justice. Mda's novel sharply exposes social ills, but participates in a non-egalitarian discourse, doing little to posit an alternative, more progressive future for South Africa. By contrast, the trajectory followed by Neo in *Queen B.E.E.* hinges on freedom attained through hard work and a determination to resist the oppression of women which prevents them from attaining their full potential, including in terms of earning-power. Matseke's representation of this character refutes discrimination on grounds of gender, race, ethnicity or sexuality, thus affirming equal rights and potentially contributing to a juster society where wealth is more equally distributed than at present.

## WORKS CITED


Abrams, M.H., & Geoffrey Galt Harpham. *A Glossary of Literary Terms* (Boston MA: Wadsworth Cengage Learning, 9th ed. 2005).

Balfour, Robert J. "Introduction: Culture, Capital and Representation," in *Culture, Capital and Representation*, ed. Robert J. Balfour (London & New York: Palgrave Macmillan, 2010): 1–15.

Coetzee, J.M. *Disgrace* (London: Secker & Warburg, 1999).

Dezső, Cristian L., David Gaddis Ross & Jose N. Uribe. "Why Are There So Few Women Top Managers? A Large-Sample Empirical Study of the Antecedents of Female Participation in Top Management," *Social Science Research Network* 11.1 (2013), https://wwwo.gsb.columbia.edu/mygsb/faculty/research/pubfiles/5848/WomeninTMT.pdf (accessed 27 June 2015).

Fincham, Gail. *Dance of Life: The Novels of Zakes Mda in Post-Apartheid South Africa* (Cape Town: U of Cape Town P, 2011): 147–58.

Hage, Dorothy. "There's Glory for You," *Aphra: The Feminist Literary Magazine* 3.3 (1972): 2–14.

Haynes, Rebecca. "SA's Mysterious 'Middle Class'," *Mail & Guardian* (31 January 2014), http://mg.co.za/article/2014-01-31-00-sas-mysterious-middle-class (accessed 27 March 2014).

Isaacson, Maureen. "In his Personal Capacity," *The Sunday Independent* (29 November 2009), Books section: 17.


---

[28] Jabulile Bongiwe Ngwenya, *I Ain't Yo Bitch* (Parkview, S.A.: Paper Bag, 2009).

Labia, Natale. "Black Diamonds Sparkle – for Some," *Mail & Guardian* (15 November 2010), http://mg.co.za/article/2010-11-15-black-diamonds-sparkle-for-some (accessed 31 March 2014).

Matseke, Lebogang. *Queen B.E.E.* (Pietermaritzburg: Otterley Press, 2015).

Mda, Zakes. *Black Diamond* (Johannesburg: Penguin, 2009).

Mda, Zakes. *The Heart of Redness* (Oxford: Oxford UP, 2000).

Mda, Zakes. *Sometimes There Is a Void: Memoirs of an Outsider* (Johannesburg: Penguin, 2011).

Ngwenya, Jabulile Bongiwe. *I Ain't Yo Bitch* (Parkview, S.A.: Paper Bag, 2009).

"Oxfam Finds 85 Elites as Rich as 3.5-billion People," *Mail & Guardian* (21 January 2014), http://mg.co.za/article/2014-01-21-oxfam-finds-85-people-as-rich-as-half-the-global-population (accessed 31 March 2014).

"Pornography of Power," *Culture Review Magazine* (2015), http://www.culture-review.co.za/pornography-of-power (accessed 13 October 2015).

Schultz, Muriel R. "The Semantic Derogation of Woman," in *Language and Sex: Difference and Dominance*, ed. Barrie Thorne & Nancy Henley (Rowley MA: Newbury House, 1975): 64–75.

*The Shorter Oxford English Dictionary on Historical Principles*, ed. William Little, H.W. Fowler & Jessie Coulson, rev. C.T. Onions, reset G.W.S. Friedrichsen (Oxford: Clarendon, 3rd ed. 1973).

Silva, Christine, Nancy M. Carter & Anna Beninger. "Good Intentions, Imperfect Execution? Women Get Fewer of the 'Hot Jobs' Needed to Advance," *Catalyst* (2012): 15–17.

Staines, Graham, Carol Tavris & Toby E. Jayaratne. "The Queen Bee Syndrome," *Psychology Today* 7.8 (January 1974): 55–70.

"Surname Mokoena," *Namespedia* (2006–2015) http://www.namespedia.com/details/Mokoena (accessed 29 June 2015).

Tangri, Roger, & Roger Southall. "The Politics of Black Economic Empowerment in South Africa," *Journal of Southern African Studies* 34.3 (2008): 699–718.

Van Onselen, Charles. "The Witches of Suburbia: Domestic Service on the Witwatersrand 1890–1914," *Studies in the Social and Economic History of the Witwatersrand 1886–1914*, vol. 2: *New Nineveh* (Johannesburg: Ravan, 1982): 45–60.

Visagie, Justin. *Race, Gender and Growth of the Affluent Middle Class in Post-Apartheid South Africa* (Economic Research Southern Africa Working Paper 395, 2013), http://www.econrsa.org/system/files/publications/working_papers/working_paper_395.pdf (accessed 31 March 2014).

❄

# The Truth on Common Poverty and Uncommon Wealth in Rural Kenya

## *Stanley Gazemba's* The Stone Hills of Maragoli[1]

Alex Nelungo Wanjala

Social inequality, specifically the contrast between extreme poverty suffered by the majority of the populace and the enormous wealth held in the hands of a few, has been a key theme in Kenyan novels since the 1960s. Whereas political discourse perpetuates the idea of the nation as one in which there are equal opportunities for growth and development for all, evidence from across the social sciences illuminates how the independence-era goal of re-creating social equality remains unattainable in contemporary Kenya due to national malpractices as well as to dramatic asymmetries in the global distribution of geopolitical power. In the twenty-first century, it is still a very small part of Kenyan society who live in wealthy gated communities whereas the rest of the nation remain without adequate shelter and basic resources. Poverty levels have stagnated in Kenya over the past thirty years: in 1981, the World Bank estimated forty-eight percent poverty; in 2006, they still found that forty-seven percent of Kenyans "were unable to meet the cost of buying the amount of calories sufficient to meet the daily nutritional requirements and minimal non-food needs."[2] On the United Nations Human Development Index, Kenya's 2013 score of 0.535 places it in the low human-development category. As recently as 2014, the World Bank president Jim Yong Kim could only reiterate this assessment:

---

[1] Part of this essay was first presented at the European Association for Commonwealth Literature and Language Studies conference, held in Innsbruck Austria in April 2014. I would like to thank the participants for their insightful comments, which helped to develop my arguments.

[2] World Bank *Kenya Poverty and Inequality Assessment Report*, ii.

> Two-thirds of the world's extreme poor are concentrated in just five countries: India, China, Nigeria, Bangladesh, and the Democratic Republic of Congo. If you add another five countries; Indonesia, Pakistan, Tanzania and Kenya, the total grows up to 80% of the extreme poor.[3]

Despite the attention paid by international observers to the persisting socio-economic disparities in Kenya, the Kenyan government has remained either blind to chronic poverty or in active denial of it as a problem which it ought to tackle. In the same year as Jim Yong Kim delivered his speech, the government claimed that Kenya was, in fact, growing richer and, after re-evaluating the country's Gross Domestic Product, the National Bureau of Statistics, in creatively unconventional terms, announced:

> The size of the economy is 25% larger than previously thought and Kenya is the now the fifth largest economy in Sub-Saharan Africa behind Nigeria, South Africa, Angola and the Sudan. [...] Kenya crossed the lower-middle income threshold in 2012.[4]

The very contradictory appraisals of Kenya's wealth[5] make it rather difficult to determine the poverty level at which its weakest members live, let alone to glean an idea of their lives. Imaginary invocations of economic strife are all the more valuable as documents complementing such projects as "Unga: The Issue," which gathered oral testimonials from across Kenya on food availability and scarcity,[6] or the survey of food security undertaken by the African Women's Studies Centre and Kenya National Bureau of Statistics. This essay isolates one particular literary text and pays attention to the special realism deployed by its

---

[3] Jim Yong Kim, "Count on Us" Speech, The World Bank (1 April 2014), http://www. world bank.org/en/news/speech/2014/04/01/speech-world-bank-group-president-jim-yong-kim-council-on-foreign-relations (accessed 11 May, 2015).

[4] Kenya National Bureau of Statistics. *Information on the Revised National Accounts* (Nairobi: Government Printer, 2014). For critiques, see John Mistiaen, John Randa & Apurva Sanghi, "Kenya's Re-based National Accounts: Myths, Facts, and the Consequences," "Kenya's Re-based National Accounts: Myths, Facts, and the Consequences," *The World Bank Data Blog*, http:// blogs.worldbank.org/opendata/kenya-s-re-based-national-accounts-myths-facts-and-consequen ces (accessed 11 May 2015); Farai Gundan, "Kenya Joins Africa's Top 10 Economies After Reassessing of its Gross Domestic Product," *Forbes* 01.10 (2014), http://www.forbes.com/sites/faraigundan/ 2014/10/01/kenya-joins-africas-top-10-economies-after-rebasing-of-its-gross-domestic-product/ #21c7fc533a25 (accessed 11 May 2015).

[5] African Women's Studies Centre, University of Nairobi & Kenya National Bureau of Statistics. *Status Report on Kenyan National Food Security* (Nairobi: Nairobi UP, 2014).

[6] I was a researcher on this 2009 project under the aegis of Storymoja publishers that was unfortunately never published. These testimonies are still in my archives.

author to assert in all clarity that poverty does exist in much of Kenya and that it is omnipresent in its rural areas, so much so that to deny it would be to deny the existence of Kenya itself.

In the process, the text in question, *The Stone Hills of Maragoli* by Stanley Gazemba, does not appeal so much to the reader's sympathy with Kenya's poor, or indulge in a sentimental portrayal of their victimization, as, in a dauntingly uncompromising manner, exposes the moral weakness of human subjects, especially those who find themselves on the brink of destitution. He explains their susceptibility to temptation, however unpromising, and their corruptibility by gain, however minimal. Crediting fiction with at least the same truth-value as historical documents, this essay seeks to isolate from Gazemba's narrative observations on Kenyan society that make the reader realize the crass discrepancy between the Kenyan state's optimistic interpretation of its economic situation and the lived experience of the many citizens who have not benefitted from Kenya's purported economic success.[7] The following has been written with Michel Foucault's idea of the intellectual in mind: a public figure partaking in the production of truth in the interest of the masses.[8] Accordingly, the analysis of *The Stone Hills of Maragoli* offered here has been conducted in the hope that it can add to the pressure that needs to be put on policy-makers to no longer deny the glaring social inequalities dividing Kenyan society, stop perpetuating stories of their country's prosperity, and start conceiving of measures of wealth re-distribution capable of alleviating the catastrophic destitution in which so many Kenyans live. This essay offers an intrinsically political reading of *The Stone Hills of Maragoli* aiming to render visible what official political discourse tries to conceal, by stressing the radical difference between the broken Kenya conjured up in Gazemba's novel and the booming Kenya construed in the narratives issued by the state's propaganda machinery. For, rather than a Kenya confidently thriving on the allegedly wholesome effects of globalization, *The Stone Hills of Maragoli* portrays a small, impoverished rural community in

---

[7] The government's interest in marketing Kenya as an emergent economy rather than in addressing poverty has political and economic repercussions: the Revised National Accounts were published just as the government was in the process of raising a bond for infrastructural development. The revision caused debt levels to fall as a proportion of GDP, thereby giving the government "some leeway for more borrowing to help finance its plans to build new transport links and repair creaking infrastructure." See George Obulutsa & Edmund Blair, "Kenya's Economy Increases by a Quarter to join Africa's Top 10," *Reuters.com* (30 September 2014), http://www.reuters.com/article/2014/09/30/kenya-economy-idUSL6N0RV1Q020140930 (accessed 11 May 2015).

[8] Michel Foucault, "The Political Function of the Intellectual," tr. Colin Gordon, *Radical Philosophy* 17 (Summer 1977): 12–14.

Kenya abandoned by its government and the rest of the world. The novel makes painfully obvious the complete absence of help, on the part both of Kenya's policy-makers and of international organizations in those places in Kenya where it would be needed most urgently. It leaves no doubt that it is from this want that the horrific stasis results in which it shows Kenya's farmers to be entrapped. As Gazemba demonstrates, external help is all the more urgently needed as Kenyan farmers' own patient and persistent efforts to help *themselves* have long ceased to be effective enough measures to avert their total bankruptcy and prevent Kenyan society from falling/breaking apart.

*The Stone Hills of Maragoli* was first published by Acacia in 2002. It is Stanley Gazemba's first novel, which he wrote while working as a gardener for an American news editor, Susan Linnee, who provided him with a typewriter when she discovered that he was composing a novel in longhand.[9] Maragoli is the place where Gazemba grew up, enjoying a relatively privileged life as child of local school-teachers before being sent away to boarding school. As an adult, Gazemba exchanged his life in security and comfort for one as manual labourer in Kiambu, Mombasa, and Nairobi. In the late 1990s, living in Kangemi, a slum on the outskirts of Kenya's capital, Gazemba began to write *The Stone Hills of Maragoli*. In 2003, one year after its publication, it earned him the Jomo Kenyatta Prize for Literature, one of Kenya's most prestigious literary awards. Though *The Stone Hills from Maragoli* was advertised as a "breakthrough novel," the initial success of the book did not enable Gazemba to leave poverty behind. In a 2010 news blog he is still portrayed as a slum-dweller and near-victim of the 2007 post-election riots. Only after the re-publication of his novel by the Kwani Trust in 2010 could Gazemba finally abandon gardening, tea-picking, and bricklaying and start to seriously pursue a career as journalist and writer of fiction.

A good measure of the slowness of change experienced by Kenya's less privileged citizens, Gazemba's own story has, of course, fed into the fictional account he gives in *The Stone Hills of Maragoli* of economic stasis crippling an entire community cut off from the rapid modernization that globalization seems to have effected everywhere else in the world. Only at first sight, however, does Gazemba's novel emulate predominantly urban Kenyan fiction and chronicle the everyday life of Kenya's poor. Unlike Meja Mwangi's *The Cockroach Dance* (1979) or *Going Down River Road* (1976) and also unlike Ngũgĩ wa Thiong'o's *A Grain of Wheat*, *The Stone Hills of Maragoli* displays an identity arguably marked by the new spirit and politics of the postcolony. Whereas earlier writers would

---

[9] "A Kenyan Writer Blossoms from a Nairobi Slum," *National Public Radio*, 31 May 2010, http://www.npr.org/templates/story/story.php?storyId=127245175 (accessed 11 May 2015).

contest either the colonial order (*A Grain of Wheat*) or neo-colonialism (*Going Down River Road*) in their descriptions of the social ills they had to face, younger writers such as Gazemba belong to a larger ensemble of African writers of whom Phyllis Taoua notes that they no longer practise the kind of "symbolic Othering that used to be organized by the outmoded colonizer–colonized boundary." Instead, she holds, they tend to apply "a new set of oppositional identities that are decidedly more dynamic in nature."[10]

In the case of *The Stone Hills of Maragoli*, these "oppositional identities" are defined wholly by socio-economic difference. For, as Richard Bartlett puts it, Gazemba's novel

> has no pretensions about attempting to address issues of modernity, of city life, of 'clash of cultures', of the rural–urban divide [...] the issues it deals with are as immediate, even if they are beyond the gaze, beyond the limits of the urbanity that attracts most writers.[11]

Gazemba's focus rests entirely on the divide between rich and poor Kenyans producing antagonisms "more dynamic" than that between colonizer and colonized insofar as they affect the coexistence of equals by race and nationality who in the postcolony are no longer united by a common enemy. This makes for complicated personal discord in which normally uncontested notions of right and wrong are called in question. As a result, the social fabric of the villages of of Ivona and Kigama, where *The Stone Hills of Maragoli* is mainly set, tears apart so that economic survival remains the sole motivation for people to continue living together.

Right at the beginning of the novel, the villagers' descent into moral and cultural bankruptcy is foreshadowed by their demure acceptance of the enormous wealth of their employer, the landowner and businessman Andimi. They tolerate the superior airs and detachment he has cultivated along with the harsh conditions of the employment he affords them. As the only representative in the area of Kenya's emergent middle class, he is respected almost beyond his due, considering that he came into wealth not by hard labour or inheritance but merely by marrying Madam Tabitha, the daughter of another rich man. Nonetheless, no one dares to challenge the methods whereby he keeps increasing his riches, using the desperation of the subsistence small farmers to his own advantage and forcing them to work more for him than on their own land.

---

[10] Phyllis Taoua, "The Postcolonial Condition," in *The Cambridge Companion to the African Novel*, ed. Irele F. Abiola (Cambridge: Cambridge UP, 2009): 211.

[11] Richard Bartlett, review of *The Stone Hills of Maragoli*, *African Review of Books* (20 April 2004), http://www.authorsden.com/visit/viewwork.asp?AuthorID=149672 (accessed 20 May 2015).

From the very opening of the novel, Gazemba casts doubt on the villagers' tacit tolerance of the manifest injustice of Andimi's prosperity as a profoundly disabling stance by introducing his main character Ombima and showing how despair after another unsuccessful harvest drives him to steal food for his family from Andimi's kitchen garden. Not even in this moment of crisis does Ombima stop to consider that his effort to save his wife and children from starvation might actually be a perfectly just and valiant attempt to right an obvious wrong. Though he is harvesting what he himself has helped to grow, and though he is driven to dishonorable action by "burning need," Ombima, gripped by anxiety and bare of any sense of entitlement, makes his way to Andimi's garden. Instead of recognizing the harmlessness of his modest plundering from a garden replete with bananas, cassava, and maize, he feels that for the first time in his life he is committing a crime and is consumed by shame at the thought that this is all he can do to make up for his failure to fend for his family honestly and without breaking the law:

> Ombima was scared – not of the approaching storm but of what he was about to do. [...] For all his life into grey-sideburned middle age, Ombima had never really stolen from anyone. He had always worked tirelessly for what little he had. Of course, there were those petty offences like pilfering fruit from a neighbour's tree and things that everyone does as a boy and which are not really considered theft. But stealing to satisfy a burning need he had never done. He had always gone out of his way to keep on his cloak of honesty, even after he got married and the hardships of looking after a family pressed. Today Ombima was going to steal. Not money, not silver. He was going to steal food. Plain life-sustaining food, and it weighed him down with such shame he could hardly keep his head straight.[12]

Echoes of the biblical fall from innocence accompany Gazemba's depiction of Ombima reaching out for forbidden fruit and vegetables in Andimi's paradisiacal garden. The profoundly ironical allusion is made even more obvious by the appearance of a female catching the poor thief in the act and using his terror at her appearance to tempt him into an amorous liaison with her: Madam Tabitha, who has been watching Ombima, steps out of the darkness, and under the threat of a punishment worse than expulsion from paradise – namely, betrayal to the unforgiving Ambimi – blackmails her victim into becoming her lover.

It is an indication of the village community's brokenness that the petty crime committed by Ombima triggers a cascade of calamities eventually impossible to

[12] Stanley Gazemba, *The Stone Hills of Maragoli* (2002; Nairobi: Kwani Trust, 2010): 11–12.

control by any of the characters involved and therefore culminating in the tragic devastation of the protagonist. The gradual progression towards the final catastrophe sets in with individual villagers undergoing personal crises, typically suffering them in secret isolation: Ombima's shocked realization that the late nights he spends pleasuring Andimi's wife have roused his wife Sayo's distrust, Sayo's growing despair as it dawns on her that Ombima might be having an affair with another woman, Tabitha's fear of her lover's rejection and her husband's revenge, Ang'ote's jealousy of Ombima and his keen wish to earn Ambimi's favour – these are all rendered in the form of interior monologue, exposing not only their distress but also their loneliness and lack of trust in the support of the community. The repeated confluence of their quiet reveries, while drawing attention to the absence of dialogue as far more than a formal choice on the part of the author, effectively accentuates their alienation from each other.

There are moments in the novel where there still seems to be hope that the efforts of some of the characters to repair apparently ruptured social bonds and even reach across class barriers can bear fruit. Madam Tabitha's involvement in village life and her personal investment in the local school, for instance, appear to hold the promise of her willingness to act as an intermediary between the farmers and her husband. Likewise, Ombima's attempts to coax his friend Ang'ote out of the depression into which he has fallen and assist him in sorting out his affairs seem to imply that civic responsibility is not yet obsolete among the farmers of Maragoli – that the wellbeing of the community is still valued. However, the opposite proves the case. Neither Madam Tabitha's nor Ombima's intervention is appreciated, instead inciting the resentment and jealousy of others. Before long they find themselves betrayed by those they trust and delivered up to Ambimi.

In the same vein, the villagers' joint labouring on Andimi's land requires to be read. The impression one obtains at first glance of their harmonious togetherness is thoroughly deceptive, yet needs little closer inspection to remind the reader that what unites the farmers as they are working on the same lot of land is merely the need to supplement their meagre incomes by doing additional work. It is in meticulous concrete detail that Gazemba describes their involuntary rather that voluntary experience of collective labour, paying special attention to the corporeal aspect of the farmer's being and doing. A wealth of auditory, tactile, and visual images brings to life the sounds and rhythms of their working day, lends materiality to the tools they need for hoeing and picking tea, renders physically imaginable the motions they perform as they apply their bodies to harvesting what the plants give with little resistance. These and the brief exchanges taking place between labourers, the silences that grow when their concentrated work forbids speech, the schemes some of them devise to escape tasks onerous to them, make for the portrait of a 'workforce' rather than a group of individuals carrying out their task almost like automata, concentrating on the wage they will earn and almost oblivious to the presence of their fellow workers:

> Conversation gradually stopped as the stained fingers plucked at the juicy tipping shoots, tough thumbnails cutting into the more stubborn twigs. The callused palms, work toughened, soon filled up, and the hand flipped over the bended shoulder into the sagging basket weighing down the picker's ravaged back. Washed by the dew covering the luxuriant leaves, the skin of the palms soon turned a corny white colour, the joints in the fingers stiffening into their gnarled angles in the plucking 'posture' as the frost bit. Their *tap-tap!* was infectious, hanging in the thin hilltop air as the huge workforce spread over the first portion of the estate, devouring the soft tender shoots as if they were the money they sought at the end of it all. Each of the workers knew only too well the importance of the productive hours of the morning, they darted their work-honed hands to and fro with deftness, determined to fill the first basket before the sun rose in the sky. Then, they knew they would have to slow down.[13]

Throughout *The Stone Hills of Maragoli*, Gazemba makes extensive use of his first-hand knowledge of farming (and, more specifically, of the procedure of tea-picking in the above passage). Indeed, so convincing are his representations of peasants at work that one feels reminded of the Kamiriithu People's Theatre Project for which Ngũgĩ wa Thiong'o recruited Kenyan peasants and had them appear in the play *Ngaahika Ndeendai* (*I Will Marry When I Want*). On stage they entered into a dialogue with him about production, agricultural and cultural. The idea was that in taking part in the play and speaking about this experience, Ngũgĩ's lay interlocutors would teach him, the author, about his own work as an activity related to their own modes of production.[14] However, unlike Ngũgĩ, Gazemba is a dedicated farmer himself, if less by origin than by dint of his life experience, and in the process of writing about this experience clearly seeks to appeal not less to other peasants than to modern Kenyans like those he would meet crossing from the Kangemi slums into the wealthy gated community in which his employer lived. It is, in the first instance, to them that his novel seeks

[13] Gazemba, *The Stone Hills of Maragoli*, 28–29.

[14] Phyllis Taoua, "The Postcolonial Condition," 216.

to communicate his knowledge of rural Kenya and his desire to alert them to the dire abjection in which the majority of Kenya's farmers still have to live.

For all their physical investment in the land (including Andimi's property), the energies of Gazemba's people of Maragoli lie fallow. The greater dynamic Phyllis Taoua discerns in the new oppositional constellation brought to the fore in *The Stone Hills of Maragoli* between ruler and ruled, exploiter and exploited, while no longer accommodating violent confrontation between natives and foreigners but instead limited to conflict within one nation, commands a new trajectory, no less devastating. It consists in the abject subject's descent into total alienation, where all hope for restoration of justice is suspended because the rift between rich and poor has become unbridgeable. In Ombima's case, this alienation is rendered horrifically final by Andimi, who, upon finding out about his wife's affair, has Madam Tabitha killed and seeks out Ombima to personally gouge out his eyes. The loss of his eyesight makes Ombima unable to work his land, let alone keep it, and forces him to use his disability as the only source of income left to him: in the final scene of *The Stone Hills of Maragoli* we see Ombima walking through the streets of Mbale, a town in Eastern Uganda, guided by his son and asking for alms. Gazemba makes sure that Ombima's lot should not be mistaken for a singular one in Kenya. After all, the final vision he offers of his protagonist repeats an earlier scene in the novel also showing the figure of a man begging.

The fact that the rich villain Andimi manages to get away with murder and mutilation and buy his way out of prison completes Gazemba's pessimistic appraisal of the state of Kenya's society and its need for change. This change seems almost impossible to bring about in the face both of the terrible immutability of the rich and the total despondency of the poor. It is hardly surprising that the only hope the latter allow themselves to have on occasion is that by mere chance the vagaries of nature may work in their favour. Whereas they have ceased to expect justice from humans, they have retained their love of the land, whose beauty they admire and in whose richness they never cease to believe even when the yield from their own allotments is so meagre that they cannot survive on it alone. They continue to farm their property, not only for want of an alternative but also in the obstinately optimistic expectation of nature offering the help they used to received and the magical change this help is able to bring about and at times still does bring about:

> He [...] made his way across the open field. It was covered in a thick carpet of coarse tough grass and shrub that the cattle turned to only during the dry season. [...] The downpour of the day before had washed the village paths of the dust and debris. There was a pleasant freshness in the

> early morning air that was partly the odour of the clean washed earth. The grass along the paths was green and fresh, sprinkled with clear droplets of morning dew that sparkled in a bright array of the colours of the rainbow when they were struck by the pearly shafts of the rising sun. The leaves were equally fresh, drooping with dew and wetness, succulent and supple with good health. [...] The night was humid and warm, pregnant with the call of cicadas upstaging the continuous droning buzz of a million other night insects. The deep purple sky was spangled with a million twinkling stars. Light cast by a thin silver moon revealed late evening shoppers hurrying from the village *duka* with purchases wrapped in old newspapers.[15]

It is difficult to take the promise of abundance unexpectedly offered by nature in this passage at face value and resist the temptation to see it in connection with the many urgent warnings voiced in recent years of desertification and prolonged droughts in Kenya caused by global warming, on the one hand, and the aiding and abetting by politicians of the destruction of Mau Forest, the largest indigenous montane forest in East Africa, on the other. Even if Gazemba does not refer to such ecological threats in *The Stone Hills of Maragoli*, awareness of them helps the reader to grasp the fragility his novel conveys of rural Kenya's last hope. What is more, it helps us form an idea of the enormous odds against which the *wananchi*, the rural peasants who constitute fifty-one percent of Kenya's population, refuse to relinquish this hope. For Gazemba, such a capacity to believe in one's environment and the perseverance that comes with it constitute assets the Kenyan government will ignore at its peril as long as its pet concern continues to be that the people of Kenya as well as the world should believe in the fiction of Kenya's boundless prosperity.

## Works Cited

African Women's Studies Centre, University of Nairobi & Kenya National Bureau of Statistics. *Status Report on Kenyan National Food Security* (Nairobi: Nairobi UP, 2014).

Anon. "Domestic Product (GDP)," *Forbes* 01.10 (2014), http://www.forbes.com/sites/faraigundan/2014/10/01/kenya-joins-africas-top-10-economies-after-rebasing-of-its-gross-domestic-product/#21c7fc533a25 (accessed 11 May 2015).

Bartlett, Richard. Review of *The Stone Hills of Maragoli*, *African Review of Books* (20 April 2004), http://www.authorsden.com/visit/viewwork.asp?AuthorID=149672 (accessed 20 May 2015).

15 Gazemba, *The Stone Hills of Maragoli*, 12, 19, and 77.

Foucault, Michel. "The Political Function of the Intellectual," tr. Colin Gordon, *Radical Philosophy* 17 (Summer 1977): 12–14.

Gazemba, Stanley. *The Stone Hills of Maragoli* (2002; Nairobi: Kwani Trust, 2010).

Gordon, David. "Indicators of Poverty and Hunger," *The UN Document*, http://www.un.org.esa/socoder/unyin/document (accessed 11 May 2015).

Gundan, Farai. "Kenya Joins Africa's Top 10 Economies After Reassessing of its Gross Domestic Product," Forbes 01.10 (2014), http://www.forbes.com/sites/faraigundan/2014/10/01/kenya-joins-africas-top-10-economies-after-rebasing-of-its-gross-domestic-product/#21c7fc533a25 (accessed 11 May 2015).

Jim Yong Kim. "Count on Us," *The World Bank* (1 April), http://www.worldbank.org/en/news/speech/2014/04/01/speech-world-bank-group-president-jim-yong-kim-council-on-foreign-relations (accessed 11 May 2015).

Kamencu, Kingwa. "How Award Winning Middle-Class Shamba Boy Got His Groove Back," *Daily Nation* (20 June 2014), http://www.nation.co.ke/lifestyleweekend/award-winning-middle-class-shamba-boy-groove-back-/1220-2356110-h8ijxaz/index.html (accessed 11 May 2015).

Kenya National Bureau of Statistics. *Information on the Revised National Accounts* (Nairobi: Government Printer, 2014).

Lewis, Libby. "A Kenyan Writer Blossoms from a Nairobi Slum," *National Public Radio* (31 May 2010), http://www.npr.org/templates/story/story.php?storyId=127245175 (accessed 11 May 2015).

Mistiaen, John, John Randa & Apurva Sanghi. "Kenya's Re-based National Accounts: Myths, Facts, and the Consequences," *The World Bank Data Blog*, http://blogs.worldbank.org/opendata/kenya-s-re-based-national-accounts-myths-facts-and-conse quences (accessed 11 May 2015).

Mwangi, Meja. *The Cockroach Dance* (Nairobi: Longman, 1978).

Mwangi, Meja. *Going Down River Road* (Nairobi: East African Educational, 1976).

Ngugi wa Thiong'o. *A Grain of Wheat* (Nairobi: East African Educational Publishers, 1966).

Ngugi wa Thiong'o. *Petals of Blood* (Nairobi: East African Educational, 1977).

Ngugi wa Thiong'o. *Weep Not, Child* (Nairobi: East African Educational Publishers, 1964).

Obulutsa, George, & Edmund Blair. "Kenya's Economy Increases by a Quarter to Join Africa's Top 10," *Reuters.com* (30 September 2014), http://www.reuters.com/article/2014/09/30/kenya-economy-idUSL6N0RV1Q020140930, (accessed 11 May 2015).

Ogot, Grace. *The Promised Land* (Nairobi, East African Educational, 1966).

Taoua, Phyllis. "The Postcolonial Condition," in *The Cambridge Companion to the African Novel*, ed. Irele F. Abiola (Cambridge: Cambridge UP, 2009): 209–24.

❄

# Neoliberalism, Water Scarcity, and Common Wealth

## *Mohsin Hamid's* How to Get Filthy Rich in Rising Asia

DAVID WATERMAN

MOHSIN HAMID'S NOVEL *How to Get Filthy Rich in Rising Asia* (2013) is both a celebration of the "resilience and potential" of Asia's young generation and a condemnation of neoliberal economic policies which guarantee wealth for a portion of Asia's people while doing little or nothing to eradicate poverty for hundreds of millions of others.[1] Presented as a self-help book, the novel is a satiric critique of neoliberalism in rapidly evolving and resource-stressed 'South Asia'. The undefined location and the topic of water privatization set the scene for exploration of the impact of the individualistic, self-help, and user-pays consumer capitalism that, since Reagan and Thatcher, has gone global in spite of the post-independence socialism envisioned by Nehru.[2] Many analysts credit the market-oriented reforms of 1991 in India, which coincided with the breakup of the Soviet Union,[3] with creating the

---

[1] Mohsin Hamid, *How to Get Filthy Rich in Rising Asia* (New York: Riverhead/Penguin, 2013): 224. Further page references are in the main text. Hamid's previous novels were *Moth Smoke* (2000) and the best-selling *The Reluctant Fundamentalist* (2007). The book under discussion here was followed by a selection of Hamid's journalism, *Discontent and Its Civilisations: Despatches from Lahore* (2014).

[2] For analysis of Nehru's ambivalent relationship to socialism and capitalism, see Brahma Chellaney, *Water: Asia's New Battleground* (Washington DC: Georgetown UP, 2011): 183–84.

[3] The disintegration of the former Soviet Union forced India to overhaul its economic philosophy, as Brahma Chellaney explains: "India's rise as a new economic giant was tied to the post-1989 events. India was so much into barter trade with the Soviet Union and its Communist allies in Eastern Europe that when the Eastern Bloc began to unravel, India had to start paying for imports in hard cash. This rapidly depleted its modest foreign-exchange reserves, triggering a severe balance-of-payments crisis in 1991. This financial crisis, in turn, compelled India to embark on radical economic reforms, which laid the foundation for its economic rise" (*Water*, 19–20).

conditions for South Asia's spectacular economic growth. As Akhil Gupta, for instance, observes,

> neoliberalism was accompanied by a new set of antipoverty initiatives that stressed self-help and emphasized that the poor could take the initiative and use the market to help themselves rather than rely on government assistance and handouts. The new buzzwords were *empowerment, microcredit*, and *entrepreneurialism.*[4]

However, a more nuanced examination of such an economic policy reveals that, in spite of a long period of economic boom, abject poverty is still far too common and far too easily accepted, and the neoliberal mantra of a rising tide lifting all boats is exposed as a lie as inequality between the nation's rich and poor increasingly widens.[5] Hamid's fiction, in the form of a satiric documentary which allows for pseudo-objective realistic commentary, begins with an image of such poverty, and reminds the reader of the overwhelming odds against escaping its vicious cycle. In spite of Asia's impressive growth, the novel introduces the protagonist and his mother in their single mud-walled room thus:

> huddled, shivering, on the packed earth under your mother's cot one cold, dewy morning. Your anguish is the anguish of a boy whose chocolate has been thrown away, whose remote controls are out of batteries, whose scooter is busted, whose new sneakers have been stolen. This is all the more remarkable since you've never in your life seen any of these things. The whites of your eyes are yellow, a consequence of spiking bilirubin levels in your blood. The virus afflicting you is called hepatitis E. Its typical mode of transmission is fecal–oral. Yum. It kills only about one in fifty, so you're likely to recover. (4)

Despite his extremely humble origins, the protagonist will indeed rise out of poverty, but in an environment of aggressive self-interest and omnipresent corruption, one must be willing to pay a very high price, take enormous risks, and make compromises along the road to wealth; self-help does not rhyme with solidarity. Even so, many of the pillars of neoliberal economic policy are not illegal – work for yourself, use debt, have an exit strategy – yet Hamid's satirical representation foregrounds a cynical attitude regarding corporate capitalism in

---

[4] Akhil Gupta, *Red Tape: Bureaucracy, Structural Violence, and Poverty in India* (Durham NC & London: Duke UP, 2012): 241–42. Gupta also refers the reader to Aradhana Sharma, *Logics of Empowerment: Development, Gender, and Governance in Neoliberal India* (Minneapolis: U of Minnesota P, 2008).

[5] Gupta, *Red Tape*, 285.

general, interrogating the moral and ethical foundations of the entire neoliberal system. Many of the novel's chapter titles, such as "Avoid Idealists," "Be Prepared to Use Violence," "Befriend a Bureaucrat" or "Patronize the Artists of War," leave no doubt as to the shady ethics involved, all the more so, given that the 'product' being peddled should, in theory, belong to everyone: water. Taken for granted until relatively recently, wasted and polluted, clean water is becoming increasingly rare – the new oil, in both economic and political/strategic terms.[6] Water-rights conflicts in South Asia are nothing new – relations between India and Pakistan have been strained due to such disagreements, dating to Partition in 1947; access to water is a primary reason for the ongoing dispute over Jammu and Kashmir. In his political satire, Hamid's novel brings the debate over neoliberalism and access to water down to a personal, human scale as a way of exposing the everyday reality of unethical wealth when a basic necessity – a common wealth – is appropriated for the benefit of the few, so that, as the above quotation makes clear, the poor do not even have access to uncontaminated water.

Poverty, according to Akhil Gupta, is a form of structural violence, in that it is "taken for granted in the routinized practices of state institutions such that it disappears from view and cannot be thematized as violence at all."[7] He suggests that poverty becomes normal through biopolitics, or the creation of a bureaucratic category of the 'poor' through statistical analysis and the definition of a 'poverty line', for example, which ultimately results in bureaucratic indifference, which is not necessarily to be taken as a synonym for uncaringness but, rather, as the fact that bureaucracy leads to arbitrary decisions, wherein some of the poor receive aid and some do not.[8] A solution, Gupta goes on to propose, would be to consider poverty-related deaths as preventable, as abnormal, as unacceptable, as a form of "thanatopolitics" which would refuse such official indiffe-

---

[6] However, unlike oil, water cannot be purchased on world markets, nor is there a substitute for water (Chellaney, *Water*, 11–12; 14; 25). Oil substitutes, in the form of biofuels, consume enormous quantities of water: "Fuel farming is not only claiming greater volumes of irrigated water but also pushing up food prices and accentuating water shortages, because it takes as much as 2,500 gallons of water to grow sufficient corn to refine just 1 gallon of ethanol" (*Water*, 14). See also Robert Glennon, "Our Water Supply, Down the Drain," *Washington Post* (23 August 2009), http://www.fbcoem.org/external/content/document/1528/315137/1/Our%20Water%20Supply,%20Down%20the%20Drain.pdf (accessed 29 December 2014).

[7] Gupta, *Red Tape*, 5. Gupta's argument applies specifically to India, although he engages with the work of theorists of the "bureaucracy of poverty" as a more general foundation to his thesis, among them Michel Foucault, Giorgio Agamben, Michael Herzfeld, Arthur Kleinman, Veena Das, and Margaret Lock. See *Red Tape*, 5–6.

[8] *Red Tape*, 42; 58; 158–59.

rence.[9] Much of South Asia's poverty exists in the villages and countryside, and, as Brahma Chellaney reminds us in *Water: Asia's New Battleground*, improved farming methods and irrigation have contributed to a certain degree of food security which "laid the foundation for Asia's rise," yet the agricultural sector has been largely neglected in terms of wealth redistribution.[10] Hamid's satire, which embellishes for dramatic effect real bureaucratic and corporate practices, highlights the "yawning gap that exists between countryside and city" (132), and makes clear that its protagonist cannot become rich if he remains in the village: "Moving to the city is the first step to getting filthy rich in rising Asia" (15).

Urbanization of the economy, the concentration of goods and services in the big cities and megacities of Asia, means that the poor very often live right next to the rich yet are not necessarily less invisible. Such proximity is one of the first things the novel's protagonist notices:

> Your city is not laid out as a single-celled organism, with a wealthy nucleus surrounded by an ooze of slums. It lacks sufficient mass transit to move all of its workers twice daily in the fashion this would require. It also lacks, since the end of colonization generations ago, governance powerful enough to dispossess individuals of their property in sufficient numbers. Accordingly, the poor live near the rich. Wealthy neighborhoods are often divided by a single boulevard from factories and markets and graveyards, and those in turn may be separated from the homes of the impoverished only by an open sewer, railroad track, or narrow alley. Your own triangle-shaped community, not atypically, is bounded by all three. (20)

Hamid portrays the enormous gap between the very rich and the very poor in big cities in stark, even shocking terms: upward mobility is construed as access to sanitation, in the young apprentice's desire to "leap from my-shit-just-sits-there-until-it-rains poverty to which-of-my-toilets-shall-I-use affluence" (78). As Gupta expands, in the urban environment where excessive fertility is not an

---

[9] *Red Tape*, 6.

[10] Chellaney, *Water*, 33. Agriculture has recorded the slowest growth rates of all sectors in the Indian economy. Gupta argues that agriculture is the only place where the vast majority of the unemployed and underemployed population can find employment in the short and medium term, but that will not happen if there is slow growth in this sector (Gupta refers the reader to Mukesh Eswaran, Ashok Kotwal, Bharat Ramaswami, and Wilima Wadhwa, "Sectoral Labour Flows and Agricultural Wages in India, 1983–2004: Has Growth Trickled Down?" *Economic and Political Weekly* 44.2 [2009]: 46–55.) Without significantly increasing growth rates in agriculture, or employing expensive new farming technologies (326), there is little chance that the poor will see a growth in their employment prospects or wages (284–85).

asset as it was in the village, overpopulation disturbs the "balance between population size and available natural resources, including water, food, and energy."[11] In the novel, the city is presented as a living, if sickly, organism, literally absorbing life from the countryside, whether from the vegetable farmer who has recently become rich by selling his land to local developers or via the freeways under construction, "dusty new arteries feeding this city, which despite its immensity is only one among many such organs quivering in the torso of rising Asia" (82). Here, Hamid signals the key issue of rapid urbanization. As Chellaney cautions, the predicted sixty-percent increase in urban population by 2025 will continue to stress vital resources, especially water. Martine Valo's point that water and energy exist in a vicious cycle is of particular importance in the planning and provisioning of ever-expanding urban spaces:

> To make water accessible, in other words to pump it, treat it, transport it, distribute it, requires energy. And to furnish energy requires water, lots of water.[12]

Once Hamid's main character has become a city dweller, one of the next self-help steps is to avoid idealists, especially those who might believe in environmental protection, following the law, or the promises of advertising. By contrast with the lauded self-interested values of the entrepreneur, the novel derides concepts of the common good that "are by their very nature anti-self" (57). Hamid's protagonist will associate, albeit briefly, with different sorts of idealists during his truncated time at university, knowing as his father did that getting ahead requires "advanced schooling and rampant nepotism" (59). In his satire's attack on the co-option of education by capitalist principles, Hamid exposes how profit-making functions in the university:

> State-subsidized though it may be, your university is exquisitely attuned to money. A small payment and exam invigilators are willing to overlook neighborly cheating. More and someone else can be sat in your seat to write your paper. More still and no writing is needed, blank exam books becoming, miraculously, a first-class result. (60)

The cynical protagonist joins an organization of religious extremists, idealists in their own way, but quickly learns to avoid them as well (60, 73). After an apprenticeship in the distribution of grocery products, in which he learns to undercut competitor's prices by selling expired foods after changing the date of

---

[11] Chellaney, *Water*, 55.

[12] Martine Valo, "Le boom de l'énergie menace les ressources en eau," *Le Monde* (23 March 2014: 8. (My tr.)

expiration (90), the protagonist decides to become self-employed – self-help, after all, implies working for oneself – and he enters the bottled-water market (99). The product, however, is no less fraudulent, as it is simply tap water packaged in used mineral-water bottles recuperated from restaurants, and the tap water is contaminated as well:

> Your city's neglected pipes are cracking, the contents of underground water mains and sewers mingling, with the result that taps in locales rich and poor alike disgorge liquids that, while for the most part clear and often odorless, reliably contain trace levels of feces and microorganisms capable of causing diarrhea, hepatitis, dysentery, and typhoid. (99)

The protagonist takes care to boil the water (101), knowing that customers falling sick will be bad for business, but also because he understands that great care must be exercised when presenting a counterfeit product. The young entrepreneur takes seriously the notion that forgeries must be more "real" than the genuine product, and understands the power of packaging; he goes so far as to install tamper-resistant caps and plastic safety wrapping (100).

Access to water provides a clear example of the coexistence of gross inequality in the city. While the rich buy water as a consumable product, the poor who cannot afford bottled water are obliged to drink contaminated tap water, often becoming very ill as a result – including Hamid's protagonist, infected with Hepatitis E from fecally contaminated water. By contrast, those better off can and do pay the protagonist for his marginally safer product: although boiling removes bacteria, it does nothing to remove other toxins, such as heavy metals and pesticides. Thus, access to safe drinking water affects the poor more than the rich, although water scarcity will become increasingly acute in the near future, affecting everyone not only in terms of drinking water but also with respect to water for agriculture, the 'virtual water' that we consume every day. The issue of increasing water consumption and subsequent scarcity, whether real or virtual, does not, however, fit neatly into a rich-versus-poor binary. Rather, in contemporary Asia as elsewhere, the burgeoning middle class indicated in Hamid's title "rising Asia" is increasingly responsible for environmentally unfriendly habits. Responding to the global capitalist imperative to consume, they equip their homes with washing machines and dishwashers, and eat much more water-intensive produce such as dairy and meat.[13] The protagonist's entrepreneurship is indeed a response to this growing demand. Shunning idealism for the rational market rules of supply and demand, the narrator surmises:

---

[13] Chellaney, *Water*, 3.

> You have thrived to the sound of the city's great whooshing thirst, unsated and growing, water incessantly being pulled out of the ground and pushed into pipes and containers. Bottled hydration has proved lucrative. (121)

The dubious ethics of this market-based rationale is ever present in the novel's satiric tone.

Gupta more directly castigates the violence hidden in the rapidly expanding market:

> In a country like India, the perpetrators of violence include not only the elites but also the fast-growing middle class, whose increasing number and greater consumer power are being celebrated by an aggressive global capitalism.

For Gupta, paraphrasing John Gledhill, market-led resource allocation is not only violent but even deadly:

> the demands imposed on Third World states by global capitalist enterprises, along with the geopolitical agendas of northern states, sometimes results in the creation of states that kill their own citizens.[14]

This strong claim is supported by statistics on water-related deaths. According to the international non-governmental organization Water.org, "the World Bank estimates that 21% of communicable diseases in India are related to unsafe water. In India, diarrhea alone causes more than 1,600 deaths daily."[15] In choosing to locate the protagonist's entrepreneurism in a product that is both essential and commodified, a right as well as a privilege, Hamid's novel exposes the clash between the idealism of on-demand, user-pays consumerism and the ethics of the vacillating political stance on water access and privatization.

Water has become a political issue; whoever controls the water supply has a strategic advantage. On the scale of an unnamed city, Hamid's novel reveals the murky and multiple layers of vested interests in the water supply chain, both public and private, communal and individual. Chapters entitled "Befriend a Bureaucrat," "Patronize the Artists of War," and "Dance with Debt" suggest that the State must be dealt with on many different levels, whether administrative, military or financial. Hamid's protagonist knows that, rather than avoid the

---

[14] Gupta, *Red Tape*, 299. See also John Gledhill, "The Challenge of Globalisation: Reconstruction of Identities, Transnational Forms of Life and the Social Sciences," *Journal of European Area Studies* 7.1 (1999): 9–37.

[15] Water.org, "India's Water Crisis," http://water.org/country/india/ (accessed 30 August 2016).

State, he must offer it a partnership if he is to succeed: "Two related categories of actor have long understood this," he explains,

> Bureaucrats, who wear state uniforms while secretly backing their private interests. And bankers, who wear private uniforms while secretly being backed by the state. You will need the help of both. (140)

If negotiations with the State bureaucracy are essential in any country, they are particularly complex in South Asia, especially when one is selling a fraudulent product which, by rights, should be provided to everyone; hence, Gupta's question "Which State?" makes sense:

> When analysts refer to the state, do they mean the state at the federal or central level, at the regional level, or at the local level? Which branch of the state are they studying: the administrative, legislative, or judicial? Which particular bureau are they focusing on: the police, the revenue department, the education department, the bureau of worker safety, the electricity department, and so forth? [...] Finally, what policies, programs, and people do they see as constituting the state?[16]

Alongside acknowledged public–private cooperation between business and political institutions, rampant corruption renders the State machine even more complex. The protagonist has learned this over the years, and has paid many bribes to remain in business: "Permits denied, inspections failed, surmounted by greasing junior and mid-level palms" (141). But now that business is even better and he is seeking a municipal contract, the stakes have been raised and the political authorities must be approached more directly. Bribes have been paid for an appointment with a politician, for access to "the courts of princes of old," where negotiations take place almost as asides to other business, and according to a protocol the protagonist does not understand but accepts: "with obsequious murmurs" and "bows of the head [...] precisely as he has been instructed to do by the bureaucrat. And that is that" (145). The narrator-protagonist's willing acceptance of the need to play the game confirms Gupta's view that corruption actually constitutes the State.[17]

Hamid's pragmatic narrator recognizes the need to cultivate an awareness of the State's violent nature:

---

[16] Gupta, *Red Tape*, 52.

[17] Gupta calls corruption, and narratives/perceptions of corruption, a "Durkheimian social fact" and insists that popular perceptions of corruption help sustain the phenomenon of corruption (*Red Tape*, 112–13; 138).

> Distasteful though it may be, it was inevitable, in a self-help book such as this, that we would eventually find ourselves broaching the topic of violence. [...] For wealth comes from capital, and capital comes from labor, and labor comes from equilibrium, from calories in chasing calories out, an inherent, in-built leanness, the leanness of biological machines that must be bent to your will with some force. (119)

The Marxist inflection of this passage, which strips the labourer of individuality, reducing him or her to a function within a profit-making rationale, may be read alongside the World Bank statistics on deaths by lack of access to clean water and sanitation. In the logic of free-market capitalism, the deaths of non-paying customers are more rational than the prospect of losing money by providing free goods and services, a proposition that renders the poor disposable in economic rather than ethical terms.

Against a backdrop of social unrest and violence, riots and bombings, in unplanned and overpopulated cities where millions of migrants come to seek a better life, the protagonist is also exposed to punctual, direct, physical violence as a result of his desire to dominate the water market (119–21). In another Darwinian struggle for supremacy, a well-connected local businessman and competitor who is losing bottled-water customers hires a thug to threaten the protagonist at gunpoint. Rather than go to the police, the protagonist responds in kind, seeking the help of a local armed faction, which furnishes him with a bodyguard; the guard will later kill the thug during a second encounter, thus frightening the local businessman into ending his ultimatum (123–35). The protagonist's business will continue to prosper, yet his brush with death has shattered his belief that wealth would shelter him from premature death, wherein the victims are almost always the poor. Observing his small son, for example, the protagonist thinks:

> for while disease or violence could of course strike down your son, the probability of his early death has, through your attainments, been reduced dramatically. (146)

The stark contrast between the protagonist's own childhood, beginning in the narrative with his "one in fifty" chance of surviving Hepatitis E, and that of his son embodies in two generations the positive discourse of development and the heralded middle class in the "rising Asia" of the title.

In the different register of global geopolitics, Chellaney analyses on an international level the conflict over water played out locally in Hamid's novel. Chellaney claims that international tensions and institutional sabre-rattling between water-haves and water-have-nots will almost certainly escalate to armed conflict in the relatively near future:

> Asia, with the world's fastest-growing economies, fastest-rising military expenditures, most dangerous hot spots, and fiercest resource competitions, seems to be the biggest potential flashpoint for water wars in the world – a concern underscored by the attempts of some countries to exploit their riparian advantage.[18]

For example, as almost all of South Asia's rivers locate their headwaters in the Tibetan Plateau, China controls the source of the major waterways, from the Indus in the west to the Mekong in the east. The opportunities for political and even military conflict are exacerbated by the fact that many of the countries affected by water scarcity are also those with dysfunctional governments, including Pakistan and Afghanistan, and the Israel-dependent Palestine.[19] Water is thus evolving from its role in non-traditional security discussions into a central strategic factor in the traditional security debate, giving rise to the possibility of armed conflict over water in the twenty-first century, in much the same way as over oil in the twentieth. Hydropolitics will, Chellaney insists, "turn ugly" and become violent, particularly if spectacular Asian economic growth begins to slow due to competition for increasingly scarce resources:[20]

> The current hyperbole about the dawn of a new Asian age obscures the geostrategic significance of the serious constraints Asia confronts on natural resources, particularly water. Indeed, the greatest potential for water-related conflict in the world exists in Asia, which faces water challenges more weighty than developing economies elsewhere put together.[21]

Indeed, for Chellaney, control over energy and other strategic resources will be the twenty-first-century version of the colonial-era 'Great Game' conflict between super-powers.[22]

Intimating the unsustainable rate of water extraction, after his "retirement," Hamid's protagonist hears news reports which hint at the increasing water scarcity to come:

---

18 Chellaney, *Water*, 15.

19 *Water*, 56; 58.

20 *Water*, 90.

21 *Water*, 47.

22 *Water*, 16; 23.

> You hear reports that the water table continues to drop, the thirst of many millions driving bore after steel bore deeper and deeper into the aquifer, to fill countless leaky pipes and seepy, unlined channels, phenomena with which you are intimately familiar and from which you have profited, but which are now contributing in places to a noticeable desiccation of the soil, to a transformation of moist, fertile, hybrid mud into cracked, parched, pure land. (204–205)

At this point of realization, Hamid's self-help book admits that helping yourself is not all, that one's fortunes are dependent on external circumstances as well and that the only self-help then advisable is to give in to fate. Self-fulfilment, in other words, is a matter of temporary luck: "For there was a moment when anything was possible. And there will be a moment when nothing is possible. But in between we can create" (219–20). This is a rather surprising recantation or renunciation of writerly authority on the part of Hamid's persona. It retrospectively calls into question the validity of his advice but also of his appraisal of economic developments in general. The reader is ultimately left with a sense of helplessness in the face of a rapidly approaching calamity. Clearly, Hamid's novel in the end appeals to individual readers to help themselves but lodges a plea for international cooperation in the solution of problems that have long ceased to be national.[23] Strong transnational institutions with a focus on long-range, holistic/biosphere planning with clearly defined norms and objectives are necessary if Asia – and especially South Asia – is to avoid serious future conflict. As Chellaney concludes his book,

> In an era of growing constraints on augmenting the supply of the most essential resource – water – Asian countries must seek sustainable, cost-effective solutions through collaborative efforts that extend beyond national borders. Competing demands for scarce water resources pose economic, social, and political threats that can be contained only through forward-looking policies. Such policies, as well as the promotion of greater interstate and intrastate water collaboration, depend on linking stakeholders together, collecting reliable data on water resources, and enunciating specific, measurable, attainable, realistic, and timely – SMART – goals.[24]

Such forward-looking policies are needed because economic prosperity and the interdependence of the global economy are not enough to ward off serious conflict over resources – in Asia as elsewhere. In the context of South Asia,

---

[23] Gupta, *Red Tape*, 239.

[24] Chellaney, *Water*, 305.

Chellaney argues that the region's current political fragmentation and "piece-meal approach that translates into an absence of urgency and accountability"[25] must be addressed in order to prevent future resource wars.

In an interview with Claudia Kramatschek, Hamid insists that the privatization of access to water goes beyond a rich/poor dichotomy; water should, quite simply, be available to everyone:

> Until recently, in much of the world, it has not been the case that drinking water was an expensive commodity. It was thought of as a public good, like air. But now, of course, we find that it is possible to sell these things. The markets have taken the commons over.[26]

Hamid's novel illustrates on an individual and local level some of the serious questions which arise when a basic necessity – water – is appropriated by a few rather than shared out fairly; those same questions are pertinent and increasingly pressing on national and international scales. Hamid's self-help satire and Chellaney's compelling call for international attention to water scarcity are both political texts that shine much-needed light on the misappropriation of water, our most basic common wealth.

## Works Cited

Chellaney, Brahma. *Water: Asia's New Battleground* (Washington DC: Georgetown UP, 2011).

Eswaran, Mukesh, Ashok Kotwal, Bharat Ramaswami & Wilima Wadhwa. "Sectoral Labour Flows and Agricultural Wages in India, 1983–2004: Has Growth Trickled Down?" *Economic and Political Weekly* 44.2 (2009): 46–55.

Gledhill, John. "The Challenge of Globalisation: Reconstruction of Identities, Transnational Forms of Life and the Social Sciences," *Journal of European Area Studies* 7.1 (1999): 9–37.

Glennon, Robert. "Our Water Supply, Down the Drain," *Washington Post* (23 August 2009), http://www.fbcoem.org/external/content/document/1528/315137/1/Our%20Water%20Supply,%20Down%20the%20Drain.pdf (accessed 29 December 2014).

Gupta, Akhil. *Red Tape: Bureaucracy, Structural Violence, and Poverty in India* (Durham NC & London: Duke UP, 2012).

Hamid, Mohsin. *How to Get Filthy Rich in Rising Asia* (New York: Riverhead/Penguin, 2013).

---

[25] *Water*, 81.

[26] Claudia Kramatschek, *Qantara.de* (10 February 2013), http://en.qantara.de/node/17039 (accessed 19 June 2015).

Kramatschek, Claudia. *Qantara.de* (10 February 2013), http://en.qantara.de/node/17039 (accessed 19 June 2015).

Sharma, Aradhana. *Logics of Empowerment: Development, Gender, and Governance in Neoliberal India* (Minneapolis: U of Minnesota P, 2008).

Valo, Martin. “Le boom de l’énergie menace les ressources en eau,” *Le Monde* (21 March 2014): 8.

Water.org. “India’s Water Crisis,” http://water.org/country/india/ (accessed 30 August 2016).

❄

# III ❄

# Indigenous Common Wealths

# Indigenous Cosmopolitanism

SNEJA GUNEW

> We learned your words and songs and stories, and never knew you didn't want to hear ours.[1]

WHY 'COSMOPOLITANISM' in a neo-cosmopolitan formulation? We think we all know the meaning of the word, that it represents a comprehensive knowledge of the world but often at the cost of abandoning the local and everyday. The concept is traditionally linked with elite mobility, hyper-consumerism, and deracination. That is emphatically not the meaning of the 'cosmopolitanism' in my title. Recent debates, particularly since 1998, have signalled their departure from these earlier senses of 'cosmopolitanism' by attaching qualifying terms such as vernacular cosmopolitanism,[2] abject cosmopolitanism,[3] subaltern cosmopolitanism[4] etc. in order to create an apparent oxymoron that functions to alert readers to the seeming contradiction of the two adjacent terms and to speculate about their relation to each other. In the anthropologist Pnina Werbner's explanation of "vernacular cosmopolitanism,"

> Vernacular cosmopolitanism [...] is at the crux of current debates on cosmopolitanism. These pose the question whether the local, parochial, rooted, culturally specific and demotic may co-exist with the translocal, transnational, transcendent, elitist, enlightened, universalist and

---

[1] Kim Scott, *That Deadman Dance* (Sydney: Picador PanMacmillan, 2010): 106.

[2] Pnina Werbner, "Vernacular Cosmopolitanism," *Theory, Culture & Society* 23.2–3 (2006): 496–98.

[3] Peter Nyers, "Abject Cosmopolitanism: The Politics of Protection in the Anti-Deportation Movement," *Third World Quarterly* 24.6 (2003): 1069–93. Imogen Tyler, "Social Abjection," in Tyler, *Revolting Subjects: Social Abjection and Resistance in Neoliberal Britain* (London: Zed, 2013): 19–47.

[4] Minhao Zeng, "Subaltern Cosmopolitanism: Concept and Approaches," *Sociological Review* 62 (2014): 137–48.

> modernist – whether boundary–crossing demotic migrations may be compared to the globe trotting travel, sophisticated cultural knowledge and moral world-view of deracinated intellectuals. (496)

In his own meditations on "vernacular cosmopolitanism," a term he may have coined, Homi Bhabha notes that it requires a "domestication of the universal" and that it is "our task to turn the movement of 'unsatisfaction' towards the 'domestic' to reveal its uncanny site/sign of the native, indigenous, as a kind of 'vernacular 'cosmopolitanism'."[5] Bhabha also refers to the concept as attempting to capture the "growing, global gulf between political citizenship, still largely negotiated in 'national' and statist terms, and cultural citizenship which is often community–centred, transnational, diasporic, hybrid."[6] He also associates this concept with minorities who don't necessarily wish to claim majoritarian belongingness and whose defining impetus is that of translating across cultures in an economy marked by iteration rather than teleology.[7] The way in which Bhabha structures these arguments pertains to his familiar dyad: the performative and pedagogical nation, in which adding to does not mean adding up.[8]

So it is with cosmopolitanism and indigeneity, the latter being often thought of as encapsulating the hyper-local (indigenous people's primary interest in their immediate lands) as distinct from the global. According to Maximilian Forte, indigenous cosmopolitans, "write against hegemonic stories of modernity that suppress coloniality and its production of differences on a planetary scale."[9] The point here is that differences are produced rather than lying there waiting to be discovered.[10] The Native-American critic Sean Kicummah Teuton argues:

> return to indigenous cosmopolitan writers [...] uncover[s] an alternative conception of indigenous nationhood, attendant to territory and

---

[5] Homi K. Bhabha, "Unsatisfied: Notes on Vernacular Cosmopolitanism," in *Text and Narration: Cross-Disciplinary Essays on Cultural and National Identities*, ed. Laura García-Moreno & Peter C. Pfeiffer (Columbia SC: Camden House, 1996): 202.

[6] Homi K. Bhabha & John Comaroff, "Speaking of Postcoloniality, in the Continuous Present: A Conversation," in *Relocating Postcolonialism*, ed. David T. Goldberg & Ato Quayson (Oxford: Blackwell, 2002): 25.

[7] Bhabha, "Unsatisfied," 202.

[8] This is reiterated in Homi Bhabha, *The Location of Culture* (London: Routledge, 1994): 139–70 (chapter eight, "DissemiNation: Time, Narrative and the Margins of the Modern Nation").

[9] Maximilian C. Forte, "Introduction" to *Indigenous Cosmopolitans: Transnational and Transcultural Indigeneity in the Twenty-First Century*, ed. Maximilian C. Forte (New York: Peter Lang, 2010): 4.

[10] The U.S. cultural critic Rey Chow refers to this logic as the "difference revolution." See Chow, *The Protestant Ethnic and the Spirit of Capitalism* (New York: Columbia UP, 2002): 128.

> peoplehood [...] a new model of the indigenous writer as a cosmopolitan engaged with the world for the sake of the community.[11]

Uncovering the cosmopolitan dimensions of those knowledges subjugated by colonialism in relation to globalism itself and including them in cultural studies has been the general goal of recent attempts to rethink cosmopolitanism. For example, the concept of vernacular cosmopolitanism has helped in the decolonizing project, which advocates the difficult task of separating oneself from a long and robust tradition of conceptualizing cosmopolitanism within Western philosophy, in which the shifting categories of human subjectivity are increasingly seen to be predicated on the exclusion of subjugated groups – slaves, indigenous peoples, refugees, and asylum-seekers.[12] Looking at the debates in cosmopolitanism as a way of reading these 'other' cultural texts is part of the larger study in which the present essay is embedded. While, on the one hand, cosmopolitan readings consist of ways of defamiliarizing hegemonic ideologies (as in Dipesh Chakrabarty's notion of "provincializing Europe"[13]), they also, on the other, convey a sense of how one might consider the world otherwise within a specifically indigenous world-view. However, in this version of globalism, a term such as the 'planetary' might be a useful substitution, in that it raises awareness of the idea that the human should not be the measure of all things (and I will return to this). So, indigenous cosmopolitanism offers both a critique of and a way to situate oneself outside familiar conceptual ideologies as well as glimpsing alternative imagined worlds.

An element central to such an imagining is the question of language, also at the heart of certain versions of postcolonial criticism and new conceptualizations of world literature. In a monolingual (and consequently often monologic) context, it is very difficult to articulate thinking otherwise, and so another language becomes an important tool for extrication from the familiar, as a way of becoming more self-reflexive about the mediatory nature of language and representation. In geopolitical national sovereignties, the question of multilingualism arises in an uncanny homology to the fate of the nomadic often

---

[11] Sean Kicummah Teuton, "Cities of Refuge: Indigenous Cosmopolitan Writers and the International Imaginary," *American Literary History* 25.1 (Spring 2013): 51. My thanks to Brendan McClure for alerting me to this essay.

[12] Agamben's notion of 'bare life' can be usefully invoked here – those not even worth sacrificing. See Giorgio Agamben, *Homo Sacer: Sovereign Power and Bare Life*, tr. Daniel Heller-Roazen (*Homo sacer: Il potere sovrano la nuda vida*, 1995; Stanford CA: Stanford UP, 1998).

[13] Dipesh Chakrabarty, *Provincializing Europe: Postcolonial Thought and Historical Difference* (Princeton NJ: Princeton UP, 2000).

associated with indigeneity. Languages run riot in spectacularly unexpected ways, hence the many anxieties that spawn policies to discipline their manifestation (one thinks here of Indigenous languages being banned in Canada's 'Indian' residential schools). The role of English, designated a global language, in this mix is complex. For example, in global English the meanings attached to linguistically enunciative positions differ (I speak; I am spoken), as do the geopolitical positions from which one speaks English. What, then, does it mean to be asked to reside precariously in another language, a language that always comes with historical (including ideological) baggage? Some of the answers depend on the "monolingualism" of the culture, as in Derrida's explanation:

> The monolingualism imposed by the other operates by relying upon that foundation, here, through a sovereignty whose presence is always colonial, which tends, repressively and irrepressibly, to reduce language to the One, that is, to the *hegemony of the homogeneous*. This can be verified everywhere, everywhere this homo-hegemony remains at work in the culture, effacing the folds and flattening the text.[14]

World English is a quintessential example of 'homo-hegemony'. Thus, it is, for example, *more* difficult to assert the legitimacy of other versions of English or the many languages associated with indigenous writing in cultures that strenuously reiterate their monolingualism, such as Australia, than officially bilingual cultures such as Canada.[15] In terms of cultural texts, there is also, increasingly, the thematization of the English language as designating a passport to global mobility.[16]

## "Moving between languages, Bobby wrote on stone"[17]

In his quest to become familiar with his own Aboriginal heritage, the Australian writer Kim Scott speaks about allowing the sounds of Noongar to reshape his corporeality from within and to link these sounds with the elements of a speci-

---

[14] Jacques Derrida, *Monolingualism of the Other or The Prosthesis of Origins*, tr. Patrick Mensah (*Le monolinguisme de l'autre: ou la prothèse d'origine*, 1996, Stanford CA: Stanford UP, 1998): 39–40. (My emphasis.)

[15] It is interesting here to consider the role of the oral/acoustic. Derrida spends a lot of time registering the 'accent' as a sign of 'impurity' within one's mother tongue.

[16] For example, as part of the larger study, provisionally titled *Back to the Future: Post-Multicultural Writers as Neo-Cosmopolitan Mediators*, I have looked at the meanings attached to 'English' in a number of novels emanating from the Chinese mainland and the Chinese diaspora.

[17] Kim Scott, *That Deadman Dance*, 1.

fic geophysical place. In his non-fictional collaborative text *Kayang and Me*, Scott traces the process of this painstaking and affective journey undertaken with his relative Hazel Brown, who gradually inducts him into the Noongar language and knowledge-system by means of their immediate family history. As he puts it, "Making the sounds of Noongar country [...] It was as though I was being reshaped from the inside out [...]."[18] In his most recent novel, *That Deadman Dance*, Scott creates a text that animates this pedagogical process differently and pushes it further to produce an affective loop that includes non-Indigenous readers, attempting to re-order their perception of Australia's colonial history. The novel concerns those years of first contact and colonial settlement on the western coast of western Australia (1833–44), the country of the Noongar nation from which Scott derives his heritage.

> Originally, that novel had the working title, *Rose a Wail*, a (poor) pun on a whale breaking from the ocean surface and the hint of an inarticulate cry of anguish. [...] The first word of the novel is an attempt by a Noongar character to render a Noongar word in English spelling; the novel concludes with the central character delivering a speech in Noongar. But even more than this sparse spattering across pages and pages of English, Noongar language influences the imagery, rhythm and characters of the novel.[19]

The book begins with the protagonist Bobby Wabalanginy's older self looking back on the years in which he and his people first helped the settlers survive by sharing their resources with them, only to be summarily ejected, in return, from their own country. At the same time, Bobby evokes the ways in which he himself studied and translated the new conceptual territory of these intruders, juxtaposing it with his own knowledge-system. So, for the reader, as modelled by the characters, the two frameworks of knowledge function to defamiliarize the homo-hegemony of English. For example, the act of writing is juxtaposed with the dancing and singing that are presented as a major form of Noongar communication, to which the title of the novel also alludes. Dance is an embodied form of communication that includes the distinctive smell of an individual – Noongar can identify each other through these individual smells; all of the senses are engaged in this formation of intimate knowledge. The "dead man dance" is itself a case of reverse appropriation in which the military drill of the colonial soldiers is borrowed by Bobby to create a dance that translates his

---

18 Kim Scott, *Kayang and Me* (Fremantle, WA: Fremantle Arts Centre Press, 2005): 257.

19 See Scott's contribution in Zable, Arnold, John Bradley, Kim Scott and Marie Munkara, "Language and Politics in Indigenous Writing," *Overland* 205 (Summer 2011): 59.

analyses and understanding of these strangers for his own community.[20] With large white clay crosses painted on their chests, the dancers are like animated tombstones carrying sticks that represent rifles. After the sticks are "fired" the men fall down but then rise again. Focus switches to the one dancer who touches them all into a more lasting death:

> People loved the experience of it. To have no will of their own but only Bobby's, briefly.
>
> By the time he was a grown man everyone knew it had never been dead men dancing in the first place anyway, but real live men from over the ocean's horizon, with a different way about them. There was difference among them, too, as a grown-up Bobby learnt too late, but this was something people argued about. (69)

Bobby is often characterized as being a consummate mimic, but the significance of his mimicry needs to be fully considered. It is a term that brings to mind Homi Bhabha's much-misunderstood notion of colonial mimicry.[21] Building on the more straightforward concept associated with V.S. Naipaul's account of creating the 'mimic men' of colonial 'native' administration, who internalize the values of the colonizer to create (in Macaulay's terms) "brown Englishmen,"[22] Bhabha argues that something else is going on in a two-way process. The mimicry of the colonizer by the colonized is indeed a kind of mockery that undoes the supposedly transcendental authority of the colonizer. In part, this mechanism works by demonstrating that the colonizer needs to have his authority mirrored back to him by the colonized in order to shore it up. This begs the question of its transcendent power, since, if it requires such support, it cannot be omnipotent and invulnerable in the first place. The mimicry is also mockery, in that it brings out the absurdity of the colonizer's actions. Indeed, the white settlers *are* rendered uneasy by Bobby's ability to mimic them:

> It was like Bobby *was* them, showing their very selves, inside their heads and singing their very sound and voices [...] Bobby could look through

[20] In a recent essay, Alison Ravenscroft contrasts the ways in which this moment of mimicry is represented in other Australian writings and in Scott's novel. See Ravenscroft, "The strangeness of the dance: Kate Grenville, Rohan Wilson, Inga Clendinnen and Kim Scott," *Meanjin* 72.4 (2014): 64–73.

[21] See Homi Bhabha, *The Location of Culture* (London: Routledge,1994): 85-92 (chapter four, "Of mimicry and man").

[22] Macaulay's infamous 1835 "Minute on Education" can be found in full at http://www.columbia.edu/itc/mealac/ pritchett/00generallinks/macaulay/txt_minute_education_1835.html.

> the eyes of anything. It made everyone unstable, surprised and hardly trusting [...]. (376)

By demonstrating that he understands both language-systems, Bobby attempts, at a pivotal moment in settler–Indigenous relations, to speak to the colonizers in their language as well as his own languages of both Dance and Noongar, whereby "he would show how people must live here, together" (390). However, in this instance his audience members turn away and the novel ends with the sound of gunshots heralding the grim future of the colonizing process that ultimately attempts to eradicate this prior world-view and culture. To give one example, the ethical structures of reciprocity that constitute the communal glue of the Noongar are perceived by the colonizers as illegal trespass, and so, when the Noongar help themselves to the occasional sheep or to flour from the stores, they feel entitled to these, since they had not hesitated to share their own resources to help the first settlers to survive. Instead, they are seen as thieves and on the strength of these 'misappropriations' are expelled from their own "country" (the term used by Aboriginal Australians to delineate specific tribal areas)[23] or, worse, executed.

In terms of reciprocal power-relations, the energy Bobby devoted to choreographing the dance may have represented a mistaken direction, as Scott suggests in an interview with Anne Brewster:

> perhaps the dance as a form is not necessarily the form that's going to powerfully speak to this mob – the ones that get up at the end of the novel, dismissively; he hasn't got them. But, just possibly, writing is [the form]. So it's not a mistake what he did there [...].[24]

In other words, the writing, more so than the dance, enables stories to live on and create a pedagogical tool that makes this history legible. The rationale for the limited power of the dance may also lie in the many ways in which mimicry is understood simply as a one-sided reflection of abject processes rather than as a subversion of authority (in Bhabha's sense). In Scott's pedagogical framework for the novel, Bobby's journal borrows from another technology and his learning is put to effective use:

---

[23] For a comprehensive discussion of 'country' in this context, see Brigitta Olubas & David Gilbey, ed. "Country" (Special Issue) *Journal for the Association for the Study of Australian Literature* 14.3 (2014).

[24] Anne Brewster, "'Can You Anchor a Shimmering Nation State via Regional Indigenous Roots?' Kim Scott talks to Anne Brewster about *That Deadman Dance*," *Cultural Studies Review* 18.1 (March 2012): 232.

> you can dive deep into a book and not know just how deep until you return gasping to the surface, and are surprised at yourself, your new and so very sensitive skin. As if you're someone else altogether, some new self trying on the words.[25]

Writing and the journal Bobby maintains add to an archive that is, for better or for worse, a recognizable form of material history for the colonizers, even though its meanings may shift over time. It is one of the ironies of history, as many analysts of decolonization have observed, that the colonial archive becomes a necessary and primary reference point because it encloses the only surviving traces of the colonized – seeds waiting to be re-activated to aid the flowering of decolonizing resistance.

## Ambiguous Archives

The notion of the archive in these contexts is worth pausing over. Archives are fragile repositories at the best of times, particularly so when linked to subaltern knowledges. What to do with books in public (including university) libraries is a problem faced all over the so-called developed world.[26] In the so-called undeveloped world there is still a hunger for books, but there are also terrifying stories of the demise of ancient libraries such as those in Iraq during the Iraqi–US war. We also think of the fragility of archives in the recent commemorations of World War One where only certain groups are recognized as part of that history. Santanu Das writes a moving account in a recent *Guardian Weekly* of the ways in which the war also claimed the lives of many (conscripted) recruits from the British Empire – Asians, Africans, and Pacific Islanders who were catapulted into European theatre of war, voyaging, in his evocative phrase, "to the heart of whiteness."[27] In her exploration of the slave trade, Saidiya Hartman gives a vivid account of the importance of reading these colonial archives against the grain:

---

[25] Scott, *That Deadman Dance*, 86.

[26] I am currently particularly concerned about these matters because after many decades of attempting to create an archive for the writings of non-Anglo-Celts in Australia (both in English and in other languages) I find that these projects have encountered severe obstacles and that the library charged and funded with collecting this material has uttered a kind of symbolic *cri de coeur* in relation to the books entrusted to it by gluing the 'surplus' into its staircases. Gluing books into the wall represents a particular kind of commemorative mausoleum practice or possibly just a variation on book burning.

[27] Santanu Das, "Eurocentric Views of the First World War," *The Guardian Weekly* (1–7 August 2014): 48.

> In other words, there is no access to the subaltern consciousness outside dominant representations or elite documents [...]. The effort to "brush against the grain" requires excavations at the margins of monumental history in order that the ruins of the dismembered past be retrieved, turning to forms of knowledge and practice not generally considered legitimate objects of historical inquiry or appropriate or adequate sources for history making and attending to the cultivated silence, exclusions, relations of violence and domination that engender the official accounts. Therefore the documents, fragments, and accounts considered here, although claimed for purposes contrary to those for which they were gathered, nonetheless remain entangled with the politics of domination. In this regard, the effort to reconstruct the history of the dominated is not discontinuous with dominant accounts or official history but, rather, is a struggle within and against the constraints and silences imposed by the nature of the archive – the system that governs the appearance of statements and generates social meaning.[28]

This need to read against the grain of the archive is particularly true of Indigenous history. In a recent documentary concerning Australian Aboriginal culture there is a moment, hard to watch, when an Arnhem Land guardian elder, explaining the importance of passing on knowledge of the Law of Dreaming to future generations, apologizes for the tears that well up during her explanation.[29] As Kim Scott's earlier novel *Benang* illustrates,[30] the traces of ancestors survive within the alien repository of the colonial administration – the humiliating permits to travel, the documents of incarceration. Scott is particularly haunted by phrases such as "the first white man born" and the "last full-blood Aborigine," which he reduces to acronyms to demonstrate the ways in which they become metonyms of colonization, a type of shorthand for making legible the authorizing framework of the colonial archive. Scott discovers no place in the archives for ontological Aboriginality, in that the thrust of the colonial administration was that they be "bred out."[31] This example brings to mind the work of critical race theorists such as Denise Ferreira da Silva who trace in Western philosophy a "logic of exclusion" that works through constitutive

---

[28] Saidiya Hartman, "Introduction" to Hartman, *Scenes of Subjection: Terror, Slavery, and Self-Making in Nineteenth-Century America* (New York: Oxford UP, 1997): 10–11.

[29] See Wade Davis, *National Geographic Specials – Life at the Ends of the Earth – Keepers of the Dream* (TV, accessed 30 August 2014).

[30] Kim Scott, *Benang: from the heart* (Fremantle, WA: Fremantle Arts Centre Press, 1999).

[31] Kim Scott, "Strangers at Home," in *Translating Lives: Living in Two Languages and Cultures*, ed. Mary Besmeres & Anna Wierzbicka (St Lucia: U Queensland P, 2007): 3–4.

*inclusion* – that is to say, in which 'others' such as slaves and the indigenous are the constitutive principle of difference upon which Western white subjectivity is founded

> Because raciality has been intrinsic to the institution of the very global (ethico-political) subjects, emancipatory projects and visions of justice grounded in (neo-)Kantian universality and self-determination will remain self-defeating because impossible goals.[32]

It is a trend in critical race theory that began perhaps with the "necropolitics" of Achille Mbembe illustrating that the discourse of human rights, the desire for marginalized groups to be 'included', are misplaced projects because such groups are constitutively excluded from a conceptual system that owes its very ontological existence to their inclusion under particular terms of abjection.[33] To explain further: a comparable logic is to consider the long tradition of defining the human by differentiating it from the animal, or the example of sexual difference. In all of these instances, the processes of installing 'difference' are, rightly, being interrogated.

## Cannibal Christianity

But let me turn to a different example of Indigenous cosmopolitanism. In the Cree writer Tomson Highway's novel *Kiss of the Fur Queen*, the defamiliarization mechanism I have been describing takes place in relation to the powerful frameworks of religious beliefs. As Thomas King suggests in his important recent book *The Inconvenient Indian*,

> Missionary work in the New World was war. Christianity, in all its varieties, has always been a stakeholder in the business of assimilation, and, in the sixteenth century, it was the initial wound in the side of Native culture. Or, if you want the positive but somewhat callous view, you might want to describe Christianity as the gateway drug to supply-side capitalism.[34]

---

[32] Denise Ferreira da Silva, "Notes for a Critique of the 'Metaphysics of Race'," *Theory, Culture & Society* 28.1 (2011): 146. See also Denise Ferreira da Silva, *Toward a Global Idea of Race* (Minneapolis: U of Minnesota P, 2007).

[33] Achille Mbembe, "Necropolitics," tr. Libby Meintjes, *Public Culture* 15.1 (2003): 11–40. My thanks to Dina Al-Kassim for alerting me to the work of the 'Afro-Pessimists'. See http://incognegro.org/afro_pessimism.html (accessed 20 September 2015).

[34] Thomas King, *The Inconvenient Indian: A Curious Account of Native People in America* (Toronto: Doubleday Canada, 2012): 103.

In Highway's example, Indigenous cosmopolitanism excavates Christianity to show its violent and cannibalistic/sacrificial roots – those who are sacrificed are the colonized Indigenous peoples. Highway is a fluent speaker of Cree and has used that language to great effect in his plays and this novel as a defamiliarization device, but in this instance it is the colonial religious belief-system that is rendered wholly strange. The novel concerns the lives of two Cree brothers, Champion and Ooneemeetee Okimasis, who are renamed Jeremiah and Gabriel by the colonial system. As Gabriel puts it,

> "Christianity asks people to eat the flesh of Christ and drink his blood – shit, Jeremiah, eating human flesh, that's cannibalism. What could be more savage – ? [...] Do you wonder why the world is so filled with blood and war and hate when it has, as its central symbol, an instrument of torture?"[35]

Some years after the novel, Highway produced a small volume on comparative mythologies in which he develops the implications of this cosmology further in a different rhetorical register of the reverse ethnographic gaze:

> And last, this male God gave us this Earth and then snatched it away from us – the narrative of eviction from a garden, because of a woman's stupidity, is a narrative that, so far as I know, exists in three mythologies, and three mythologies only – Christian, Judaic, and Islamic – the only three mythologies extant on the Earth, so far as I know, that, not quite coincidentally, are monotheistic in structure, that have one God only. Space, in other words was taken from us, and time is our curse.[36]

In *Kiss of the Fur Queen*, the brothers undergo the increasingly familiar catalogue of horrors perpetrated in residential schools. In the Australian contexts, children considered to be part-white were summarily hunted down and kidnapped and taken to missions and mission schools,[37] whereas in the Canadian context parents were coerced into believing that this was the only survival strategy for their children, and at least the children were occasionally permitted to return home, as did the brothers in Highway's novel. Jeremiah watches the repeated nightly abuse of his brother Gabriel by the presiding priest at the

---

[35] Tomson Highway, *Kiss of the Fur Queen* (Toronto: Doubleday Canada, 1999): 184.

[36] Tomson Highway, *Comparing Mythologies* (Charles R. Bronfman Lecture in Canadian Studies; Ottawa: U of Ottawa P, 2003): 31–32.

[37] See *Bringing Them Home: The Stolen Children Report* (1997) at https://www.humanrights.gov.au/publications/bringing-them-home-stolen-children-report-1997 (accessed 20 September 2015).

residential school and transforms the image into the Weetigo, a cannibalistic spirit,

> A dark hulking figure hovered over him like a crow. Visible only in silhouette, for all Jeremiah knew it might have been a bear devouring a honey-comb, or the Weetigo feasting on human flesh. (79)

The Weetigo, also referred to as Windigo, is a mythological figure across First-Nations cosmologies. In his text *Drawing Out Law*, the Anishinabek legal scholar John Borrows refers to "Windigos as people who went mad and took the lives of others, becoming cannibals. They're also a symbol of greed and consumption because they are constantly hungry and devour all around them, but are never satisfied."[38]

In a remarkable passage in the novel, the abused Gabriel turns the tables by exposing the Communion Mass in terms of a cannibalistic orgy:

> Flailing for his soul's deliverance, the priest thrust out a hairy trembling hand. And by immaculate condensation [...] a length of raw meat dangled from his fingers. What was a humble caribou hunter's son to do? He exposed himself. And savoured the dripping blood as it hit his tongue [...] Up the aisle Gabriel bumped and clattered, his mouth spewing blood, his bloated gut regurgitant, his esophagus engorged with entrails. At every step he took, ghost-white masks and gaping mouths lunged and shrieked: "Kill him! Kill him! Nail the savage to the cross, hang him high, hang him dead! Kill him, kill him [...]." (131)

Against the world of abusive priests is set the trickster figure of Indigenous beliefs – the shape-changing gender-morphing vixen/fur queen. Peeling off the usual white beauty-queen skin, she reveals the animal beneath as something to be respected, someone who is "running the goddamn show" and not the usual "grumpy, embittered, sexually frustrated old fart" (233–34). As Highway explains in his comparative-mythology volume:

> Christian mythology arrived here on the shores of North America in October of the year 1492. At which point God as a man met God as a woman – for that's where she'd been kept hidden all this time, as it turns out – and thereby hangs a tale of what are probably the worst cases of rape, wife battery, and attempted wife murder in the history of the world as we know it. At that point in time, in other words, the circle of

38 John (Kegedonce) Borrows, *Drawing Out Law: A Spirit's Guide* (Toronto: U of Toronto P, 2010): 224. See chapter fifteen, "Windigos" (216–27). My thanks to Margery Fee for alerting me to the work of John Borrows.

> matriarchy was punctured by the straight line of patriarchy ... Circles, however, and fortunately, can be repaired. Or an erect phallus can be ... um ... doused with ice water? Severed completely? – before it's too late.[39]

The trickster figure in *Kiss of the Fur Queen* and other Highway texts (notably his plays) is Nanabush, a gender-morphing deity who is unpredictable, to say the least, but always life-affirming.[40]

## The Planetary

But how do these versions of indigenous cosmopolitanism change conceptualizations of globalism? One answer is that they substitute the planetary for the global; what are the implications of this? In the postcolonial critic Paul Gilroy's version of cosmopolitanism, the planetary is associated with becoming more reflexively critical of one's own culture by cultivating an estrangement from within. He locates a blueprint in Montesquieu's *Persian Letters*, conflating its perspectives on 'Muslim' visitors to Paris in the eighteenth century with the figure of George Orwell, whose scathing critiques of colonialism from within its borders continue to be of great use to the decolonizing process.[41] Gayatri Spivak's "planetarity" speaks of "an imperative to re-imagine the subject as planetary accident [...] rather than global agents."[42] In order to skirt the problems connected with imagining alterity, Spivak considers the planet from an outside vantage point as a way of emphasizing that it is not up to the human subject to imagine the Other. The moment the Other is imagined into being, a hierarchy slides into place or an "onto-epistemology" of subjugation (in Denise da Silva's terminology). Instead, Spivak refers to the Islamic concept of '*haq*' as a birthright that confers the responsibility to care for others. She differentiates this inherent responsibility from the concept of rights. Arguing for the rights of others is dubious because it constitutively reinforces the gulf between those who have rights and those who don't. Such a process sets up an ethics inevitably

---

[39] Highway, *Comparing Mythologies*, 47–48.

[40] In his analysis of comparative Indigenous legal frameworks in Canada and Australia, John Borrows has a chapter (12, "Iskugaewin") in which the distinctions are conveyed via stories that involve the collaboration of Nanabush and Dingo, an equivalent trickster figure in Australian Indigenous knowledge (Borrows, *Drawing Out Law*, 169–86).

[41] See Paul Gilroy, *After Empire: Melancholia or Convivial Culture?* (New York: Routledge UP, 2006).

[42] Gayatri Chakravorty Spivak, "Imperative to Re-imagine the Planet," in Spivak, *An Aesthetic Education in the Era of Globalization* (Cambridge MA: Harvard UP, 2012): 339. Spivak invokes the 'planetary' as well in the final chapter of her *Death of a Discipline* (New York: Columbia UP, 2003).

haunted by an imperialist dynamic, whereas the concept of inherent responsibility to and for others sets up a different ethical dynamic.[43] How one relates this conceptual apparatus to literary interpretation is a challenge – Spivak conveys it through Mahasweta Devi's novella "Pterodactyl, Pirtha, and Puran Sahay," via indigeneity and geological allochthonic demographic patterns – basically, rocks that migrate.[44] Recall here Kim Scott's reference to Bobby's writing on stone and Tomson Highway's statement (above): "Space [...] was taken from us, and time is our curse."

These conceptions of the planetary connect with the growing literature on the post-human and the fundamental questioning of the old notion of the human as the measure of all things. The idea that everything is animated is a staple of indigenous cosmologies, where features of the landscape are recognized as living links with ancestral creation stories as well as being invoked as participating in communal consultations and decision-making. One thinks here of such work as that of the Andean anthropologist Marisol de la Cadena, who describes what she terms "a pluriversal politics" which includes other than human actors, whom she terms "earth beings."

> A reading of the Andean ethnographic record along epistemic lines shows that earth-practices are relations for which the dominant ontological distinction between humans and nature does not work [...]. The "things" that indigenous movements are currently "making public" [...] in politics are not simply nonhumans, they are also sentient entities whose material existence – and that of the worlds to which they belong – is currently threatened by the neoliberal wedding of capital and the state. Thus, when mountains – say Quilish or Ausangate – break into political stages, they do so also as earth-beings.[45]

In other words, we encounter "earth-beings demanding a place in politics" (346). To put it differently: whereas much of the cosmopolitan debate is concerned with rethinking notions of individualism – as citizens, as having access to rights, to cultural franchise – there is another fruitful trajectory that links up with debates concerning the post-human, in which responsibilities are ex-

---

[43] Spivak is at pains to point out that she is not speaking for Islam but merely trying to conceptualize a different ethical relationship from those associated with arguing for 'human rights'.

[44] This brings to mind Mel Chen's notion of "animacy," deriving from linguistics, where rocks and other forms of the posthuman also have agency. See Mel Y. Chen, *Animacies: Biopolitics, Racial Mattering, and Queer Affect* (Durham NC: Duke UP, 2012).

[45] Marisol de la Cadena, "Indigenous Cosmopolitanism in the Andes: Conceptual Reflections beyond 'Politics'," *Cultural Anthropology* 25.2 (April 2010): 341–42.

tended beyond traditional Western concepts of the 'human'. And it is here that indigenous cosmopolitanism has a great deal to offer. As Kim Scott puts it, "Rocks can set a narrative in motion, animate the stone."[46]

## Deep Time

The implication for thinking in planetary terms is nothing less than a restructuring of time and space. While I have given a brief indication of what this means for the spatial, in relation to temporality we encounter the concept of 'deep time' usually associated with geological processes. In her study of American literature across deep time, the American critic Wai-chee Dimock came up with this concept for the following reasons:

> What this highlights is a set of longitudinal frames, at once projective and recessional, with input going both ways, and binding continents and millennia into many loops of relations, a densely interactive fabric.[47]

Later in her study, she explains further:

> What is the advantage of using geological time as a human measure? One effect, it seems, is that it compels us to rethink the phenomenology of race itself, seeing it retrospectively, against the history of the planet. Three million years ago there was no such thing as Homo sapiens in the world. And when this class of primate finally emerged, there was no such thing as Asians or Europeans or Americans. All of us came from Africa, the ancestral home of Homo sapiens in prehistoric times (177).

But, as I have indicated in the references to animated rocks, deep time cannot simply be relegated to the past. Here, for example, is the opening of the Australian Aboriginal writer Alexis Wright's monumental novel *Carpentaria*,[48] which

---

[46] Scott, *Kayang and Me*, 248.

[47] Wai-chee Dimock, *Through Other Continents: American Literature Across Deep Time* (Princeton NJ: Princeton UP, 2006): 3–4.

[48] Alexis Wright, *Carpentaria* (Artarmon, NSW: Giramondo, 2006). For those unfamiliar with her text, here is a summary from the publisher's website:

> Alexis Wright is a member of the southern highlands of the Gulf of Carpentaria. *Carpentaria* is her second novel, an epic set in the Gulf country of north-western Queensland, from where her people come. The novel's portrait of life in the precariously settled coastal town of Desperance centres on the powerful Phantom family, leader of the Westend Pricklebush people, and its battles with old Joseph Midnight's renegade Eastend mob on the one hand, and the white officials of Uptown and the neighbouring Gurfurrit mine on the other. Wright's storytelling is operatic and surreal: a blend of myth and scripture,

deals with contemporary Aboriginal lives threatened by rampant mineral resource extraction, among other erosions of their cultures:

> The ancestral serpent, a creature larger than storm clouds, came down from the stars, laden with its own creative enormity. It moved graciously – if you had been watching with the eyes of a bird hovering in the sky far above the ground. (1)

Wright goes on to illustrate the ways in which her Indigenous characters constantly re-animate what is called the 'Dreaming' in Australian Aboriginal belief-systems that are passed down to each generation and pervade their lives by means of songs, dances, and rituals.[49] In other words, the ancestral Dreaming is constantly remade through each generation and there is a custodial relationship between each generation and their country or nation. This is why the Aboriginal elder from Arnhem Land was weeping at the thought that this custodial link might be interrupted. The deep time of such belief-systems is certainly beyond the human and connects in interesting ways with the Islamic concept of '*haq*' (responsibility) mentioned earlier. This custodial relationship to the land is the background for Kim Scott's novel and through the dance of the title is a tactful reminder of the centuries of complex beliefs contained in that particular cosmopolitan belief-system. Alexis Wright's novel is also arguably a rejoinder to iconic Australian novels concerning colonial race relations produced by white Australia, such as Xavier Herbert's *Capricornia* and *Poor Fellow My Country*. While no doubt well-meaning, Herbert's versions casts the Indigenous peoples into an inescapable abject history, whereas Wright's text restores agency on many levels. Although there is no room here for a detailed analysis, let me draw attention to another example in Wright's text where rocks have agency (as do all her characters, needless to say). At a critical moment, when one of the main characters is about to be killed by a vengeful white emissary of the mining company,

> the yellow-haired man tripped. Instantly, his head was split open at the temple by a rock that had, up to that moment, lain on the ground, embedded in soil that was thousands of seasons old, untouched by humankind since the ancestor had placed it in this spot, as if it had planned to do this incredible thing. (405)

---

farce and politics. The novel teems with extraordinary characters ... figures that stride like giants across this storm-swept world.

[49] See Irene Watson, "Spirituality," in *Aboriginal Australia & the Torres Strait Islands: Guide to Indigenous Australia*, ed. Sarina Singh et al. (Footscray, Victoria: Lonely Planet, 2001): 106–12.

Kim Scott, Tomson Highway, Alexis Wright, and other Indigenous writers offer to induct non-Aboriginal readers into their cosmopolitanism – a blueprint for survival in the face of the risks the planet faces.

## Works Cited

Agamben, Giorgio. *Homo Sacer: Sovereign Power and Bare Life*, tr. Daniel Heller–Roazen (*Homo sacer: Il potere sovrano la nuda vida*, 1995; Stanford CA: Stanford UP, 1998).

Bhabha, Homi K. *The Location of Culture* (London: Routledge, 1994).

Bhabha, Homi K. "Unsatisfied: Notes on Vernacular Cosmopolitanism," *Text and Narration: Cross-Disciplinary Essays on Cultural and National Identities*, ed. Laura García-Moreno & Peter C. Pfeiffer (Columbia SC: Camden House, 1996): 191–207.

Bhabha, Homi K., & John Comaroff. "Speaking of Postcoloniality, in the Continuous Present: A Conversation," in *Relocating Postcolonialism*, ed. David T. Goldberg & Ato Quayson (Oxford: Blackwell, 2002): 15–46.

Borrows, John (Kegedonce). *Drawing Out Law: A Spirit's Guide* (Toronto: U of Toronto P, 2010).

Brewster, Anne. "Can You Anchor a Shimmering Nation State via Regional Indigenous Roots?" Kim Scott talks to Anne Brewster about *That Deadman Dance, Cultural Studies Review* 18.1 (March 2012): 228–46.

*Bringing Them Home: The Stolen Children Report* (1997) https://www.humanrights.gov.au/publications/bringing-them-home-stolen-children-report-1997 (accessed 20 September 2015).

Cadena, Marisol de la. "Indigenous Cosmopolitanism in the Andes: Conceptual Reflections beyond 'Politics'," *Cultural Anthropology* 25.2 (15 April 2010): 334–70.

Chakrabarty, Dipesh. *Provincializing Europe: Postcolonial Thought and Historical Difference* (Princeton NJ: Princeton UP, 2000).

Chen, Mel Y. *Animacies: Biopolitics, Racial Mattering, and Queer Affect* (Durham NC: Duke UP, 2012).

Chow, Rey. *The Protestant Ethnic and the Spirit of Capitalism* (New York: Columbia UP, 2002).

Das, Santanu. "Eurocentric Views of the First World War," *The Guardian Weekly* (1–7 August 2014): 48.

Davis, Wade. *National Geographic Specials – Life at the Ends of the Earth – Keepers of the Dream* (TV, accessed 30 August 2014).

Derrida, Jacques. *Monolingualism of the Other or The Prosthesis of Origins*, tr. Patrick Mensah (*Le monolinguisme de l'autre: ou la prothèse d'origine*, 1996; Stanford CA: Stanford UP, 1998).

Devi, Mahasweta. "Pterodactyl, Pirtha, and Puran Sahay," in Devi, *Imaginary Maps: Three Stories*, tr. & intro. Gayatri Chakravorty Spivak (London & New York: Routledge, 1995): 95–196.

Dimock, Wai-chee. *Through Other Continents: American Literature Across Deep Time* (Princeton NJ: Princeton UP, 2006).

Forte, Maximilian C. "Introduction" to *Indigenous Cosmopolitans: Transnational and Transcultural Indigeneity in the Twenty-First Century*, ed. Maximilian Forte (New York: Peter Lang, 2010): 1–16.

Gilroy, Paul. *After Empire: Melancholia or Convivial Culture?* (New York: Routledge, 2006).

Hartman, Saidiya. "Introduction" to *Scenes of Subjection: Terror, Slavery, and Self-Making in Nineteenth-Century America* (New York: Oxford UP, 1997): 3–14.

Highway, Tomson. *Comparing Mythologies* (Charles R. Bronfman Lecture in Canadian Studies; Ottawa: U of Ottawa P, 2003).

Highway, Tomson. *Kiss of the Fur Queen* (Toronto: Doubleday Canada, 1999).

King, Thomas. *The Inconvenient Indian: A Curious Account of Native People in America* (Toronto: Doubleday Canada, 2012).

Mbembe, Achille. "Necropolitics," tr. Libby Meintjes, *Public Culture* 15.1 (2003): 11–40.

Nyers, Peter. "Abject Cosmopolitanism: The Politics of Protection in the Anti-Deportation Movement," *Third World Quarterly* 24. 6 (2003): 1069–93.

Olubas, Brigitta, & David Gilbey, ed. "Country" (Special Issue) *Journal for the Association for the Study of Australian Literature* 14.3 (2014).

Ravenscroft, Alison. "The Strangeness of the Dance: Kate Grenville, Rohan Wilson, Inga Clendinnen and Kim Scott," *Meanjin* 72.4 (2014): 64–73.

Scott, Kim. *Benang: from the heart* (Fremantle, WA: Fremantle Arts Centre Press, 1999).

Scott, Kim. "Disputed Territory," in *Those Who Remain Will Always Remember: An Anthology of Aboriginal Writing*, ed. Anne Brewster, Angeline O'Neill & Rosemary van den Berg (Fremantle, WA: Fremantle Arts Centre Press, 2000): 162–71.

Scott, Kim. *Kayang and Me* (Fremantle, WA: Fremantle Arts Centre Press, 2005).

Scott, Kim. "Strangers at Home," in *Translating Lives: Living in Two Languages and Culture*, ed. Mary Besmeres & Anna Wierzbicka (St.Lucia: U of Queensland P, 2007): 1–11.

Scott, Kim. *That Deadman Dance* (Sydney: Picador PanMacmillan, 2010).

Silva, Denise Ferreira da. "Notes for a Critique of the 'Metaphysics of Race'," *Theory, Culture & Society*, 28.1 (2011): 138–48.

Silva, Denise Ferreira da. *Toward a Global Idea of Race* (Minneapolis: U of Minnesota P, 2007).

Spivak, Gayatri Chakravorty. *Death of a Discipline* (New York: Columbia UP, 2003).

Spivak, Gayatri Chakravorty. "Imperative to Re-imagine the Planet," in Spivak, *An Aesthetic Education in the Era of Globalization* (Cambridge MA: Harvard UP, 2012): 335–50.

Teuton, Sean Kicummah. "Cities of Refuge: Indigenous Cosmopolitan Writers and the International Imaginary," *American Literary History* 25.1 (Spring 2013): 33–53.

Tyler, Imogen. "Social Abjection," in Tyler, *Revolting Subjects: Social Abjection and Resistance in Neoliberal Britain* (London: Zed, 2013): 19–47.

Watson, Irene. "Spirituality," in *Aboriginal Australia & the Torres Strait Islands: Guide to Indigenous Australia*, ed. Sarina Singh et al. (Footscray, Victoria: Lonely Planet, 2001): 106–12.

Werbner, Pnina. "Vernacular Cosmopolitanism," *Theory, Culture & Society* 23.2–3 (2006): 496–98.

Wright, Alexis. *Carpentaria* (Artarmon, NSW: Giramondo, 2006).

Zable, Arnold, John Bradley, Kim Scott & Marie Munkara. "Language and Politics in Indigenous Writing," *Overland* 205 (Summer 2011): 55–60.

Zeng, Minhao. "Subaltern Cosmopolitanism: Concept and Approaches," *Sociological Review* 62 (2014): 137–48.

❄

# Colonial Capitalism's 'Disvaluation' of Indigenous Australians' Uncommon Wealth

## *Scholarly Analyses and Literary Representations*

Sheila Collingwood–Whittick

> In themselves, and as the bearers of unique and unrepeatable social forms and culture, [Aboriginal Australians] were and still are disvalued by our conventional European outlook; not just *under*-valued but *dis*valued.[1]

Of the many disturbing statistics published on 18 January 2015 in Oxfam International's issue briefing on economic inequality, the following gave particular pause for thought: by 2016, the report predicted, the richest one percent of the world's population would be wealthier than the remaining ninety-nine percent put together.[2] Yet, despite the mind-boggling asymmetry these figures expose, and regardless of the many socio-cultural differences that demarcate the world's heterogeneous populations, most societies have, in varying degrees, succumbed to the "lie-dream" of international capitalism.[3] Wealth, universally understood today as an enviable surfeit of material and monetary assets, has become a global obsession. The poor have been taught to crave it, while those who possess it on an unimaginable scale are driven to amass increasingly surreal reserves of it.

Among isolated pockets of resistance to this planetary phenomenon are certain indigenous populations; peoples whose absence from the Gadarene rush

[1] W.E.H. Stanner, "Aborigines and Australian Society," in Stanner, *The Dreaming and Other Essays* (Melbourne: Black Inc., 2009): 246.

[2] Oxfam Issue Briefing, *Wealth: Having It All and Wanting More* (Oxford: Oxfam International, January 2015): 2.

[3] Stuart Jeffries, "*The Men Who Made Us Spend* Review," *The Guardian* (14 July 2014).

can be explained both by their recent hunter–gatherer past and by a world-view that privileges human welfare, psychosomatic wellbeing, and general happiness (all notions encompassed by the Middle English meaning of 'wealth') over monetary abundance. It is the dichotomy between this now uncommon vision of human plenitude and the predominant usage of the term 'wealth' to signify an exclusively material affluence that constitutes the point of departure for the present essay.

The view of wealth expressed by many Aboriginal Australians seems, prima facie, to have much in common with the Aristotelian concept of *εὐδαιμονία* – the state of 'human flourishing' to which good health, wellbeing, and happiness give rise. One significant difference, however, is the Aboriginal belief that human flourishing is indissociable from the fulfilment of each person's sacred duty to ensure the wellbeing or flourishing of 'country'. What exactly 'country' (zero article) denotes in Aboriginal English is concisely rendered by the Aboriginal elder Mick Dodson as "all the values, places, resources, stories and cultural obligations" that Indigenous Australians associate with the land to which they belong.[4] In Aboriginal understandings of the world, "country [...] is a self-organizing system that brings people and other living things into being, into action, into sentience itself."[5] As Victoria Strang explains, Indigenous people's powerful sense of being an organic part of their country results in their

> discuss[ing] their ancestral land as if it were kin: 'this rock is my father'; 'this tree is my mother'. In doing so [...], they also refer to a basic Aboriginal concept that, in emerging from the spiritual forces held within the land, they have been 'grown up' by that place. As well as providing the spark of life enervating the foetus in the womb, the land also 'feeds' people in spiritual and economic terms throughout their lives.[6]

Thus, the massive land-grab that followed the British invasion of 1788 can in no way be legitimized (as it was at the time) on the grounds that settlers were simply re-routing to other territories a primitive nomadic population for whom

---

[4] Mick Dodson, "My People and Place: Why Does Place Matter?" conference talk, Sydney, 29 April 2003. The anthropological archive abounds in lyrical explanations of both the signification and the cultural and spiritual significance of 'country' for Aboriginal people. One memorable example is the much quoted passage in Stanner's "After the Dreaming," *The Boyer Lectures 1968* (Sydney: ABC, 1969): 44–45.

[5] Deborah Bird Rose, "An Indigenous Philosophical Ecology: Situating the Human," *Australian Journal of Anthropology* 16.3 (2005): 303.

[6] Veronica Strang, "Showing and Telling: Australian Land Rights and Material Moralities," *Journal of Material Culture* 5.3 (2000): 283.

one part of the country held no greater significance than any other. From the perspective of the continent's First Peoples, deracination from "the communicative matrix of country [within which they] respond to the patterns of connection and benefit, nurturing their own lives and the lives of others,"[7] represented no less than the complete destruction of their common wealth.

Crucial to any understanding of Australia's post-contact history is, then, the recognition that the arrival of British settlers on the continent resulted first and foremost in a head-on collision between two radically different epistemologies. It is the ontological fallout from that primary clash that explains why colonization has left such a deep and ugly, unhealed wound on the body of Aboriginal Australia.

Late-eighteenth-century Anglo-Celtic apprehensions of land were, naturally, the product of a very different tradition from that of the Aboriginal peoples whose territories British settlers had invaded. Already shaped by centuries of sedentarization and the practice of agriculture, the European world-view had, in the wake of the Scientific Revolution, been radically transformed by "the twin notions of 'humanity' as somehow separate from 'nature', and nature as an abstract other that must be mastered."[8] Older beliefs in the self "as an integral part of a close-knit harmony of organic parts united to the cosmos and society"[9] had, by that time, given way to a mind-set illuminated by what the environmentalist Val Plumwood describes as "hegemonic anthropocentrism."[10]

Perceiving land as an alienable resource, a commodity to be exploited to the maximum, Australia's first immigrants were, Deborah Bird Rose observes, blind to "the living presence of the living country in its own flourishing particularity."[11] Sensorially handicapped by their own interpretative perspective on the natural world, all that settlers could see in Aboriginal culture, then, was its astonishing backwardness, its lamentable inability to recognize, let alone take advantage of, the vast expanses of valuable real estate that begged to be developed. What moral objection could there possibly be to taking 'uncultivated' land, land that had remained 'unimproved' under a nomadic hunter–gatherer regime that had,

---

[7] Rose, "An Indigenous Philosophical Ecology," 300.

[8] John Jervis, *Transgressing the Modern: Explorations in the Western Experience of Otherness* (Oxford: Blackwell, 1999): 136.

[9] Carolyn Merchant, *The Death of Nature: Women, Ecology, and the Scientific Revolution* (New York: HarperCollins, 1980): 214, quoted in Jervis, *Transgressing the Modern*, 140.

[10] Deborah Rose, "An Indigenous Philosophical Ecology," 302, summarizing Val Plumwood, *Environmental Culture: The Ecological Crisis of Reason* (New York, Routledge, 2002).

[11] Deborah Bird Rose, *Reports from a Wild Country: Ethics for Decolonisation* (Sydney: U of New South Wales P, 2004): 9.

for millennia, ignored its capacity for wealth production?[12] As an article published in the *Port Phillip Herald* in 1842 indignantly asserted,

> *it cannot be improper* [...] to reclaim their grounds from a useless waste to a state of fertility giving employment to the idle, food to the hungry, and quick sure return to the adventurist capitalist.[13]

Colonial conjecture postulating the tenuousness of the natives' attachment to territories – whose apparent potential for pastoral or agricultural development the appraising European eye had swiftly detected – was, in fact, entirely *counterfactual*. Apart from providing everything on which these hunter–gatherer societies depended for their physical survival, country was the very ground in which Aboriginal identity, both individual and collective, was rooted. Regulated by a dense nexus of spiritual and ethical obligations, their relationship with land was the very opposite of parasitic. Indeed, as sometimes documented in early exploration literature, Indigenous Australians carried out multiple quotidian and seasonal tasks that were clearly destined to maintain the environmental health of country to which they belonged.

"Their firestick farming, their organisation of the country, their protection of refuge and breeding zones, and other action that kept country productive"[14] were all, Rose explains, part of their sacred duties as custodians of land on which their Dreaming ancestors had placed them for eternity. Dispossession thus involved far more than 'just' robbing Aboriginal peoples of material property or depriving them of their means of subsistence. It effectively denied them the possibility of caring for country – the most important spiritual obligation their belief-system required them to fulfil and the principal source of their well-being.[15]

---

[12] Veronica Strang quotes an Anglo-Australian grazier complaining in 1992 that "[Aborigines] have got all this prime country, and what are they doing with it? Nothing!" *Uncommon Ground, Cultural Landscapes and Environmental Values* (Oxford: Berg, 1997): 266.

[13] Quoted in John Rickard, *Australia: A Cultural History* (London & New York: Longman, 1988): 59. (My emphasis.)

[14] Deborah Bird Rose, *Sharing Kinship with Nature: How Reconciliation is Transforming the NSW National Parks and Wildlife Service* (Canberra: Centre for Resource and Environmental Studies, Australian National University, 2003): 86–87.

[15] Even today, communities in a position to maintain traditional lifeways consider hunting and gathering as "a way of attending to, re-enacting and ensuring the physical and mythical reproduction of the environment, the human body and the social group. The health and productivity of land or sea country depends on regular human visits; sites must be occupied, used and talked about." Stephen T. Garnett, Bev Sithole, Peter J. Whitehead, C. Paul Burgess, Fay H. Johnston & Tess Lea, "Healthy Country, Healthy People: Policy Implications of Links between Indigenous

❄

Like much Aboriginal literature, the novels of the Waanji author Alexis Wright and the Nyoongar novelist Kim Scott perform the salutary pedagogical function of instructing non-Indigenous readers in the wealth of knowledge that informs Indigenous Australian cultures and the benefits (physical, moral, and spiritual) that being in country affords Aboriginal people. The two authors also use their writing to demonstrate the extent to which Indigenous peoples have been ontologically destabilized both by colonization and by the concomitant environmental toll that settler-colonial agriculture, pastoralism, resource-extractive industries, and urban development have taken on their ancestral estates. On the other hand, many of the Aboriginal characters in their respective works are clearly portrayed as rejecting the plutocentric world-view that dominates colonial culture, preferring by far the ecocentric values of their own cosmology.

Alexis Wright's *Plains of Promise*,[16] for example, shows how Aboriginal beliefs and practices persist in the face of biopolitical schemes destined to eradicate them. When a suicide epidemic strikes the forcibly interned Aboriginal residents of a Christian Mission, the community elders immediately link the problem to the recent violent death of one of their fellow internees. Sending Elliot (one of the novel's protagonists) as an emissary on a journey to the country from which colonial authorities had earlier removed the dead woman, they charge him with investigating and putting right the "big mob of sorry business affecting them all" (43). The multiple protocols Elliot is seen to observe as he makes his way through "dangerous country" provide important insights into the awe with which Aboriginal people regard natural phenomena and the power (at once magical and malignant) they ascribe to the spirit of country. Interestingly, they also constitute a clear demonstration of what the genocide scholar Mark Levene and the sociologist Daniele Conversi describe as subsistence societies' "precognitive alertness of nature's unpredictable and capricious power." What cosmologies of subsistence societies thus transmit, Levene and Conversi suggest, is the ecologically invaluable warning that "to ignore or defy nature is to bring down its wrath on the whole community with cataclysmic force."[17]

---

Human Health and Environmental Condition in Tropical Australia," *Australian Journal of Public Administration* 68.1 (2009): 54.

[16] Alexis Wright, *Plains of Promise* (St. Lucia: U of Queensland P, 1997). Further page references are in the main text.

[17] Mark Levene & Daniele Conversi, "Subsistence Societies, Globalisation, Climate Change and Genocide: Discourses of Vulnerability and Resilience," *International Journal of Human Rights* 18.3 (2014): 292.

Other important information about Aboriginal relationships with land is also communicated via the narrative of Elliot's journey. Traditional methods of navigation are revealed, for instance, in the description of Elliot "singing the songs taught by his father and uncle fathers, each step through the song-map unlocking the land" (43). Defining him as a man "trained in religious knowledge of the land by the thoughts of the elders, through a straight line of law since time began and the land and everything in had been created" (73), the narrator indicates that, for someone of Elliot's epistemological inheritance, the journey on which he is engaged takes place on more than one level. As well as traversing geographical terrain, Elliot simultaneously travels in the mythical space of his ancestral "Dreaming line" (72). "Slip[ping] into unconsciousness" (79) at a critical point on his journey, he enters an inner psychic space where, immune from the pervasive influence of settler-colonial culture "and its ability to reshape mind" (82), he is able, finally, to "rejoin the deeper world of his birthright" (82).

Kim Scott's prize-winning novel *Benang: from the heart*, a fictionalized account of the author's own Nyoongar family history, similarly foregrounds both the strength of Aboriginal peoples' connections to country and their struggle to survive biopolitical strategies designed to sever those all-important links. Placing particular emphasis on Western views of land as no more than a means to material enrichment, Scott records how the "culture of profit"[18] introduced by settler colonialism has translated into incommensurable environmental loss. At once "neglected" and "grazed, razed, shaved and plucked,"[19] "ground by the steel wheels of loaded wagons and the tramp of heavy draught horses" (284), the earth and the fragile ecosystem it supports have been reduced to powder. Irrigation systems, introduced to facilitate the mass-production of wheat, have resulted in the widespread salinization "betrayed" by the numbers of white and dying trees lining the roads along which Harley, the novel's narrator, travels (34). Lethally polluted by the pesticide-laden river that flows into it, a pool once known by Nyoongars for its "acres and acres" of mullet (22) can no longer support such prolific life. Foot-made trails on which the subsistence economy of Australia's nomadic hunter–gatherer peoples depended are obliterated by the "massive, clunking chains," "ripping machines," and dynamite (366) used to pave the way for urban development. In diametric opposition to Western myths that construct colonization as "productivity, growth and civilisation [...] in

---

[18] John Kinsella, "Scapegoats and Feral Cats" (2001), in Kinsella, *Spatial Relations: Essays, Reviews, Commentaries, and Chorography*, ed. & intro. Gordon Collier (Cross/Cultures 162; Amsterdam & New York: Rodopi, 2013), vol. 2: 434.

[19] Kim Scott, *Benang* (Fremantle, WA: Fremantle Arts Centre Press, 1999): 272. Further page references are in the main text.

places where these purportedly had not existed before,"[20] *Benang* shows us the destructive predatoriness of the settler vision of land. As the following passage attests, Australia's colonization has not only resulted in widespread environmental devastation, it has also led to the shocking impoverishment and degradation of Indigenous Australians:

> The telegraph line, railway line, wheel tracks everywhere. Rubbish and bad smells. Trees gone, grass grazed to the ground, the earth cut, shifting, not healed and not yet sealed; vegetation left too long without flames and regeneration. Dust coated the leaves. So many places seemed empty or had new inhabitants. [...] [Nyoongar] people huddled in groups, dressed in the rags of white people. They held out their hands to strangers and were herded about like sheep and cattle, though less well fed. (478–79)

Deeply concerned by the 'trashing' of Australia's landscapes, Germaine Greer was driven in 2004 to write a book-length essay challenging her white compatriots to "sit on the ground [...] and think, think about salination, desertification, dieback, deforestation, species extinction, erosion, suburbanisation, complacency, greed and stupidity." [21] Settler Australians' abusive exploitation of the natural environment is, she argued, a direct consequence of their repressed feeling that the country "belongs to someone else."[22] But if Greer's excoriating analysis succeeded in generating a storm of angry debate on the issue, it was actually no more than the polemical expression of an unease that began to emerge in Anglo-Australian literature from the early-twentieth century onwards. Consider the following randomly selected examples.

Highlighting the environmental desolation produced by settlers' "unholy hunger" for gold, Henry Handel Richardson's *Australia Felix*, published in 1917,[23] illustrates "the pioneering paradox that what is gained occurs at the price of irremediable loss."[24] Ravaged by the gold-diggers' "loveless schemes of robbing and fleeing" (11), the Ballarat landscape's former "pristine beauty" has become a nightmarish scene of "strange, repellent ugliness," its hills and valleys "feverishly

---

20 Rose, *Reports from a Wild Country*, 62.

21 Germaine Greer, *Whitefella Jump Up: The Shortest Way to Nationhood* (London: Profile, 2004): 231–32.

22 Greer, *Whitefella*, 117.

23 Henry Handel Richardson, *Australia Felix* (1917; Sydney: University of Sydney Library, 1997): http://setis.library.usyd.edu.au/ozlit. Further page references are in the main text.

24 Paul Carter, *The Road to Botany Bay: An Exploration of Landscape and History* (1987; Minneapolis: U of Minnesota P, 2010): 171.

disembowelled" by the miners' "wanton disturbing of earth's gracious, green-spread crust" (8).[25]

It is to the same lexicon of catastrophe that the narrator of Rodney Hall's *The Second Bridegroom* turns when confronted by the unconscionable destruction caused by European settlement in the fledgling colony of New South Wales. Looking down at land disfigured by gaping lacerations, charred tree-stumps, and the ugly scar made by a road cut through a landscape of dunes and forest, he struggles to find language capable of articulating the depths of his dismay at "the horror of it, the plunder, the final emptiness. [...] the sheer scale of violence" of "an assault on the earth beyond anything [he] might have been ready for."[26]

Set in Western Australia almost two centuries later, Tim Winton's short story "Aquifer" similarly records, though in less anguished terms, the environmental destruction attendant upon the (sub)urbanization of Australia's landscapes. The environmental ignorance of early European residents, planting their gardens with introduced species, the pumping of water to keep non-Indigenous vegetation alive, the vandalistic dumping of car wrecks in the local swamp, the ecological violence of bulldozers, mowing down native trees and shrubs with their "great chains and steel balls," [27] are all, Winton shows, key factors in the destruction of Australia's native bush, which has, as the narrator observes, "peeled back like the sea before Moses."[28]

Other ecocritical views of settler Australians' exploitative relationship with the land can be noted in Janette Turner Hospital's *Oyster*,[29] which presents an apocalyptic vision of the Australian outback, devoured from the surface to the core by, respectively, pastoralists and opal miners; and Alex Miller's *Journey to the Stone Country*,[30] which similarly references both the cattle industry's earlier poisoning of North Queensland's "sweet boxforest country" (34) and the environmental damage destined to result from equipment currently used in the

---

[25] Note Greer's description of gold mining: "Of all the transitory devastators of country, miners must be the worst. They arrived like locusts, stripping every vestige of vegetation off the ground that they believed to be hiding their lode, riddling it with holes and tunnels and pimpling it with mullock heaps, reducing it to mud and dust at best, and poisonous slime dumps at worst" (*Whitefella Jump Up*, 115).

[26] Rodney Hall, *The Second Bridegroom* (London: Faber & Faber, 1992): 43.

[27] Tim Winton, "Aquifer," in Winton, *The Turning* (London: Picador, 2006): 47.

[28] Winton, "Acquifer," 52

[29] Janette Turner Hospital, *Oyster* (London: Virago, 1997).

[30] Alex Miller, *Journey to the Stone Country* (London: Hodder & Stoughton, 2002). Further page references are in the main text.

modern coal-mining industry: "Eighty million dollars worth of hydraulic hoists and conveyors [...] thundering through the seam twenty-four hours a day, three-hundred and sixty-five days of the year" (22).[31]

For Anglo-Australia's ecocentric poets, it is agricultural development that is probably the most frequent cause of anger and distress. Showing how settler Australians' interactions with the natural environment have produced "dead country," "acres / Drowned in salt," Dorothy Hewett graphically figures cultivated land as "falling into the cash register / Raped and eroded, thin and black as a myall girl on a railway siding."[32] Though the perpetrators of the despoliation Hewett describes are the poet's own grandparents, she gives them no quarter, remembering her grandfather as "an old man on a ginger horse who filled his till / And died content with a desert" and her grandmother as the "Little and pitiless" wife who "kept the till, / Counted the profits, and stacked the bills of sale."[33] Other equally damning assessments of the impact of settler agriculture are articulated in the writing of the poet Judith Wright (an early and life-long environmentalist), the "ecocritical concern" with which many of Les Murray's poems are permeated,[34] and the "eco-anarchist critique of colonialism"[35] that constitutes the driving force behind much of John Kinsella's poetry.

But it is perhaps Xavier Herbert's novel *Poor Fellow My Country*, published in 1975, that offers the most comprehensive, sustained, and fiercely critical portrait of the profit-driven ecocide of which Australia has been the victim since the earliest days of colonization.[36] Studded with penetrating insights into Aboriginal cosmology (and the wealth of interconnections with natural phenomena to which such understandings give rise), and suffused from start to finish with the author's rage and despair at settler colonial rapacity, *Poor Fellow My Country* is a truly visionary novel for its era.

---

[31] As Stanner observes, while pastoralism was the "great wrecker" of Aboriginal land and culture in the 1860s and 1870s, the explosion of extractive industries a century later was the twentieth-century equivalent of pastoral expansion writ large (*After the Dreaming*, 197, 213).

[32] Dorothy Hewett, "Legend of the Green Country," in Hewett, *Collected Poems 1940–1995* (1995), http://www.poetrylibrary.edu.au/poets/hewett-dorothy/legend-of-the-green-country-0050048 (accessed 18 August 2016).

[33] Hewett, "Legend of the Green Country".

[34] See Nicholas Birns' review of "Ecopoetics 6/7," *Jacket Magazine* 40 (2010): http://jacketmagazine.com/40/r-ecopoetics-rb-birns.shtml (accessed 26 August 2016).

[35] See Gary Clark, "Environmental Themes in Australian Literature," in *A Companion to Australian Literature Since 1900*, ed. Nicholas Birns & Rebecca McNeer (Rochester NY: Camden House, 2009): 439.

[36] Clark sees the novel as "arguably one of the most significant engagements with ecological thought and environmental aesthetics in Australian literature" ("Environmental Themes," 431).

Since the inordinate length (one third greater than *War and Peace*)[37] of this ambitious life-work and the densely ideological vision that underpins it militate against summary analysis, I simply indicate, in passing, Herbert's magisterial critique of settler-colonial culture's way of seeing Australia as "inert territory (*terra nullius*) available for exploitation and profiteering,"[38] "a country to loot,"[39] as Wright puts it. And while the "will to force the earth to deliver up its riches and its products in obeisance to an ideology is," as John Martin reminds us, "not a uniquely Australian will," the Australia Herbert depicts reflects, in every respect, Martin's argument that, in Australia, the natural environment is "accorded no status whatsoever."[40]

❄

The market economy that settler colonialism introduced to Australia is, as Stanner suggests,[41] utterly incompatible with the world-view of Aboriginal Australians, people who have never ceased to consider their relationship with 'country' as the key to their flourishing. As a trans-disciplinary group of researchers reported in 2009, Aboriginal Australians continue, almost two and a half centuries after being struck down by the seismic impact of colonization, to express "a high sense of obligation to country, and feel that their wellbeing, especially health, is inextricably connected to their execution of those obligations."[42] Given this belief in the absolute interconnectedness between human and telluric wellbeing, it is hardly surprising that the health of the large numbers of dispossessed Aborigines whose lives are now disconnected from ancestral territories is today seriously degraded by a wide range of life-threatening diseases, alcohol and substance abuse, and suicide.

---

[37] See Frances Devlin–Glass's excellent essay, "The Eco-Centric Self and the Sacred in Xavier Herbert's *Poor Fellow My Country*," *Journal of the Association for the Study of Australian Literature* 8 (2008): 46.

[38] Jane Gleeson–White, "Capitalism versus the Agency of Place: An Ecocritical Reading of *That Deadman Dance* and *Carpentaria*," *Journal of the Association for the Study of Australian Literature* 13.2 (2013): 3.

[39] Judith Wright, "Towards the Bicentennial Landscape," in *Born of the Conquerors*, 42.

[40] John Martin, "A Dark History," *Arena* 96 (August–September 2008): 21.

[41] "Ours is a market civilisation, theirs not. Indeed there is a sense in which The Dreaming and the Market are mutually exclusive"; Stanner, "Continuity and Change among the Aborigines," in Stanner, *After the Dreaming*, 163.

[42] Garnett, Sithole et al., "Healthy Country," 54.

Although numerous commentators have underlined the robust and healthy appearance of Indigenous people at the time of first contact,[43] the gap between Indigenous life expectancy and that of non-Indigenous Australians is now approximately seventeen years, a fact that makes Australia "unique among comparable post-colonial societies in failing to make substantive reductions to the indigenous/non-indigenous health differential."[44] Australia, one of the richest nations in the world today,[45] was reported in 2007 as having "the lowest rank among wealthy nations working to improve the health and well-being of aboriginal peoples."[46]

As in Canada, where "the high rates of suicide, alcoholism, and violence, and the pervasive demoralization seen in Aboriginal communities can be readily understood as the direct consequences of a history of dislocations and the disruption of traditional subsistence patterns and connection to the land,"[47] so the self-destructive forms of behaviour manifested in large swathes of Australia's Indigenous peoples are symptomatic of the psychological injuries resulting from the savagery of the colonial process.

In the last few decades, Indigenous literature has insistently demonstrated how deeply Aboriginal cultures (commonly perceived as inimical to mainstream values) and Aboriginal wellbeing have been affected by the assimilation programmes consistently enforced by successive Commonwealth governments. Whether life-histories or novels, what all such narratives highlight are the marginalized and chaotic lives, the ruined childhoods, the broken families, the fractured identities, the economic distress, and the (sometimes) anomic forms of behaviour that have become the norm in Aboriginal communities since settler-colonial Australia embarked on the elimination of their 'backward' cultures.

In Kim Scott's *Benang*, the 'mixed-race' narrator repeatedly affirms how his British grandfather's obsessive attempts to turn him into a white man have made him "so much less than [he] might have been" (90). Mirroring the bio-

---

[43] See, for instance, Ethel (Wara) Alderete, *The Health of Indigenous Peoples* (Geneva: WHO, 1999): 26; Kim Scott's *Kayang and Me* (Fremantle, WA: Fremantle Arts Centre Press, 2005): 93.

[44] NACCHO & Oxfam Australia, 2007, quoted in Dominic O'Sullivan, "Justice, Culture and the Political Determinants of Indigenous Australian Health," *Ethnicities* 12.6 (2012): 688.

[45] *The* richest according to one report published in 2013. See A.A.P., "Australians retain title as world's richest, according to wealth report," *The Guardian*, 9 October 2013: http://www.theguardian.com/world/2013/oct/09/australia-worlds-richest (accessed 3 September 2016).

[46] Garnett et al. "Healthy Country," 53.

[47] Laurence J. Kirmayer, Gregory M. Brass & Caroline L. Tait, "The Mental Health of Aboriginal Peoples: Transformations of Identity and Community," *Canadian Journal of Psychiatry* 45.7 (September 2000): 609.

political objectives settler Australia has pursued since the beginning of the twentieth century, Ern Scatt's project of assimilating his grandson is, the latter points out, based on the genocidal principle of depriving him of his Aboriginal heritage. Forced to undergo the "inexorable process [...] of we becoming I. [The] reduction of a rich and variously shared place to one fragile impoverished consciousness" (31), the young Harley, like countless other 'beneficiaries' of bio-cultural absorption, feels that his life has been profoundly diminished.

> Nyoongar language. Culture. .... I thought of all the things that I did not have. Unsettled, not belonging [...] I thought I was the only one. I thought it was just me – a solitary full stop. (109)

In the course of the narrative, the identity his grandfather stole from him is finally restored to Harley by his Nyoongar uncles, Jack and Will. Like the cyclical nomadic itineraries followed by their Aboriginal predecessors, the repeated journeys the old men undertake with their nephew are used to transmit traditional Indigenous knowledge of country. By demonstrating the resourcefulness of their common ancestors in managing both to keep alive traditional cultural values and to preserve their all-important links with Nyoongar country, the old men's stories function as parables, teaching their young relative the means of his own survival. In a very real sense, then, Jack and Will are Harley's saviours. It is their continual efforts to familiarize him with his Aboriginal kin and country that enable him to overcome the crippling sense of alienation from which he suffers, and thus return him to a state of spiritual and physical health.

❄

Interestingly, numerous academic studies conducted over the past two decades confirm Scott's vision of the healing power of Aboriginal culture. The many pathological conditions currently afflicting indigenous populations (not just in Australia but worldwide) are, specialists from a wide spectrum of disciplines have begun to suggest, neither inevitable nor entirely irreversible. Indeed, the general consensus now is that, while "loss of control over land has had ongoing, serious negative impacts on health,"[48] indigenous wellbeing can be significantly improved by such protective factors as cultural continuity and the maintenance of links with traditional territories.

---

[48] Australian Indigenous Doctors' Association and Centre for Health Equity Training, Research and Evaluation, UNSW, *Health Impact Assessment of the Northern Territory Emergency Response* (Canberra: Australian Indigenous Doctors' Association, 2010): 28.

In their ground-breaking epidemiological study of the high incidence of suicide among the youth of Canada's First Nations, Michael Chandler and Christopher Lalonde found, for instance, that in those Indigenous communities which had made "a collective effort to rehabilitate and vouchsafe the cultural continuity of these groups" youth suicide rates were "dramatically lower."[49] In the specific case of Australia, stronger attachment to traditional culture has not only been shown to result in higher levels of Indigenous health but has also been linked with better educational outcomes, improved employment prospects, and a "lower likelihood of engaging in risky alcohol consumption."[50] "Cultural identity," the economist Alfred Dockery asserts, "has robust associations with well-being."[51]

The function of language as a vehicle for transmitting culture is the subject of David Malouf's "The Only Speaker of His Tongue," a short story that powerfully attests to the incommensurability of language loss.[52] But whereas Malouf depicts the extinction of Indigenous Australian languages as one of the inevitable consequences of frontier massacres, the "Coolangatta Statement on Indigenous Peoples' Rights in Education" approaches this important question from a less fatalistic perspective, focusing instead on ways of ensuring "the survival and revival of Indigenous languages." Nonetheless, as the Coolangatta signatories take care to underline, such an objective can only be achieved through "the protection, transmission, maintenance and preservation of Indigenous knowledge, cultural values and wisdom."[53]

---

49 Michael J. Chandler & Christopher E. Lalonde, "Cultural Continuity as a Hedge against Suicide in Canada's First Nations," *Transcultural Psychiatry* 35.2 (1998): 191. Alderete also underlines the fact that studies on a wide range of health issues (including infant mortality, cancer, high blood pressure, diabetes, blood lipid levels, stress and substance abuse) have consistently revealed "an association between maintenance of culture and decreased rates of [ill-health]" (*The Health of Indigenous Peoples*, 40).

50 Alfred M. Dockery, "Culture and Well-Being: The Case of Indigenous Australians," *Social Indicators Research* 99.2 (November 2010): 329.

51 Dockery, "Do Traditional Culture and Identity Promote the Wellbeing of Indigenous Australians? Evidence from the 2008 NATSISS," in *Survey Analysis for Indigenous Policy in Australia*, ed. Nicholas Biddle & Boyd Hunter (Canberra: Australian National UP, 2012): 298.

52 David Malouf, "The Only Speaker of His Tongue," in Malouf, *Antipodes: Stories* (Ringwood, Victoria: Penguin, 1986): 68–72.

53 See "The Coolangatta Statement on Indigenous Peoples' Rights in Education," quoted in *What Good Condition: Reflections on an Australian Aboriginal Treaty 1986–2006*, ed. Peter Read, Gary Meyers & Bob Reece (Canberra: ANU E-Press, 2006): 235. See also the observations of the Canadian Task Force on Aboriginal Languages and Cultures quoted in Darcy Hallett, Michael J.

For their part, Hallett, Chandler, and Lalonde conclude that language use "as a marker of cultural persistence" is not only "a strong predictor of health and wellbeing in Canada's Aboriginal communities" but that "high language knowledge" among young Indigenous Canadians helps protect them from suicide.[54] Conversely, in Australia, where biopolitical schemes have systematically aimed at the deracination of Aboriginal people and where, as a result, "the blackman's language" is, as Wright observes in *Plains of Promise*, "dying away because it [is] no longer tied to his traditional country" (74), the rate of Indigenous people committing suicide is now the highest in the world.[55]

Considering the centrality of land in indigenous cultures, an increasing volume of research has, in recent years, been concerned with assessing the potentially therapeutic value of the so-called 'homelands' or 'outstation' movements in Australia – movements whose main aim is to assist Aboriginal people in reconnecting with 'country'.[56] And, encouragingly, results show that Indigenous Australians who choose to return to their homelands benefit from better mental and physical health, are less prone to substance abuse, have a more functional family life, and are generally more at peace with themselves than Aboriginal Australians who are, for whatever reason, prevented from doing so.[57]

---

Chandler & Christopher E. Lalonde, "Aboriginal Language Knowledge and Youth Suicide," *Cognitive Development* 22 (2007): 393.

[54] Hallett et al., "Aboriginal language knowledge," 398. The Australian linguist Rob Amery refers to a mass of evidence indicating the positive health benefits accruing to Indigenous people who are fluent in their own language. See House of Representatives Standing Committee on Aboriginal and Torres Strait Islander Affairs, "The Role of Indigenous Languages," in *Inquiry into Language Learning in Indigenous Communities*," 2.69, 26: http://www.aph.gov.au/Parliamentary_Business/Committees/House_of_Representatives_Committees?url=atsia/languages2/report.htm (accessed 15 January 2015).

[55] Helen Davidson, "Indigenous suicide: 'prevention should focus on cultural reconnection,'" *The Guardian* (17 November 2014), http://www.theguardian.com/australia-news/2014/nov/17/indigenous-suicide-prevention-should-focus-on-cultural-reconnection (accessed 3 September 2016).

[56] According to the Blanchard Report of 1987, 'homelands' are "small, relatively permanent, decentralised communities consisting of closely related individuals which have been established by Aboriginal people with a strong traditional orientation." Quoted in Rachel E. Reilly, Joyce Doyleb, Di Bretherton & Kevin G. Rowley, "Identifying Psychosocial Mediators of Health Amongst Indigenous Australians for the Heart Health Project," *Ethnicity & Health* 13.4 (September 2008): 353.

[57] Aboriginal people electing to live permanently or even partially on homelands have been reported as having "lower rates of diabetes, cardiovascular risk factors, hospitalisation and death" than those noted among the residents of "more centralised communities". Robyn McDermott, Kerin O'Dea, Kevin Rowley, Sabina Knight & Paul Burgess, "Beneficial Impact of the Homelands

One of the dominant themes of Aboriginal life-writing – retrieving a cultural heritage largely erased by more than two hundred years of colonial occupation through the undertaking of a journey back to territorial origins – bears out these findings by demonstrating the homeland's power to heal. In addition to his portrayal of Harley's fictional journey in *Benang*, Kim Scott also describes his own visits to ancestral territory in *Kayang and Me*, an autobiographical narrative in which Scott's travels with his elderly Aboriginal Auntie teach him to understand that "the bush gave [Indigenous Australians] respite from the hostility of white society. It let you feel good about yourself, and it was that part of your country you might still call home." Ultimately, returning to country is, he observes, "about recovery, in both senses of the word: reclaiming a heritage and restoring health."[58] In her polyphonic, auto-ethnographical work *My Place*, Sally Morgan similarly remarks on the therapeutic value of the journey she and her mother make to their ancestors' country. "How deprived we would have been if we had been willing to let things stay as they were," she reflects, "We would have survived but not as a whole people."[59]

Yet, as Morgan's narrative shows, there is another side to this inspirational story, her grandmother Daisy's traumatic life-history having placed the old lady beyond the reach of such a healing experience. Removed, like thousands of young Aboriginals, from her native milieu at the age of fourteen, Daisy spent most of her days as the live-in servant of a powerful family of white pastoralists; people who, in Daisy's own word, "owned" her (342). Although Morgan avoids explicitly saying so, her grandmother, subjected to the abuse with which Aboriginal domestics were typically treated, was sexually molested by her master (who, it is strongly insinuated, is Daisy's own father). Full of self-hatred, treated "rotten, real rotten" (344) all her life, and brainwashed through her long immersion in settler-colonial culture into rejecting her Aboriginal identity, Daisy refuses to accompany her daughter and granddaughter on their visit to the land of her birth. "All you'll be lookin' at," she tells them, "is dirt. Dirt and scrub" (211).

As Michael Griffiths has recently suggested,

> the motif of healing resonates on a personal level for both Sally and Daisy as the novel closes with their mutual understanding brought about by Daisy's eventual decision to tell her part of the story before her death.[60]

---

Movement on Health Outcomes in Central Australian Aborigines," *Australian and New Zealand Journal of Public Health* 22.6 (1998): 657.

[58] Scott, *Kayang and Me*, 119 and 217.

[59] Sally Morgan, *My Place* (Fremantle, WA: Fremantle Arts Centre Press, 1987): 230. Further page references are in the main text.

[60] Michael Griffiths, "Indigenous Life Writing: Rethinking Poetics and Practice," in *A Companion*

Maybe so, but the bitterly reductive words Daisy uses to refer to her birthplace indicate to me that 'country', the axis around which Aboriginal cosmology turns, no longer holds any value in her eyes, and, thus, that the healing power of land is irretrievably lost to her. As her brother Arthur explains, "she's bin with whitefellas too long. They make her feel 'shamed, that's what white people do to you" (146).

Thanks to the new ways of seeing that have emerged from research linking cultural continuity to indigenous health, a growing number of international declarations, charters, and conventions now acknowledge the right of First Peoples to "practise and revitalize their cultural traditions and customs."[61] But, while the landmark (if merely hortatory) United Nations Declaration on the Rights of Indigenous Peoples (UNDRIP) has pressured white-settler nations like Australia into adjusting their stance on indigenous rights, there exist numerous powerful lobbies and ideological currents within contemporary Australia that persist in denouncing what they see as the "destructive naïveté"[62] of self-determination policies introduced in a more optimistic era. Since, this line of argument insists, it is their traditional cultural practices that are mainly responsible for the catastrophic situation in which Indigenous communities find themselves today, the only sensible option is to force Aboriginal Australians to abandon such practices and yield to the power of the mainstream – a world that, as Altman and Hinkson remind us, is "increasingly geared towards producing mobile, formally educated, individualized Aboriginal citizens who will embrace the values of the free market."[63]

Predictably, much of the hostility towards the maintenance of Aboriginal cultural practices stems from the domains of finance and industry. When it comes to exploiting natural resources located on Aboriginal-owned land, these corporate interest groups find little of value in the significance traditional Indigenous peoples attach to their custodianship of ancestral territories. Consequently, both the Native Title Act (NTA) introduced by the Keating government in 1993 and the Aboriginal Heritage Act designed to protect sites considered to be either sacred or of cultural importance to Indigenous people have come

---

*to Australian Aboriginal Literature*, ed. Belinda Wheeler (Rochester NY: Camden House, 2013): 27.

[61] Article 11, United Nations Declaration on the Rights of Indigenous Peoples (March 2008).

[62] See Peter Sutton, "After Consensus," *Griffith Review* 21 (2008).

[63] Jon Altman & Melinda Hinkson, "Very Risky Business: The Quest to Normalise Remote-living Aboriginal People" in *Risk, Welfare and Work* ed. Greg Marston, Jeremy Moss & John Quiggin (Carlton, Victoria: Melbourne UP, 2010): 188.

under repeated attack from the all-powerful mining and pastoral organizations.[64]

Capitulating to the massive political clout such groups wield, John Howard's government made considerable amendments to the NTA in 1998, stripping it of much of its original power. The Aboriginal Heritage Act (AHA) has undergone similar assaults and proved to be equally ineffective in repelling the challenges of industrialists. The Indigenous academic Jillian Marsh argues that "laws aimed at protecting indigenous sacred sites are generally tokenistic and toothless."[65] The Native Title specialist David Ritter agrees, suggesting that neither Act can "provide traditional owners with the ability to satisfy aspirations to protect Indigenous cultural heritage."[66]

The current situation in the Burrup Pensinsula (WA) constitutes striking evidence of the accuracy of such assessments. Despite the Burrup's status as a treasure-house of ancient Aboriginal rock art (one declared worthy of World Heritage listing), the landscape's cultural significance has, over the past couple of decades, been trampled underfoot as ruthless industrial exploitation of the area – one rich in natural gas – has flourished unchecked. To date, some twenty-five percent of the 10,000-year-old petroglyphs[67] located there since time immemorial have been destroyed.

Over the last few years, in the light of the aggression to which all of Australia's ecosystems – land, sea, and air – continue to be subjected, conservationists and politicians worldwide have strongly condemned the Commonwealth government's "environmental vandalism."[68] The consequences of such vandalism for Indigenous Australian lives fail, on the other hand, to provoke any comparable expressions of indignation. Judged incompatible with the goals of industrial development, limitless economic growth, and the uninhibited accumulation of riches which, like most modern capitalist societies, Australia aspires to attain,

---

[64] For a wide-ranging discussion of the mining industry's attacks on Aboriginal land rights, see Jon Altman, "Indigenous Communities, Miners and the State in Australia," in *Power, Culture, Economy: Indigenous Australians and Mining*, ed. Jon Altman & David Martin (Canberra: Australian National UP, 2009): 17–49.

[65] Lisa Martin, "Aboriginal cultural laws 'tokenistic'," *The Age* (19 April 2011), http://www.smh.com.au/breaking-news-national/aboriginal-cultural-laws-tokenistic-20110419-1dnby.html (accessed 28 August 2015).

[66] "Many Bottles for Many Flies: Managing Conflict over Indigenous People's Cultural Heritage in Western Australia," *Public History Review* 13 (2006): 139.

[67] It is important to note that, for Aborigines, these represent their title to the land.

[68] See Zachary Davies Boren, "Australia scraps shark protections – and continues its backwards environment policy," *The Independent* (21 January 2015).

the cultural and spiritual wellbeing that Aboriginal peoples derive from their relationship with land is dismissed as "acceptable loss."[69]

❄

In 2001, this populist view received unexpected intellectual backing when the anthropologist Peter Sutton revealed his conversion to the now-common wisdom that Aboriginal culture is the cause of, rather than the solution to, material destitution and psycho-social dysfunction in Indigenous communities. Comforted by Sutton's unequivocal indictment of the "progressive rights-oriented view of Indigenous policy" that prevailed in the 1970s,[70] public opinion on the question of Aboriginal self-determination has hardened considerably.

Gillian Cowlishaw's explanation that self-determination policies of that period were "saturated with culturally specific ideas of progress, development and economic viability which were taken to be invariant characteristics of the world"[71] cuts no ice with settler Australians who have always perceived the indigeneity and socio-cultural difference of Aboriginal peoples as undermining the legitimacy of their own presence. Nor are Australia's 'whitefellas' receptive to any appeal suggesting that, after more than two hundred years of being subjected to practices that have physically exterminated, dislocated, segregated, decultured, biologically managed, stigmatized, and oppressed them along with removing their children, Aboriginal Australians may need somewhat more than a mere couple of decades to recover.

On the contrary, "the settler hostility to Indigenous people that," according to the Aboriginal leader Patrick Dodson, "bubbles beneath the surface of Australian civil society"[72] received a further boost in 2007 when John Howard ordered a sudden and brutal military intervention in Indigenous communities living in what is considered, by knowledgeable Australians, to be the heartland of

---

[69] As defined by Kerry Arabena, "acceptable loss" signifies "negative outcomes that are considered tolerable against the achievements of a particular strategy or tactic." Quoted in David Cooper, *Closing the Gap in Cultural Understanding: Social Determinants of Health in Indigenous Policy in Australia* (Darwin: Aboriginal Medical Services Alliance of the Northern Territory (AMSANT), 2011): 34.

[70] Sutton, "After Consensus."

[71] Gillian Cowlishaw, "Erasing Culture and Race: Practising 'Self-Determination'," *Oceania* 68.3 (March 1998): 151.

[72] Patrick Dodson, "Whatever Happened to Reconciliation?" in *Coercive Reconciliation: Stabilise, Normalise, Exit Aboriginal Australia*, ed. Jon Altman & Melinda Hinkson (Melbourne: Arena, 2007): 25.

'traditional' Aboriginal cultures.[73] Although Howard's decision was ostensibly justified on the grounds that it was an "emergency response" to widespread sexual abuse of Indigenous children, this allegation was later shown to be largely unfounded.[74]

What *is* certain is that there are vast deposits of uranium on Aboriginal land in the Northern Territory and that "a month after the [NTER] legislation to seize the land was passed, Australia signed a uranium deal with China and Russia."[75] Also germane to the issue is the Indigenous law professor Irene Watson's observation that "prior to the announcement of the emergency response" there had been a "long Australian media campaign waged against Aboriginal culture and law."[76] My own contention is, then, that the NT intervention was, as Altman and Hinkson assert, "clearly imagined as establishing the pre-conditions for the production of a new kind of disciplined Aboriginal subject: one who would embrace the individualised aspirations of neo-liberalism."[77]

Today, a heterogeneous cohort of both Anglo-Australian and media-approved Indigenous intellectuals[78] is vociferous in its condemnation of the 'progressivist' thinking that allegedly *made* Aborigines perennial victims of colonization.[79] Like rabbits from hats, spurious concepts such as 'post-ethnicity' are produced to delegitimize any approach to Indigenous disadvantage that favours the preservation of Aboriginal identity. The idea of cultural continuity is claimed to be not only out of touch with "the post-ethnic reality of Aborigines' lives," it is actually accused of exacerbating the deplorable conditions that exist in many Indigenous communities.[80]

---

73 The 'Intervention' is also commonly referred to as the NTER (Northern Territory Emergency Response).

74 See Sabine Kacha, "The NT Intervention: Does the End Justify the Means?" *Aboriginal and Social Justice Issues* (August 2009): 13–15.

75 Sinem Saban, quoted in Anna Bruce-Lockhart, "New Dawn for the Aborigines?" *Guardian Weekly* (3 December 2007); https://www.theguardian.com/world/2007/dec/03/australia-humanrights (accessed 3 September 2016).

76 "In the Northern Territory Intervention: What is Saved or Rescued and at What Cost?" *Cultural Studies Review* 15.2 (September 2009): 54.

77 "Very Risky Business," 193.

78 The latter include the high-profile academics Marcia Langton and Noel Pearson, and the prominent politician Warren Mundine.

79 See A. Dirk Moses, "Time, Indigeneity, and Peoplehood: The Postcolony in Australia," *Postcolonial Studies* 13.1 (2010): 9–32.

80 See Terry Moore, "Misadventures with Aboriginalism," *Social Identities: Journal for the Study of Race, Nation and Culture* 17.3 (2011): 423–41.

At the present time, majority opinion is that, if Indigenous people are ever to recover from their present grievous condition, they must blank out the trauma of the colonial past, shed their 'perverse' attachment to outdated cultural mores, and become, in the words of the economist Helen Hughes, "normal Australians [...] living normal lives like we do."[81] For Hughes, this means "integrat[ing] into the economy [...] living in their own houses [and] buying their houses."[82] Meanwhile, Aborigines unimpressed by a value-system that prizes individual success and the accumulation of material riches at the expense of environmental integrity are constructed as *ab*normal people who cannot be accommodated within the modern nation. It is a view in which we can hear distinct echoes of the notorious A.O. Neville's eugenicist proposal that, as there was "*no* place for Aboriginal people in Australian society," the visible signs of their identity should be systematically bred out.[83]

The circumstances in which large numbers of Indigenous Australians live today are catastrophic. That human beings can suffer such extreme levels of poverty, squalor, disease, and psycho-social desolation in an industrially developed, wealthy, First-World nation like Australia defies comprehension. Yet what the anthropological, medical, sociological, and economic research that I have referred to throughout this essay contends, and what Aboriginal Australian literature vigorously asserts, is that such problems would eventually disappear if only Indigenous people were allowed to live on and care for their own land, speak their own languages, and follow their own rich cultural practices.

And, contrary to what advocates of coercive assimilation and theorists of 'post-ethnicity' argue, this is not the naive fantasy of rights-obsessed idealists. It is the conclusion reached by Joseph Kalt and Stephen Cornell, who, after more than two decades of research into Native-American economic development,[84] find that Indigenous Americans are finally beginning "to break long-standing patterns of dependency and second-class status."[85] Far from seeing this achieve-

---

[81] See Helen Hughes, "Aboriginal Homelands," *Counterpoint*, ABC TV b28 May 2007), http://www.abc.net.au/radionational/programs/counterpoint/aboriginal-homelands/3246514 (accessed 3 September 2016).

[82] Hughes, "Aboriginal homelands."

[83] See Scott, *Kayang and Me*, 197. Chief Protector of Aborigines for Western Australia in the 1930s, Neville masterminded the policy that led to the Stolen Generations.

[84] Professors in, respectively, International Political Economy and Sociology and Public Administration.

[85] Stephen Cornell & Joseph P. Kalt, "American Indian Self-Determination: The Political Economy of a Successful Policy," *The Harvard Project on American Indian Economic Development* (Tucson: University of Arizona, October 2010): 27. Further page references are in the main text.

ment as "the product of the cultural assimilation of Native Americans into non-Indian society and norms" (11), Cornell and Kalt categorically affirm that: "after a century or more of failed efforts to improve the lives of the U.S. indigenous people, the only strategy that has worked" is that of "federal promotion of tribal self-government under formal policies known as "*self-determination*" (15).

In Australia, however, it is business as usual in the administrative realm of Indigenous Affairs. In 2008, hard on the heels of the NTER, the Commonwealth government announced its latest scheme – 'Closing the Gap' – for addressing the enormous differences that, according to mainstream indicators of socio-economic wellbeing, separate Indigenous experience from that of non-Indigenous Australians. Yet, like key measures introduced by NTER legislation, 'Closing the Gap' policies are, Cooper argues, "contributing to the processes of cultural loss, alienation and disengagement that are themselves critical impediments to achieving Closing the Gap goals."[86]

In "the dominant narrative" of neoliberalism which insists that "the market can resolve almost all social, economic and political problems," the rich, George Monbiot observes, "are the new righteous; the poor are the new deviants, who have failed both economically and morally and are now classified as social parasites."[87] Since, in Australia – now the world's richest nation in terms of median wealth[88] – Aborigines are not just the poor but the extravagantly, scandalously poor, it is they who bear the brunt of this damning rhetoric of material and moral failure. Construed as impure anachronisms, the worthless vestiges of a primitive, communal, land-based being-in-the-world, they are considered an offensive anomaly, unfit for the affluent, modern world of White Australia. Lacking the individualistic, environmentally insensitive, hyperconsumerist reflexes that colonial capitalism encourages, they are being inexorably pushed "towards a 'vanishing future', away from an Aboriginal being, and relationships or connections to country."[89]

❄

Like the rest of the world, Australia is struggling today with the consequences of planetary climate change. After two and half centuries of what the Native-

[86] Cooper, "Closing the Gap," 32.

[87] George Monbiot, "Sick of this market-driven world? You should be," *The Guardian* (5 August 2014), https://www.theguardian.com/commentisfree/2014/aug/05/neoliberalism-mental-health-rich-poverty-economy (accessed 3 September 2016).

[88] See A.A.P., "Australians retain title."

[89] Watson, "In the Northern Territory Intervention," 49.

American scholar Glen Coulthard calls "the pathological drive for accumulation that fuels colonial-capitalist expansion,"[90] significant areas of Australia's natural environment are, moreover, in very poor shape. "The link between Australia's natural resources (that is, the land), regional trade, economic policy, and governmentality is," Philip Mead underlines, "part of an ecocidal ideology of growth and prosperity at any cost."[91] The problem is that the non-Indigenous mainstream shows no sign of wanting to stop, or even slow down, this reckless plunder, for settler Australians' blinkered vision of what constitutes wealth effectively blinds them to the worth of the environmentally intelligent relationship with land that is the backbone of Aboriginal cultures. Dismissing the idea that such cultures might still have value or relevance today as a vacuous New-Age romance, mainstream settler society demands that Indigenous peoples conform to the dominant capitalist world-view.

Yet, as a major investigation into worldwide language loss has recently confirmed, there are "extraordinary parallels between linguistic diversity and biodiversity." It is, the researchers Jonathan Loh and David Harmon argue, Indigenous epistemologies that have hitherto ensured the biological abundance and species diversity that *all* life-forms, humans included, need to survive. Thus, if the neoliberal project of cultural homogenization is not arrested in the near future, it is not just biodiversity but humanity *tout court* that could be facing "an extinction crisis." While linguists and ethnobiologists are busy recording a few precious elements of the vast wealth of knowledge Indigenous peoples possess, "the most important conservation," Harmon stresses, "takes place on the ground as part of a *living* culture."[92] Paradoxically, it is, ultimately, in the interests of their *own* survival that non-Indigenous Australians would be well advised to support the flourishing of Aboriginal cultures.

---

90 Glen Coulthard, "Place Against Empire: Understanding Indigenous Anti-Colonialism," *Affinities: A Journal of Radical Theory, Culture, and Action* 4.2 (Fall 2010): 82.

91 Philip Mead, "The Geopolitical Underground: Alexis Wright's *Carpentaria*, Mining and the Sacred," in *Decolonizing the Landscape: Indigenous Cultures in Australia*, ed. Beate Neumeier & Kay Schaffer (Cross/Cultures 173; Amsterdam & New York: Rodopi, 2013): 203.

92 This and preceding quotations from a draft of Jonathan Loh & David Harmon, *Biocultural Diversity: threatened species, endangered languages* (Zeist: WWF-Netherlands, 2014), are taken from: John Vidal, "As forests are cleared and species vanish, there's one other loss: a world of languages," *The Observer* (8 June 2014). My italics.

## Works Cited

A.A.P. "Australians retain title as world's richest, according to wealth report," *The Guardian* (9 October 2013), http://www.theguardian.com/world/2013/oct/09/australia-worlds-richest (accessed 3 September 2016).

Alderete, Ethel Wara. *The Health of Indigenous Peoples* (Geneva: World Health Organisation, 1999).

Altman, Jon. "Indigenous Communities, Miners and the State in Australia," in *Power, Culture, Economy: Indigenous Australians and Mining*, ed. Jon Altman & David Martin (Canberra: Australian National UP, 2009): 17–49.

Altman, Jon, & Melinda Hinkson. "Very Risky Business: The Quest to Normalise Remote-living Aboriginal People," in *Risk, Welfare and Work*, ed. Greg Marston, Jeremy Moss & John Quiggin (Carlton, Victoria: Melbourne UP, 2010): 185–211.

Australian Indigenous Doctors' Association and Centre for Health Equity Training, Research and Evaluation, UNSW. *Health Impact Assessment of the Northern Territory Emergency Response* (Canberra: Australian Indigenous Doctors' Association, 2010).

Birns, Nicholas. "Ecopoetics 6/7," *Jacket Magazine* 40 (2010), http://jacketmagazine.com/40/r-ecopoetics-rb-birns.shtml (accessed 26 August 2016).

Boren, Zachary Davies. "Australia scraps shark protections – and continues its backwards environment policy," *The Independent* (21 January 2015), http://www.independent.co.uk/environment/australia-scraps-shark-protections–and-continues-its-backwards-environment-policy-9992367.html (accessed 3 September 2016).

Bruce–Lockhart, Anna. "New Dawn for the Aborigines?" *Guardian Weekly* (3 December 2007), https://www.theguardian.com/world/2007/dec/03/australia-human-rights (accessed 3 September 2016).

Carter, Paul. *The Road to Botany Bay: An Exploration of Landscape and History* (1987, Minneapolis: U of Minnesota P, 2010).

Chandler, Michael J., & Christopher E. Lalonde. "Cultural Continuity as a Hedge against Suicide in Canada's First Nations," *Transcultural Psychiatry* 35.2 (June 1998): 191–219.

Clark, Gary. "Environmental Themes in Australian Literature," in *A Companion to Australian Literature since 1900*, ed. Nicholas Birns & Rebecca McNeer (Rochester NY: Camden House, 2009): 429–43.

Cooper, David. *Closing the Gap in Cultural Understanding: Social Determinants of Health in Indigenous Policy in Australia* (Darwin: Aboriginal Medical Services Alliance of the Northern Territory [AMSANT], 2011).

Cornell, Stephen, & Joseph P. Kalt. "American Indian Self-Determination: The Political Economy of a Successful Policy," *The Harvard Project on American Indian Economic Development* (Tucson: University of Arizona, October 2010), http://www.hks.harvard.edu/var/ezp_site/storage/fckeditor/file/pdfs/centersprograms/centers/wiener/wps/Kalt_Cornell_on_American_Indians_for_JOPNA_102010.pdf (accessed 30 August 2016).

Coulthard, Glen. "Place Against Empire: Understanding Indigenous Anti-Colonialism," *Affinities: A Journal of Radical Theory, Culture, and Action* 4.2 (Fall 2010): 79–83.

Cowlishaw, Gillian. "Erasing Culture and Race: Practising 'self-determination,'" *Oceania* 68.3 (March 1998): 145–69.

Davidson, Helen. "Indigenous suicide: 'prevention should focus on cultural reconnection,'" *The Guardian* (17 November 2014), http://www.theguardian.com/australia-news/2014/nov/17/indigenous-suicide-prevention-should-focus-on-cultural-reconnec tion (accessed 3 September 2016).

Devlin–Glass, Frances. "The Eco-Centric Self and the Sacred in Xavier Herbert's *Poor Fellow My Country*," *Journal of the Association for the Study of Australian Literature* 8 (2008): 45–63.

Dirk, Moses A. "Time, Indigeneity, and Peoplehood: The Postcolony in Australia," *Postcolonial Studies* 13.1 (2010): 9–32.

Dockery, Alfred M. "Culture and Well-Being: The Case of Indigenous Australians," *Social Indicators Research* 99.2 (November 2010): 315–32.

Dockery, Alfred M. "Do traditional Culture and Identity Promote the Wellbeing of Indigenous Australians? Evidence From the 2008 NATSISS," in *Survey Analysis for Indigenous Policy in Australia*, ed. Nicholas Biddle & Boyd Hunter (Canberra: Australian National UP, 2012): 281–305.

Dodson, Mick. "My People and Place: Why Does Place Matter?" keynote address at the PPP2 Conference, Sydney, 28–29 April 2003.

Dodson, Patrick. "Whatever Happened to Reconciliation?" in *Coercive Reconciliation: Stabilise, Normalise, Exit Aboriginal Australia*, ed. Jon Altman & Melinda Hinkson (Melbourne: Arena, 2007): 21–29.

Garnett, Stephen T., Bev Sithole, Peter J. Whitehead, C. Paul Burgess, Fay H. Johnston & Tess Lea. "Healthy Country, Healthy People: Policy Implications of Links between Indignous Human Health and Environmental Condition in Tropical Australia," *Australian Journal of Public Administration* 68.1 (2009): 53–66.

Gleeson–White, Jane. "Capitalism versus the Agency of Place: An Ecocritical Reading of *That Deadman Dance* and *Carpentaria*," *Journal of the Association for the Study of Australian Literature* 13.2 (13): 1–12.

Greer, Germaine. *Whitefella Jump Up: The Shortest Way to Nationhood* (London: Profile, 2004).

Griffiths, Michael. "Indigenous Life Writing: Rethinking Poetics and Practice," in *A Companion to Australian Aboriginal Literature*, ed. Belinda Wheeler (Rochester NY: Camden House, 2013): 15–33.

Hall, Rodney. *The Second Bridegroom* (London: Faber & Faber, 1992).

Hallett, Darcy, Michael J. Chandler & Christopher E. Lalonde. "Aboriginal Language Knowledge and Youth Suicide," *Cognitive Development* 22 (2007): 392–99.

Herbert, Xavier. *Poor Fellow My Country* (Sydney: William Collins, 1975).

Hewett, Dorothy. "Legend of the Green Country," in Hewett, *Collected Poems 1940–1995* (1995), http://www.poetrylibrary.edu.au/poets/hewett-dorothy/legend-of-the-green-country-0050048 (accessed 18 August 2016).

Hospital, Janette Turner. *Oyster* (London: Virago, 1997).

House of Representatives Standing Committee on Aboriginal and Torres Strait Islander Affairs. "The Role of Indigenous Languages," *Inquiry into Language Learning in Indigenous Communities* (2012), http://www.aph.gov.au/Parliamentary_Business/ Committees/ House_of_Representatives_Committees?url=atsia/languages2/report.htm (accessed 3 September 2016).

Hughes, Helen. "Aboriginal Homelands," *Counterpoint*, ABC TV (Monday 28 May 2007), http://www.abc.net.au/radionational/programs/counterpoint/aboriginal-homelands/3246514 (accessed 3 September 2016).

Jeffries, Stuart. "The Men Who Made Us Spend Review: the true story of how we became unremitting consumers," *The Guardian* (14 July 2014), https://www.theguardian.com/tv-and- radio/2014/jul/14/the-made-who-made-us-spend-review (accessed 3 September 2016).

Jervis, John. *Transgressing the Modern: Explorations in the Western Experience of Otherness* (Oxford: Blackwell, 1999).

Kacha, Sabine. "The NT Intervention: Does the End Justify the Means?" *Aboriginal and Social Justice Issues* (August 2009), http://stoptheintervention.org/uploads/files_to_download/The-NT Intervention-25-8-2009.pdf (accessed 3 September 2016).

Kinsella, John. "Scapegoats and Feral Cats," in Kinsella, *Spatial Relations: Essays, Reviews, Commentaries, and Chorography*, ed. & intro. Gordon Collier (Cross/Cultures 162; Amsterdam & New York: Rodopi, 2013), vol. 2: 433–37. First published in *Island Magazine* 86 (Winter 2001): 53–58.

Kirmayer, Laurence J., Gregory M. Brass & Caroline L. Tait. "The Mental Health of Aboriginal Peoples: Transformations of Identity and Community," *Canadian Journal of Psychiatry* 45.7 (September 2000): 607–16.

Levene, Mark, & Daniele Conversi. "Subsistence Societies, Globalisation, Climate Change and Genocide: Discourses of Vulnerability and Resilience," *International Journal of Human Rights* 18.3 (2014): 281–97.

Loh, Jonathan, & David Harmon. *Biocultural Diversity: threatened species, endangered languages* (Zeist: WWF-Netherlands, 2014).

McDermott, Robyn, Kerin O'Dea, Kevin Rowley, Sabina Knight & Paul Burgess. "Beneficial Impact of the Homelands Movement on Health Outcomes in Central Australian Aborigines," *Australian and New Zealand Journal of Public Health* 22.6 (1998): 653–58.

Malouf, David. "The Only Speaker of His Tongue," in Malouf, *Antipodes: Stories* (Ringwood, Victoria: Penguin, 1986): 68–72.

Martin, John. "A Dark History," *Arena* 96 (August–September 2008): 17–21.

Martin, Lisa. "Aboriginal cultural laws 'tokenistic,'" *Sydney Morning Herald* (19 April 2011), http://www.smh.com.au/breaking-news-national/aboriginal-cultural-laws-tokenistic-20110419-1dnby.html (accessed 28 August 2015).

Mead, Philip. "The Geopolitical Underground: Alexis Wright's *Carpentaria*, Mining and the Sacred," in *Decolonizing the Landscape: Indigenous Cultures in Australia*, ed. Beate Neumeier & Kay Schaffer (Cross/Cultures 173; Amsterdam & New York: Rodopi, 2013): 185–206.

Merchant, Carolyn. *The Death of Nature: Women, Ecology, and the Scientific Revolution* (New York: HarperCollins, 1980).

Miller, Alex. *Journey to the Stone Country* (London: Hodder & Stoughton, 2002).

Monbiot, George. "Sick of this market-driven world? You should be," *The Guardian* (5 August 2014), https://www.theguardian.com/commentisfree/2014/aug/05/neo liberal ism-mental-health-rich-poverty-economy (accessed 3 September 2016).

Moore, Terry. "Misadventures with Aboriginalism," *Social Identities* 17.3 (2011): 423–41.

Morgan, Sally. *My Place* (Fremantle, WA: Fremantle Arts Centre Press, 1987).

O'Sullivan, Dominic. "Justice, Culture and the Political Determinants of Indigenous Australian Health," *Ethnicities* 12.6 (2012): 687–705.

Oxfam Issue Briefing. *Wealth: Having It All and Wanting More* (Oxford: Oxfam International, January 2015), https://www.oxfam.org/sites/www.oxfam.org/files/file_attachments/ib-wealth- having-all-wanting-more-190115-en.pdf (accessed 3 September 2016).

Plumwood, Val. *Environmental Culture: The Ecological Crisis of Reason* (New York: Routledge, 2002).

Read, Peter, Gary Meyers & Bob Reece, ed. *What Good Condition? Reflections on an Australian Aboriginal Treaty 1986–2006* (Canberra: ANU E-Press, 2006).

Reilly, Rachel E., Joyce Doyleb, Di Bretherton & Kevin G. Rowley. "Identifying Psychosocial Mediators of Health amongst Indigenous Australians for the Heart Health Project," *Ethnicity & Health* 13.4 (September 2008): 351–73.

Richardson, Henry Handel. *Australia Felix* (1917; Sydney: University of Sydney Library, 1997), http://adc.library.usyd.edu.au/data-2/p00041.pdf (accessed 3 September 2016).

Rickard, John. *Australia: A Cultural History* (London: Longman, 1988).

Ritter, David. "Many Bottles for Many Flies: Managing Conflict Over Indigenous People's Cultural Heritage in Western Australia," *Public History Review* 13 (2006): 125–42.

Rose, Deborah Bird. "An Indigenous Philosophical Ecology: Situating the Human," *Australian Journal of Anthropology* 16.3 (2005): 294–305.

Rose, Deborah Bird. *Reports from a Wild Country: Ethics for Decolonisation* (Sydney: U of New South Wales P, 2004).

Rose, Deborah Bird. *Sharing Kinship with Nature: How Reconciliation is Transforming the NSW National Parks and Wildlife Service* (Canberra: Centre for Resource and Environmental Studies, Australian National University, 2003).

Scott, Kim. *Benang: from the heart* (Fremantle, WA: Fremantle Arts Centre Press, 1999).

Scott, Kim. *Kayang and Me* (Fremantle, WA: Fremantle Arts Centre Press, 2005).

Stanner, W.E.H. "After the Dreaming," *The Boyer Lectures 1968* (Sydney: ABC, 1969).

Stanner, W.E.H. *The Dreaming and Other Essays* (Melbourne: Black Inc., 2009).

Strang, Veronica. "Showing and Telling: Australian Land Rights and Material Moralities," *Journal of Material Culture* 5.3 (2000): 275–99.

Strang, Veronica. *Uncommon Ground: Cultural Landscapes and Environmental Values* (Oxford: Berg, 1997).

Sutton, Peter. "After Consensus," *Griffith Review* 21 (2008), http://griffithreview.com/edition-21-hidden-queensland/after-consensus (accessed 3 September 2016).

United Nations. *Declaration on the Rights of Indigenous Peoples* (UNDRIP) (March 2008), http://www.un.org/esa/socdev/unpfii/documents/DRIPS_en.pdf (accessed 3 September 2016).

Vidal, John. "As forests are cleared and species vanish, there's one other loss: a world of languages," *The Observer* (8 June 2014), https://www.theguardian.com/environment/2014/jun/08/why-we-are-losing-a-world-of-languages (accessed 3 September 2016).

Watson, Irene. "In the Northern Territory Intervention: What is Saved or Rescued and at What Cost?" *Cultural Studies Review* 15.2 (September 2009): 45–60.

Winton, Tim. "Acquifer," in Winton, *The Turning* (London: Picador, 2006): 37–53.

Wright, Alexis. *Plains of Promise* (St. Lucia: U of Queensland P, 1997).

Wright, Judith. "Towards the Bicentennial Landscape," in Wright, *Born of the Conquerors: Selected Essays* (Canberra: Aboriginal Studies, 1991): 33–43.

❄

# Weal/th in the Land

## *Re-Imagining Indigenous Land-Use in Australia*

GEOFF RODOREDA

GENERATIONS OF AUSTRALIANS have been taught to think of their country as an empty, uncultivated landmass before the arrival of the British in 1788. Right up until the last decades of the twentieth century, school history books with titles like *The Land They Found* (1983) were in abundance.[1] The title itself encapsulates the myth of Australia as a lost, uninhabited world, only 'found' when the enterprising British went looking for it. In this state-sanctioned text, students are introduced to a quiet, empty land, lying around somewhere in the netherworlds of geography and history, waiting to be discovered and imagined into existence by visionary Europeans. With regard to land – that land the British found – we are told:

> When the white man came to Australia, he found an open country, with huge unfenced areas suitable for grazing and farming. It was only natural that in time men would turn their eyes to this land and want to settle on it.[2]

The British colonizer is cast here as an innocent acquirer of vast holdings that are simply there for the taking. Further, it is the laws of *nature* that compel the white man to do something about what is perceived to be an unproductive wilderness. Texts like *The Land They Found* have continued to propagate what Alastair Pennycook calls "the standard tropes of colonial discourse": tropes describing how "peaceful farmers moved into empty lands with no rivals."[3] For Europeans, Australian soil only contained value when it produced wealth: its

---

[1] Ronald Laidlaw, *The Land They Found: Australian History for Secondary Schools* (1979; South Melbourne: Macmillan, 2nd ed. 1983).

[2] Laidlaw, *The Land They Found*, 110.

[3] Alastair Pennycook, *English and the Discourses of Colonialism* (London: Routledge, 1998): 10.

ownership mapped and delineated with fences, worked over by labourers, cultivated with European seed, and stocked with imported species such as sheep and cattle. A more recent recognition of *Indigenous* land management and ownership regimes only began to emerge in the 1960s and 1970s. The constitutional recognition of Aboriginal Australians in 1967, the activism and creativity of the Aboriginal land-rights movement, the growth of Indigenous poetry, autobiographical writing, and art, and an expansion of research into colonial history and violence on the frontier – this all contributed to a greater acknowledgment of Aboriginal claims to land-use through the 1980s.

Responding to changing perceptions of the environment, nature, and land-use in recent years, both Indigenous and non-Indigenous writers are (re)writing histories of Indigenous land-use, in both fiction and non-fiction. In particular, geographers, historians, archaeologists, and novelists are re-interpreting the journals of colonial-era inland explorers for what they say about Aboriginal management of land. To varying degrees across the continent, these early explorers observed Aboriginal people cultivating the soil, harvesting grain, farming eels and fish, and engaging in animal husbandry on a grand scale; it was labour on the land that the colonial-era writers were unwilling to interpret within the European agricultural framework. Re-interpreting such texts in recent scholarship, Bill Gammage argues that Aboriginal people's extensive and sustained cultivation practices created "The Biggest Estate on Earth."[4] Taking up from Gammage and others, the present essay examines changing perceptions of Aboriginal investment in labour in the land in non-fiction writing and in recent Australian fiction. I begin by tracing a shift from seeing the Aborigines as proprietors of the soil in the early decades of colonization to non-owners and non-cultivators of land beginning in the 1830s. More recently, the landmark Mabo decision, delivered by the High Court of Australia in 1992,[5] has been primarily responsible for once again altering settler perceptions of Aboriginal connections to country and Aboriginal concepts of wealth in the land.

By 'wealth in the land', I specifically mean wealth accruing from resource management *on the surface* of the land, not *underneath* it: that is to say, the changing perceptions of agricultural/farming wealth, and the historical denial of

---

[4] Bill Gammage, *The Biggest Estate on Earth: How Aborigines Made Australia* (Melbourne: Allen & Unwin, 2011).

[5] In *Mabo and Others v. Queensland* (*No.* 2) the High Court found in favour of a claim led by Indigenous Australian Eddie Mabo for customary ownership of his land. In recognizing Mabo's rights, the Court also recognized the native-title rights of all Indigenous Australians prior to British settlement in 1788. As well, native-title rights were deemed by the Court to have remained intact in some places where traditional owners could demonstrate a continuing attachment to land.

its widespread practice by Aboriginal people, rather than wealth extraction through mining and digging. While the extractive industries were also important in solidifying colonial land rights and private property, it was the perception of whether or not Aboriginal people created wealth from agricultural and farming practice – whether they cultivated the soil or not – that became central to arguments that served to deny them proprietorship. The use of the word 'wealth' with regard to Aboriginal land and Aboriginal agricultural produce derived from it is contentious here. Aboriginal people have a "very different ontological relationship to land" from that of non-Aboriginal Australians.[6] Deborah Bird Rose says that Indigenous people think of their land or their 'country' as "nourishing terrain." It is "a place that gives and receives life […] it is lived in and lived with."[7] Therefore, Indigenous Australians do not necessarily possess the land or gather the produce they extract from it in order to acquire commodity assets or monetary forms of 'wealth'; the latter reflects, rather, a Western concept of wealth in the capitalist logic of never-ending accumulation and (re) investment. Instead, to return to the origins of the word 'wealth' and its derivatives, the land yielded (and continues to yield) not so much wealth as *weal*, a "sound, healthy, or prosperous state [of] well-being" for Aboriginal people.[8] Thus, the land itself *is* the wealth rather than a primary resource to be appropriated and used to generate abstracted wealth, which Karl Marx called the "primitive accumulation" that made capitalist relations possible.[9] Furthermore, the land is the principal 'common weal' for indigenous people, which is by definition intended for the "benefit or interests of all members of a […] community."[10] This Indigenous understanding of the land's weal/th has not diminished over time.

Before considering contemporary thinking about Aboriginal land-use, it is important to reconstruct the shift in colonial discourse on Aboriginal ownership of the land that occurred in the early colonial period. When the British arrived in 1788 they did *not* seek to deny Aboriginal proprietorship of the soil, at least

---

[6] Jon Altman, "Indigenous Futures on Country," in *People on Country: Vital Landscapes, Indigenous Futures*, ed. Jon Altman & Sean Kerins (Sydney: Federation Press, 2012): 221.

[7] Deborah Bird Rose, *Nourishing Terrains: Australian Aboriginal Views of Landscape and Wilderness* (Canberra: Australian Heritage Commission, 1996): 7.

[8] "Weal," in *Merriam–Webster* online Dictionary, http://www.merriam-webster.com/dictionary/weal (accessed 1 June 2017).

[9] Karl Marx, *Capital: A Critique of Political Economy*, vol. 1, Part II: *The Process of Capitalist Production* (1867; New York: Cosimo, 2007): 784.

[10] "Common weal," in *Oxford Dictionaries* online, http://www.oxforddictionaries.com/de/definition/englisch/weal (accessed 1 June 2017).

discursively. Denial of Indigenous ownership of the land only began to emerge forty to fifty years after invasion, at precisely the moment when the colonizers needed to justify their sudden and massive seizure of the lush pasturelands of south-eastern Australia.[11] Understanding this earlier shift from token acknowledgement to forceful denial of Aboriginal land ownership is important for two reasons. First, it serves to explain why *terra nullius* became a legally codified doctrine *when* it did. Second, it reveals how adept the colonizer was or is at changing perceptions, altering arguments, and even amending the law to conveniently suit colonizing ends.

Comments by British settlers about Aboriginal people on the land demonstrate they did recognize Indigenous proprietorship of the soil, even if they never respected property rights in practice. Captain John Hunter, within a few months of landing in Sydney in 1788, noted that the Aborigines had "one fixed residence, and the tribe takes its name from the place of their general residence."[12] Sydney's first judge, David Collins, stated: "strange as it may appear, [the Aborigines] have also their real estates," noting that they possessed a "kind of hereditary property, which they retained undisturbed."[13] In 1807, Governor King wrote: "I have ever considered [the Aborigines] the real Proprietors of the Soil."[14] The same line of thinking persists well into the 1820s. A leader article in the *Sydney Gazette* of August 1827 describes the Aborigines as the "original proprietors of the soil," and argues:

> This country has now been established as a dominion of Great Britain for about 40 years, and we have gradually been rising into importance, at the expense of the unfortunate aborigines – the real proprietors of the soil – who [...] are entitled to our warmest sympathies; instead of which we go on urging them further into the interior, thus robbing them of their property.[15]

---

[11] For discussion of the change in perception and its legal repercussions, see Merete Borch, "Rethinking the Origins of Terra Nullius," *Australian Historical Studies* 32.117 (2001): 222–39, and *Conciliation, Compulsion, Conversion: British Attitudes Towards Indigenous Peoples 1763–1814* (Cross/Cultures 72; Amsterdam & New York: Rodopi, 2004.).

[12] John Hunter, *An Historical Journal of the Transactions at Port Jackson and Norfolk Island* [1793], *Project Gutenberg Australia*, http://gutenberg.net.au/ebooks/e00063.html (accessed 1 June 2017): Chapter III.

[13] David Collins, *An Account of the English Colony in New South Wales*, vol. 1 (1798; University of Sydney Library, 2003), online: Appendix IX.

[14] Quoted in Stuart Banner, "Why *Terra Nullius*? Anthropology and Property Law in Early Australia," *Law and History Review* 23.1 (Spring 2005): 116.

[15] Anon., "Three Millions of the Human Family Perishing in the Midst of Plenty!!!," *Sydney Gazette and New South Wales Advertiser* (22 August 1827): 2. *National Library of Australia*, http://

Such statements reflect a general acceptance in the first decades of colonization that Aborigines were the original inhabitants, the owners of the soil, and the proprietors of the land. In none of these early acknowledgments is proprietorship linked to any need for the inhabitants to till the soil or otherwise work on it. Ownership is not conditional on agricultural practice. It is, rather, an *unconditional* recognition that as the original inhabitants of the land the Aborigines are its first possessors and owners.[16]

Throughout the 1820s, however, the colonial economy began to undergo substantial change. Growing demand in England for Australian wool drove the search for more grazing land. Stockholders gradually began moving inland, beyond Sydney, and the number of sheep increased from 100,000 in 1820 to one million by 1830.[17] Meanwhile, in Van Diemen's Land (Tasmania), which had been established as a penal settlement in 1803 and had become a separate British colony in 1825, colonists had largely removed Aboriginal people from the land and set up huge and profitable sheep-farming enterprises. Hungry for more land, a group of entrepreneurs from Van Diemen's Land crossed Bass Strait in 1835 to establish a settlement on the southern coast of the Australian mainland at what is now Melbourne. As the historian James Boyce has argued, it was from this settlement – at first illegal but later sanctioned by colonial authorities – that the richest grazing land of the continent became fully opened up to conquest.[18] The government policy, up to that time, of confining settlement to an official 'limits of location' was abandoned and "the continental land rush began" (xiii). Land-takers, who became known as squatters, seized millions of hectares "of the most productive and best-watered Aboriginal homelands, comprising most of the grasslands" of south-eastern Australia (xiv). As Boyce puts it: "Between 1835 and 1838 alone, more land and more people were conquered than in the preceding half century" (xiii).

---

nla.gov.au/nla.news-page496057 (accessed 1 June 2017).

[16] There were some arguments, voiced in the 1820s, that began to attach conditions to Indigenous proprietorship. In the *Sydney Gazette* in 1824, 'Amicitia' argued the Aborigines had no notion of property as a territorial possession. They merely "wandered about [...] had no civil polity, no regular organized frame of society [...]. They were *inhabitants*, but not the *proprietors* of the land." This statement shows that conceptions of the Aborigines as property owners were at least being contested in the public arena at this time. (See Amicitia, "To the Editor of the Sydney Gazette," *Sydney Gazette and New South Wales Advertiser* [19 August 1824]: 4. National Library of Australia, http://nla.gov.au/nla.news-page494908 [accessed 1 June 2017]. Emphasis in the original.)

[17] Stuart Macintyre, *A Concise History of Australia* (1999; Cambridge & New York: Cambridge UP, 2nd ed. 2004): 57.

[18] James Boyce, *1835: The Founding of Melbourne and the Conquest of Australia* (2011; Collingwood, Victoria: Black Inc., 2012): xiii. Further page references are in the main text.

At the same time as this "frenzied land grab" was underway (xiv), both public discourse on proprietorship of the land began to change, and the law institutionally began the process of dismissing any suggestion that Aboriginal people had a legal claim to land. The key legal decision came in a murder case before the Supreme Court of New South Wales in 1836. British jurisdiction over the Aborigines and their lands was disputed in this murder case, but the judge argued that Aboriginal people had not "appropriated the territory" and that it could therefore be "taken into the King's possession."[19] In another judgement, in 1847, the appropriation of the land was legally backdated: "the waste lands of this colony are, and ever have been, from the time of its first settlement in 1788, in the Crown [...] there is no other proprietor of such lands."[20] It is with these legal decisions that the formation of what later came to be known as *terra nullius* begins to take shape in Australian law.

A change in public discourse on Aborigines and the land is reflected in a letter to the *Sydney Herald* in 1838. The writer dismisses any claims to Aboriginal proprietorship of the soil by contrasting the *use* of land by Indigenous people in North America to that of Indigenous people in Australia: "The American Indians were divided into nations having fixed localities – they cultivated the ground, and understood the right of property." The "natives of New Holland," on the other hand, "bestowed no labour upon the land and that – and *that* only – it is which gives a right of property to it." According to the writer, the land had remained "an unproductive wilderness" until the arrival of the British.[21] The colonial imperative that land be appropriated at whatever cost necessitated new arguments to justify its wholesale seizure from people who were previously acknowledged as rightful owners, regardless of whether they cultivated the soil or not. This change in colonial discourse was eventually reflected in legal doctrine with a Privy Council decision in 1889 that the Australian landmass was "practically unoccupied, without settled inhabitants or settled law" when the British arrived.[22]

The succession of sweeping statements from the 1830s onwards about Aborigines lacking the capacity to cultivate the ground was based on deliberate misreadings of reality. The journals of the inland explorers reveal how Aboriginal

---

[19] *R v Murrell and Bummaree* (1836) 1 Legge 72; NSWSupC 35. *Division of Law, Macquarie University*, http://www.law.mq.edu.au/research/colonial_case_law/nsw/cases/case_index/1836/r_v_murrell_and_bummaree/ (accessed 1 June 2017).

[20] Quoted by Justice Brennan in *Mabo and Others v Queensland* (No. 2) [1992] 107 ALR 1: 16, 17.

[21] Anon., "Crown Lands," *Sydney Herald* (7 November 1838): 2. *National Library of Australia*, http://nla.gov.au/nla.news-page1525292 (accessed 1 June 2017). (Emphasis in original.)

[22] Quoted by Justice Brennan in *Mabo and Others v Queensland* (No. 2) [1992] 107 ALR 1: 24.

people across the continent worked to extract wealth from the soil. The Surveyor-General of New South Wales, Thomas Mitchell, in his *Three Expeditions Into the Interior of Eastern Australia*, reported on Aboriginal people working the land.[23] In what is now western Victoria, Mitchell found "hills round and smooth as a carpet, meadows broad" of either emerald green "or of a rich golden colour, from the abundance" of yam daisy (211). He even saw a woman digging for yams in what he described as "this splendid valley, resembling a nobleman's park on a gigantic scale" (212). This turn of phrase – a nobleman's park – is revealing. A park is *created*. It is manufactured landscape not a product of 'nature'. Aboriginal people had clearly worked this ground; they were seen reaping the rewards of their labour upon the land as Mitchell rode by. Along the Darling River, Mitchell noticed grass that "had been pulled, to a very great extent and piled in hay-ricks" so that it looked like, as he put it, a "hay-field [...] we found the ricks, or hay-cocks, extending for miles" (237). All of this "hay" (native millet) was collected, "not a spike of it was left in the soil, over the whole of the ground" (238). On his final expedition, in 1846, into what is now south-central Queensland, Mitchell acknowledged the considerable effort Aboriginal people had gone to in order to create pasturelands for hunting kangaroo:

> The extensive burning by the natives, a work of considerable labour, [...] left tracts in the open forest, which had become green as an emerald with the young crop of grass. These plains were thickly imprinted with the feet of kangaroos, and the work is undertaken by the natives to attract these animals to such places.[24]

The cultivation of millet, and the making of food from it, was seen by the explorer Augustus Gregory in 1858 on the Cooper Creek in Queensland. He wrote: "Fields of 1,000 acres are there met with growing this cereal."[25] In western Australia, the explorer George Grey saw many square kilometres of fertile land overrun with yams, stretching as far as he could see. He wrote: "[More] had here been done to secure a provision from the ground by hard manual labour than I could have believed it in the power of uncivilized man to accomplish."[26]

---

[23] Thomas Mitchell, *Three Expeditions Into the Interior of Eastern Australia*, vol. 2 (London: T. & W. Boone, 2nd ed. 1839), online. Further page references are in the main text.

[24] Thomas Mitchell, *Journal of an Expedition into the Interior of Tropical Australia* (London: Longman, Brown, Green & Longmans, 1848), online: 306.

[25] Quoted in Rupert Gerritsen, *Australia and the Origins of Agriculture* (Oxford: Archaeopress, 2008): 42.

[26] George Grey, *Journals of Two Expeditions of Discovery in North-West and Western Australia*, vol. 2 (London: T. & W. Boone, 1841), online: 12.

Rupert Gerritsen's *Australia and the Origins of Agriculture* (2008), Bill Gammage's *The Biggest Estate on Earth* (2011), and Bruce Pascoe's *Dark Emu* (2014) are just three works of recent scholarship which draw heavily on the explorers' journals to demonstrate the extent of Aboriginal labour invested in the land.[27] These texts work to counter persistent notions of Aboriginal people as almost exclusively nomadic hunter–gatherers who did not engage in any forms of agriculture.[28] Gerritsen argues that "at the time of the British colonization of Australia at least 19 different species of plant were being cultivated by at least 21 different identifiable indigenous groups."[29] Gammage concludes:

> Agriculture spread more widely over Australia than now [...]. Nothing was accidental or incidental: people acted deliberately to improve quality and yield.[30]

These newer historical narratives of Indigenous land-use reflect a broader paradigm shift that has occurred in Australian society as a result of the 1992 Mabo decision, which overturned the discriminatory colonialist fiction of *terra nullius*. The settler-majority population has had to reconsider its view of Indigenous people's relationship with and proprietorship of the land, just as earlier generations of settlers did in response to historical developments. The Mabo decision has also triggered a re-assessment of representations of Aboriginal land-use in Australian novels published since 1992. Accordingly, I would like to look at just two examples of post-Mabo fiction in which Indigenous peoples' attachment to land and extraction of wealth from the soil are depicted.

Kate Grenville's novel of first settlement, *The Secret River* (2005), represents the land as being occupied, cultivated, and owned by Aboriginal people when

---

27 Eric Rolls might be cited here as a forerunner of the writers of these more recent histories of Aboriginal land use. See, for example, Rolls, "The Nature of Australia," in *Ecology and Empire: Environmental History of Settler Societies*, ed. Tom Griffiths & Libby Robin (Edinburgh: Keele UP, 1997): 35–45.

28 Such persistent notions are found, for example, in Jared Diamond's Pulitzer Prize-winning book *Guns, Germs, and Steel* (1997; London: Vintage, 2005). According to Diamond, Aboriginal people "never reached the stage of farming" (107), but were "evolving in a direction that might have eventuated in food production" (309). Through 'firestick farming', Aborigines "managed the surrounding landscape in ways that increased its production of edible plants and animals, without resorting to cultivation" (309).

29 Rupert Gerritsen, "Evidence for Indigenous Australian Agriculture," *Australasian Science* (July–August 2010): 36.

30 Gammage, *The Biggest Estate on Earth*, 289, 297.

the British arrived.[31] Grenville's protagonist is the convict William Thornhill. After serving out his convict term in Sydney, Thornhill moves with his family to the Hawkesbury River north-west of Sydney to begin a new life as a pioneer farmer on land he considers his for the taking. But, as Eleanor Collins puts it, the "familiar flow and shape of the pioneer myth is regularly interrupted [...] by the appearances of the Darug people, who already live on the Hawkesbury."[32] Conflicts arise over the land, ending in Thornhill's involvement in a violent massacre of the Darug. This massacre is the climax of the novel, situating *The Secret River* as a text that primarily seeks to show how the early settlers violently dispossessed Aboriginal people from their lands.[33] However, my interest in this novel, for the purposes of this essay, is to consider Grenville's portrayal of conflicting concepts of property and weal/th in the soil.

As Thornhill begins the process of farming the land he comes to realize that Aboriginal people are reaping sustenance from the same land with much more aplomb than he is, and that they have been doing so over a much longer period of time. Early on in his time in Sydney, Thornhill is shown to be captive to the myth of believing the Aborigines to be uncivilized savages. "They wandered about, naked as worms" (92), he observes. "They caught their feeds of fish [...] then moved on" (92). Thornhill, initially, does not see the Aborigines as landowners, because for him they are nomads who do not seek to extract wealth from the soil:

---

[31] Kate Grenville, *The Secret River* (New York: Canongate, 2005). Further page references are in the main text.

[32] Eleanor Collins, "Poison in the Flour: Kate Grenville's *The Secret River*," in *Lighting Dark Places: Essays on Kate Grenville*, ed. Sue Kossew (Cross/Cultures 131; Amsterdam & New York: Rodopi, 2010): 168.

[33] *The Secret River* attracted a lot of scholarly attention as it was published at a time of intense public debate over the extent of frontier violence in Australian history, known as the History Wars. For an overview of the History Wars, see Stuart Macintyre & Anna Clark, *The History Wars* (Carlton, Victoria: Melbourne UP, 2004). For a discussion of Grenville's dispute with historians, resulting from Grenville's suggestion that her novel might be superior to historical accounts of first settlement, see Sarah Pinto, "History, Fiction, and *The Secret River*," in *Lighting Dark Places: Essays on Kate Grenville*, ed. Sue Kossew (Cross/Cultures 131; Amsterdam & New York: Rodopi, 2010): 179–97. For Grenville's own rebuttal of the historians' critique, see: "Academic Fictions," *kategrenville.com* (2009), http://kategrenville.com/node/50 (accessed 1 June 2017). Other critical essays include Sue Kossew, "Voicing the 'Great Australian Silence': Kate Grenville's Narrative of Settlement in *The Secret River*," *Journal of Commonwealth Literature* 42.7 (2007): 7–18, and Adam Gall, "Taking/Taking Up: Recognition and the Frontier in Grenville's *The Secret River*," in *Journal of the Association for the Study of Australian Literature* (Special Issue: The Colonial Present, 2008): 94–104.

> There were no signs that the blacks felt the place belonged to them. They had no fences that said *this is mine*. No house that said, *this is my home*. There were no fields or flocks that said, *we have put the labour of our hands into this place*. (93)

Thornhill's view in this work of fiction is, in fact, contradicted by the historical record, which shows that Europeans first saw evidence of Aboriginal land-care and cultivation of the soil on the banks of the Hawkesbury River, the secret river of the book's title. Captain John Hunter was part of an expedition on the Hawkesbury in July 1789. He noted:

> The natives here, appear to live chiefly on the roots which they dig from the ground; for these low banks appear to have been ploughed up, as if a vast herd of swine had been living on them. We put on shore, and examined the places which had been dug, and found the wild yam in considerable quantities.[34]

These murnong or yam daisy are now considered to have been a vital food source for Aboriginal people across large parts of south-eastern and south-western Australia. According to Beth Gott, "Despite a popular view of hunting as the major food source, foods of vegetable origin were important in the diet and were always fallback foods."[35] Roots like murnong "constituted the staple foods [...] available virtually year-round."[36] Lesley Head notes that maintaining a constant yield of murnong required hard work ploughing up the ground: "The continual digging maintained a loose, well-aerated soil, while burning of the grass to better see the aboveground rosettes fertilized the soil and stimulated rapid regeneration."[37]

In *The Secret River*, Grenville places her protagonist in a field of Hawkesbury yam daisies on his first full day as a farmer. At first light, Thornhill is up with his young sons to plant a crop on a strip of ground that is flat and clear of trees. But one of his sons notices that the ground has already been worked over, that a "few daisies lay loose, their thick roots broken" (140). Thornhill's first thought is that some other settler has beaten him to 'his' piece of land. But then he notices the "dirt was not dug in a square, the way a man with a pick would do," and that a fellow settler "would not have left the daisies lying loose in the dirt where they

---

[34] Hunter, *An Historical Journal of the Transactions at Port Jackson and Norfolk Island*, Chapter VI.

[35] Beth Gott, "Indigenous Use of Plants in South-Eastern Australia," *Telopea* 12.2 (2008): 216.

[36] Gott, "Indigenous Use of Plants," 216.

[37] Lesley Head, *Second Nature: The History and Implications of Australia as Aboriginal Landscape* (Syracuse NY: Syracuse UP, 2000): 57.

could grow again, but would have pulled them out and thrown them to one side" (140–41). Thornhill suggests to his sons that moles had probably dug up the ground. However, his son Dick says aloud what his father is also considering: "*It's them savages. Planting them things like you would taters*" (141). Thornhill wonders how this could be, when "everyone knew the blacks did not plant things. They wandered about, taking food as it came under their hand" (141). Uncomfortably challenged by his own very limited experience and understanding, Thornhill responds to the contradiction by telling Dick to shut up.

Thornhill's course of action in this scene – staking out his claim by cultivating the soil on his first day on the land – conveys European colonialist ways of converting space into propertied place. This sense of place was shaped by European political philosophy, which served to rationalize the appropriation of land in the colonization of Australia. In his discussion of property in the seventeenth century, John Locke proposed that: "As much Land as a Man Tills, Plants, Improves, Cultivates, and can use the Product of, so much is his property."[38] For Rousseau, writing in the eighteenth century, property in land was deemed to be precisely what distinguished civilized human beings from the uncivilized:

> The first man who, having enclosed a piece of ground bethought himself of saying 'This is mine,' and found people simple enough to believe him, was the real founder of civil society.[39]

In *The Secret River*, Thornhill never quotes Locke or Rousseau, but is portrayed as beholden to their powerful discourses on ownership of the land. Although he realizes that 'his' field is probably a native yam crop, he refuses to reconcile what he sees with what he 'believes'. He maintains that "like children, [the blacks] did not plant today so that they could eat tomorrow" (141). As a colonial farmer Thornhill cannot acknowledge, at least early on in his experience, that Aboriginal people were labouring over the land, for he may then have to concede that it was their legal property.

However, if Thornhill refuses to believe in Aboriginal yam harvesting, based on what he saw on his first day as a farmer, he realizes that he cannot deny the ingenuity of Aboriginal fire-stick farming practices. One day, the Thornhills see Aboriginal people setting fire to a dry, grassy area near their hut. At first, the family thinks this might be an attack with fire, an attempt to burn them out. But Thornhill notices that this fire "was a different species altogether, a small tame thing" that the Aborigines were controlling (221). Thornhill realizes that this firing of the grass "had the look of a routine that had happened countless times"

[38] Quoted in Head, *Second Nature*, 62.

[39] Quoted in *Second Nature*, 63.

(221). A few days later, it rains and fresh grass begins to grow, turning the blackened earth into a carpet of green, attracting kangaroos to graze (223). Thornhill sees that the Aborigines have established grazing grounds to provide a seasonal supply of fresh meat, and he concludes:

> the blacks were farmers no less than the white men were. But they did not bother to build a fence to keep animals from getting out. Instead they created a tasty patch to lure them in. (229)

Thus, Grenville seeks to discredit European perceptions of the Aborigines as mere wanderers over the land, as people who did not practise any forms of agriculture or animal husbandry. Thornhill comes to realize that particular pieces of land have particular value for specific Aboriginal groups, that the land he is on has already been identified as a wealthy terrain, a rich source of sustenance for those who were there long before him. In the end, none of these realizations leads him to desist from taking part in the massacre. In the violent climax of the novel, Grenville shows the power of nineteenth-century colonizing discourses on race, culture, and property to hold sway over individual insight into Aboriginal use of the land.

Grenville is a non-Aboriginal author seeking to re-imagine managed Aboriginal landscapes from a white-settler perspective. The Aboriginal Noongar author Kim Scott's novel *That Deadman Dance* (2010) is a narrative of Noongar first contact with white settlers in what is now Albany, Western Australia, from 1826 onwards.[40] The story centres on "early, co-operative, black–white relations"[41] in a place referred to by historians as the 'friendly frontier'.[42] Anne Brewster argues that if the frontier was friendly for a time, Scott's novel suggests that "it was so largely because of Noongar hospitality, diplomacy and generosity in offering assistance and labour to the settlers, a diplomacy the settlers did not by and large reciprocate."[43]

Scott mostly presents a local Noongar perspective of frontier relations throughout the novel. The reader becomes acquainted with Aboriginal charac-

---

40 Kim Scott, *That Deadman Dance* (Sydney: Picador, 2010). The following page references are in the main text.

41 Stephen Romei, "Second Dance for Miles Franklin Winner Kim Scott," *The Australian* (23 June 2011), http://www.theaustralian.com.au/news/second-dance-for-miles-franklin-winner-kim-scott/story-e6frg6n6-1226080238431 (accessed 1 June 2017).

42 Kim Scott acknowledges the widespread use of this term in an "Author's Note," explaining that *That Deadman Dance* was "inspired by the history of early contact" in the area of Albany, Western Australia, "a place known by some historians as the 'friendly frontier' " (397).

43 Anne Brewster, "Whiteness and Indigenous Sovereignty in Kim Scott's *That Deadman Dance*," *Journal of the European Association of Studies on Australia* 2.2 (2011): 60.

ters who are connected to their country. At one point in the narrative, Bobby Wabalanginy, the central character, travels away from his home territory by sea to the larger, more-established white settlement of Cygnet River Colony (Perth). As he wanders through country that belongs to another Noongar clan, Wabalanginy notices that the land is not being cared for as it should be:

> Bobby was surprised to see so few signs of birds and wallabies [...] although there were plenty of yams: enough to feed many people and they would soon be ready for digging. He wondered why fire had not yet been put through here. (23)

The land around Cygnet River has been colonized more extensively for a longer period of time, and is falling into a state of disrepair. The observation can only be made by an Aboriginal character visiting 'foreign' Noongar land with knowledge of local and seasonal agricultural practices, an insider position that Scott privileges in his novel. Through Bobby, readers are able to see the upkeep of the land, or its lack of upkeep, through Noongar eyes, interpreted through a Noongar world-view.

Through switches in focalization, Scott also presents the way in which *Wadjela*, white settlers, see the land. Some of them see evidence of Noongar labour in the land, others do not. Dr Cross, for example, sees the land as belonging to the Noongar: "It is their home" (87). He begins to understand Noongar relationships with each other and to the land, explaining to another settler: "Almost everyone seems related, in one way or another. Even to birds and animals, and plants and things in the sea" (39). Cross also notices feats of human engineering in the landscape, such as an elaborate stone weir construction across a river: "Man-made?," he ponders (100). A little later he sees rocks dividing the river to form "what appeared to be a lock such as characterised the rivers of home," and he realizes that these are Noongar-engineered fish traps (104). By contrast, another settler, Geordie Chaine, looks at the same engineering work on the river and sees merely "a set of natural weirs" (363). Chaine first spies the land from a ship and considers it as "Empty, [...] Trackless. Waiting for him" (15). On an expedition inland, he sees soft, fine grass on a plain, and describes it as "almost a cultivated landscape" (47). The newly arrived, entrepreneurial settler has neither the experience nor the desire to understand what he sees around him. Chaine, here, is not willing to concede the possibility that Aboriginal people might have created this grassy plain, that they could have "cultivated" anything. To capitulate to this view would be tantamount to forfeiting the right to claim the land exclusively for himself.

As relations deteriorate between the colonizers and the colonized, the Noongar are depicted as having retained ties to the land and the natural world even though much of it has been stolen from them. Although they are restricted from using the land for hunting and cultivation, for what might be considered the extraction of *wealth*, the land's common *weal* remains integral to their lives. Throughout the novel, the Noongar are portrayed as maintaining an intimate, spiritual connection with the land independently of its use-value. For example, on a trek through his homeland, Wooral is heard to have "addressed the bush as if he were walking through a crowd of diverse personalities, his tone variously playful, scolding, reverential, affectionate" (46). For Wooral, the land has human qualities. Elsewhere, Aboriginal characters are shown to be at one with the land and everything in it. After returning from another journey, Bobby Wabalanginy feels wholly refreshed on reaching home again:

> Bobby closed his eyes, felt the wind tugging at his hair and rushing in the whorls of his ears. Breathed this particular air. *Ngayn Wabalanginy moort, nitjak ngan kaarlak* ... Home. (238)

It is not only "this particular air" that connects Wabalanginy to this particular place but also language. Noongar language, in Scott's text here, is used as soon as Wabalanginy enters home territory, to register connection or re-connection to place that defines an individual's belonging and identity. This intimate connection between people and land is evoked in a moving scene in the final part of the novel. Wabalanginy wakes one morning excited about a ceremonial dance he will take part in later in the day. He can smell the earth, and he feels the blood flow through his body

> connecting him to this place, this perpetual moment. Fingertips tingled, and his body hummed with the voices all around him, of bees, cicadas and crickets; of whispering wind and rustling leaves; of bird song and wingbeat; the creak and hiss of reptiles; the breath and various footfalls of animals; the murmur of waves upon the sand; the exhalation of porpoise and whale; of water welling and spilling playful paths across rock, through and beneath the sand. (334)

A Noongar cosmology is thus depicted in which the body becomes infused with the land and all of the creatures, smells, tastes, and sounds in it. Jane Gleeson-White notes that, in this way, *That Deadman Dance* works to "recover the land through imagination" in foregrounding "the landscape and seascape as active participants in the historical process."[44] This model of an active land clashes

[44] Jane Gleeson-White, "Capitalism versus the Agency of Place: An Ecocritical Reading of *That Deadman Dance* and *Carpentaria*," *Journal of the Association for the Study of Australian Literature* 13.2 (2013): 3.

"with the Western understanding of 'land' as inert territory (*terra nullius*) available for exploitation and profiteering."[45]

This brief examination of representations of an Indigenous sense of place in two historical novels is not meant to imply that Indigenous connection to country is a thing of the past. Aboriginal people in many parts of Australia retain an understanding of, and connection to, weal/th in their land. The social scientist Jon Altman says that economists remain largely ignorant of the wealth being accrued in Aboriginal lands as a result of the "land titling revolution" of recent decades.[46] According to Altman, land-rights legislation and native-title laws have resulted in a "tumultuous shift in Australia from illegal indigenous dispossession [...] to legal repossession."[47] Altman works with Indigenous communities to map land-values, not only with regard to assets but also in consideration of the value of the land for indigenous health, nutrition, sustainable livelihoods, custom, and culture.[48] Even where Aboriginal people do not live on their so-called 'traditional lands', knowledge of country is being revived, maintained, and celebrated. The Indigenous lawyer and activist Irene Watson argues that Aboriginal peoples' relationships to land "are more complex than owning and controlling a piece of property":[49]

> The non-indigenous relationship to land is to take more than is needed, depleting ruwi [land] and depleting self. Their way with the land is separate and alien, unable to understand how it is we communicate with the natural world.[50]

Through acts of state sovereignty, according to Watson,

> The land becomes enslaved and a consumable which is traded or sold in and out of existence. We are the natural world; it is a mirror of our self, our Nunganess [Aboriginality], so how can we sell our self?[51]

Indigenous views of the land, voiced in the writings of Irene Watson and found in the more recent histories of land-use and in the fiction writing examined in

---

45 Gleeson–White, "Capitalism versus the Agency of Place," 3.

46 Jon Altman, "Mapping Indigenous Land Wealth: The Revolution We Had to Have," *Crikey* (4 July 2013), http://www.crikey.com.au/2013/07/04/mapping-indigenous-land-wealth-the-revolution-we-had-to-have/ (accessed 1 June 2017).

47 Altman, "Mapping Indigenous Land Wealth," np.

48 See *People on Country: Vital Landscapes, Indigenous Futures*, ed. Jon Altman & Sean Kerins (Sydney: Federation Press, 2012).

49 Irene Watson, "Buried Alive," *Law and Critique* 13 (2002): 256.

50 Watson, "Buried Alive," 256.

51 Watson, "Buried Alive," 256.

this essay, serve to challenge still-dominant notions of both wealth and land in the Australian public domain. They articulate a way of seeing the land as a source of common weal rather than as a marker of accumulated wealth.

## WORKS CITED

Altman, Jon. "Indigenous Futures on Country," in *People on Country: Vital Landscapes, Indigenous Futures*, ed. Jon Altman & Sean Kerins (Sydney: Federation Press, 2012): 213–31.

Altman, Jon. "Mapping Indigenous Land Wealth: The Revolution We Had to Have," *Crikey* (4 July 2013), http://www.crikey.com.au/2013/07/04/mapping-indigenous-land-wealth - the-revolution-we-had-to-have/ (accessed 1 June 2017).

Altman, Jon, & Sean Kerins, ed. *People on Country: Vital Landscapes, Indigenous Futures* (Sydney: Federation Press, 2012).

Amicitia. "To the Editor of the Sydney Gazette," *Sydney Gazette and New South Wales Advertiser* (19 August 1824), *National Library of Australia*, http://nla.gov.au/nla.news-page494908 (accessed 30 January 2015).

Anon. "Crown Lands," *Sydney Herald* (7 November 1838): 1–4, *National Library of Australia*, http://nla.gov.au/nla.news-page1525292 (accessed 1 June 2017).

Anon. "Three Millions of the Human Family Perishing in the Midst of Plenty!!!," *Sydney Gazette and New South Wales Advertiser* (22 August 1827): 1–4, *National Library of Australia*, http://nla.gov.au/nla.news-page496057 (accessed 1 June 2017).

Banner, Stuart. "Why *Terra Nullius*? Anthropology and Property Law in Early Australia," *Law and History Review* 23.1 (Spring 2005): 95–131.

Borch, Merete. *Conciliation, Compulsion, Conversion: British Attitudes Towards Indigenous Peoples 1763–1814* (Cross/Cultures 72; Amsterdam & New York: Rodopi, 2004).

Borch, Merete. "Rethinking the Origins of *Terra Nullius*," *Australian Historical Studies* 32/117 (2001): 222–39.

Boyce, James. *1835: The Founding of Melbourne and the Conquest of Australia* (2011; Collingwood, Victoria: Black Inc., 2012).

Brewster, Anne. "Whiteness and Indigenous Sovereignty in Kim Scott's *That Deadman Dance*," *Journal of the European Association of Studies on Australia* 2.2 (2011): 60–71.

Collins, David. *An Account of the English Colony in New South Wales*, vol. 1 (1798; University of Sydney Library, 2003) online.

Collins, Eleanor. "Poison in the Flour: Kate Grenville's *The Secret River*," in *Lighting Dark Places: Essays on Kate Grenville*, ed. Sue Kossew (Cross/Cultures 131; Amsterdam & New York: Rodopi, 2010): 167–78.

"Common weal," in *Oxford Dictionaries* online, http://www.oxforddictionaries.com/de/definition/englisch/weal (accessed 1 June 2017).

Cotton, John. *Gods Promise to His Plantation* (1630), in *Electronic Texts in American Studies*, Paper 22 (Lincoln: Libraries at University of Nebraska–Lincoln), online.

Diamond, Jared. *Guns, Germs, and Steel* (1997; London: Vintage, 2005).

Fraser, Morag. "*That Deadman Dance*," *Sydney Morning Herald* (13 January 2011), http://www.smh.com.au/entertainment/books/that-deadman-dance-20110113-19p63.html (accessed 1 June 2017).

Gall, Adam. "Taking/Taking Up: Recognition and the Frontier in Grenville's *The Secret River*," *Journal of the Association for the Study of Australian Literature* (Special Issue: The Colonial Present, 2008): 94–104.

Gammage, Bill. *The Biggest Estate on Earth: How Aborigines Made Australia* (Melbourne: Allen & Unwin, 2011).

Gerritsen, Rupert. *Australia and the Origins of Agriculture* (Oxford: Archaeopress, 2008).

Gerritsen, Rupert. "Evidence for Indigenous Australian Agriculture," *Australasian Science* (July–August 2010): 35–37.

Gleeson–White, Jane. "Capitalism versus the Agency of Place: An Ecocritical Reading of *That Deadman Dance* and *Carpentaria*," *Journal of the Association for the Study of Australian Literature* 13.2 (2013): 1–12.

Gott, Beth. "Indigenous Use of Plants in South-Eastern Australia," *Telopea* 12.2 (2008): 215–26.

Grenville, Kate. "Academic Fictions," in *kategrenville.com* (2009), http://kategrenville.com/node/50 (accessed 1 June 2017).

Grenville, Kate. *The Secret River* (New York: Canongate, 2005).

Grey, George. *Journals of Two Expeditions of Discovery in North-West and Western Australia*, vol. 2 (London: T. & W. Boone, 1841), online.

Head, Lesley. *Second Nature: The History and Implications of Australia as Aboriginal Landscape* (Syracuse NY: Syracuse UP, 2000).

Hunter, John. *An Historical Journal of the Transactions at Port Jackson and Norfolk Island* [1793], *Project Gutenberg Australia*, http://gutenberg.net.au/ebooks/e00063.html (accessed 1 June 2017).

Kossew, Sue. "Voicing the 'Great Australian Silence': Kate Grenville's Narrative of Settlement in *The Secret River*," *Journal of Commonwealth Literature* 42.7 (2007): 7–18.

Laidlaw, Ronald. *The Land They Found: Australian History for Secondary Schools* (1979; South Melbourne: Macmillan, 2nd ed. 1983).

*Mabo and Others v Queensland (No. 2)* [1992] 107 ALR 1.

Macintyre, Stuart. *A Concise History of Australia* (1999; Cambridge & New York: Cambridge UP, 2nd ed. 2004).

Macintyre, Stuart, & Anna Clark, ed. *The History Wars* (Carlton, Victoria: Melbourne UP, 2004)

Marx, Karl. *Capital: A Critique of Political Economy*, vol. 1, Part II: *The Process of Capitalist Production* (1867; New York: Cosimo, 2007)

Mitchell, Thomas. *Journal of an Expedition into the Interior of Tropical Australia* (London: Longman, Brown, Green & Longmans, 1848), online.

Mitchell, Thomas. *Three Expeditions Into the Interior of Eastern Australia*, 2 vols. (London: T. & W. Boone, 2nd ed. 1839), online.

Pascoe, Bruce. *Dark Emu, Black Seeds: Agriculture or Accident?* (Broome, WA: Magabala, 2014).

Pennycook, Alastair. *English and the Discourses of Colonialism* (London: Routledge, 1998).

Pinto, Sarah. "History, Fiction, and *The Secret River*," in *Lighting Dark Places: Essays on Kate Grenville*, ed. Sue Kossew (Cross/Cultures 131; Amsterdam & New York: Rodopi, 2010): 179–97.

*R v Murrell and Bummaree* (1836) 1 Legge 72; NSWSupC 35. *Division of Law, Macquarie University*, http://www.law.mq.edu.au/research/colonial_case_law/nsw/cases/case_index/1836/r_v_murrell_and_bummaree/ (accessed 1 June 2017).

Rolls, Eric. "The Nature of Australia," in *Ecology and Empire: Environmental History of Settler Societies*, ed. Tom Griffiths & Libby Robin (Edinburgh: Keele UP, 1997): 35–45.

Romei, Stephen. "Second Dance for Miles Franklin Winner Kim Scott," *The Australian* (23 June 2011), http://www.theaustralian.com.au/news/second-dance-for-miles-franklin-winner-kim-scott/story-e6frg6n6-1226080238431 (accessed 1 June 2017).

Rose, Deborah Bird. *Nourishing Terrains: Australian Aboriginal Views of Landscape and Wilderness* (Canberra: Australian Heritage Commission, 1996).

Scott, Kim. *That Deadman Dance* (Sydney: Picador, 2010).

Watson, Irene. "Buried Alive," *Law and Critique* 13 (2002): 253–69.

"Weal," in *Merriam–Webster* online Dictionary, http://www.merriam-webster.com/dictionary/weal (accessed 1 June 2017).

❄

# Indigenous Degrowth and Global Capitalism

## *Exploring Notions of Development in New Zealand Literature*

Paola Della Valle

The economic crisis that has affected the Western world in the past decade demands a serious reflection on the notion of development. The 2008 debacle of international finance and subsequent global recession exposed serious flaws in the dominant doctrines of the capitalist economic model. Capitalism is based on the central idea that development consists in endless economic growth. Political leaders in Europe and the USA keep claiming that the only way to get out of the present quagmire is by rekindling growth and helping the GDP (Gross Domestic Product) to increase. However, the GDP, which uses growth as an indicator of a country's per-capita wealth, is an abstract parameter in which growth is an incontrovertible value. This forgets that the earth and its resources are finite and ignores the negative side-effects of profit-seeking on pollution, resource depletion, and the creation of inequality, as the profits and rewards are retained in the hands of the few. Among the various arguments against GDP measurement and the privileging of growth as the best indicator of economic wellbeing, 'degrowth' theory has been gaining traction, particularly since the 2008 global crisis. Originating in the early 1970s from the ideas of the European social philosophers Ivan Illich, André Gorz, and Cornelius Castoriadis, and the economist François Partant,[1] degrowth promotes the passage to an economic system based on a radically different notion of progress and welfare. This concept has many elements in common with the view of indigenous peoples from different parts of the earth regarding their approach to the environment, social relationships, and development. In the context of

[1] Serge Latouche, *La scommessa della descrescita* (*Le pari de la décroissance*, 2006; Milan: Feltrinelli, 2007): 10.

Aotearoa New Zealand, this vision is elucidated in the novels *Potiki* and *Dogside Story* by the Māori writer Patricia Grace (1937–), as well as in the earlier works of two Pākeha[2] New Zealanders, Roderick Finlayson (1904–92) and Noel Hilliard (1929–97), who published most of their writings before the great wave of the Māori Renaissance in the 1970s. Both Finlayson and Hilliard had lived in close contact with Māori communities; it is no accident that they became harsh critics of the Western concept of development ahead of their time.

This essay offers a brief exploration of degrowth theory before turning to works by the above-mentioned authors in order to highlight the affinities between degrowth and the Māori view. My point is to show how a number of Western thinkers who question the viability of the growth-based capitalist system introduced to the 'New World' by European colonization have reached conclusions indirectly entailing a re-valorization of values and principles that constitute the cultural basis of indigenous communities repressed by the dominant economic structures. The cultural importance of this system of values for Māori people today is evidenced by the application of some of its ideologies in Māori business, particularly in the 'Economy of Mana', an ethically based economic model that conjugates the historical Māori view of business with a will to succeed and thrive in the present.

The economist Kenneth Boulding's ironic aphorism "Anyone who believes that exponential growth can go on forever in a finite world is a madman, or an economist" succinctly illustrates resistance to the dominant economic espousal of growth.[3] Certainly even today, in the light of the 2008 crisis, most economists still believe that there is no other way to overcome the current impasse of growth but growth itself. Serge Latouche, one of the leading thinkers of *décroissance*, argues the contrary. A French academic and economist, Latouche has long rejected the Western myth of an assumed superiority of the West on account of its modernity. Instead, Latouche reasons,

> while the grand society has allowed a great number of people to escape from conditions that seem subhuman to us, it also condemns a greater number of people to a radically inhuman condition than any other society found in history.[4]

---

[2] 'Pākeha' means a New Zealander of European origin as opposed to Māori.

[3] Maurizio Pallante, "What Is Degrowth?," Movimento per la Decrescita Felice (Happy Degrowth Movement): 2, http://decrescitafelice.it/wp-content/uploads/Degrowth.pdf (accessed 20 October 2016).

[4] Serge Latouche, *In the Wake of the Affluent Society: An Exploration of Post-Development*, intro. & tr. Martin O'Connor & Rosemary Arnoux (*La Planète des naufragés: Essai sur l'après-développement*, 1991; London: Zed, 1993): 87. See also Latouche, *The Westernization of the World: Signi-*

Capitalism has created enormous and increasing disparities between the Global North and South. It is producing a "Fourth World International" in the neighbourhoods of the North itself; that is, the cross-national mass of

> our own disinherited, our own unclaimed baggage, our outcasts, our marginals. The wounded and the victims of development [who] are before our doors; [...] we run into them in our own backyards.[5]

Latouche's claims are supported by statistical evidence: in 1970, the richest twenty percent of the world population earned thirty times the income of the poorest twenty percent; in 2004, the gap has become seventy-four to one. In 1960, twenty percent of the world population earned seventy percent of the total world income, thirty years later they earned eighty-three percent.[6] Widespread inequalities are also present in Western societies, where the gulf between the rich and the poor keeps widening. As reported by the *Wall Street Journal*, in the USA

> wealth inequality has deepened over time. The top three percent held 54.4 percent of all wealth in 2013, up from 44.8 percent in 1989. The bottom 90 percent held 24.7 percent of wealth last year [2013], down from 33.2 percent in 1989.[7]

According to Latouche, Western capitalism and liberal economy preach the emancipation of human beings from poverty through progress and advanced technology, but the focus on material prosperity, productivity, and infinite growth chains people to a logic of profit, the aim of which seems to be the perpetuation of the system itself rather than the welfare of people. Growth economics necessarily devalue anything that cannot be traded in hard cash as a distraction from productivity. Accordingly, it fosters competition over cooperation and solidarity. The logic of growth is based on a merely quantitative evaluation and does not take into account fundamental aspects of human life such as spirituality, creativity, and 'relational goods', a term that refers to assets or goods that may not produce profit or contribute to increasing the GDP, but which

---

*ficance, Scope and Limits of the Drive Towards Global Uniformity* (*L'occidentalisation du monde: Essai sur la signification, la portée et les limites de l'uniformisation planétaire*, 1989; Cambridge: Polity, 1996): passim.

[5] Latouche, *In the Wake of the Affluent Society*, 235–36.

[6] Latouche, *La scommessa della descrescita*, 37.

[7] Ben Leubsdorf, "Fed: Gap Between Rich, Poor Americans Widened During Recovery," *Wall Street Journal* (4 September 2014), http://www.wsj.com/articles/fed-gap-between-rich-poor-americans-widened-during-recovery-1409853628 (accessed 25 July 2015).

satisfy one's material or emotional needs. Latouche claims that growth measures 'well-having' (affluence and monetary value) rather than 'wellbeing'. Growth economy discourages productive self-sufficiency, self-sustainability, and non-market exchanges.

It is important to stress that degrowth does not mean recession. The privative prefix 'de' may evoke a negative connotation, but what decreases is not necessarily bad. If cancer decreases, it is good news; if you are on a diet and lose weight, it is a positive result. In Latin America, desirable degrowth has been called '*buen vivir*' (a good life). Degrowth must not be seen as a denial of progress and technology; rather, it signifies a selective choice of what is good and useful in them. The first and most important aspect is the passage from a quantitative to a qualitative criterion in economy. This entails valorizing 'relational goods', conviviality, solidarity, gift, and reciprocity that may not contribute to increasing GDP but may be fulfilling on other levels of social interaction that consumerism ignores, including the cultural, emotional, and spiritual. It means de-globalizing and re-localizing, retrieving know-how and practical competence instead of inducing people to buy everything in the form of commodities. It means encouraging cooperation and economic self-sufficiency, differentiating and integrating people's abilities and roles, and thereby rejecting the orthodoxy of what Latouche calls 'growthism', as if this were a faith or quasi-religion highlighting the quasi-worship of capitalist economics. Degrowth also implies that we should not dedicate the most and best of our energies to productivity and competition, but should learn to appreciate values such as free time, social relationships, cultural experiences, and being part of a community.

Maurizio Pallante, the best-known Italian degrowth theorist, points out that even for Simon Kuznets, who devised the GDP indicator in the context of the 1929 crash, GDP was never meant to be an indicator of wellbeing. Pallante's argument is based on a distinction between the Italian words *merci* and *beni*. The term *merci* can be translated both as 'goods' and as 'commodities': tradable products, produce, and merchandise. By contrast, *beni* is only apparently similar to 'goods' (both words retaining their root *bene* or 'good'), because it means merchandise, possessions, and property (as in English) but also valuable things and services that meet a need or satisfy a desire but cannot be bought or sold (for example, love, affection, relational or cultural assets). He then argues that GDP includes *merci* (goods) that are not *beni* and excludes *beni* that cannot be obtained as *merci* (goods) – in other words, that cannot be bought. The GDP is therefore a monetary indicator and can only account for the economic value of commodities exchanged for money during a specified time period, not for the real living condition of people or the quality of their life.[8]

Whereas Latouche coined the term 'well-having' to define what was measured according to growth logic, Pallante prefers the expression 'much-having' and describes it as follows:

> An economy focused on 'much-having' cannot but generate 'ill-being,' as industrial growth presupposes an increase in the consumption of commodities, so people are conditioned to conceive that buying things is the only purpose in life, to never be content with what they already have, to discard newly bought items more and more rapidly in exchange for even newer products which become available, to consider each innovation an improvement without which they can never be happy, and to envy those who possess more.[9]

Whereas the double meaning of the Italian word *beni* is still present in corresponding terms in other Latinate languages, such as Spanish and French *bien*, the English word 'goods' has completely lost the idea that something valuable, important, and necessary can be available without charge. To evoke Adam Smith's distinction, the "value in use" of any item has been wholly overshadowed by its "value in exchange."[10] Arguably, this may be attributed to the early emergence of a liberal capitalist economy in Great Britain and/or to the Calvinist-Puritan persuasion of the middle class promoting it.

Degrowth theory overcomes the left/right dualism that has characterized the political arena since the advent of the Industrial Revolution and capitalism. Latouche criticizes capitalism as well as Marxism, liberal and socialist economies alike, since in his view they still belong to the same cultural paradigm. Marxism promotes a different distribution of wealth but within the same productive system. Growth is even reinforced within a socialist or state economy, in which productivism is encouraged and directed at state or national development. Latouche's vision of degrowth and his practical programme for an alternative society are also more radical than many ideas of sustainable or 'green'

---

[8] Pallante, "What Is Degrowth?," 2–3. Pallante is the author of several books on the topic of degrowth. He is also the founder of MDF, Movimento per la Decrescita Felice (Happy Degrowth Movement), a very active, non-political, militant organization, promoting degrowth principles in theory and practice. MDF is the main point of reference of degrowth in Italy.

[9] "What Is Degrowth?," 3.

[10] Adam Smith, *The Wealth of Nations*, in *The Works of Adam Smith*, vol. 2 (London: Cadell & Davies, 1812): 42.

development that do not dare reject the capitalist model.[11] His notion of the shared good severely limits or removes 'diseconomies' – costs incurred by the activity of one player but borne by the community at large. These include internalizing transport costs, relocalizing all forms of activity, especially participation in local community politics, returning to small-scale farming, reducing energy waste, re-orienting scientific and technical research according to new aspirations, and stimulating the production of "activities that depend on strong interpersonal relationships" rather than on the exploitation of resources.[12] While these suggestions are anathema to current capitalist political economy, many resonate with indigenous practices, values, and beliefs. As the environmentalist Paul Hawken contends,

> indigenous cultures may show us an image of a future by which we can escape our present. If a culture does not become like us, it may not be a failure but a *gift* to what is now an uncertain future.[13]

Hawken points to the converging objectives of environmentalists and indigenous populations in agitating against "a global economy hooked on *growth*" that can only conceive of native lands as "sources of natural gas, oil, nuclear waste disposal sites, and deposits of coal, timber, water, and minerals"[14] or as potential tourist resorts developed and run by multinational corporations. The defence of these territories by native peoples is aimed at their own cultural and material survival, grounded in an intimate relationship to the land, in a convivial life in small self-sufficient communities, and in experiential knowledge "diligently gleaned from generations of interaction with the natural world."[15] In the Māori context, Hawken argues that the Treaty of Waitangi Settlements, which have increased Māori control of land and income, are one such positive result of historical battles against assimilation and global homogeneity.[16] The American activist is not advocating the return to a pristine pre-colonial and pre-industrial past. However, Hawken thinks that indigenous diversity can become a model to

---

[11] The British degrowth scholar Tim Jackson, for example, argues that while moving from heavy industry to services, using renewable energy, recycling, or increasing energy and material efficiency may reduce the usage of finite natural resources, they only delay the expenditure of the reserves at our disposal. Jackson, *Prosperity Without Growth* (London: Earthscan, 2009): 67–86.

[12] Latouche, "The Globe Downshifted," *Le Monde diplomatique*, http://mondediplo.com/2006/01/13degrowth (accessed 24 July 2014).

[13] Paul Hawken, *Blessed Unrest* (New York: Penguin, 2008): 99. (My emphasis.)

[14] Hawken, *Blessed Unrest*, 102–103. (My emphasis.)

[15] *Blessed Unrest*, 100.

[16] *Blessed Unrest*, 113.

recuperate values lost to Western civilization, including the non-monetary valuation of natural resources: this is the *gift* outlined above. They can help Western people embrace an economic and ontological system relevant for humankind as a whole, and question the materialistic view encouraged by capitalism. Patricia Grace depicts such a gift in her fiction.

The first Māori woman to publish a book (*Waiariki and Other Stories*, 1975), Grace describes the conditions causing a minority group to risk physical and cultural extinction and reconstructs the spirit of *Māoritanga* (cultural heritage). Her writings constitute political weapons to affirm the right of Māori to self-determination, but also convey an alternative view of development, which involves notions of wellbeing and welfare close to degrowth principles. They forcefully criticize the logic of growth for growth's sake, promote small-scale local economy, and attribute great importance to social, creative, and spiritual needs in determining the right balance between individuality and membership in a community. *Potiki* (1986), probably her most 'militant' work, opposes two economic and ontological views: the materialistic arrogance of a corporation against a small self-sustaining Māori community. The novel reflects the rise of Māori activism in the mid-1970s and, in effect, calls upon Māori people to take their destiny into their own hands. The later *Dogside Story* (2001) similarly advocates for local and traditional values that conflict with modern desires for money-making opportunities and openness to globalization. Besides conveying a political and ecological message, both stories are framed in Māori myth or legend, which contextualizes the events and interacts with the story in the present. Myth anchors and gives meaning to the community's belonging to their home territory, which is typical of Māori holistic culture, in which myth and history overlap.

*Potiki* tells of a rural extended family, the Tamihanas, holding on to the 'old ways' and selecting from modernity what they find useful or necessary. They apply a form of subsistence-economy model, which allows them to be self-sufficient in a period of economic crisis and unemployment, without losing their cultural bearings. Instead of joining the urban proletariat of mainstream Pākeha New Zealand, they have re-established vegetable gardens, using the agricultural knowledge handed down to them by their elders, and supplemented by the modern implements of tractor and truck. Their sources of sustenance are agricultural produce, which they also sell at the market, and the fish they catch in the sea, which is still unpolluted and not over-fished. Every member – including the very young, the elders, and the disabled – plays a part in and can be useful to the community. Everyone is seen as an individual and has something to give in his/her uniqueness. Old skills such as carving and weaving are revalued and taught to the young by the elders. The family have also built a *wharenui* (meeting-house) according to tradition, and use it as a community centre for social gatherings, celebrations, and the sharing of stories. These include accounts of experiential knowledge, songs about the land and their ancestors, and tales learnt at school or derived from current events.[17] Mediating between past and present, tradition and modernity, the *whanau* (extended family) chooses what nurtures their wellbeing and their identity as Māori. Typically, they sell their cars, because there is no money for repairs, but keep the truck and tractor. When their televisions break down, they save the expense of fixing them and instead support one of their members studying law (106). Thus, the community seems to follow degrowth principles: a selective choice of what progress offers; self-sustainable production and economic autonomy; the retrieval of experiential know-how and practical competence; close interaction between its members, who are treated as individuals (not consumers), feel part of a community, and are tied to one another by bonds of reciprocity and conviviality; and the valorization of creative and spiritual values, as shown by the building of the *wharenui* and the revival of time-honoured skills.

The life of the community proceeds smoothly until private developers, represented by the evocatively named 'Dollarman', start building a tourist resort in the neighbourhood and try every possible way, legal and illegal, to force the Tamihanas to sell some of their land for them to obtain better access to the site under development. The community turns down Dollarman's million-dollar offer. In response, the developers flood the community vegetable gardens and graveyard, set fire to the meeting-house, and finally place a bomb at the rebuilt *wharenui*, which kills the last-born, or *potiki*, of the family. The symbolic destruction of their source of material sustenance and subsequently of their spiritual and cultural sites is followed by physical assault, as the final challenge to the Māori philosophy of acceptance, prompting Potiki's sister Tangimoana, representative of a new, reactive, and activist attitude, to launch a counter-attack that effectively calls a halt to Dollarman's invasive and criminal enterprise. Dollarman's attack on the structures ensuring the community's economic independence, the sites providing nurture to their social and spiritual life, and the natural environment in which the community lives imposes a material logic by force, taking for granted the superiority of the growth paradigm and excluding the existence of 'goods' that cannot be traded or merchandized as commodities but have an absolute value in use, such as an unpolluted environment, econo-

---

17 Patricia Grace, *Potiki* (1986; Honolulu: U of Hawai'i P, 1995): 37–41. Further page references are in the main text.

mic self-sustainability, the sense of belonging to a community. In depicting two contrasting visions of development, wellbeing, and wealth during the encounters between Dollarman's delegates and the community, the novel validates the latter's rejection of Dollarman's lucrative offer as an endorsement of a form of progress impossible for the Pākehā developer to envisage. Aware of the futility of even trying to explain their idea of progress to an outsider like Dollarman, they resign themselves to the fact that their values are incomprehensible to him. "Not to you. Not in your eyes," they concede, adding, "But what we're doing is important. To us. To us that's progress" (90).

This crucial difference between Māori and Pākeha ways of viewing progress is reinforced by a Māori spokesman who explains how the proposed venture would result in his people's regression rather than their advancement and accuses Dollarman of failing to look to the future and "looking back, looking back, all the time" (90) because of his mistaken assumption that land development has yet to happen, when in reality the Māori way of using their land sustainably has long formed the basis of their own development. The final part of the dialogue throws into relief the contrast between the Western notion of land as property to be developed and exploited for material gain and the spiritual and conservative Māori attitude recognizing also the vital cultural importance of the 'land':

> "I didn't expect you to be so unreasonable…."
>
> "Unreasonable? Perhaps it is yourself that is being unreasonable if you think we would want pollution of the water out there, if you think we would want crowds of people, people that can afford caviare and who import salmon, coming here and using up the fish…."
>
> "And jobs…."
>
> "As we've told you, we have work. You want us to clean your toilets and dig your drains or empty your rubbish bins but we've got more important…."
>
> "I didn't say … And I wasn't … And you're looking back, looking back, all the time."
>
> "Wrong. We're looking to the future. If we sold out to you, what would we be in the future?"
>
> "You'd be well off. You could develop land, do anything you want."
>
> "I tell you if we sold to you we would be dust. Blowing in the wind." (93)

To use Latouche and Pallante's categories, the *iwi* spokesman affirms the primacy of 'quality' over 'quantity', 'wellbeing' over 'well-having' or 'much-having', 'the good' over 'goods'. He underscores the moral responsibility that his people have for the environment and the generations to come, and how their mode of living would affect cultural identity. He also realizes that the job opportunities produced by Dollarman's markedly Western model of progress would only result in a regression like that of Johnny Wairua, the eponymous hero of one of Finlayson's stories, who undergoes a tragic change from working his own land to being a waged undertaker.[18]

Set in 1999, in the same kind of rural environment on the east coast of New Zealand's North Island as *Potiki*, Grace's novel *Dogside Story* explores the life of a community swiftly diminishing as its members leave for urban areas in search of employment. One plot strand revolves around a fraud first devised by a Pākeha con-artist and then adopted and exploited by the Māori community themselves. The fraud entails using Māori property and renting it as campsites to tourists wanting to be the first people in the world to see the dawn of the New Millennium.[19] The idea proves profitable and allows the community to finance the construction of a new *wharekai* (dining-hall). In Grace's shift from rejecting Western development outright, in *Potiki*, to harnessing competitive profit-making ventures for their own ends, in *Dogside Story*, the critic Holly Walker claims that the author moves from a post-development approach to one of participatory development. While degrowth theory belongs to the former, rejecting development discourse that does not take into consideration factors like resourcefulness, environmental impact, or democracy, participatory development may be seen as an inflection of traditional development, managed by local communities that possess a large degree of autonomy.[20] Another way of reading the Māori relationship to growth economics is to acknowledge the possibilities of Māori development through the appropriation of Western tools to advance traditional beliefs and cultural values. In the Millennium Business in *Dogside Story*, a one-off venture pursued for a specific purpose, Grace encourages the use of Western development models only as a last resort. Renegotiating a form of development aligned especially with the Māori principle of respect for the environment, the model implied in *Dogside Story* is closer to post-development than to participatory development, insofar as it effectively resists the logic of profit for profit's sake. After all, the *kaupapa* or purpose is that of financing the

---

[18] Roderick Finlayson, *Brown Man's Burden and Later Stories* (Auckland: Auckland UP, 1973).

[19] The Gisborne area in New Zealand is supposed to be the first place in the world to see the sunrise. For this reason it was inundated with tourists from all over the world on New Year's Eve 1999.

[20] Holly Walker, "Developing Difference: Attitudes towards Maori 'Development' in Patricia Grace's *Potiki* and *Dogside Story*," *Kunapipi* 27.2 (2005): 216–18.

*wharenui*, a decision guided democratically by a communal *hui* or assembly, and limited in its impact on the environment.

Grace's two stories experiment with different beliefs in and uses of capitalist accumulation that contemporary Māori communities are confronted with. Seduced by New Zealand's embrace of global neoliberalism, Māori have become increasingly savvy in business, particularly following Waitangi Tribunal reparations that have in many cases paid out multi-million dollar lump sums, and in capitalizing on culture through regulating the Māori brand, Toi Iho, and intellectual property rights.[21] Māori have been encouraged to apply a capitalist logic in their business practices. A controversial example is that of Ngāi Tahu, the main tribe in the South Island, with 33,000 signed-up members, many of whom live outside the tribal territory, elsewhere in New Zealand or in Australia. Following a compensation settlement of $170 million in 1998, the tribe invested in tourism, property, seafood businesses, and shares, seeing its total assets grow to $400 million by 2004.[22]

Ngāi Tahu's interests reflect cosmopolitanism as much as tribal identity. The tribe is likely to become a global corporate over the next fifty years and to enter into business partnerships with international companies on the global market. Jeffrey Sissons underlines the controversial nature of such business practices:

> cultural nationalists in New Zealand, Hawai'i, Canada, the United States and Latin America have vigorously denounced this tribal capitalism and its right-leaning ideology. Market forces and individualism, it is argued, are the very antithesis of fundamental indigenous values such as co-operation and kin-group belonging.[23]

On the other hand, Ngāi Tahu's attempts to incorporate Māori values into their corporate management illustrate the constant negotiation at work in indigenous modernity. Ngāi Tahu's Board of Directors is organized as a *runanga* or tribal council, in which decision-making and the distribution of wealth are organized through linkages between the tribe's urban-based leaders and its eighteen rural communities.[24] The corporation also targets health, education,

---

[21] Toi Iho is the registered and globally recognized trademark of quality and authenticity of Maori art and artists.

[22] Jeffrey Sissons, *First Peoples: Indigenous Cultures and Their Future* (London: Reaktion, 2005): 152–53.

[23] Sissons, *First Peoples*, 153.

[24] See Ngāi Tahu's website, http://ngaitahu.iwi.nz/te-runanga-o-ngai-tahu/(accessed 20 October 2016).

savings, and housing improvements for its members, which includes funding scholarships, pension schemes, and the underwriting of home loans.[25]

The considerable controversy over and contestation of Māori business management practices[26] such as those of Ngāi Tahu points to complex issues at the heart of assumptions about indigenous authenticity, attachment to tradition, engagement with change, and assimilation to Western norms and expectations. In particular, their adoption of capitalistic business models is assumed to clash with expectations of indigenous sustainability and communalism.

Manuka Henare's concept of the Economy of Mana, which conjugates employment and wealth-creation with Māori ethical and cultural values, comes close to the philosophy of degrowth. For Henare, tradition informs the discussion of what constitutes the ethical and moral basis of a 'good life', which is the ultimate purpose of economic activity and business for Māori people. Their notion of development involves the enhancement of the four wellbeings according to *Māoritanga* – spiritual, environmental, socio-cultural or kinship, and economic – because the indigenous developmental approach "will consider the whole, dynamic, cyclic nature of spiritual, human and environmental ecologies."[27] This implies reformulating indicators to quantify the development of enterprises and to measure performance, assess risk, and reduce cost, which also means re-organizing the value-system in qualitative as well as quantitative terms. Henare explains that the Māori economy has undergone a remarkable development since the 1970s, particularly with regard to small-to-medium enterprises, which constituted ninety-seven percent of the total business in 2010, with an asset base of $36.9 billion.[28] He adds that new models of doing business have risen in the twenty-first century for indigenous people that meet their customary requirements. In particular, social enterprises, social businesses, and business groups represent a better way to understand capital,

---

[25] See Ngāi Tahu, "Whanau: Holistic Wellbeing," http://ngaitahu.iwi.nz/whanau/and "Mata ruanga: Education," http://ngaitahu.iwi.nz/education/ (accessed 4 June 2017).

[26] For a Māori analysis of Maori business models, see Pita Sharples, "Needs Analysis: Maori Business and Management," *Maori Qualifications Services*(December 2013), http://www.nzqa.govt.nz/assets/qualifications-and-standards/qualifications/Bus-qual-review/FINAL-Maori-Business-Needs-Analysis.pdf, Annette Sykes, "2010 Bruce Jesson Lecture," http://www.brucejesson.com/?page_id=349, and Hautahi Kingi, "Illuminating Inequality," in *The Piketty Phenomenon: New Zealand Perspectives* (Wellington: Bridget Williams, 2014): 42–47.

[27] Manuka Henare, "Lasting Peace and Good Life: Economic Development and the 'Ata noho' Principle of Te Tiriti o Waitangi," in *Always Speaking: The Treaty of Waitangi and Public Policy*, ed. Veronica M.H. Tawhai & Katarina Gray–Sharp (Wellington: Huia, 2011): 435.

[28] Henare, "Lasting Peace and Good Life," 426–28.

investment, and development and, ultimately, of "humanising capitalism."[29] They create "markets with meaning" and pursue "profits with purpose." Henare concludes that, while according to the capitalist approach to business "profit is the end in itself and capital buys labour," the social enterprise mode of business "views profit as a means to an end and labour buys capital."[30]

Many of the principles enunciated in Henare's article "Lasting Peace and Good Life" are identifiable as principles of degrowth: they are socially oriented rather than profit-oriented, attentive to spiritual and affective needs as well as material aspects, concerned about the environment, and focused on wellbeing. The essay affirms "the ability to be diversely authentic,"[31] which, in Sissons's words, consists in a repossession of Māori agency and the search for a Māori economy in a globalized market. It is precisely in this respect that the search for balance between tradition and modernity in Grace's novels gestures towards such an economy.

Consideration of the interplay between Western capitalist and traditional indigenous social formations is not, however, a recent phenomenon, nor is it confined to Māori interests. Throughout the mid-twentieth century, until the neoliberal turn and the biculturalism emergent in the New Zealand of the 1980s, Pākeha writers also explored indigenous concepts of degrowth and their validity for mainstream society. As a result of their close contacts with Māori communities, the Pākeha writers Roderick Finlayson and Noel Hilliard became harsh critics of the Western notion of development. Finlayson established long-lasting friendships with Māori families living near the farm where he spent all his childhood summers. Hilliard married a Māori woman. Both were among the first Pākeha writers to deal with Māori culture without falling into the predominantly negative white preconceptions or stereotypes that cast Māori as culturally inferior to Pākeha. Their insight into Māori life enabled Finlayson and Hilliard to cultivate political and environmental positions that prefigure degrowth theory.

Finlayson is foundational to New Zealand's national literature as it grew out of the 1930s Depression. Writers of this period were to varying degrees committed to socialist or communist ideals in the inter-war period, which was also the heyday of Marxism in Aotearoa New Zealand. Although the movement was leftist and progressive, it was largely indifferent to the concerns of the indigenous people, with the key exception of Finlayson, who chronicled the dis-

---

29 Henare, "Lasting Peace and Good Life," 433–34.

30 "Lasting Peace and Good Life," 434–35.

31 Sissons, *First Peoples*, 148.

orientation of a race in danger of losing its roots and its identity. As he explains in the 1938 foreword to his first collection, *Brown Man's Burden*, Finlayson deliberately chose to write mostly about Māori life, and to expose the dispossession of Māori by Europeans. He further believed that the indigenous people were "still more truly of the land"[32] than the whites who had dispossessed them. He propagated a return to a life informed by spirituality and imaginative power and looked to Māori culture as a model to follow. Furthermore, he identified European "modern materialism" and "scientific barbarism"[33] as the forces that had nearly annihilated indigenous culture,[34] concluding:

> the author himself belongs to the remnant of a race not defeated in battle, but more surely defeated by an alien and material society, which may explain in part, why he loves his brother of the 'Iwi Maori'.[35]

Bill Pearson, in his introduction to a later Finlayson collection, *Brown Man's Burden and Later Stories* (1973), underlines the fact that Finlayson "was the first to want to write of Maoris as living fellow men and to see in their way of life qualities the Pakeha might envy"[36] and that his achievement has been "to address himself repeatedly to a problem that is important in every part of the world that has been touched by the industrial revolutions, old and new." Already by the 1970s, Pearson finds a "renewed relevance" in Finlayson's oeuvre in the wake of current protests against "the ethos of success and materialism."[37]

It was not, however, until a generation after Finlayson that literature captured and critiqued accelerating capitalism and the coincident destruction of Māori ways of life, compellingly evoked in Hilliard's fiction of the 1960s and 1970s. Shaped by his working-class origins and active involvement in the Labour and Communist parties, Hilliard's preoccupation with race relations is linked to the increasing presence of Māori in urban areas and the concomitant increase of racial unrest, Māori dislocation and trauma, disempowerment and criminality. Whereas in 1936 only around eleven percent of Māori lived in towns, by 1970 the number had risen to nearly sixty-nine percent.[38] Hilliard's first novel, *Maori*

---

32 Roderick Finlayson, *Brown Man's Burden* (Auckland: Unicorn, 1938): ii.

33 Finlayson, *Brown Man's Burden*, i–ii.

34 Finlayson extrapolates his attack on the spread of industrialism, consumer society, and capitalism in a later essay, *Our Life in This Land* (Auckland: Griffin, 1940).

35 Finlayson *Brown Man's Burden*, ii. *Iwi* means 'tribe' in Maori.

36 Finlayson, *Brown Man's Burden and Later Stories* (Auckland: Auckland UP, 1973): xv.

37 *Brown Man's Burden and Later Stories*, vii (both quotations).

38 Michael King, *Nga Iwi O Te Motu: 1000 Years of Maori History* (1997; Auckland: Reed, 2001): 101–102.

*Girl* (1960), sparked considerable controversy for its unfashionable revival of the realist literature of the 1930s and its open treatment of the topic of race relations. Lawrence Jones, for example, argued that Hilliard's realism belongs to the literature of "protest" rather than "accommodation," implying thereby "a criticism of social and political systems."[39] *Maori Girl* is the first volume of a tetralogy that follows the separate lives of a Māori girl and a Pākeha boy, Netta and Paul, who grow up, get to know each other, and marry. *Maori Girl* sets the rural childhood of Netta Samuel against a background of poverty, but also of warm affection, close communal relationships, and shared values. As an adolescent, Netta feels the pull of city life, which, to her, seems to hold out the promise of economic independence, modernity, and emancipation from traditional Māori life. A child of the Depression, Netta moves to Wellington to witness New Zealand's transformation under the impact of major technological advances, straddling two worlds as a typically 'amphibious' Māori youth. The second volume, *Power of Joy* (1965), recounts Paul Bennett's upbringing in a railway construction village. He belongs to a white working-class family with social ambitions and lives a life defined by materialism, puritanical restraint, emotional repression, and failed communication. Combining all of these features, Paul's mother stands in sharp contrast to the characters nurturing Netta in *Maori Girl* during her childhood. It is from the claustrophobic world of his childhood that Paul eventually escapes by marrying a Māori woman.

The third volume, *Maori Woman* (1974), continues the depiction of the hardships Netta suffers in the city and records the degradation of urban Māori, particularly in the character of Netta's partner, Jason. At the end of the novel, Netta and Paul meet and finally fall in love. In the last volume of the tetralogy, *The Glory and the Dream* (1978), Hilliard juxtaposes Netta's and Paul's world-views and analyses the cultural gap determining the nature of their marriage. The differences recorded in the process anticipate later accounts of cultural otherness in Māori literature that translate social alterity into an epistemological difference manifested in specific notions of time, money, ownership, family, communality, education, rationality, imagination, and spirituality. Paul, a left-wing trade-union member working at a paper mill, is preoccupied with the future to the point of obsession. His constant saving and planning are counterpointed with Netta's easy-going attitude. Netta wants to live and not just to stay alive.[40] She believes Paul's forward orientation to be the cause of his dissatisfaction with

---

[39] Lawrence Jones, *Barbed Wire & Mirrors* (1987; Dunedin: U of Otago P, 1990): 33.

[40] Noel Hilliard, *The Glory and the Dream* (London: Heinemann, 1978): 85. Further page references are in the main text.

the present (240) and that money is made to be spent on useful or concrete things, not accumulated. For Paul, the family is made up of two persons; for Netta, it is made up of relations, "not only the ones living now but all the other ones way back" (91). Paul has formal relationships with his friends and is jealous of Netta's spontaneous conviviality. He tends to rationalize everything, while she has an intuitive approach to people and knowledge. Paul's knowledge is bookish, while Netta's is practical and experiential. He is an atheist, believing in individual man, not religious institutions, which he views as instruments to avoid making personal choices and delegating responsibility. She believes in God and enjoys going to a Māori church service, although her approach to religion and spirituality is not tied to any particular dedomination but is, rather, an undefined experience of emotional and social wellbeing. For Netta, church service is "a feeling" (93) and "a real family gathering" (94). Her view prefigures degrowth principles in its prioritizing of a convivial society and the fulfilment of spiritual and creative needs, as well as in her disdain for a life centred on accumulation, profit for profit's sake, and the obsession with material needs to be satisfied by consumerism.

Hilliard depicts Netta and Paul's political differences as stemming from their cultural backgrounds. Paul's working-class roots make him left-wing and politicized, whereas Netta's convictions come from her cultural heritage, which is not represented in mainstream politics and which thus gives the impression that she is apolitical. However, her views encompass a much more radical vision of society than Paul's. Netta's lack of a sense of ownership, her focus on communality and reciprocity both between human beings and between humans and nature, and her emphasis on the quality of life that makes up for the quantity of money one can earn, take her in a direction diametrically opposed to Western notions of progress and development based on growth. The difference Paul traces between his job at the paper mill and Netta's work at home, "one producing surplus value for profit," the other "creating use value" (130), still operates within the same logic, although he may side with the proletariat rather than the bourgeoisie. Paul's left-wing leanings advocate a redistribution of profit but do not allow him to question the way profit is produced, nor do they change the exploitative approach to natural resources. Hilliard's analysis clearly probes two different views, Western materialism and indigenous holism, both of which need to be reconsidered in the light of today's pressing issues of environmental degradation and accelerating inequality.

In many respects, post-development theories, especially of degrowth, are compatible with indigenous cultures. Both foster relations to humans and the environment as a value that can compensate for the individualism promoted by consumer society, encourage environmental consciousness, and support the benefits of globalization that enhance the wellbeing of nature and humankind. Neither degrowth nor indigenous cultural praxis is against progress *tout court*, but both are against a notion of progress that impoverishes a great number of people in material and spiritual terms while enforcing the privileges of a minority. Growing poverty in the Western world suggests the probable failure of a system that is profoundly inequitable. By contrast, as Latouche writes, in indigenous communities solidarity rather than hierarchy works on a vertical axis, because the obligations that define them are embedded in values that are anchored in long traditions with multi-generational obligations. This automatically limits competition for material wealth and instead encourages efforts to secure social and cultural capital. In Western communities, solidarity is generally applied horizontally, within the nuclear family, close relations, or voluntary associations of individuals.[41] Degrowth, by comparison, encourages vertical solidarity as well. Accordingly, Pallante compares degrowth to the work of a farmer "who is grateful for fruit he eats from the trees he didn't plant," and so "plants trees whose fruit he won't eat himself."[42] Such a convergence of views between indigenous and Western post-development world-views is evidenced in a long-running counter-narrative in New Zealand fiction, from Finlayson in the 1930s to Grace in the 2000s, that urges the adoption of alternatives to capitalism and the development of economic and ecological models privileging the common good over individual goods.

## Works Cited


Beatson, Peter. "Noel Hilliard: The Public and the Private Self," *Sites* (March 1988): 103–10.

Finlayson, Roderick. *Brown Man's Burden* (Auckland: Unicorn, 1938).

Finlayson, Roderick. *Brown Man's Burden and Later Stories*, intro. Bill Pearson (Auckland: Auckland UP, 1973).

Finlayson, Roderick. *Our Life in This Land* (Auckland: Griffin, 1940).

Grace, Patricia. *Dogside Story* (Honolulu: U of Hawai'i P, 2001).

Grace, Patricia. *Potiki* (1986; Honolulu: U of Hawai'i P, 1995).

Hawken, Paul. *Blessed Unrest* (New York: Penguin, 2008).

Henare, Manuka. "Lasting Peace and Good Life: Economic Development and the 'Āta noho' Principle of Te Tiriti o Waitangi," in *Always Speaking: The Treaty of Waitangi*


[41] Latouche, *In the Wake of the Affluent Society*, 237–38.

[42] Pallante, "What is Degrowth?" 3.

*and Public Policy*, ed. Veronica M.H. Tawhai & Katarina Gray-Sharp (Wellington: Huia, 2011): 422–44.

Hilliard, Noel. *The Glory and the Dream* (London: Heinemann, 1978).

Hilliard, Noel. *Maori Girl* (London: Heinemann, 1960).

Hilliard, Noel. *Maori Woman* (London: Robert Hale, 1974).

Hilliard, Noel. *Power of Joy* (London: Michael Joseph, 1965).

Jackson, Tim. *Prosperity Without Growth: Economics for a Finite Planet* (London: Earthscan, 2009).

Jones, Lawrence. *Barbed Wire & Mirrors* (1987; Dunedin: U of Otago P, 1990).

King, Michael. *Nga Iwi O Te Motu: 1000 Years of Maori History* (1997; Auckland: Reed, 2001).

Kingi, Hautahi. "Illuminating Inequality," in *The Piketty Phenomenon: New Zealand Perspectives* (Wellington: Bridget Williams, 2014): 42–47.

Latouche, Serge. "Degrowth Economics," *Le Monde diplomatique*, http://mondediplo.com/2004/11/14latouche (accessed 24 July 2015).

Latouche, Serge. "The Globe Downshifted," *Le Monde diplomatique*, http://mondediplo.com/2006/01/13degrowth (accessed 24 July 20015).

Latouche, Serge. *In the Wake of the Affluent Society: An Exploration of Post-Development*, intro. & tr. Martin O'Connor & Rosemary Arnoux (*La Planète des naufragés: Essai sur l'après-développement*, 1991; London: Zed, 1993).

Latouche, Serge. *La scommessa della decrescita* (*Le pari de la décroissance*, 2006; Milan: Feltrinelli, 2007).

Latouche, Serge. *The Westernization of the World: Significance, Scope and Limits of the Drive Towards Global Uniformity* (*L'occidentalisation du monde: Essai sur la signification, la portée et les limites de l'uniformisation planétaire*, 1989; Cambridge: Polity, 1996).

Leubsdorf, Ben. "Fed: Gap Between Rich, Poor Americans Widened During Recovery," *Wall Street Journal* (4 September 2014), http://www.wsj.com/articles/fed-gap-between-rich-poor-americans-widened-during-recovery-1409853628 (accessed 25 July 2015).

Ngāi Tahu. Website, http://ngaitahu.iwi.nz/te-runanga-o-ngai-tahu/ (last accessed 20 October 2016).

Pallante, Maurizio. *La decrescita felice* (Rome: Edizioni per la decrescita felice, 2009).

Pallante, Maurizio. "What Is Degrowth?," http://decrescitafelice.it/wp-content/uploads/Degrowth.pdf (accessed 24 July 2015).

Sharples, Pita. "Needs Analysis: Maori Business and Management," *Maori Qualifications Services* (December 2013), http://www.nzqa.govt. nz/assets/qualifications-and-standards/qualifications/Bus-qual-review/FINAL-Maori-Business-Needs-Analysis.pdf (accessed 24 July 2015).

Sissons, Jeffrey. *First Peoples: Indigenous Cultures and Their Future* (London: Reaktion, 2005).

Smith, Adam. *The Nature and Causes of the Wealth of Nations*, in *The Works of Adam Smith*, vol. 2 (1776; London: Cadell & Davies, 1812).

Sykes, Annette. "2010 Bruce Jesson Lecture," http://www.brucejesson.com/ ?page_id =349 (accessed 24 July 2015).

Walker, Holly. "Developing Difference: Attitudes towards Maori 'Development' in Patricia Grace's *Potiki* and *Dogside Story*," *Kunapipi* 27.2 (2005): 215–30.

❄

# IV

# The Location of Wealth in Culture

# Wards and Rewards

## *Adoptability and Lost Children*

John McLeod

On a chilly Thursday in early December 1969, my Irish-born birth-mother signed a statement in which she acknowledged that in surrendering her new son for adoption, "I fully understand that the effect will be irrevocable and permanently deprive me of my parental rights."[1] This statement came at the end of a long document in which she also confirmed that her assent to the adoption was "given freely and without pressure from any other person." The following month, the County Court which confirmed the adoption received a report from the guardian *ad litem* (the figure who represents adoptees in UK court proceedings) in which it was confirmed that "no payment or other reward is involved in consideration of the adoption." Phrases like these have been crucial to the judicial contracting of adoptions in a number of countries. They express the legal requirement that financial incentives must not be involved in the transfer of parental rights from a (biogenetic) parent to a new (adoptive) one. One cannot buy children. But at the same time, the notion of adoption as a practice which has nothing to do with the wedded worlds of wealth and privation is itself something of a fiction, regardless of what the law would have its participants confirm.

According to the paperwork, my birth-mother surrendered me because she was "unable to provide for the child." As a single unmarried twenty-year-old woman in late-1960s London earning a meagre salary, she desired for me "a more secure future being adopted." When reporting this information to the County Court in January 1970, the guardian *ad litem* also included details of my new parents' economic standing and financial security: annual salaries, mort-

[1] This quotation, and those that follow regarding my adoption, are taken from the file of documents that I received in April 2014 when I actioned my legal right as UK citizen to access my initial (pre-adoption) birth certificate.

gage details, even the condition of the amenities at their home ("bathroom, separate w.c. and an attached garage"). Money may not have changed hands, but wealth and its lack played a part in rendering me both adoptable and eventually adopted (not all those rendered adoptable find new families, of course). Like thousands of others at the time, the contracting of my adoption relocated a child born to a working-class mother in a middle-class household. The requirement that my birth-mother declare her consent to surrender me "freely," without incurring or declaring charges, masks the irrevocable complicity, oft-noted by several adoption scholars, between the contracting of adoption and the circumstances of wealth and impoverishment.[2] Adoption occurs amidst – indeed, is legitimated by – the seemingly altruistic desire to secure a better financial future for adoptees by surrendering them to wealthier strangers. In securing "the best interests of the child," another kind of interest can be counted in terms of economic empowerment: the perceived added value of relocating a person in terms of class and wealth. The notion of adoption as a mode of rescue is partly derived from this contradictory scenario in which economic empowerment is cited to support the claim that no money is involved in the act of transferring parental rights which birth-mothers give up "freely." Such fantasies of altruism and rescue conceal the brutal facts of inequality which lie behind nearly all incidences of adoption, especially those that happen transnationally or transculturally, and which recast severance as salvation. As the San Salvador-born Patrick McDermott has remarked when reflecting upon his adoption by white parents,

> In the United States, Salvadoran adoptees are seen mostly as success stories. Anglo Americans generally view adoptees as having barely escaped growing up in poverty and not as having been separated from their birth families and birth countries.[3]

No money has to change hands between biogenetic and adoptive parents for adoption to be understood in terms of financial constraint and opportunity.

As Margaret Homans has argued, bluntly and brilliantly, all acts of parenthood are economically circumscribed, and it is hardly possible to disentangle love from money. "Love is not separate from the economic," she reminds us.

---

[2] For example, see Margaret Homans, *The Imprint of Another Life: Adoption Narratives and Human Possibility* (Ann Arbor: U of Michigan P, 2013).

[3] Patrick McDermott, "Disappeared Children and the Adoptee as Immigrant," in *Outsiders Within: Writing on Transracial Adoption*, ed. Jane Jeong Trenka, Julia Chinyere Oparah & Sun Yung Shin (Cambridge MA: South End, 2006): 109.

> Raising children, adopted or not, requires resources, and raising them with that emotional overflow called "love" requires additional resources: think of what it would cost to provide even the conditions of possibility for "love" [...] for every child in every orphanage in the world.[4]

As she explains, in adoption contexts the issue of wealth is particularly sensitive, not least because adoption, often a costly act which incurs legal and other fees, is contrasted with 'natural' (read: biogenetic) parenthood deemed remote from matters of the market, even though "middle-class parenthood enmeshes families in daily acts of consumption, from diapers to prom dresses."[5] Adoptive relations are considered discomfiting by some because they demythologize biogenetic parenting and expose the difference presumed between consanguineous and adoptive families in normative discourses of family-making:

> The naturalising of bio-family love, its rendering invisible of the economic cost of "love," makes the expenses of adoption seem very conspicuous and sets up an apparent binary opposition between adoptive and biological families. Although, as I am arguing, all family life involves expenditure, adoptive parents bear the uncomfortable burden of making visible the connection between love and money [...].[6]

Homans reads a selection of recent representations of adoption, endogamous and transcultural, as often attempting to conceal the economic particulars of adoptability behind a celebration of adoptive "falling-in-love."[7] A proximate task preoccupies me in this essay, although in what follows I wish to think about three recent representations of transcultural adoptability which expose rather than erase the centrality of wealth and impoverishment to both family-making and -breaking.[8] In making plain the lines of connection between love and money, to rent Homans' phrase, in their different ways Martin Sixsmith's *The Lost Child of Philomena Lee* (2009), Stephen Frears's film adaptation *Philomena* (2013), and Caryl Phillips's recent novel *The Lost Child* (2015) invite us to attend to the rendering as vulnerable certain mothers and their children whose

---

[4] Homans, *The Imprint of Another Life*, 25–26.

[5] *The Imprint of Another Life*, 26.

[6] *The Imprint of Another Life*, 26.

[7] See *The Imprint of Another Life*, 24–58.

[8] In a recent monograph, I have explained my preference for using the phrase 'transcultural adoption' instead of the concomitant but *not* readily interchangable terms 'transracial adoption' or 'transnational adoption'. I hold to that preference in this essay, while also acknowledging that I must turn to concomitant terms when required by context. See John McLeod, *Life Lines: Writing Transcultural Adoption* (London: Bloomsbury, 2015): 7–10.

identities, as a consequence of the machinations of the market, are refashioned into the serrated selves of 'birth-mother' and 'adoptee' and subsequently costed in starkly different cultural and social terms.

Adoptions which cross the lines of race, nation, or culture have become a point of concern for those keen to challenge the vocabularies of altruism and rescue that conceal the material inequalities and unequal relations without which adoptability could not be confected. While much of this concern is directed towards child-trafficking and illegal baby markets, state-sponsored or recognized adoption services are regarded by some as different in legal status but not in kind. The Korean-born US-raised adoptee Kim Park Nelson has starkly described lawful adoptions as the product of a shadowy service industry that encases intimate transpersonal relations in the routine equation of supply and demand:

> While the equation might be simple, this is a complicated exchange, where children, the governments of the two nations, both sets of parents (birth and adoptive), (usually) two adoption agencies, adoption workers, social workers, childcare providers, attorneys, and a host of other intermediaries may be involved. Typically, everyone is compensated, either monetarily, or socially, creating a complex economic relationship. [...] The demand [for children] is met with supply from poorer nations around, where the potential to procure healthy infants is great and the possibilities for realizing a healthy profit are just as great.[9]

While one might take issue with the view that "everyone is compensated," particularly those women in recent decades whose only recompense for surrendering infants was the avoidance of social stigma as unmarried or unwed mothers, Nelson's observation draws together the interests of families, adoption agencies, and often the state. As such, the attempt to profit through adoption, by procuring adoptable children as part of a strategy of financial gain, often crosses the thin line that divides lawful from illegal behaviour in this context; so, we must accept, in Laura Briggs's words, that intercountry adoption practices "do not resolve neatly into categories of coercive and innocent, good and bad."[10] Indeed, Briggs opens her remarkable exploration of transracial and transnational adoption by making mention of the attempts by two American groups to procure for adoption children left vulnerable by the chaos of the Haitian earthquake of

---

[9] Kim Park Nelson, "Shopping for Children in the International Marketplace," in *Outsiders Within*, 89.

[10] Laura Briggs, *Somebody's Children: The Politics of Transracial and Transnational Adoption* (Durham NC: Duke UP, 2012): 4.

2010. One of these, a Pittsburgh-based evangelical group which airlifted fifty-four children from Haiti's BRESMA orphanage and had the support of the Pennsylvania governor Ed Rendell, was initially praised for its act of child rescue but was later revealed as seeking to procure children for adoption without the consent of birth-parents or the Haitian government. Briggs describes how the children in the orphanage were mostly not orphans at all but had been placed there often temporarily by single mothers as a coping strategy. In addition,

> While much was made of the fact that the children were "in process" for adoption, it turned out that twelve of them were not (and were hence unadoptable, because they lacked the proper court orders and visas). Furthermore, what it means that children's adoptions were not complete is that there were still supposed to be legal opportunities for their mothers to object, to ask for their children back.[11]

As Briggs regards things, such opportunism is typical of the practices of adoption across a number of contexts which disenfranchise black, Latina, working-class, and immigrant mothers. "Adoption," she declares, "was indispensible to the neoliberal economic and political order" and "is an index of political and social vulnerability" rather than a blessed act of philanthropy ever to be applauded.[12]

Briggs's detailed and polemical study rarely pauses to think about how adoptees and adoptive families might choose to function in defiance of neoliberal ideology and *make* something from the circumstances which have underwritten their family-making. In contrast, Barbara Yngvesson's study of transcultural adoption in Sweden examines the activities of a group of intercountry adoptees at an Adoption Centre workshop who took an opportunity to point out the paradoxes of belonging and identity they experienced as a way of critiquing the state's appropriation of adoption as an assimilative act by which immigrants are legitimated as national citizens, culturally compliant and securely placed in one culture rather than between at least two.[13] That said, the coercive and complicit parameters of adoption that Briggs traces in the USA have a long history in Europe, particularly in those countries, such as Britain, which for a while enjoyed a global presence as a colonial power. In Margaret Humphreys' silence-breaking account of the exporting of children from the UK to Australia in the mid-twentieth century, especially in the years immediately after the Second

---

11 Briggs, *Somebody's Children*, 3.

12 *Somebody's Children*, 13, 14.

13 See Barbara Yngvesson, *Belonging in an Adopted World: Race, Identity, and Transnational Adoption* (Chicago: U of Chicago P, 2010): 123–27.

World War, there emerges a grim history of state collusion in depriving mothers of their children for the purpose of adoption. Although lodging in orphanages, many of these children were not orphans at all but had been placed there by parents as a short-term measure while they contended with the challenging and austere conditions of a country recovering from the exhaustion left by war. Many were sent without proper parental consent and grew up in former settler colonies such as Canada, Australia, and New Zealand having been told (falsely) that their biogenetic relations had died. As the children grew, many were made to work as labourers, which saved money for landowners and employers, and were routinely exposed to forms of physical and sexual abuse, not least by members of the Catholic Church. As Humphreys discovers with alarm, the rhetoric of rescue was used by the institutions involved – including nearly every UK child-care agency and charity – to conceal a history of harm:

> Children in Britain and Ireland were being "rescued" from difficult conditions for the greater good of themselves and the Empire. [...] As victims of poverty, illegitimacy or broken homes, these children were regarded as "deprived" and considered a burden on society.[14]

Intercountry adoption was an effective means of shifting the burden of welfare away from the state and charitable institutions in the UK to the private realm of family-making overseas, as well as "restocking the empire" with European-descended (read: white) infant settlers.[15] Years later, helped by Humphreys and other members of the Child Migrants Trust which she founded, some of these 'orphans' met their biogenetic parents or siblings again; but others found that their birth-mothers had died only a few years before they instigated their attempt to trace them after decades of silence, and in some cases only a few short years after they had discovered they were not orphans at all.[16]

---

14 Margaret Humphreys, *Empty Cradles* (1994; London: Corgi, 1995): 80.

15 Briggs has written extensively in *Somebody's Children* about the use of adoption to privatize child care and reduce welfare budgets in the USA, and her argument influences my reading of the parallel context of child migration in the Empire.

16 This appalling history of state-sponsored severance was recently the focus of a profoundly moving exhibition, inspired work of the Child Migrants Trust, titled *On Their Own: Britain's Child Migrants* that opened between October 2015 until June 2016 at the V&A Museum of Childhood, Bethnal Green, London. The exhibition was a collaborative enterprise between the V&A, National Museums Liverpool and the Australian National Maritime Museum. In 2010 Humphrey's *Empty Cradles* was made into a film, *Oranges and Sunshine*, directed by Jim Loach (son of the esteemed director Ken Loach).

Post-Independence Ireland was complicit in such acts of deprivation for financial gain, thanks to the collusion of government with the Catholic Church. In his excellent account of twentieth-century Ireland's oppression of unwed mothers and recent cultural responses to this silenced history, *Ireland's Magdalen Laundries and the Nation's Architecture of Containment* (2007), James M. Smith soberingly records the complicity of Church and State in the creation of a post-Independence nationalist chauvinism which seized upon the figure of the pure, compliant female as epitomizing an idealized vision of Irish motherhood. This manoeuvre wedded moral and religious piety to cultural purity at the heart of postcolonial political discourse, while shifting the provision of welfare for unwed mothers, punitively criminalized for their sexual behaviour (despite the fact that some pregnancies were the result of rape), often from the State to the Catholic Church. The institutionalization of these women, writes Smith, "contributed to the containment of embodied sexuality crucial to the project of national identity formation."[17] It was a practice which

> proved mutually beneficial to Ireland's powerbrokers, which explains the state's abdication of responsibility for the women and children placed under church control. [...] Containing sexual immortality, specifically, illegitimacy and prostitution, behind the walls of Ireland's mother and baby homes and Magdalen asylums helped to constitute and to perpetuate the fiction of Irish cultural purity.[18]

The origins of Ireland's Magdalene Laundries lie in the post-Famine context of the nineteenth century, and these institutions were never subject formally to external inspection or control (the last one closed in 1996). The mother and baby homes, by contrast, were a Free State-endorsed initiative often run by nuns and in receipt of funding, and deemed suitable for women considered 'first offenders' and capable of 'rehabilitation', whereas the Laundries incarcerated women considered morally beyond the pale. While the silence surrounding the latter began to be broken with the release of Peter Mullen's 2002 film *The Magdalene Sisters*, life in the mother and baby homes has been brought to international awareness most recently by Stephen Frears's film *Philomena*, a dramatization of Martin Sixsmith's book *The Lost Child of Philomena Lee*. Significantly, both the book and the film convey the centrality of capital, deprivation, and

---

[17] James M. Smith, *Ireland's Magdalen Laundries and the Nation's Architecture of Containment* (2007; Manchester: Manchester UP, 2008): 19.

[18] Smith, *Ireland's Magdalen Laundries*, 19. Smith's research informs my brief account of the Laundries and the mother and baby homes throughout this paragraph.

wealth as at the heart of the childcare economy in which Ireland's religious institutions willingly invested.

Both texts record the romantic encounter between Philomena Lee, a young unmarried Irish girl, and John McInerney, whose meeting at Limerick Carnival in October 1951 resulted in Philomena's pregnancy and confinement at Sean Ross Abbey mother and baby home in Roscrea. Her son Anthony was born in 1952 and adopted by American birth-parents. In 2004, Philomena decided to trace his whereabouts, aided by Sixsmith – only to discover that Anthony, who had been renamed Michael Hess, had died of AIDS in 1995, having enjoyed a successful career in Washington DC. The central sections of Sixsmith's book are concerned with Philomena's 'lost child' and piece together the life-story of Anthony as Michael Hess, while Frears's film maintains a closer focus on Philomena by dramatizing the impact of her efforts to trace her son, in the process discovering the details of his life. Frears also makes Sixsmith a significant character in the film, whereas in the book he is a much less intrusive presence who only sporadically speaks of himself. This marks an important difference between the two texts, with major consequences to which I'll return, and is the key means by which Frears foregrounds both the pragmatics and the ethics of tracing adoptable children. In addition, and important for our purposes, Sixsmith's cinematic portrayal as a character in his own right provides opportunities for the film to dwell upon the *challenges of making narratives* from, and for, those whose filial lines of connection have been severed by the bureaucratic particulars of adoption. As Mark Jerng has argued, representing adoption triggers a crisis for conventional narratives and often appears in cultural texts as "a problem of narrative form in which the capacity of narrative to 'take in' the adoptee opens up issues central to the political and social conditions of personhood."[19] In Frears's film, the issue of narrative is foregrounded in two ways: through the interest that Philomena Lee (Judi Dench) takes in popular romance fiction, the plots of which she enjoys recounting to a bemused Martin Sixsmith (Steve Coogan), and through the conversations Sixsmith has with his editor Sally Mitchell (Michelle Fairley) concerning how he might turn the matter of Philomena's travails into a 'human interest story'. While Sixmith's book is generally less self-conscious about such matters, *The Lost Child of Philomena Lee* nonetheless concludes its various parts by drawing attention to the challenges facing Sixsmith in researching and writing Philomena's tale, and assembling it

[19] Mark C. Jerng, *Claiming Others: Transracial Adoption and National Belonging* (Minneapolis: U of Minnesota P, 2010): xxviii.

from "sporadic traces and disparate evidence"[20] amidst an environment of secrecy and the reluctance of the several agencies and institutions involved to provide information about Anthony's life. But both texts attend firmly to the matter of money, which sits at the heart of Philomena's experiences and is an important point of confluence between them, with Frears clearly keen to foreground Sixsmith's account of the financial context of the mother and baby homes, how they were used by the Catholic Church to acquire wealth through forcibly removing children.

Early in Sixsmith's book there is mention of the so-called Jane Russell affair, when the childless Hollywood actress attempted to adopt a child from Ireland with the full support of the state, during which "large amounts of money were involved" (9). This incident frames the subsequent account of Philomena and Anthony's sundering in terms of financial advantage, so that the loss of the child might be imagined as part of an obscene balance-sheet where privation is offset against fiscal gain. We soon learn that Philomena gives birth in the mother and baby home in July 1952 where she is expected to work "to pay for your sins" (19) while having contact with Anthony for short periods each day, and she can only leave upon payment of £100 (an unlikely, enormous sum at the time for any family with modest means). When her father, Patrick, visits Philomena at Sean Ross Abbey, she imagines for a moment that she and Anthony might move back home, but in addition to the scandal she would have to bear, "the council house on Connolly's Terrace was small and Patrick Lee had not the space for her to sleep or the means for her to eat" (83). When researching how Anthony's adoptive parents came to visit Roscrea and considered adopting the Abbey's children, Sixsmith unearths a letter from one Monsignor O'Grady in which the latter makes plain the financial realities of Ireland's intercountry adoption system and the wealth it brought the Catholic Church:

> While neither the NCCC [National Conference of Catholic Charities] nor Sean Ross Abbey charge any fees, it is customary for the adopting party to make a donation to the Sisters of the Sacred Hearts of Jesus and Mary, the size of which may be determined in consultation with the Superioress of the Order. (55)

Whether the source is birth-mother or prospective adopters, it is clear that the infant Anthony may not leave Roscrea without money changing hands.

---

[20] Martin Sixsmith, *The Lost Child of Philomena Lee* (2009; London: Pan, 2010): 193. Further page references are in the main text.

In these opening pages, Sixsmith also intersplices Philomena's years at the home with a fictionalized account of Joe Coram, who works for the Free State's minister for External Affairs and is asked to write a briefing paper, prompted by the Russell matter, that details Ireland's trafficking in children overseas, which has come to alarm the minister (this is not dramatized in Frears's film). Interestingly, the vignette reveals some tension as well as collusion between Church and State and suggests that, where the trade in children was concerned, the queasiness of the government could be circumvented by the Catholic hierarchy when it came to drafting adoption policy in 1950s Ireland, not least due to the formidable influence of the Archbishop of Dublin, John Charles McQuaid.[21] As well as reporting on the minimal assessment of adoptive parents' suitability by the Church, over which the Department of External Affairs had no jurisdiction, Sixsmith cites the comments in Coram's paper on the lucrative element of intercountry adoption for the Catholic hierarchy, which finds good business in its demonizing and delegitimating of unwed mothers and motherhood:

> *The Church's financial stake is substantial. The nuns receive payment from the adopting parents, particularly those from the USA, and few checks are made on the suitability of the homes they are sent to. The Jane Russell case is the tip of a rather large iceberg*. (24; italics in original)

Anthony must appear adopted for free, not for a fee, through the conveniences of "donation," which almost mask the market that the Irish Catholic Church has made from birth-mother misery. As such, Sixsmith sets the emotional price paid by Philomena in surrendering her son in relation to the financial costs to the Church of his relocation overseas as a way of challenging the rhetoric of piety used to legitimate severed relations and exposing the hard knot of hypocrisy definitive of the Church's practices at the time.

In his film *Philomena*, Frears attends to the matter of wealth in two particularly important ways. First, as well as providing information as the film progresses about the cost of living in and leaving Sean Ross Abbey, including the brutal laundry work which Philomena and the other girls pursue each day, he offers visual evidence of the mother and baby home's business of profiting from loss in two telling details that are located at the heart of the Abbey. The first is a

[21] In recent years, McQuaid's reputation has suffered greatly in the light of the various child abuse and adoption scandals which took place during his tenure as Archbishop between 1940 and 1972, and which he is regarded by some actively to have covered up. In 1999, John Cooney's biography of McQuaid sensationally suggested that the Archbishop may himself have been a paedophile (a view which many have since contested). See John Cooney, *John Charles McQuaid: Ruler of Catholic Ireland* (Dublin: O'Brien Press, 1999).

signed photograph of Jane Russell that hangs on the wall in the Abbey's reception room, and which anticipates Sixsmith hearing about the baby-selling scandal in a pub in a later scene. The second concerns the contemporary Abbey's shop, which, Sixsmith notices early in the film, sells a modest range of trinkets and religious paraphernalia which plays a small but important role in the film's climax when he returns with Philomena to Roscrea armed with the news that Michael Hess has been buried there at his own request (the nuns have told Philomena, falsely, that they did not know what had happened to him once he left the Abbey). The appearance of the shop during the first visit positions the Abbey as a place of both purchase and piety, with the spiritual realms of devotion and faith contextualized by the cash register. A couple of minutes later, Philomena hands Sixsmith a copy of the contract presented to her in 1952 during her audience with the nuns, a contract in which she had agreed to surrender Anthony in perpetuity and which she signed "with my own free will." The film's critique of the treatment of unwed mothers contests the extent to which Philomena's act of surrender was ever really 'free' – the fiction of non-coercion which Philomena still sadly subscribes to fifty years later – while Frears's decision to make proximate the glimpse of the shop with Sixsmith's glance at the contract heavily ironizes Anthony's adoption as one of freedom of exchange.

At the film's climax, having confronted the elderly, odious, and unrepentant Sister Hildegarde (Barbara Jefford) about her role in the adoption of Anthony and many others, Sixsmith voices his anger while Philomena movingly pronounces her forgiveness of the aged nun and asks to be taken to her son's grave. Having calmed down, he pauses at the shop: "I just want to buy something," he says to a young nun (Wunmi Mosaku). By Michael's frost-fringed grave, Sixsmith hands Philomena the small plastic model of Jesus he has just bought, partly as a peace offering after their disagreement about whether Sister Hildegarde deserves forgiveness. The model, simultaneously saccharine and profound in its toy-like vision of reverence, figures something of the necessary future required for all those involved in Ireland's common trade in sundered children: an admission of that history without which contrition is impossible, the hard business of apology and forgiveness, a ready acknowledgement of the capital made from coerced adoptability, and (especially for women like Philomena) an attempt to recover from the exploitation of their religion something of the emotional and spiritual values that underwrite their personhood and faith.

With admirable and ethical intelligence, Frears remains acutely aware throughout *Philomena* of another kind of exploitation which may result from the surrendering of Anthony and Philomena's desire to find him: namely, the cultural capital that may accrue from turning Philomena's circumstances into a readily digestible 'human-interest' story written for the purposes of entertaining newspaper readers (and, indeed, cinema-goers). If there was money to be made from rendering Anthony adoptable, then the accounting of this suppressed history also affords the chance to garner wealth. On this point, the narrative self-consciousness of the film takes on a vital purpose as the chief means by which Frears attempts laudably to distance his film from profiting unthinkably from the losses of others. It is made clear from the opening of *Philomena* that Sixsmith, once a BBC foreign correspondent and recently Director of Communications as part of Tony Blair's government, is down on his luck, having lost his job. He agrees to research Anthony's adoption in order partly to revive his fortunes, even though he takes a mostly withering view of the clichéd nature of human-interest stories to begin with. In convincing his editor Sally to fund the research, he pitches the narrative he envisages writing as cheaply emotional and entirely predictable:

> Well, it's about a little old Irish lady, a retired nurse, who is searching for her long-lost son, who was taken – snatched – from her at birth by evil nuns. [...] Either he's Chairman of IBM or a hobo, it doesn't matter. *The years melted away as a fifty-year silence was broken by two simple words: hello mum.* I could write it now.[22]

Even Sally regards this comment as "cynical." Frears suggests a connection between Sixsmith's cynical pragmatism and his economic standing in relation to Philomena, to emphasize how the narratorial encasement of her life-story could quickly become complicit in the machinery of economic disenfranchisement which contributed to her confinement in Roscrea. Sixsmith is Oxford-educated, middle-class, and secular, while Philomena lives modestly amidst her faith and memories and enjoys a number of phenomena which seem to make Sixsmith uncomfortable, such as romantic fictions and Harvester Inns replete with 'all you can eat' salad buffet bars. He is also something of a snob. When discussing accompanying Philomena to Roscrea, Sixsmith elects not to travel in the family Vauxhall Cavalier but hires a BMW instead. Philomena moves equally awkwardly when taken into Sixsmith's world. On the flight to Washington DC, she only accepts a Bucks Fizz when she learns it is complimentary – "you have to pay for everything on Ryanair," she says – while in Washington we are con-

[22] The film's dialogue I have transcribed from the UK DVD release. See Stephen Frears, dir., *Philomena* (Pathé Films, UK | USA | France 2013; 98 min.).

stantly shown Philomena's startled response to the luxury of the hotel, from TV channels to the chocolates left on the pillow.

These important class dynamics mark out Sixsmith as potentially exploitative and beckon into the film an ethical cognizance of what we might call Philomena's potential birth-mother subalternity, spoken for by affluent others who appropriate her pain. Frears emphasizes this in a scene at the Lincoln Memorial when Philomena admits to having reservations about turning her private family business into a published story. Sixsmith deflects these as he tries to take Philomena's photograph: "[Families] are very private, but tracking them down is a rather expensive business and, er, so it's like quid pro quo, isn't it?" It is important, then, at the film's climax as the two characters stand before Michael's grave, that Sixsmith renounces his desire to publish Philomena's story, prompted by the showdown in front of the wheelchair-bound Sister Hildegarde when Philomena challenges him for losing his temper: "It happened to me, not you. It's up to me what I do about it. It's my choice." In refusing his offer and asking that her story be told after all, Philomena ends the film both in possession of her story and in charge of its dissemination, on which she will work with Sixsmith collaboratively. At the same time, Sixsmith's middle-class secularism is presented as principled and essential to the gathering of information which might break the silences and so support oppressed women like Philomena, yet also as too brittle and rigid to accommodate the compassionate response which Philomena makes to Sister Hildegarde's inflexible, bankrupted pieties by forgiving her. Philomena's culturally modest standpoint may be of more value than Sixsmith's educated outrage, owing to the wealth of compassion it contains. The delicacy with which Frears's film foregrounds this important matter of representation as exploitation is one reason why *Philomena* works so effectively in providing a narrative of severance that exceeds the confines of the human-interest story and seeks out an ethical vantage from which to tell proper tales of adoptability.

Both *The Lost Child of Philomena Lee* and *Philomena* have something to tell us about the appropriation of intimacy in the public sphere, where the sexual lives of women were marshalled in twentieth-century Ireland partly as a consequence of Empire's legacy. Smith has argued that the construction of the morally refined Irish woman as a central icon in "postindependence Ireland's nativist nationalist imaginary"[23] was deliberately set against colonial clichés of the country's lax character. In moving to my last point of focus, Caryl Phillips's novel *The Lost Child*, we encounter a parallel example of how imperial legacies have

[23] Smith, *Ireland's Magddalen Laundries and Nation's Architecture of Containment*, 3.

helped make children vulnerable and sanctioned their adoptability due to the deprivations visited upon vulnerable mothers. As in much of his fiction, in *The Lost Child* Phillips pursues what I term a poetic of proximation by combining in the same fictional frame a variety of narratives that are not always obviously linked, in order to expose hidden connections between disparate yet overlapping contexts and to prompt critical reflection upon the ways one might conventionally conceive of and constellate an always-already entangled past. In Stephen Clingman's terms, Phillips's writing helps broker a new grammar of identity that moves transgressively in a rhizomatic, horizontal fashion across the border-lines and -logic of the imperial imagination, shaped by

> an interest in all those asymmetrically marginalized and excluded people of whatever origins whose routes cross in ways that shift from the complex and complementary to the jagged, tangential and disjunctive.[24]

In *The Lost Child,* Phillips brings together the imaginative world of Emily Brontë's *Wuthering Heights* (1847), set in the late-eighteenth century, the mid-nineteenth-century world of the Brontë family's home in Haworth, West Yorkshire, and late-twentieth-century Oxford, London, and Leeds, with this last location shadowed by the 'Moors Murders' committed between 1963 and 1965 by Myra Hindley and Ian Brady. In making ambiguous the distinction between fact and fiction, Phillips invites attention to the grimly recurring matter of vulnerability for a number of lost children who often suffer fatal fortunes: a young mixed-race boy struggling in Liverpool during the slave trade whose black mother dies destitute and who recalls the fictional figure of Heathcliff; the last days of Emily Brontë, fragile and ailing amidst her family on the moors; and two mixed-race boys, Ben and Tommy, who enter foster care as their mother, Monica Johnson, struggles to cope with loneliness and hardship, only for Tommy to disappear in 1972 and meet a sorry end on the bleak Yorkshire moors.

The fortunes of Ben and Tommy are framed by poverty and class, as Phillips attends to the knotted constraints that bind together economic deprivation and racial discrimination. Initially, Monica lives in comfortable surroundings as the daughter of a grammar-school master and, later, as an undergraduate student at Oxford University. Freighted with her father Ronald's upwardly mobile ambitions, she quietly rebels against his attempts to direct the shape of her life and finds herself cut off from the family when Ronald learns of her relationship at Oxford with Julius Wilson, founder of the University's Anti-Colonial Club. As

[24] Stephen Clingman, *The Grammar of Identity: Transnational Fiction and the Nature of the Boundary* (Oxford: Oxford UP, 2009): 77.

her life develops, Monica finds herself progressively abandoned by men: her relationship with Julius, who prioritizes his political ambitions over his family responsibilities, breaks down while they live in insalubrious surroundings with their two new sons in London, and by the late-1960s she has moved to Leeds to raise her sons on her own in an environment notable for its austerity:

> They wandered by dismal-looking pubs and corner shops with paint peeling from their facades and windows that were securely grilled [...]. After four years as a librarian in this run-down city that, despite the evidence of increased poverty, recently had the temerity to host the Commonwealth Games, she was quietly desperate to escape.[25]

There is little 'common wealth' here. Consequently, Monica's compressed life – she, too, is something of a lost child – sees her seeking solace on nights out with her friend Pamela, often leaving her sons to fend for themselves. On one such night, she meets a suitor, Derek Evans, who will eventually kidnap and kill Tommy on the moors. Phillips dwells on the complexity of Monica's descent towards destitution (and an untimely death) and does not absolve her of some responsibility for her sons' fortunes – she can be uncommunicative, silent, and stubborn, and to this extent she shares some of the inflexible personality traits of her father. In shaping the tale of the Johnson family, Phillips attends to the intersection of the wider social dispensation, prejudicial and unforgiving, with matters of individuated and ethical action, especially on the part of filial relations who each contribute to their children's vulnerability.

As ever, Phillips invites us to enter into a complex procedure of understanding those circumstances and actions that have produced a life of loss and pain, rather than to assume a pious position of uninformed judgment wrought from ethical cliché. Monica's attenuated mothering as she struggles with the economic and emotional cost of struggling to make ends meet propels her sons into the care of the local authorities, as they are fostered by a Mrs Swinson in her "beautiful home" (149). This temporary transfer from the impoverished parental home to more comfortable surroundings is a reminder of the unsettling class dynamics of both adoption and fostering. In a parallel fashion to the case of Philomena Lee, financial inequalities and the lack of economic means and support threaten mother–child relations. Ben and Tommy are not rendered vulnerable as a sole consequence of poor parenting or, remembering Tommy's fate, by sinister and deviant forms of adult behaviour. The wider class condition of

---

[25] Caryl Phillips, *The Lost Child* (London: Oneworld, 2015): 66. Further page references are in the main text.

postwar England has a part to play in the sundering of consanguineous relations.

Once Tommy disappears, Ben's adoptability is quickly formalized and, while he is not adopted, he enters the care of a second foster family, the Gilpins. Monica is kept away from her remaining son by the authorities, so she takes to menacing the Gilpins and disrupting Ben's education. As he remarks with distress and frustration,

> a posh woman in a fancy twinset came to see me and told me that Mam was disrupting the Gilpins' household. [...] Things got worse when Mam turned up outside of school, and the teachers wouldn't let me out until she'd gone, and I just wanted the whole thing to end. (179)

Yet the Gilpins' household is no refuge from the privations of his previous dwellings, and in the foster home Ben lives in an environment where support, nurturing, and care are in scant supply. Mrs Gilpin's silent antipathy in particular seems to phrase an undercurrent of prejudice, sourced in attitudes to class and race, that is most notably discerned when she discovers Ben – lonely, adolescent, curious, confused – going through her thirteen-year-old daughter Helen's clothes as he looks for something to wear to a David Bowie concert in 1973:

> Before I knew what I was doing, I was fingering [Helen's] cuddly toys, and then I started pulling open the drawers and touching her clothes. [...] I'd never even touched a bra. Her underwear felt so soft and comfortable, and so I picked some up and smelled them and rubbed them against me a little, and then I could sense somebody standing behind me. I put the pile of panties back into the drawer and turned and saw Mrs Gilpin staring at me. [...] I'll never forget that look on her face. She was glaring at me like she'd finally sized me up and found out who I really was and there was no hiding it now. (181)

In discovering Ben opening and exploring her daughter's drawers, Mrs Gilpin has an opportunity to instruct the pubescent youth on inappropriate behaviour as well as to open a conversation about the changes and challenges which puberty brings; and she might, on reflection or at that moment, understand Ben's longing to experience softness and comfort as sourced in the pain of his austere upbringing and separation from his mother, rather than as evidence of sexual arousal or perceived deviance. But this is 1973, when the placing of black and mixed-race boys in white families with daughters was often discouraged by social workers due to racist assumptions about their libidinous nature. For example, in his 1962 account of life as a Child Welfare Officer in London titled *Paid Servant* – a book which Phillips knows – E.R. Braithwaite records with stunned disdain the attitudes of one of his colleagues who counsels him against seeking to have a mixed-race child adopted by a white family. "Well," she says,

> "there is the problem of placing him in a family where there might be girls. [...] I've had to work among Asians and Africans and West Indians in London and before that in Cardiff, and I know how they feel about things like sex, quite different from the way we English people feel."[26]

Although Phillips does not make it explicit, Mrs Gilpin's silent staring and the impression it makes on Ben that she has found out "who I really was" suggests the presence of such prejudicial attitudes. Rather than regard Ben as bemused, isolated, and pining for the warmth of contact, however inappropriate his unsolicited exploration of Helen's things may be, Mrs Gilpin's subsequent coldness towards Ben "as though I'd somehow interfered with her precious daughter" (183) seems beholden to the dispiriting attitudes towards vulnerable black and mixed-race children at the time as innately sexually threatening – as depraved rather than deprived, unworthy of patient unprejudiced parenting.

Phillips's poetic of proximation means that Ben and Tommy's predicament finds an historical analogue in the seemingly remote travails of the infant Heathcliff figure, whom Phillips fictionalizes as the child of Brontë's Mr Earnshaw and an unnamed slave woman, and whose fortunes open and close *The Lost Child*. Here, too, is a child whose vulnerability and adoptability are established, first, by his living in destitution with an ailing mother near the insalubrious docks in late-eighteenth-century Liverpool, and, second, by her death as a consequence of poverty, neglect, and sexual exploitation:

> Her poor son, who lay with his body curled tightly and his desperate hands clasped over his ears. (My child what have I done to you in this place? Will you ever forgive me?) (11)

As such, the child's predicament foreshadows that of Monica Johnson and her sons and suggests that prejudices of class, gender, and race have firm colonial-crafted antecedents which resound dispiritingly across the centuries.

That said, Phillips concludes *The Lost Child* with deliberate and welcome ambiguity, when he depicts Mr Earnshaw walking from the Yorkshire moors to Liverpool and back to claim the seven-year-old child and bring him into the Earnshaws' home after his mother dies. Phillips's Earnshaw appears a complex

---

[26] E.R. Braithwaite, *Paid Servant* (1962; London: Four Square, 1965): 8. Phillips makes reference to this book in his introduction to the Vintage reissue of Braithwaite's memoir *To Sir, With Love* (1959; London: Vintage, 2005): x. For an extended reading of *Paid Servant*, see McLeod, *Life Lines*, 92–103.

figure who defies ready judgment. On the one hand, his affair with the former slave woman is extra-marital, so his behaviour seems at one with that of many other men in Liverpool who, with scant conscience, use women solely for sexual pleasure. When she becomes pregnant and asks him to send her back to the West Indies, he attempts to procure passage for her, perhaps to remove the inconvenience of her pregnancy from his presence. On the other hand, Earnshaw takes it upon himself after her death to take responsibility for his son by removing him from the dangers of the docks, where he might be pressed into joining a ship or carted off to the workhouse, and finding for him a safer space of refuge in his own home. Rather than impose a vision of delinquency upon him, as did Mrs Gilpin on Ben with her silence and staring, Earnshaw discerns a different kind of look with this mixed-race child:

> There is a luminosity to the boy, as though he is cognizant of something that others cannot see, and this knowledge bequeaths upon him a full awareness of his destiny. (252)

Readers know from *Wuthering Heights* that Heathcliff's destiny will be difficult, to be sure, and this knowledge hinders a reading of Earnshaw's intervention in both novels as purely a laudable form of rescue. Nonetheless, Phillips's presentation of Earnshaw's commitment to his son seems stronger and longer-lasting than the behaviour of the novel's other father figures such as Ronald Johnson, Julius Wilson, and, indeed, Emily Brontë's father, Patrick. "It was his duty," thinks Earnshaw, "to take the scruffy lad into his care and protect him" (257). Without this commitment, such children will remain ever lost.

Yet Earnshaw's commitment only stretches so far, and as *The Lost Child* concludes, Phillips anticipates the deprivations that await the child at Wuthering Heights. Will the Heathcliff figure ever secure personhood or does he exist in some degree as property, as a product of the business that takes Earnshaw regularly to Liverpool? As Earnshaw walks with the child across the moors towards Yorkshire, they are forced to take shelter in a stranger's cottage as a storm rages. The stranger finds them at his door, the ill-dressed child seeming "adrift and lost" (256), and he invites them inside, noting that Earnshaw "gently pushed the boy ahead of him" (256). The stranger senses the child's distress and loneliness in such unfamiliar surroundings, separated from his mother, and offers him comfort: "I have only a little food, some dry bread and milk, but whatever I have I'm disposed to share" (258). When Earnshaw refuses and says they cannot stay long, the stranger baulks a little at his brusque manner and worries about the welfare of the boy, who seems reluctant to depart, leading him to propose that "the boy is welcome to stay" (258). This moment of unconditional reception, of hospitality offered without a price, indeed makes an "asylum of this old man's cottage" (258), a location preferable to the unhappy environs of Wuthering Heights, where the Heathcliff figure is heading. It is the closest we get in Phillips's novel to the salvation of loss, where new relations might be brokered beyond the constraints of class, cost, prejudice, and "duty," where from out of the loss of a parent there might emerge new reciprocal relations, sourced in sadness but compassionate and without preconditions. Instead, Earnshaw deports Heathcliff to an unsettled future of broken belonging where entering his home is not the same as being at home – a sombre predicament captured in the novel's final sentence, which points to a fearful future of displaced dwelling:

> The boy stares now at the man in whose company he has suffered this long ordeal, and he can feel his eyes filling with tears. *Please don't hurt me*. Come along now. There's a good lad. We're nearly home. (260)

In the mother and baby home, Philomena Lee found cruelty and severance, and could not afford to return to her father's house. Her son, Anthony who became Michael, made a new home in the USA but asked after his death to be flown to Ireland and buried at Roscrea, where Philomena eventually found him despite the best efforts of the nuns, in a distant country and a location he had come to think of in terms of home. Phillips's characters find little enduring love at the various homes between which they are shunted, whether it is Monica moving from Oxford to London and then to Leeds, eventually hospitalized and confined as her mental state fragments, or Ben's passing from home to home, ending up at Oxford shunning the overtures of his grandfather. My birth-mother could not take me home: we stayed together for eight days before I was taken to a foster home across London, and forty-five years would pass until she saw me again. These confinements and journeys are part of the cost of adoptability, far beyond the merely fiscal, which is created when those in authority seek rewards from the losses they created in the first place by compelling some to sign up to their own deprivation, "given freely." It would be some solace to regard the stories we have thought about in this essay as an 'uncommon wealth', exceptional and extreme, but they are not. All instances of unequal and intercultural encounters produce adoptable children, vulnerable and exposed to a life lived amidst loss. The hard work of exposing these histories and telling such tales, as the texts I have discussed evidence, has only just begun.

## WORKS CITED

Braithwaite, E.R. *Paid Servant* (1962; London: Four Square, 1965).

Braithwaite, E.R. *To Sir, With Love* (1959; London: Vintage, 2005).

Briggs, Laura. *Somebody's Children: The Politics of Transracial and Transnational Adoption* (Durham NC: Duke UP, 2012).

Clingman, Stephen. *The Grammar of Identity: Transnational Fiction and the Nature of the Boundary* (Oxford: Oxford UP, 2009).

Cooney, John. *John Charles McQuaid: Ruler of Catholic Ireland* (Dublin: O'Brien Press, 1999).

Frears, Stephen, dir. *Philomena* (Pathé Films, UK | USA | France 2013; 98 min.).

Homans, Margaret. *The Imprint of Another Life: Adoption Narratives and Human Possibility* (Ann Arbor: U of Michigan P, 2013).

Humphreys, Margaret. *Empty Cradles* (1994; London: Corgi, 1995).

Jerng, Mark C. *Claiming Others: Transracial Adoption and National Belonging* (Minneapolis: U of Minnesota P, 2010).

McDermott, Patrick. "Disappeared Children and the Adoptee as Immigrant," in *Outsiders Within: Writing on Transracial Adoption*, ed. Jane Jeong Trenka, Julia Chinyere Oparah & Sun Yung Shin (Cambridge MA: South End, 2006): 105–14.

McLeod, John. *Life Lines: Writing Transcultural Adoption* (London: Bloomsbury, 2015).

Park Nelson, Kim. "Shopping for Children in the International Marketplace," in *Outsiders Within: Writing on Transracial Adoption*, ed. Jane Jeong Trenka, Julia Chinyere Oparah & Sun Yung Shin (Cambridge MA: South End, 2006): 89–104.

Phillips, Caryl. *The Lost Child* (London: Oneworld, 2015).

Sixsmith, Martin. *The Lost Child of Philomena Lee* (2009; London: Pan, 2010).

Smith, James M. *Ireland's Magdalen Laundries and the Nation's Architecture of Containment* (2007; Manchester: Manchester UP, 2008).

Yngvesson, Barbara. *Belonging in an Adopted World: Race, Identity, and Transnational Adoption* (Chicago & London: U of Chicago P, 2010).

❄

# Exploring the European 'Common' Wealth

## *A Black British Literary and Artistic Tour*

Francesco Cattani

In one of her most recent essays about the creolization of Europe, Fatima El-Tayeb stresses how "Being European without being white and Christian does not only put one in a strange place, but also in a strange temporality: Europeans who lack one or both of these qualities tend to be read as having just arrived or even as still being elsewhere – if not physically, then at least culturally."[1] Being elsewhere and just arrived is exactly what the black-British texts to be discussed in the following submit to examination: the travel diary *The European Tribe* by Caryl Phillips, the novel *Soul Tourists* by Bernardine Evaristo, and the two installations *A Fictional Tourist in Europe* by Keith Piper and *Gallantry and Criminal Conversation* by Yinka Shonibare. All four stage a more or less fictional journey across European space and history. Producing a collision between colour and whiteness, between those who have 'always belonged' and those who have 'newly arrived', these texts choreograph a strange encounter[2] with what is unfamiliar not because it is alien, but because it has been denied or hidden. They interpellate the idea of Europe as "a historically situated discourse and not a genetic inheritance,"[3] and in the process deconstruct old stereotypes while imagining new patterns of representation in order to recover the hybridized nature of the continent. At the same time, they question its homogenizing narrative, and its underlying ideas of what constitutes Europe, by right or by concession, and what should remain outside or unseen:

---

[1] Fatima El-Tayeb, "European Others" (2015), *Eurozine* (22 February 2017), http://www.eurozine.com/european-others/ (accessed 7 June 2017).

[2] The expression is derived from Sara Ahmed's volume *Strange Encounters: Embodied Others in Post-Coloniality* (London & New York: Routledge, 2000).

[3] Ella Shohat & Robert Stam, *Unthinking Eurocentrism: Multiculturalism and the Media* (London & New York: Routledge, 1994): 4.

what makes up European heritage and the common cultural wealth it represents. Phillips, Evaristo, Piper, and Shonibare demand access to Europe not as new members of the club but as an historical part of it,[4] and in so doing redefine the idea of European citizenship.

In his essay "What is This 'Black' in Black Popular Culture?" Stuart Hall critiques this idea and its underlying colourblindness. He touches on the difference between America and Europe, underlining how, while the former has always been conscious of its composite ethnic origins "and consequently, the construction of ethnic hierarchies has always defined its cultural politics," "Western Europe did not have, until recently, any ethnicity at all. Or didn't recognize it had any."[5] To help create an awareness of Europe's ethnic diversity, Fatima El-Tayeb[6] analyses the way Europeans of colour interrogate and transform essentialist definitions of Europeanness as well as the continent's perception of itself as a racially homogeneous formation. In the introduction to her volume *European Others*, she maintains:

> To reference race as native to contemporary European thought, [...], violate the powerful narrative of Europe as a colourblind continent, largely untouched by the devastating ideology it exported all over the world.
>
> The ideology of "racelessness" is the process by which racial thinking and its effect are made invisible. Race, at times, seems to exist anywhere but in Europe, where racialized minorities have traditionally been placed outside of the national and by extension continental community.[7]

According to El-Tayeb, Europeans of colour have been (and still are) constructed as "'impossible' subjects in heteronormative discourses of nation as well as migration."[8] As a consequence, they have to operate through fissures and cracks to create alternative, 'disobedient' narratives and build their own archive.

---

[4] I want to underline the ambiguity of the expression 'to be recognized', which implies a concession while, as I hope to illustrate, in the works under discussion in this essay, recognition is more a case of self-affirmation.

[5] Stuart Hall, "What is This 'Black' in Black Popular Culture?" in *Black Popular Culture*, ed. Gina Dent (Seattle WA: Bay Press, 1992): 22.

[6] I owe thanks to Fatima El-Tayeb for the valuable inroads she has given me into the texts analysed here and for her useful advice on literature of relevance to my work.

[7] Fatima El-Tayeb, "Theorizing Urban Minority Communities in Postnational Europe," in El-Tayeb, *European Others: Queering Ethnicity in Postnational Europe* (Minneapolis: U of Minnesota P, 2011): xv, xvii.

[8] El-Tayeb, "Theorizing Urban Minority Communities in Postnational Europe," xxxv.

Their pervasive presence, the ever-increasing volume of their voices, their insistence on recuperation and re-vision operate towards a queering of European ethnicity: a troubling of conventional imaginaries, a questioning of what has remained unquestioned so far. Such queering leads to processes of "alternative community building":[9] constantly linking traces, fragments, stories, it undermines received narratives perpetuating monoculturalism and colourblindness and militates against established notions of authenticity and "uncomplicated belonging."[10]

In *We, The People of Europe?* Étienne Balibar describes the production of Europe as the "constitution of a *fictive ethnicity*"[11] predicated on the "characteristic nationalisation of societies [...], and thus of cultures, languages, genealogies."[12] For him, Europe is the product of a process of 'europeanization', of imagining a community and defining its heritage in terms that confirm the fantasy of a monolithic white identity. Instead of acknowledging this identity's adaptability to constantly changing circumstances, its discursive production has insisted on construing Europe as fixed, durable, stable or, in Shohat and Stam's words, "as the unique source of meaning, as the world's centre of gravity, as ontological 'reality' to the rest of the world's shadow."[13]

Already in 1994, Shohat and Stam observed that the conception of Europe as centre of everything was "forcing cultural heterogeneity into a single paradigmatic perspective,"[14] and generating "a geographical fiction that flattens the cultural diversity even of Europe itself."[15] This idea was reiterated in 2012 by Neil Lazarus, who argued that "'Europe' is defined (and, indeed, asserted) in civilizational terms against other 'civilizations' which are not only misrepresented, of

---

9 El-Tayeb, "Theorizing Urban Minority Communities," xxx.

10 "Theorizing Urban Minority Communities," 30. I will come back to the process of queering European ethnicity in the last part of this essay.

11 The expression comes from his 1988 volume, *Race, Nation, Class: Ambiguous Identities*, co-written with Immanuel Wallerstein.

12 Étienne Balibar, *We, the People of Europe? Reflections on Transnational Citizenship*, tr. James Swenson (*Nous, citoyens d'Europe? Les Frontières, l'État, le peuple*, 2001; Princeton NJ: Princeton UP, 2004): 8.

13 Shohat & Stam, *Unthinking Eurocentrism*, 1–2. See also Vita Fortunati & Francesco Cattani, *Questioning the European Identity/ies: Deconstructuring Old Stereotypes and Envisioning New Models of Representation* (Bologna: Il Mulino, 2012).

14 Shohat & Stam, *Unthinking Eurocentrism*, 1.

15 *Unthinking Eurocentrism*, 4.

course, but construed as categorically lesser or inferior."[16] Drawing on Paulo de Madeiros' suggestions, Lazarus underlines the resulting tension:

> 'There are two related flaws' in it where 'Europe' is concerned: first, the amalgamation of everything European into a fictive unity that, even if it might have some correspondence to the dream of homogeneity, has no real counterpart in a fragmented and divided Europe, more often than not torn against itself and amongst its constituent members; second, the forgetting exactly of those parts of Europe that 'Europe' itself tends to forget, its own, anything but central, dominated others.[17]

Neither the collapse of the Eastern bloc nor the progressive expansion of the European Union has disrupted the zealous 'editing' of European identity as a homogeneous formation, and it remains to be seen how the current challenges of the European refugee crisis and Brexit will affect the routine denial of Europe's internal diversity. In a conversation with Balibar, Sandro Mezzadra analyses the European present in terms of a crisis calling into question both the nation-state system and the Enlightenment ideal of tolerance on which the "European social model" hinges. He insists that "the 'whiteness' of the European citizen" has not been put in question by multiculturalism but only "rhetorically 'weakened'" to enable a coexistence with 'non-white' citizens which, however, must remain strictly hierarchical.[18] Therefore, the 'non-white' continues to be viewed as Other, as someone from outside, granted entry but not inclusion to a point where the continent's perceived whiteness must change.[19] The assumption of Europe's immutability is a fallacy increasingly difficult to sustain as European thinkers such as Balibar are conceptualizing Europeans as "a new type of people yet to be defined."[20]

The transformation of the Westphalian nation-state system into the European Union and the influx of immigrants from Africa and the Middle and Near

---

[16] Neil Lazarus, "Spectres Haunting: Postcommunism and Postcolonialism," *Journal of Postcolonial Writing* 48.2 (2012): 123.

[17] Lazarus, "Spectres Haunting," 126.

[18] Étienne Balibar & Sandro Mezzadra, "Borders, Citizenship, War, Class: A Dialogue with Étienne Balibar and Sandro Mezzadra," *New Formations* 58 (2006): 16.

[19] See Rey Chow, commenting on the production of ethnicity in a late capitalist Western society: "Ethnicity as a cultural boundary easily transforms into a type of temporal/historical discrimination, which is laced with self-congratulatory moral righteousness: although 'ethnics' are 'humans' (like us), they are so only because of our *benevolent tolerance* and acceptance of their stubborn difference." Chow, *The Protestant Ethnic & the Spirit of Capitalism* (New York & Chichester: Columbia UP, 2002): 28. (My emphasis.)

[20] Balibar, *We, the People of Europe?*, 2.

East have necessitated a reorganization of the European space by a redrawing of its borders and redefinition of the place of the racial and cultural Other within these borders. According to Balibar, "*borders have changed place*" in the event:

> Whereas, traditionally, [...] they should be *at the edge of a territory*, marking the points where it ends, it seems that borders and the institutional practices corresponding to them have been transported *into the middle of political space*.[21]

This, he submits, has significantly intensified their "socially discriminatory function"[22] and, one might add, reinforced established practices of denial and forgetting. As El-Tayeb notes, according to official discourse there are no minorities in Europe, only migrants[23] – others who have only 'just arrived':

> The ideology of colourblindness is not a passive attitude but an active process of suppression [...]. Encounters with the repressed presence of non-white Europeans – be it through a chance meeting on the subway or TV images of burning cars in neighbourhoods the average European has never visited – are not necessarily forgotten but rather decontextualized, denied any relevance for and interaction with one another by being defined as singular.[24]

Accordingly, encounters with non-whites figure in the dominant European imaginary as unusual, even curious, incidents, as spectacular and outside the 'everyday', and as insistently prompting the question "Where are you from?" which, for El-Tayeb, constitutes the primary scene for a person's erasure from the landscape of Europeanness.[25] Within this landscape, the notion of sharing the European heritage is starkly constricted, implying a magnanimous concession granted by white Europeans on condition that the non-white Other embrace their culture without expecting to become part of it, let alone to be recognized as an historically relevant contributor to its formation.

The texts analysed in the following displace "the European narratives of racelessness by bringing the forgotten history to the fore."[26] Their authors explore Europe's geography for clues to to how their own identity has been shaped by

---

21 Balibar, *We, the People of Europe?*, 109.

22 *We, the People of Europe?*, 113.

23 El-Tayeb, "Theorizing Urban Minority Communities," xxi.

24 "Theorizing Urban Minority Communities," xxiv.

25 As El-Tayeb notes, "the 'true' answer, 'I am from here', is precisely the one that is not acceptable as it falls outside of the logical, the thinkable and thus speakable" (*European Others*, 168).

26 El-Tayeb, "Theorizing Urban Minority Communities," xxvi.

the experience of being labelled 'non-European' or 'new-European'. To question and undo 'official' acts of erasure and restore the impurity of the continent's cultural DNA, they undertake journeys along routes of longstanding popularity among European travellers, claiming these as their own itineraries, as places in which they, too, enact and participate in the European cultural practice of getting to know the continent.

Balibar's definition of European apartheid is useful here, as it allows one to understand the works by Keith Piper and Caryl Phillips as "intentionally provocative expression[s]" signalling "the contradiction between [...] inclusion and exclusion, [...] stigmatization and repression of populations whose presence within European societies is nonetheless increasingly massive and legitimate."[27] Indeed, Keith Piper's *A Fictional Tourist in Europe* may be seen as addressing the same "reduplication of external borders in the form of 'internal borders'" that Balibar identifies as crucial to Europe's policy of covert racial segregation. It speaks directly to the post-1985 Schengen Agreement devised to gradually remove national borders and ease the flow of material goods and, at the same time, curb that of humans. According to Ginette Verstraete, the unlimited mobility of a very limited group of "propertied nationals" has come at the price of a "massive erasure [...] of local particularities of nationality, race and ethnicity."[28] From the beginning symbolically marked by white national identity and territory,"[29] it, in effect, automatically rendered the migrant, the refugee, and the Other illegal, illegitimate, not belonging.

Being black and British, the artist Keith Piper sees his own entitlement to extended residence in Europe as a privilege, but he is also aware that his physical characteristics will still continue to subject him to identification as non-European.[30] *A Fictional Tourist in Europe* was conceived for the exhibition *Unpacking Europe* held in 2001 at the Museum Boijmans Van Beuningen in Rotterdam.[31]

---

[27] Balibar, *We, the People of Europe?*, x.

[28] Ginette Verstraete, "Technological Frontiers and the Politics of Mobility in the European Union," in *Uprooting/Regrounding: Questions of Home and Migration*, ed. Sara Ahmed, Claudia Castañeda, Anne–Marie Fortier & Mimi Sheller (New York: Berg, 2003): 227.

[29] Verstraete, "Technological Frontiers," 232–33.

[30] Keith Piper, "A Fictional Tourist in Europe," in *Unpacking Europe: Towards a Critical Thinking*, ed. Salah Hassan & Iftikhar Dadi (Rotterdam: Museum Boijmans Van Beuningen/NAj Publishing, 2001): 386–87. The visibility of difference is a key focus in Piper's art, especially in *Surveillances: Tagging the Other* (1991), a four-channel video installation, where black subjects are scrutinized by the searching and classifying gaze generated by new technologies, while phrases appear in the background such as: "subject object reject," "Fixing the Boundaries of a New Europe...".

[31] For the occasion, different artists were asked to interrogate the contemporary and historical meanings of Europe as well as the construction of Europeanness. Among these artists were María

This is how Piper has explained the discourse as part of which he expects his installation to be comprehended:

> It is against the backdrop of the official text of Europe, bolstered by the constant activation and reactivation of ancient xenophobic anxieties around the racial 'other,' that 'New Europeans,' Europeans of colour, have for decades presented their labour and have established their presences. Those presences have thrown, and will continue to throw notions of what constitutes 'Europeanness' into flux.[32]

The multimedia installation is composed of a series of projections from a random computer-generated selection of images and texts re-presenting the journey undertaken by a migrant across different European cities, from Italy up to the North of England. Piper describes this journey as "a touristic odyssey through a series of geographic locations and fictionalized moments, some humorous, some terrifying, some nonsensical."[33] The installation creates a tension between tourism (as authorized travel) and migration (as unauthorized movement). One projection presents a map on which iconic touristic landmarks are replaced by the typical stop-overs through which migrants/Europeans of colour have to pass. Each comes with a caption saying "was stopped here," "was intimately searched here," or "was detained here." Thus, a narrative is produced that collides and conflicts with official imaginings and representations of Europe, and meshes with self-consciously aesthetic renderings and memories of other times and places, other landscapes:

> We are seen [...] to be enclosed within an urban space by the abrasive forces of policing, by technologies of surveillance and by the hostile gaze of the 'locals', whilst at the same time being able to transform space through presence, through aesthetics, and through the nostalgic memory of other places.[34]

A similar atmosphere of conflict and collision dominates, albeit in a less humorous way, in Caryl Phillips's autobiographical travelogue *The European Tribe* (1987). Reflections collected by Phillips after an international tour across Europe coalesce into an account of a journey across European apartheid, uncovering a violence that seems endemic to Europeanness and hence part of a European

---

Magdalena Campos–Pons, Coco Fusco, Fiona Hall, Isaac Julien, Nalini Malani, Anri Sala, Yinka Shonibare, Vivan Sundaram, and Fred Wilson.

32 Piper, "A Fictional Tourist in Europe," 388.

33 "A Fictional Tourist in Europe," 387.

34 "A Fictional Tourist in Europe," 387.

transnational common heritage. As Phillips states in the "Preface," the journey he recorded was not simply a tracking of other blacks and Europeans of colour like him, or an attempt to understand what the continent meant to him. Rather, it was an exploration of the tension between himself and his environment and a narrative of how Europe came to define "the parameters of [his] 'problem'."[35] Trying to resolve this cultural confusion and the contradiction of feeling British while being constantly reminded that he does not belong, Phillips sensed that he had to go across and beyond national borders and to encounter his predicament through an experience of the continent, so as to confront Europeans and "the European Academy that ha[d] shaped [his] mind."[36] Feeling "like a transplanted tree that had failed to take root in foreign soil,"[37] he consciously sought to suspend his emotional attachment to his Caribbean origins while searching for his intellectual and cultural roots elsewhere in order to grow what he calls his European "branches."[38]

Phillips realizes that his presence in Europe is precarious not because it is new, but because of the destructive forces he believes are still at work in Europe and capable as ever of erasing his being at any time.[39] Paradoxically, it is in this precariousness that he discovers a connectedness with other non-European minorities, who have been living in consistent non-recognition in Europe for centuries. His identification with other Others brings to mind Françoise Lionnet and Shu-mei Shi's notion of "transnational minorities," emergent "in opposition to a dominant discourse," building horizontal networks and dialogues "vis-à-vis each other and other minority groups."[40] Transnational minorities are groups routinely rejected as alien and relegated to the margins of continents, nations, and regions. This, however, is a condition Phillips thinks no one should accept.

---

[35] Caryl Phillips, *The European Tribe* (London & Boston MA: Faber & Faber, 1987): xiii.

[36] Phillips, *The European Tribe*, 9.

[37] *The European Tribe*, 9.

[38] *The European Tribe*, 9.

[39] Before describing his experience of Amsterdam, Phillips recounts how when he was fifteen he watched a television programme about "the Nazi occupation of Holland and the subsequent rounding up of the Jews," and suddenly realized "the enormity of the crime perpetrated, and the precariousness of my own position in Europe" (*The European Tribe*, 66).

[40] Françoise Lionnet & Shu-mei Shi, *Minor Transnationalism* (Durham NC: Duke UP, 2005): 2. Phillips draws on "the Jewish experience" in order to better understand his own predicament: "As a child, in what seemed to me an hostile country, the Jews were the only minority group discussed with reference to exploitation and racialism, and for that reason I naturally identified with them. [...] I vicariously channelled a part of my hurt and frustration through the Jewish experience" (*The European Tribe*, 54). And later, describing Paris's Belleville, he states, "Here the Jew and Arab exist side by side aware of a common enemy" (63).

In conscious defiance of European colourblindness, he emphatically lays claim to the right to be visibly part of Europe. "History," he declares, "has decreed that we must dig deep for the evidence of our equally great contribution, and cling to it in the face of ignorance" (128).

*The European Tribe* recounts a tour across a continent scarred by division, repression, and suppression. It takes the reader from Morocco to the Russian Empire, through the geographical anomaly and cultural schizophrenia of Gibraltar, into a Moorish Spain now conquered by herds of English "settlers":[41] tourists disrespectful of the local culture.[42] Phillips experiences the antisemitism of Venice and Amsterdam, the hypocritical and selective *egalité–fraternité* of France, and a Northern Ireland impoverished by and entrenched in religious conflict. He passes through a Germany reconstructed by *Gastarbeiter* who do not exist officially and therefore have no civil rights, stays in a still-divided Berlin, and finally reaches the northern border of 'white' Norway. The travel diary becomes a journey through a series of geographical and cultural ghettos. The Europe that emerges is devoid of the civility it is usually attested: its constants are, rather, the rejection, denial, and deletion of its Others. Of course, the tension Phillips senses at the beginning of his journey is provoked by his own ethnic difference. Still, it becomes increasingly clear to him that the cause of the hostility he encounters is external to him, that it does not reside in his otherness but in a history of violence against the non-white Other so pervasive that it has become an integral part of Europe's cultural heritage.

According to Phillips, "very little seems to have changed in the heart of Europe"[43] since the rise of twentieth-century fascisms. In the last chapter, the author returns to a Great Britain haunted by its colonial legacy and desperately striving to re-assess its position in the world.[44] He has acquired a new consciousness of what Europe is and can be critical not only of its racist mentality and its continued toleration of racism, but also of its "defective" eyesight.[45] He

---

[41] Phillips, *The European Tribe*, 35.

[42] *The European Tribe*, 37.

[43] *The European Tribe*, 69. Indeed, in "Revisiting *The European Tribe*," he stressed that nothing has really changed since he undertook his journey in the 1980s. See lecture held at the Institute of English Studies of the University of London on 4 October 2013, on occasion of the fourth Afroeurope@ns conference, 'Black Cultures and Identities in Europe: Continental Shifts, Shifts in Perception', repr. in *The Cross-Cultural Legacy: Critical and Creative Writings in Memory of Hena Maes–Jelinek*, ed. Gordon Collier, Geoffrey V. Davis, Marc Delrez & Bénédicte Ledent (Cross/Cultures 193; Leiden & Boston MA: Brill | Rodopi, 2016): 121–35.

[44] See Phillips, *The European Tribe*, 119–20.

[45] See *The European Tribe*, 128.

believes that Europe is blind to its own past and only by confessing its sins will learn to appreciate its heterogeneity and cultural diversity. It is important for Phillips to keep stressing that the absence of people of colour from Europe and its history is a mere construct and that the creation and perpetuation of this construct, as much as the invisibility of non-white Europeans it has caused, has "perverted" the continent's past.[46] "It is a false history," he notes, "an unquestioning and totally selfish one."[47]

The idea of a falsified history also permeates the works of Bernardine Evaristo and Yinka Shonibare and the historical as well as geographical journeys across and 'within' the continent they describe. To better understand their narrative manoeuvres, it seems worth considering first of all the essay "Europe's Other Self," in which Stuart Hall analyses the impact of fundamentalism and Third-World migration on European identity and redefines European history as a product of discursive construction. In particular, he shows how the continent has narrated, and thus created, its modernity as an "internalist story," "self-generating," "growing from its womb," evolving "from within its own body," denying its central external/internal relations with the Other.[48] Its characteristically introspective acts of remembrance have produced a highly ambivalent European cultural identity informed by both the enduring fantasy of a homogeneous community and the actual coexistence of so many unequals. To resolve the confusion resulting from this complex blending of imagined sameness with lived diversity, it is vital that plural pasts and plural histories should be constituted creatively:

> The construction of alternative local histories and cultures can be a resource for building the future, not just a return to the 'safe haven' of the past: an *invention* rather than simply a rediscovery of tradition, which provides marginalised people with cultural means to construct new identities and counter-narratives without which they cannot survive, let alone contest and negotiate with the West on anything approaching equal terms.[49]

---

[46] 'Pervert' and 'perfect' are verbs used by Caryl Phillips in *The European Tribe* (89, 116). In particular, the latter is chosen to refer to the Soviet state and its rewriting of history in order to order to suppress facts and figures not deemed worth retaining. "The rewriting of Soviet history," Phillips observes accordingly, "has been perfected until it is now a fine art" (116). Likewise, in their volume, Ella Shohat and Robert Stam employ the verb 'to sanitise': "Eurocentrism sanitises Western History while patronising and even demonising the non-West," *Unthinking Eurocentrism*, 3.

[47] Phillips, *The European Tribe*, 120.

[48] Stuart Hall, "Europe Other's Self," *Marxism Today* 35.8 (Autumn 1991): 18.

[49] "Europe Other's Self," 19.

Eight years later, in his essay "Whose Heritage?," Hall posits quite specifically the need to rethink Britishness so as to take into account "the 'Black British' presence and the explosion of cultural diversity and difference."[50] Even if, according to Hall, heritage implies "preservation and conservation,"[51] it is not a fixed essence but an "on-going process" through which a nation builds a "collective social memory" for itself. In particular, Hall defines "storying" as the method nations use to "construct identities by selectively binding their chosen high points and memorable achievements into an unfolding 'national story'. This story is what is called 'Tradition'."[52] Hall also stresses the need for alternatives to the discursive exclusion of ethnic minorities by mis- or non-representation of their alterity and calls for a redefinition of majorities (a category applicable to nations as much as to Europe as a whole) in 'truer' and more inclusive[53] terms:

> There is the demand that the majority, mainstream versions of the Heritage should revise their own self-conceptions and rewrite the margins into the centre, [...]. This is not so much a matter of representing 'us' as of representing more adequately the degree to which 'their' history entails and has always implicated 'us', [...], and vice versa. (10)

"An invention rather than simply a rediscovery of tradition" and a more adequate representation of intertwined pasts is exactly what Bernardine Evaristo undertakes in *Soul Tourists* (2005), a novel in verse and prose mixing imagination and historical documentation. In "CSI Europe," an essay which appeared in the 2008 *Wasafiri* issue dedicated to African Europeans, the author

---

[50] Stuart Hall, "Whose Heritage? Un-Settling 'the Heritage', Re-Imagining the Post-Nation," *Third Text* 13/49 (1999): 3. Despite the essay's focus on the necessity to reconsider the idea of a British national heritage, its principal arguments are also readable as a plea for a new understanding of the European continental heritage.

[51] "Whose Heritage?," 3.

[52] "Whose Heritage?," 5. Here Hall returns to concepts also explored by David Scott and Raymond Williams before him.

[53] I find it important to underline how the concept of 'inclusion' retains a certain degree of ambiguity, as it implies an externality that is transformed into an internality, a position outside rather than one already within the nation-state. This is perfectly expressed by Jo Littler in his introduction to *The Politics of Heritage*, where he notes: "Rethinking national heritage does not only mean 'including' 'other' heritages by simply tacking them on to an official national story that is already sealed, [...] it instead involves *revising* Britain's island stories to acknowledge their long and intertwined histories with complex patterns of migration and diaspora." Jo Littler, "Introduction" to *The Politics of Heritage: The Legacies of 'Race'*, ed. Jo Littler & Roshi Naidoo (London & New York: Routledge, 2005): 1. (My emphasis.)

meditates on her roots and on the necessity of finally opening the eyes of white Europeans to the forgotten history of black presence:

> As a novelist and a poet I am enriched and captivated by the multiple histories unearthed by researchers digging out that which has been lost, forgotten or deliberately overlooked. And I am dismayed and frustrated by the absences which invalidate the black history of the world's Great White Continent. This social amnesia was one of the spurs for my novel, *Soul Tourists*.[54]

Evaristo's novel tells of a road trip through Europe that the protagonist, Stanley, a black Briton, undertakes after the death of his father. He is accompanied by his new lover, Jessie, also a black Briton, who will guide him and open his eyes. The geographical journey immediately turns into a 'voyage in': both into the past of the continent and into the protagonist's genetic and cultural origins. It involves a series of supernatural encounters with historical figures representing the cultural and racial Other of Europe. Evaristo defines them as "whispers, winds, [...] ethereal beings" waiting to be made whole and to make the protagonist whole.[55] Among these historical spectres one finds not only Lucy Negro, the Dark Lady of Shakespeare's sonnets, or Louise Marie, the Black Nun of Moret, believed to be the daughter of Maria Theresa of Spain (the wife of Louis XIV), but also Mary Seacole, the Jamaican nurse of Scottish-African descent whose charitable work has always been outshone by that of Florence Nightingale. There is also Queen Charlotte, wife of George III, whom Evaristo has claim that, thanks to her progeny and their marriages into nearly all the Royal European courts, "there's a little bit of me spread out all over the continent" (286). Evaristo's desire to give visibility to women is obvious, but does not amount to the total exclusion of male figures of black European history. She also conjures up Alessandro de' Medici, Queen Marie Thérèse's black valet Nabo, and Pushkin's grandfather Ibrahim Gannibal.

Evaristo renders audible the unrecorded whispers of these forgotten African ancestors,[56] delivering them from their marginalization as mere objects of

---

[54] Bernardine Evaristo, "CSI Europe," *Wasafiri* 23.1 (2008): 3. The essay was inspired by her participation in the project *Literature Express 2000* that enabled 107 European writers to travel across the continent by train, stopping at various cities from Lisbon to Moscow to hold literary events.

[55] Bernardine Evaristo, *Soul Tourists* (London: Hamish Hamilton, 2005): 70. Further page references are in the main text.

[56] In her essay "CSI Europe," she states, "I was fuming [...] at the tacit historical practice of presenting prominent individuals of African heritage as conveniently racially neutral, aka white.

gossip and thereby also challenging the stigmatization of offspring of extramarital affairs and other 'improper' relations. Thus, she creates a space for Joseph Boulogne, an esteemed musician and the first black colonel in the French Army, to implore Stanley that he should "make of [him] a memory once more," that he should "let [him] be known" (121); or for Zaryab, the Persian composer exiled to Moorish Córdoba, to request that he be recognized for his part in civilizing Europe. "I helped make everyday life a little more beautiful," he claims, "a little more practical, a little more sophisticated, a little more luxurious, a little more learned. This is how great civilizations are created, by little men like myself" (157).

At the same time, the journey becomes an opportunity for Stanley to discover his own otherness: to search for what school never taught him, to re-read History and find the traces of those who 'look like' him, who are visibly his relatives. In the process, the mechanisms of repression and denial Evaristo exposes turn out to pervade private discourse, too – the family history, for instance, passed down to Stanley by his parents. This history, Stanley realizes, is also one shaped by denial, by suppression of what his father considered shameful and therefore unworthy of recollection:

> my people came from a straggly, disgruntled queue
> of slaves, masters and indentured servants,
> of whom I was never allowed to speak –
> the hoe, the road, the rape, the tongue split by a knife,
> then slowly ripped apart like the tough, succulent
> flesh of the yucca
>
> shame, shame, shame *Doan go raking up the past Stanley* […]
>
> [… they] taught me
> to honour my parents but not those who went before,
> stuffed anonymously into an airless attic trunk
> with moth-eaten clothes and discarded mementoes
>
> shame, shame, shame. (122)

Stanley's quest becomes an endeavour of creative re-vision, which ultimately yields what cannot be found in officially approved maps and history books. His constant negotiation between being and becoming, remembering and forget-

---

Take the novelist Alexandre Dumas *père* […] France most widely read and widely filmed novelist. His father was the mixed-race son of a Haitian slave – Marie Céssette. Now, how many people know that?" (3).

ting leads to what Paul Gilroy has defined as "a historical and experiential rift between the location of residence and the location of belonging."[57] Nonetheless, the process of uncovering his roots does not lead to Stanley's break with Europe; rather, it proves to be a wholesome and enriching experience eventually allowing Stanley to develop a new sense of belonging to Europe. Such belonging is what Evaristo herself remembers finding when she finally visited Nigeria, her father's home-country and her own imaginary but unknown 'homeland'.[58] Having been to Africa, she can travel Europe with a difference and appropriate it as hers: "Criss-crossing the continent by car was somehow akin to claiming it. Travelling over thousands of miles of European roads *demystified* and *familiarised* it."[59]

As he explores the past, Stanley becomes aware that the past is exploring him, too, and that his ethereal travel companions have returned to reclaim their place in history and to unsettle Europe's colourblind memory and obstinately "internalist"[60] retrospection. At the beginning of *Soul Tourists*, Stanley is living in an apartment he has furnished with only the absolute essentials and has redecorated in plural shades of white:

> Bone white, white lead, blond, *blanc d'argent*, *blanc de fard*, *blanc fixe*, antimony white, titanium white, strontium white, Paris white, zinc oxide, zinc sulphide. Before I moved into this place and redecorated I never knew there were so many official shades of white. (11)

The asceticism he has cultivated is a mask concealing his personality but also disallowing him to develop any sense of true belonging and ownership. In leaving his colourless abode and setting out on his journey, he is forced to overcome his chromophobia and love of "pure emptiness" (11) and cultivate a love of colour and fullness, of an affluence of images and voices. Constantly challenging him to "stop acting like a resident without a permit" (51), his companion Jessie assists him in finding a way of seeing this affluence as entirely his.

Thus, the recognition of full entitlement replaces the stance of demurely grateful acceptance of "benevolent tolerance."[61] Stanley no longer needs to think of his European heritage as a gift bestowed on him in a process of decolonization but can regard it as a possession that has never been anyone else's, as a lost

---

[57] Paul Gilroy, *Between Camps: Nations, Culture and the Allure of Race* (London & New York: Routledge, 2000): 124.

[58] Evaristo, "CSI Europe," 4–5.

[59] "CSI Europe," 5. (My emphasis.)

[60] See Hall, "Europe's Other Self," 18.

[61] Chow, *The Protestant Ethnic*, 28. See also note 11.

treasure returned to its rightful owner. Jessie teaches Stanley that it is not only the fact of being born and bred in Britain that has made him "just another Englishman" (51). History has actually bestowed on him the right to be British and to be considered British. As Jessie suggests to him,

> "Think that slavery and the colonies were a pipeline of liquid fertilizer pumping away into the British soil for four hundred years so that the money trees on this fair isle could grow big and strong. Think that gives us land rights, don't you?" (51–52)[62]

Through his encounter with all those spectres of the past, history ceases to be a pure abstraction for Stanley and becomes a concrete reality, as 'corporeal' as his blackness. The "visitations" from the past change not only the protagonist but also the 'face' of Europe, transforming its history into a non-linear genealogy based on affiliation rather than concession:

> Maybe you didn't have to blend in or be accepted to belong. You belonged because you made the decision to and if you truly believed no one could knock it out of you. These visitations came from inside the body of history, turning its skin inside out and writing a new history upon it with a bone shaved down to a quill dripped in the ink of blood. Europe was not as it seemed, Stanley decided, and for him, at least, Europe would never be the same again. (189)

Stanley's journey through actual space turns into an exercise in imaginary historiography that questions the homogenizing fiction Europe has been telling itself. It is a form of rediscovery and interrogation, but also of identification and

---

[62] This brings to mind Stuart Hall's often quoted statement on the UK's connection to its colonies being defined not by separate outside/inside histories but by a unique, common history:

> People like me who came to England in the 1950s have been there for centuries; symbolically, we have been there for centuries. I was coming home. I am the sugar at the bottom of the English cup of tea. I am the sweet tooth, the sugar plantations that rotted generations of English children's teeth. There are thousands of others beside me that are, you know, the cup of tea itself. Because they don't grow it in Lancashire, you know. Not a single tea plantation exists within the United Kingdom. This is the symbolization of English identity – I mean, what does anybody in the world know about an English person except that they can't get through the day without a cup of tea?
>
> Where does it come from? Ceylon – Sri Lanka, India. That is the outside history that is inside the history of the English. There is no English history without that other history.

—Stuart Hall, "Old and New Identities, Old and New Ethnicities," in *Culture, Globalization and the World-System: Contemporary Conditions for the Representation of Identity*, ed. Anthony D. King (Basingstoke & London: Macmillan, 1991): 48–49.

"disidentification," as envisaged by El-Tayeb, who proposes seeing the latter not as rejection but as the creation of a moment of "disruption" or "reorientation."[63] Similarly, José Esteban Muñoz conceives of a minority group's disidentification as a dialogic engagement with normative citizenship constitutive of a new cultural space, a "counterpublic sphere,"[64] that displaces the nation and the continent (or, indeed, any normative space), thereby legitimizing presences that neither strictly oppose the norm nor assimilate to it unconditionally.[65]

Such a presence is constituted in the work of the British-Nigerian artist Yinka Shonibare. I will not concentrate on the most recognized feature of his art – his ironical play on received assumptions of 'African authenticity' in his tableaux of headless mannequins wearing opulent dresses made from wax fabric produced in Europe for an African market.[66] This play is part of a larger scheme to reproduce cultural stereotypes and thereby fashion works of art as Trojan horses with which the artist may enter mainstream culture, as Shonibare puts it, unnoticed until they "wreak havoc."[67] His videos, photographs, and installations are not counter-histories but intrusions into officially recorded History. They seek to "draw attention to […] incomplete cultural histories, prompting the politicized and transitive spectator to play a more reflexive role in humanizing contemporary and future [and past] narratives."[68]

It seems appropriate, therefore, to approach Shonibare's art as decollage rather than collage. By painting layers of fragmented images onto a lacerated

---

63 El-Tayeb, "Theorizing Urban Minority Communities," xxxiii–xxxiv.

64 José Esteban Muñoz, *Disidentifications: Queers of Color and the Performance of Politics* (Minneapolis & London: U of Minnesota P, 1999): 7.

65 By way of reference to the theories of the linguist Michel Pêcheux, Muñoz states: "Disidentification is the third mode of dealing with dominant ideology, one that neither opts to assimilate within such a structure nor strictly opposes it; rather disidentification is a strategy that works on and against dominant ideology. Instead of buckling under the pressure of dominant ideology […] or attempting to break free of its inescapable sphere […], this 'working on and against' is a strategy that tries to transform its cultural logic from within" (11).

66 Shonibare has often recounted the story of how he began his career. Born in Great Britain to Nigerian parents who moved back to Lagos when he was still a child, he relocated to London for his studies. Asked by one of his teachers why his artwork, clearly influenced by the anti-Thatcherism of the 1980s, was not African in theme, and intrigued by the idea that as a person of African origin he should make African art, he started to interrogate what 'africanness' was. This gave him the idea of dressing headless mannequins in (usually) Victorian garments made of textiles, African in design yet produced in Indonesia for Dutch and British manufacturing companies and distributed from there to West Africa.

67 "Yinka Shonibare by Anthony Downey," *BOMB* 23 (Fall 2005).

68 Grant Pooke, *Contemporary British Art: An Introduction* (London: Routledge, 2011): 161.

canvas, decollage aims to expose the palimpsestic nature of reality, its composition of different versions of the past that connect, clash, and contrast with each other. Just as his colourfully costumed mannequins create a symbolic disruption of European History, Shonibare's videos and photographs reveal what has traditionally been concealed, such as the wealth Britain accumulated by exploitation of her colonies. As Robert Stilling phrases it, Shonibare's narratives "achieve historical depth [...] by meticulously imagining historical impossibilities that reveal hidden connections."[69]

In *Scramble for Africa* (2003), Shonibare thematizes Europe's oblivion to its colonial past and re-stages the 1884–85 Berlin Conference. It assembles fourteen headless mannequins, representing the political powers involved in the Partition, dressed in Victorian garments made of 'African' print textiles and gathered around a table whose surface shows a map of Africa. In Stilling's words, Shonibare's installation casts the colonial subject as a central character in Europe's drama of self-definition[70] and turns the history of Europeans scrambling for Africa into fiction. The artist's counter-history is no more truthful than European accounts, but parodies in bitterly ironic manner the Europeans' unashamed distortions of the past, provocatively claiming a place in what appears to be a perfectly accepted and, indeed, much-honoured practice of imaginative confabulation. In the event of such ironic imitation or mimicry, the truth of European historiography's untruthfulness is not merely noted but put into play to bleakly comical effect.

Created in 2002 for the eleventh edition of Kassel's *Documenta*, Shonibare's *Gallantry and Criminal Conversation* (2002) advances a particularly confrontational idea of a journey across Europe by subjecting the popular motif of the historical Grand Tour to radical transformation and distortion. The installation is composed of a carriage suspended from the ceiling over several groups of headless mannequins dressed in 'African-Victorian' costumes. Lying scattered among trunks, their bodies assume varying sexual positions. The carriage above them provocatively suggests that, while advertised as serving the purpose of higher education and cultural refinement, the Grand Tour was really a form of sex tourism.[71] At the same time, the African fabrics worn by the mannequins invite a Saidian contrapuntal reading not only as a commentary on the morality of

---

[69] Robert Stilling, "An Image of Europe: Yinka Shonibare's Postcolonial Decadence," *PMLA* 128.2 (March 2013): 305.

[70] Stilling, "An Image of Europe," 316.

[71] Yinka Shonibare, "Setting the Stage: Yinka Shonibare MBE in Conversation with Anthony Downey," in *Yinka Shonibare MBE* (Munich, London & New York: Prestel, 2008): 42.

Europe's first 'tourists' and the nature of the entertainment they were offered but also as tongue-in-cheek references to wealth gathered in the colonies and spent lavishly by members of Europe's affluent classes on tour in foreign places closer to home. Thus, conjuring up an 'impossible fictional alternative' to official history, *Gallantry and Criminal Conversation* debunks Europe's claims to civilizing superiority, suggesting instead hitherto unthought-of affinities between Europe and the colonies in the form of physical intimacies performed and endured by Shonibare's mannequins, which symbolically also insinuate intimacies of another order – among different stories, histories, and geographies.

By postulating the presence of the Other at the European centre well before the implosion of Europe's Empires, the works by Shonibare, Phillips, and Evaristo destabilize any idea of European 'normativity'. One could say, in Neil Lazarus' words, that

> the attempt made is not to 'unthink Eurocentrism' or to 'provincialize Europe' or to promote and advocate for a 'post-European perspective' or a 'post-Occidentalism,' but, on the contrary, to seek to install oneself at the very heart of 'Europe' – as 'core European'.[72]

In this respect, their works perform a queering of ethnicities as described by Fatima El-Tayeb: a critical confrontation with a cultural heritage based on the exclusion and denial of a supposed difference that never existed in reality:

> The queering of ethnicity, diversion, situational communities and diasporic intersubjectivities employed by racialized minorities all work against the attempt to cohere them out of existence, resisting not only their erasure from the contemporary European landscape but also from its past. The queering of ethnicity has the dual function of inserting European minorities into the ongoing debate around the continent's identity and of reclaiming their place in its history, with the creation of alternative archives working as a bridge between the two.[73]

Queering the European past as well as the European present not only implies a breaking with or refusal of the European common wealth and the majority culture on which it is based, but acknowledges the necessity of a continuous negotiation and redefinition of Europe's cultural wealth. It is a strategy not simply of survival but of regeneration by validation of a history of otherness as a commonly shared resource rather than a trauma that needs to be overcome.

---

[72] Lazarus, "Spectres Haunting," 127.

[73] El-Tayeb, "Creolizing Europe."

## Works Cited


Ahmed, Sara. *Strange Encounters: Embodied Others in Post-Coloniality* (London: Routledge, 2000).

Balibar, Étienne. *We, the People of Europe? Reflections on Transnational Citizenship* (*Nous, citoyens d'Europe?: Les Frontières, l'État, le peuple*, 2001; Princeton NJ: Princeton UP, 2004).

Balibar, Étienne, & Sandro Mezzadra. "Borders, Citizenship, War, Class: A Dialogue with Étienne Balibar and Sandro Mezzadra," *New Formations* 58 (2006): 10–30.

Chow, Rey. *The Protestant Ethnic & the Spirit of Capitalism* (New York: Columbia UP, 2002).

Downey, Anthony. "Yinka Shonibare," *BOMB* 23 (Fall 2005), http://bombmagazine.org/article/2777/yinka-shonibare (accessed 23 February 2015).

El-Tayeb, Fatima. "European Others," *Eurozine* (22 February 2017), http://www.eurozine.com/european-others/ (accessed 7 June 2017). Original, slightly different version as "Creolizing Europe," *Manifesta Journal* 17 (2013), http://www.manifestajournal.org/issues/creolizing-europe-0# (accessed 23 February 2015).

El-Tayeb, Fatima. "Introduction: Theorizing Urban Minority Communities in Postnational Europe," in El-Tayeb, *European Others: Queering Ethnicity in Postnational Europe* (Minneapolis: U of Minnesota P, 2011): xi–xlvi.

Evaristo, Bernardine. "CSI Europe," *Wasafiri* 23.1 (2008): 2–7.

Evaristo, Bernardine. *Soul Tourists* (London, Hamish Hamilton, 2005).

Fortunati, Vita, & Francesco Cattani. *Questioning the European Identity/ies: Deconstructuring Old Stereotypes and Envisioning New Models of Representation* (Bologna: Il Mulino, 2012).

Gilroy, Paul. *Between Camps: Nations, Culture and the Allure of Race* (London: Routledge, 2000).

Hall, Stuart. "Europe Other's Self," *Marxism Today* 35.8 (Autumn 1991): 18–19.

Hall, Stuart. "Old and New Identities, Old and New Ethnicities," in *Culture, Globalization and the World-System: Contemporary Conditions for the Representation of Identity*, ed. Anthony D. King (Basingstoke: Macmillan, 1991): 41–68.

Hall, Stuart. "What is This 'Black' in Black Popular Culture?," in *Black Popular Culture*, ed. Gina Dent (Seattle WA: Bay Press, 1992): 21–33.

Hall, Stuart. "Whose Heritage? Un-Settling 'the Heritage', Re-Imagining the Post-Nation," *Third Text* 13/49 (1999): 3–13.

Lazarus, Neil. "Spectres Haunting: Postcommunism and Postcolonialism," *Journal of Postcolonial Writing* 48.2 (2012): 117–29.

Lionnet, Françoise, & Shu-mei Shi. *Minor Transnationalism* (Durham NC: Duke UP, 2005).

Littler, Jo. "Introduction" to *The Politics of Heritage: The Legacies of 'Race'*, ed. Jo Littler & Roshi Naidoo (London: Routledge, 2005): 1–19.

Muñoz, José Esteban. *Disidentifications: Queers of Color and the Performance of Politics* (Minneapolis & London: U of Minnesota P, 1999).

Phillips, Caryl. *The European Tribe* (London: Faber & Faber, 1987).

Phillips, Caryl. "Revisiting *The European Tribe*" (October 2013), in *The Cross-Cultural Legacy: Critical and Creative Writings in Memory of Hena Maes–Jelinek*, ed. Gordon Collier, Geoffrey V. Davis, Marc Delrez & Bénédicte Ledent (Cross/Cultures 193; Leiden & Boston MA: Brill | Rodopi, 2016): 121–35.

Piper, Keith. "A Fictional Tourist in Europe," in *Unpacking Europe. Towards a Critical Thinking*, ed. Salah Hassan & Iftikhar Dadi (Rotterdam: Museum Boijmans Van Beuningen/NAj Publishing, 2001): 386–91.

Pooke, Grant. *Contemporary British Art: An Introduction* (London: Routledge, 2011).

Shohat, Ella, & Robert Stam. *Unthinking Eurocentrism: Multiculturalism and the Media* (London: Routledge, 1994).

Shonibare, Yinka. "Setting the Stage: Yinka Shonibare MBE in Conversation with Anthony Downey," in *Yinka Shonibare MBE* (Munich: Prestel, 2008): 39–45.

Stilling, Robert. "An Image of Europe: Yinka Shonibare's Postcolonial Decadence," *PMLA* 128.2 (March 2013): 299–321.

Verstraete, Ginette. "Technological Frontiers and the Politics of Mobility in the European Union," in *Uprooting/Regroundings: Questions of Home and Migration*, ed. Sara Ahmed, Claudia Castañeda, Anne–Marie Fortier & Mimi Sheller (New York: Berg, 2003): 225–49.

❄

# Alpenreich | Alpine Riches

*Writing Back Mountain Stories*

Eva–Maria Müller

Although my part-German, part-English title contains the concepts 'alpine' and 'rich', the two compounds "Alpenreich" and "Alpine Riches" mean very different things.[1] In English, the term 'alpine riches' refers generally to the idea of wealth, taking into account the material and immaterial abundance that makes mountainous regions valuable for humans. The German word 'Alpenreich' is more complex: 'reich', and its capitalized twin 'Reich', denotes both 'rich' *and* 'empire'. Therefore, in German the concept of alpine riches – despite all its negative implications – already contains the echo of empire, and it is that echo that the present essay explores in addressing the industries capitalizing on mountains by focusing on how alpine spaces are represented (and misrepresented) in literature. With a view to exploring how certain contemporary writers in Austria and Canada offer a postcolonial critique of alpine riches in the shadow of empire, I will set out my argument in three individual steps culminating in a concluding ascent. The first step is a mountain story set in Innsbruck, Austria.

In the time of the giants, as all Tyroleans know, there lived high on the mountains above present-day Innsbruck a giant queen, whose name was Frau Hitt. Her empire was composed of magnificent forests and her palace was so rich and sumptuous that it looked like a tower of diamonds. One day a beggar woman with a child in her arms stopped Frau Hitt and asked her for a piece of bread. Frau Hitt laughed scornfully, took a piece of rock, and hurled it at the woman. But the giant queen had a child as well, and one day it happened that her beloved son fell into a swamp while he was playing in the nearby forest. When the

[1] I owe enormous thanks to my guide into the world of alpine fictions, Stephen Slemon. This article could not have been written, had it not been for him, and the extraordinary literary scholar, postcolonial thinker, and mountain-lover that he is.

boy returned to the palace covered in dirt, Frau Hitt ordered her servants to clean his body with bread and milk. This filled up the measure[2] of Frau Hitt's life-long extravagance, and as her servants executed her sinful command, a heavy thunderstorm built up in the alpine valley, enveloping everything in a dreadful darkness. Earthquakes shook the whole mountain, the palace of Frau Hitt was blown into smithereens, and enormous boulders of rock and avalanches began to fall. Within a few hours, her paradisiacal 'Alpenreich' was destroyed, and all around, nothing was to be seen but a large stone desert. Frau Hitt was changed into a rock, and there she stands to this day, holding her petrified son in her arms, and thus she must remain until the end of the world.

Frau Hitt is one of the most prominent and storied peaks in Tyrol and the tale of its origin has been passed down for centuries. One would, indeed, be hard-pressed to find a point of departure more fitting to start critical reflections about empire, literature, and alpine riches, not only because the fable explains how the uneven distribution of wealth and power can lead to the destruction of a natural and cultural environment but also because it is evidence of the cultural practice employed to produce or, rather, preserve a specific sense of place. It is a sense of place predicated on the understanding that places reflect existing power-structures.

Apart from being used in stories exposing injustice and the failings of the powerful, mountains have also been used in popular narratives to inspire respect for the powers of nature. Until the disenchantment of the world in the eighteenth century, the forces of nature that cause landslides, avalanches, and rock-falls were ascribed to the power of sinister mythical beings – to beasts, dragons, gods, and giantesses.[3] Stories about mountains are saturated with them, thus constituting a very particular human history of knowledge, affect, and memory mainly for the purpose of teaching locals to stay at a safe distance from the mountains.

The second step in my argument starts where "Frau Hitt" leaves off – in the nineteenth century, when the alpine wasteland turned from an obstacle to the traveller's progress into a traveller's destination in its own right, due a renewed interest in science, a change in the overall understanding of what was beautiful, and an insatiable colonial appetite for exploration. Despite the fact that Romantic and Victorian writers often had an anthropological interest in folk-tales (not

---

[2] Given that mountains have been frequently understood as spiritual spaces, it is no coincidence that the tale of Frau Hitt uses the biblical concept of filling up the measure of sins, guilt, and iniquities (Genesis 15:16, Matthew 23:32, Thessalonians 2:16, Jeremiah 44:22) along with the idea of divine retribution.

[3] Robert Macfarlane, *Mountains of the Mind* (New York: Pantheon, 2003): 205.

to mention a pronounced interest in the supernatural), their colonial selves won out, so that, in their experience of the mountain, they erased local legends and imposed their own narratives of colonial conquest in obedience to a distinctly colonial aesthetics. The second step in my argument, therefore, engages with stories of empty space.

Under the influence of the Romantics, who assigned sublime and picturesque qualities to uncultivated nature and glorified the individual, as well as concepts of solitude and liberty, mountains moved from the periphery of scientific discourse and cultural production into the light of a growing mountaineering culture. Early-nineteenth-century 'grand tourists,' such as William Wordsworth, S.T. Coleridge, and Percy Bysshe Shelley, returned home from their passage across the Simplon Pass, shaken by the 'joyful terror' and 'terrible beauty' which they felt in the presence of mountains. Between 1800 and the 1820s, a wave of Romantic literature pertaining to the Alps reached the British (and German)[4] upper-middle classes, and prompted in the well-educated reading audience the desire to gaze at "these primaeval mountains"[5] and see for themselves "the immeasurable height of woods decaying, never to be decayed, the stationary blast of waterfalls,"[6] "the summit of Mont Blanc," and "the wondrous Vale of Chamony."[7] Rendering their travel experiences in poetry, Shelley, Wordsworth, and Coleridge sparked in their privileged readers a curiosity for what was to them a largely unknown but strangely compelling place at the heart of Europe. When they depicted mountains as a "desert peopled by the storms alone,"[8] these writers suppressed the meaning that mountains had for those who lived at their feet, and even went so far as to erase the physical presence of locals themselves. Shelley's famous projection of Mont Blanc as inhabited only by natural and climatic forces is just one indication that mountains were becoming a place which was, for the travelling eye, first and foremost, empty.

The Alps, which appealed to the nineteenth-century mind in the same way as the distant, mysterious, and exotic places of imperial conquest had, could be

---

[4] German equivalents of Wordsworth, Coleridge, and Shelley are undoubtedly Johann Wolfgang von Goethe and Albrecht von Haller, whose poem *Die Alpen* (1729) was one of the earliest signs for the rising appreciation of mountains.

[5] Percy Bysshe Shelley, "Mont Blanc: Lines Written in the Vale of Chamouni" (1816), in *The Complete Poetic Works of Percy Bysshe Shelley*, ed. Thomas Hutchinson (Oxford: Oxford Wordsworth, 1914): 29.

[6] William Wordsworth, *The Prelude, or Growth of a Poet's Mind: An Autobiographical Poem* (London: Edward Moxon, 1850): 161.

[7] Wordsworth, *The Prelude*, 157.

[8] Shelley, "Mont Blanc," 28.

reached in a single day-long journey, thanks to the railways that provided easy access in the 1830s and '40s.[9] If a person wanted to feel like an explorer, he no longer had to board a ship, sail to the farthest places of the empire, and roam distant jungles; he could simply board a train to the Alps, hire a guide, and climb an 'unconquered' mountain. Exploration became an affordable leisure and Victorian travellers swarmed over the Alps, equipped with quotations from Romantic poetry and with the nationalist heroic and imperialist ideology of their age. In most nineteenth-century British writing pertaining to the Alps, mountains were written about as places that have no intrinsic value and only gain worth when they can be taken, exploited, and related to the self. With a few exceptions,[10] the stories that were told about mountains from the mid-nineteenth century onwards were narratives about reaching summits and conquering heights, and authored by those who could afford to read, write, travel, and climb for pleasure – a privilege enjoyed by few of those who lived at the feet of these peaks.

Despite the local imaginaries, which were infused by an appreciation for the inherent spiritual value of mountains, the wealth of nineteenth-century travel literature and the cacophony of colonial voices whitened out local narratives and transformed mountain landscapes into a blank canvas on which new stories could be drawn, stories that would eventually transform mountains from feared trading routes into centres of commerce. One of the strongest and most influential Victorian voices was undoubtedly Virginia Woolf's father Leslie Stephen, co-founder of the British Alpine Club, who contributed to the semantic manufacture of mountains. When he wrote about the Alps as a *Playground for Europe* (1871), he made mountains into an alpine empire for recreation – an 'Alpenreich'.

The title of Stephen's book fosters the impression that the Alps, although at the geographical centre of the continent, are not part *of* Europe but a pleasure periphery *for* its imperial centre. Accordingly, the second step in my argument addresses 'the imperial' in 'Alpenreich', with the aim of showing that mountain regions – whether they are located in the far-away places of the British Empire or at the crowded heart of Europe – have been successfully turned into tourist

---

[9] John Urry & Jonas Larsen, *The Tourist Gaze 3.0* (London: Sage, 2011): 14.

[10] In another essay, it would be interesting to analyse how British and German women writers, unlike their male fellow mountain travellers, acknowledged mountain knowledge by including local legends into their travelogues. Marie Alker von Günther's and R.H. Busk's renderings of the late-nineteenth-century Tyrol would invite such a study. See Marie Alker von Günther, *Tales and Legends of the Tyrol* (London: Chapman & Hall, 1874), and R.H. Busk, *The Valleys of Tirol: Their Traditions and Customs and How to Visit Them* (London: Longmans, Green, 1874).

destinations by being charged with one of the most culturally violent key concepts of imperial conquest: namely, the idea of understanding foreign land as a *terra nullius* – land of no one. At the core of this notion lies the postcolonial doctrine of the first hour – that "imperialism means thinking about, settling on, controlling land that you do not possess,"[11] and that this land that is "owned by others"[12] is taken into possession by those in power, and with supreme disregard for any local claims to it. This notion of empty space is an obvious one in postcolonial scholarship, but one that remains to be explored in regard to alpine environments. It provides a productive tool for analysing the hegemonic forces at work in mountain spaces today, and invites reflection on the discipline itself, as it shows that colonialism is not only about torrid, extra-European zones, but that the imperialist mode extended even into cold and intra-European regions. Alpine spaces were laid claim to in precisely the sequence that Edward Said suggests: they were first thought of, dreamt of, and written about by those who did not know the land. Then they were settled by means of the colonial symbolism of flag and cross,[13] and ultimately controlled by external capital through the development of a tourist infrastructure with an outfitting industry, pack animals, local guides, hotels, and guidebooks.

Colonial settling was not limited to written representation. An equally invasive, and much more visible, form of settling is the physical act of claiming land. Much of alpine Europe carries temporary or permanent visual symbols of colonial (dis)possession. Helga Ramsey–Kurz explains how the Austrian Alps were invaded with the logic of the conquest of far-away islands, where "the conviction has survived that the last uninhabited (or least inhabitable) spaces in Central Europe must bear noticeable signs of [colonial] consecration."[14] Edmund Hillary's burying of a miniature crucifix on top of Mountain Everest, the highest mountain on the edge of empire, was part of a tradition of placing crucifixes and flags on mountaintops – both of them imperial gestures that survived the historical demise of the British Empire.[15] The colonizing mission was to define and create a space that "Europeans proceed to fill [...] with the evidences of

---

[11] Edward W. Said, *Culture and Imperialism* (New York: Vintage, 1994): 7.

[12] Said, *Culture and Imperialism*, 7.

[13] See, for example, Stephen Slemon, "Tenzing Norgay's Four Flags," *Kunapipi* 34.2 (2012): 32–41, and Helga Ramsey–Kurz, "Tokens or Totems? Eccentric Props in Postcolonial Re-Enactments of Colonial Consecration," *Literature and Theology* 21.3 (2007): 302–16.

[14] Helga Ramsey–Kurz, "Tokens or Totems?," 302–303.

[15] Stephen Slemon, "Tenzing Norgay's Four Flags," 32–41.

their culture."[16] When Said says that "the idea that the earth is in effect one world, in which empty, uninhabited spaces virtually do not exist," his theory suggests an application to alpine spaces.

In the centennial year of the beginning of the First World War, when the Austrian Alps are being commemorated as battlegrounds, it becomes important to show that alpine battles today, as much as in the nineteenth century, are not "about soldiers and cannons but also about ideas, about forms, about images and imaginings."[17] The ideas and forms that wrote mountains into being in the nineteenth century are just as powerful and destructive a weapon as a military invasion, and the narratives of empty space have turned mountain regions today into combat zones in which investors, locals, and travellers fight for their share at the cost of local cultures and fragile ecosystems. The fact that the democratization of modern travel and the resulting invasion of alpine spaces has not dismantled the colonial imagery of untouched wilderness and empty landscape can be attributed to the special dynamics of representation and circulation. Here my approach accords with that of Anthony Carrigan, who states that the realities of tourist sites acquire their texture by way of repetition of their various representations. Such repetitions are central to producing the cliché of the empty mountain that feeds the tourism industry, and implies the re-activation and perpetuation of colonial concepts.[18] I want to extend what Carrigan explains in regard to tropical islands and tourist brochures to alpine spaces and their literary representations, since mountains, like other spaces, are constituted by the narratives that envelop them.

In Austria and Canada, a number of contemporary writers have been problematizing the Alpenreich by undertaking a telling-back of their own mountain stories. Imperialist thinking has produced not only a wealth of texts on mountain explorations but also a wealth of writing protesting against such exploration and the usurpation following it. The third and final step in my argument is therefore about the riches of narrative, and shows how contemporary mountain literature of the Austrian Alps and the Canadian Rockies addresses the imperialist rhetoric of *terra nullius* and harkens back to a time in which mountains were ruled by myth and legend, rather than by the economy of tourism. To illustrate

---

[16] Alan Frost, "Old Colonisations and Modern Discontents: Legacies and Concerns," in *Proceedings of the Inaugural Conference of The Samuel Griffith Society, Hillton-on-the-Park, Melbourne,* 24–26 July 1992, http://www.samuelgriffith.org.au/papers/html/volume%201/chap11.htm (accessed 15 February 2015).

[17] Said, *Culture and Imperialism,* 7.

[18] Anthony Carrigan, *Postcolonial Tourism: Literature, Culture, and the Environment* (London: Routledge, 2011): 26.

this movement, I have chosen to discuss Angie Abdou's *The Canterbury Trail* (2011) and Elfriede Jelinek's *In den Alpen* (2002), but I should add that other Canadian and Austrian mountain narratives, such as *Icefields* (1995) by Thomas Wharton and *Die Piefke Saga* (1991) by Felix Mitterer, also support my argument.

In *The Canterbury Trail*, Abdou imagines a backcountry ski trip in the Canadian Kootenays as a pilgrimage, and offers a black comedy of ski culture in which mountain travellers from all walks of life compete with each other in their attempt to reach the summit and claim dominion over the mountain. Rednecks, ski bums, hippies, realtors, locals, and city-dwellers, all set out for Camelot, a mountain cabin off Coalton, a fictionalized version of Fernie, British Columbia, with very distinct expectations of what their last springtime ascent should be like. Despite their different ideas and ideals, all of them seek solitude and follow the perennial pioneering desire to be the first. But Camelot proves to be as illusory and resistant to harmony for this 'unselect few' as its ironically chosen mythic Arthurian template.

To convey a sense of how mountains are still valued for the seeming absence of humans in the twenty-first century, Abdou emphatically renders the alpine landscape as empty in the eyes of her characters. Shanny, the pilgrim introduced as "the rad chick," leaves Coalton early in the morning, hoping to find the mountain "untracked."[19] As she unloads her gear at the foot of the hill,

> Shanny's mouth [was] salivating, at the virgin blanket of sparkling white fluff covering the ground, piling up high on the road signs, coating the branches of all the cedar trees, transforming them to shimmering ghosts. The gradual slope before her beckoned, completely untracked, a perfect marshmallow landscape with not a single footmark in sight. (*CT* 67)

To enforce this atmosphere of mountains as untouched, the author resorts to such expressions as "virgin blanket" (*CT* 67) and has Shanny ascribe value to the landscape because there is "not a single footmark in sight" (*CT* 67). Similarly to the Victorian mountaineers who were eager to claim the first ascent of the Swiss and Austrian peaks, Shanny "wanted her footprints to be the first, each step up the mountain clearly marking her ascent, nothing but untracked beauty before her and only her own imprints in the fresh snow behind her" (*CT* 67). A few paragraphs down, the imperialist motive becomes even more apparent when Abdou frames Shanny as a queen and the landscape as her kingdom:

---

[19] Angie Abdou, *The Canterbury Trail* (Victoria, BC: Brindle & Glass, 2011): 67. Further page references are in the main text after '*CT*'.

> Shanny hoped [...] she could get a healthy lead and be alone in the candied landscape, globs of vanilla ice cream plopped on top of fallen logs, perfect strips of whipped cream sitting along every tree branch. She imagined herself the Queen of the Jujubes, rolling through her Candied Kingdom. (*CT* 68)

Apart from Shanny's wish for the absence of others, the atmosphere of this scene, with its substantial comparisons to candy, leaves no doubt that she comprehends the alpine landscapes as something that tempts leisure explorers to consume. In addition, the reference to the jujube, here a gum-drop but a word derived from a fruit tree native throughout the Indian subcontinent, South-East Asia, and Africa, hints at Shanny's Orientalist appreciation of space and her imperial dominance over it, as these continents, which she imagines to rule as queen, are inseparably linked to British imperial history.

That the narratives of empty space also persist in areas that lie outside what is conventionally perceived as (post)colonial terrain becomes clear in Elfriede Jelinek's *In den Alpen*. The play is based on one of the most tragic accidents in postwar Austria, in which 155 people, who were on their way to the Kitzsteinhorn Glacier, burned to death on 11 November 2000 due to cost-cutting, defective repair of a cable car. Jelinek addresses the destructive forces of mountain tourism and offers a post-imperialist narrative in which the image of the Alps as an empty space is challenged. Despite recent travel statistics revealing that western Austria hosts thirty-four million travellers a year, the Alps are effectively rendered as *terra nullius* in tourist rhetoric.[20] A perfect reaction to this phenomenon is contained in the following passage, which openly suggests that tourists continue to undertake pilgrimage to the Alps with images of an empty 'Alpenreich' before their eyes:

> Das müssen Sie doch zugeben, wenn Sie versucht haben vom Becher des Todes zu nippen, so wie ich, wenn ich die Pistenabsperrung mißachte und drunter durchtauche und mich in den vollkommen unberührten Tiefschnee stürze. Es gibt nichts, das mich sonst so berühren könnte, wie das Unberührte.

"There is nothing that can touch me as much as the untouched,"[21] says the child protagonist, who remembers that she frequently ignored the avalanche barriers,

---

[20] Rainer Ribig, *Tourismus in Zahlen: Österreichische und Internationale Tourismus- und Wirtschaftsdaten* (Vienna: Wirtschaftskammer Österreich, Statistik Austria, 2012): 45.

[21] Elfriede Jelinek, "In den Alpen," in Jelinek, *In Den Alpen: Drei Dramen* (Berlin: Berlin Verlag, 2002): 45. Further page references are in the main text after '*IDA*'. All in-text translations from the

willing to risk her life for a few minutes in untouched powder snow. The tourist industry effectively mobilizes the imagery of colonial mountaineering involved in being the first to set foot on unknown land in order to, paradoxically, attract a crowd. The privilege – the uncommon privilege, one might say – of being the 'first' is thus doled out again and again, becoming a commodity.

The consequences of the abundance of travellers and the wealth of mountain misrepresentation constitute my third move towards the conclusion, as Jelinek and Abdou work not only *with* but especially *against* the imperialist imagery surrounding mountain travel: they show just how crowded alpine regions really are today, unearth the violent history that emptied mountain regions of their inhabitants, and demonstrate that mountain regions with extensive tourism have become emptied of life through their participation in the money-making industry.

At the same time as Abdou and Jelinek show how imperial gestures prevail in mountain travel, their work testifies to the colonial imaginary of mountains as empty spaces failing to hold. As Shanny continues her climb, "the hum of snowmobiles shatter[ing] her illusion that this mountain [is] hers to consume in its frosting-covered entirety" (*CT* 69), she hears the presence of others and must realize that the mountain is not the empty space that she has imagined it to be. Heinz Wittinger, "the hermit," who finds refuge in the mountain wilderness, experiences something similar when "he sip[s] on his purified creek water and gaze[s] across the valley, so untouched that he could convince himself he was the only man on earth" (*CT* 47). Heinz's idea of being "the only man on earth" is merely a construct of his imagination. Abdou's narrative suggests that it would need heavy convincing to think of the mountain as empty:

> he knew, though, that he had not been the first. The hawthorn bushes lay trampled in spots, and the occasional boot imprint in mud, or in the few remaining patches of snow, stood as evidence that others had bushwhacked their way up here. (*CT* 47)

When the different pilgrims finally reach the mountain cabin, they realize that mountains are far from empty. To convey their sense of disillusionment, Abdou describes Loco's physical repulsion at the presence of others when he enters Camelot: "Loco felt his stomach make contact with his throat as the sour smell of the overcrowded room hit him" (*CT* 232). Abdou and Jelinek indicate that what is being sold is the idea of blissful solitude when characters directly or in-

---

German in the remainder of this essay (with the original provided only selectively in the running text or footnotes) are my own.

directly wish "to be alone in the candied landscape" (*CT* 68) and state, "Am liebsten wär ich allein" (*IDA* 33).

The untouched has become a commodity and the tourism industry is aware that it has to guarantee at least the illusion of solitude for its business to continue. It caters to this wish by maintaining the false assumption that mountains are the uninhabited deserts Shelley described in *Mont Blanc*, which is why evidence for human history often finds limited space for the conceptualization and promotion of alpine regions. Few of these thirty-four million travellers who play explorer on the Austrian peaks each year are aware of the violent history that is covered up by the layers of snow and ice (Ötzi being perhaps a signal exception). As border zones and symbols of national meaning-making, mountains have held a contested position in the politics of space throughout the past two decades. In *In den Alpen*, as well as in *The Canterbury Trail*, the layers of snow and ice that allow one to imagine these environments as empty are brushed and hacked away, and a carefully concealed and inconvenient history is exposed. Abdou does this by drawing attention to the indigenous presence that predates colonial exploration through the character F-Bomb, "the ski bum" with native roots. During a dispute over the narratives regarding Coalton's past and future, F-Bomb states: "*My people were here before coal mines, my people were here before tourism*" (*CT* 103, emphasis in the original). Jelinek, in her play, unfolds the national socialist history surrounding the construction of the Kaprun reservoir power station. Hundreds of war prisoners lost their lives during the construction of the dam, and former Nazis found employment at the station after World War Two, a fact that was carefully concealed in the postwar years. Jelinek casts into relief the practice of instructed forgetting by having the child protagonist point towards how "the white fluttering will soon devour the cabin, the houses, the church, and suck it all into a milky nothingness" (*IDA* 47).[22] For a dam project like the one at Kaprun, human presence was an obstacle that had to be removed at all costs. Therefore, the author not only refers to the conceptual transformation of alpine landscapes but also intimates the social, cultural, and territorial aggression that the practice of relocation and the flooding of homes entails.[23] These stories of loss and aggression, along with the evidence of settlement, were, of necessity, buried by the tourism industry in order for the regions

---

[22] "Schauen Sie, es schneit, das weiße Rieseln frißt bald die Hütte auf, die Häuser, die Kirche, saugt es ein in ein milchiges Nichts" (*IDA* 47).

[23] Indeed, the culturally disputed issue of dam constructions and its relations to literary manifestations and discourses was addressed by Helga Ramsey–Kurz in her talk "Dam Stories: When literature becomes concrete and concrete becomes literature" (Edmonton, University of Alberta, 16 October 2012).

to remain what Joseph Conrad, referring to the terra incognita of Africa, called "blank spaces [...] a white patch for a boy to dream gloriously over."[24]

Dreaming over a seemingly primal landscape has undoubtedly become a highly prized privilege in the twenty-first century, a factor Abdou points out in the following passage in which F-Bomb criticizes the visitors' willingness to pay for this experience as much as he attacks Michael, "the developer," for his participation in a business that empties mountains to fill pockets:

> F-Bomb knew the foundation [of their rented miner's shack] had to be sinking. It sure wouldn't be the only rental property in town with a sinking foundation, all the landlords holding fast to their slums, waiting for the new golf course, the ski hill upgrades, something to drive real estate up, up, and up. Soon the land would be worth a fortune, and the landlord would sell to some city slickers ('shitty' slickers, more like it) who'd tear the shack down and build themselves a million-dollar mountain chalet to match the million-dollar view – shimmering snowcapped peaks in every direction. Then they'd act like they'd discovered Coalton, like the whole place sat empty before they arrived. Columbus had nothing over these arrogant pricks from the big shitty. (*CT* 9)

By showing that the highest value of alpine land is its emptiness, and by equating the visitors who are willing to pay for "the million-dollar view" (*CT* 9) with Columbus, Abdou points, with unambiguous clarity, at the colonial power structure that lies at the root of the commodification of alpine land, and thus invites an equation of mountain travel with neo-colonial practices. That the *terra nullius* principle is at the forefront of this venture is indicated when F-Bomb criticizes how travellers behave as if "the whole place sat empty before they arrived" (*CT* 9). As they unearth dark histories and challenge the *terra nullius* doctrine, Abdou and Jelinek protest neocolonial interventions in alpine spaces by showing that mountains, after two hundred years of strategic emptying of meaning, have, in fact, become emptied of life. The consequences of external capital exercising pressure on a local society are revealed when Loco argues with Michael:

> 'Tourism doesn't keep a community alive. Those jobs - $8.50 an hour. That's what they pay. You tell me how you're gonna support a family on that? Not when the houses cost a million dollars.' (*CT* 217)

This passage openly addresses one of the many socio-cultural problems that mass tourism brings, with Michael expressing what John Akama notes is a

---

[24] Joseph Conrad, *Heart of Darkness & Other Stories* (1902; Hertfordshire: Wordsworth, 1995): 36.

typical feature of postcolonial tourism: namely, that "the local people, who bear most of the costs of tourism development [...], do not receive any form of direct monetary benefits from the tourism industry."[25] In the passage above, the character is effectively demonizing the tourism industry and local participation, and showing the kind of consequences it has for a community if its market value, rather than intrinsic qualities, dictates the significance of people's lives. If a community cannot be kept alive, as Loco states, then it is bound to slowly die. To heighten this atmosphere of an alpine community in decay, Abdou has her characters turn to alcohol and drugs in order to fill up the emptiness that extensive tourism created, not only for the landscape but also for its people. Ultimately, the narrative invites comparison of the drunk bodies with corpses, as when Shanny looks "like a corpse propped up on snowshoes" (*CT* 241) after a night at Camelot.

Jelinek even goes a step further: she makes it clear from the start of her play that her main characters are corpses, all victims of the Kaprun disaster(s), speaking to each other in the cable-car terminal. Most of their conversations centre on a reflection of their having become as much a commodity as the landscape they sought. This finds clear expression when the unnamed helper bags the talking dead body remains as if packing commodities into a shopping bag (*IDA* 30). The plastic bags carry numbers to indicate that the people have lost their identity. "I have a bag for you as well," says the helper, "which one was it again?" he asks, and demands that the body tell him which bag is meant for her (*IDA* 30). When the dead body inquires whether "you mean, the bag tells you your number" (*IDA* 30),[26] the atmosphere of the scene creates the impression that what matters most to those working at the station is numbers and quantities, and not human identities, or lives. As much as this passage refers to the national-socialist history surrounding Kaprun (the identification numbers of inmates and the burning of bodies in Nazi concentration camps), it shows that even at the moment of death, humans are but "easily inflammable material" (*IDA* 15) for the ski-lift cooperative and the tourist industry. With this in mind, it seems to be no coincidence that none of the characters Jelinek pours onto the stage, in the fashion of a glacial stream, bears a name. She takes the characterological flatness that Abdou partly adopts to an extreme, and clearly shows

---

[25] John Akama, "Neocolonialism, Dependency and External Control of Africa's Tourism Industry," in *Tourism and Postcolonialism: Contested Discourses, Identities and Representation,* ed. Michael Hall & Hazel Tucker (London: Routledge, 2004): 149.

[26] "Ich habe auch schon den Sack für dich, welcher war es nun gleich? Kannst du mir bitte deinen Nummer sagen? Sei doch nicht so blöd, auf dem Sack steht sie doch drauf! Außen! Du meinst, der Sack sagt dir die Nummer, die für dich vorgesehen ist?!" (*IDA* 30).

that the characters' bodies have to fulfil the money-making "purpose" (*IDA* 25.). The way in which the author introduces "the young woman" supports such a claim, as the stage direction states that the character could "as well be a young man, which might even be better, and then swap gender during the act. Gender irrelevant, body: purpose" (*IDA* 25).[27] Hereby, *In den Alpen* shows just how much mountains have ceased to be a means to an end in travelling and have become an end that justifies all means. To reinforce this atmosphere of mountains as being haunted by, and continuously producing, death, the author uses a variety of expressions referring to mountains as accumulations of dead bodies. There is mention of the skull of a lost hiker spiked to a signpost (*IDA* 10), of bodies being caught up by concrete pumps (*IDA* 10), of "victims of mountains" (*IDA* 21), of broken chains and bones (*IDA* 14), and, most explicitly, of "the dead of the mountains" (*IDA* 14).

At this moment of death, both narratives, themselves counter-responses to neo-colonial interventions, invite reflection on the role of storytelling. The third step in my argument, for which I have withheld the title until now, is about the 'alpine riches' of narrative (and the lack thereof). The lack of plot in *In den Alpen* itself provides a diagnosis: that mountain regions are suffering from a loss of stories. *In den Alpen* lacks real characterological dialogue and plot; instead, the story is conveyed in shreds of conversation, melted in fire and frozen in ice and time. The play is a demonstration of ruin. What Jelinek achieves in form, Abdou achieves in content, when she, much like Chaucer in his *Canterbury Tales*, has her pilgrims engage in a storytelling contest. The contest, however, fails due to anger, accusations, and the mountain enthusiasts' inability to listen (*CT* 198).

As *In den Alpen* and *The Canterbury Trail* unearth the violence of silencing, of monetary exploitation, of ownership, and empire, they demystify the cliché of mountains as *terra nullius*. This is in keeping with Uta Degner's remark about the deconstruction of myths central to the aesthetics of Jelinek's writing.[28] It would, however, ascribe little value to the productive force of the literary imagination, and do little justice to the constructiveness of Jelinek and Abdou's narratives, if I were to end my analysis with an image of montane dystopia. And that is because, despite their open engagement with death and destruction, the

---

[27] "Kann auch ein junger Mann sein, wäre vielleicht sogar besser. Dann Geschlecht des Sprechens ändern! Geschlecht egal, Körper: der Zweck" (*IDA* 25).

[28] "Das Verfahren der Mythendekonstruktion mit seinen unterschiedlichen Gegenstandsbereichen [...] zählt zu den zentralen Charakteristika der Ästhetik Jelineks, ja gilt gar als Schlüssel für ihr Gesamtwerk." Uta Degner, "Mythendekonstruktion," in *Jelinek-Handbuch*, ed. Pia Janke (Stuttgart: J.B. Metzler, 2013): 41.

endings of the two narratives, as devastating as their depiction of mountain reality may be, in fact invite a return to the beginnings of mountain imaginaries.

Jelinek, for instance, does not simply erode romantic and imperial myths surrounding mountains, as Degner suggests, but engages in their *re*mystification by expressly inviting a remembering of spiritual and mythical mountain stories. To support a reading of mountains as places ruled by mythical beings, Jelinek plays strategically with the original name of the cable car, "Gletscherdrachen" (*IDA* 38), 'Glacier Dragon', when she compares the rope – a symbol of mountaineering comradeship, which snaps in the light of commercialization[29] – to a dragon's tail, whipping towards the valley like a fiery fuse:

> Und dann hat das Seil selbst nicht gehalten. Wie eine feurige Lunte ist es ins Tal gepeitscht, sein eigener Drachenschwanz, dabei war es in diesem Augenblick alles, was uns mit dem Leben verband. (*IDA* 51)

Evoking the image of the dragon, Jelinek refers to the burning of a sense of community and the destruction of wildlife under the pressure of tourism. The German '*Lunte*', apart from its sense of 'fuse', denotes a fox or marten's tail in hunting jargon, which suggests that wildlife is just as willingly sacrificed to the market as human life. Jelinek's imagery surrounding the dragon unleashes mountain wildness, as indicated in the following passage, in which 'the young woman' realizes that the dragon must escape into the wild: "der Gletscherdrachen mußte wieder raus ins Freie" (*IDA* 38); Jelinek has us return to a space in which stories acknowledge 'wildness', rather than culturally constructed 'wilderness'.[30] All those who capitalize on the domestication of nature burn to death in the tunnel, the dragon's throat, and are spat out at the foot of the mountain, in the station that poses as purgatory. Jelinek thus reframes the mountain not only as a mythical space but also as a spiritual one. This notion of mountains as religious spaces is reinforced when those who survive do not go skiing but stay in the valley to pray – "Derzeit beten sie" (*IDA* 17).

In a less morbidly convoluted way, *The Canterbury Trail* calls for a return to the past riches of mythical and spiritual alpine stories. This is most conspicuous

---

[29] For a discussion of the commodification of the mountaineering principle of the 'brotherhood of the rope' and its masculine and nationalistic undercurrents, see Stephen Slemon, "The Brotherhood of the Rope: Commodification and Contradiction in the 'Mountaineering Community'," in *Renegotiating Community: Interdisciplinary Perspectives, Global Contexts*, ed. Diana Bryon & William D. Coleman (Vancouver: U of British Columbia P, 2008): 237–71.

[30] Following William Cronon, I am using the term 'wildness' instead of 'wilderness', which evokes histories of cultural domestication of natural environments. See Cronon, "The Trouble with Wilderness: Or, Getting Back to the Wrong Nature," *Environmental History* 1.1 (1996): 7–28.

in the title, which is obviously a reference to Chaucer's narrative poem and foregrounds the pilgrimage, the earliest form of travel. But Abdou's novel does much more than simply adopt Chaucerian narrational devices and characters, as she offers a pilgrimage through the breadths and depths of medieval literature while managing to reconsider a sense of mountain place. The reference to Chaucer is but one of many to pre-modern texts: influences from Boccaccio's *Decameron*, elements from Norse mythology, and symbols from Arthurian legend frequently occur in the story. Abdou's reliance on pre-modern literature distinguishes her novel from most contemporary mountain fiction, which normally exploits alpine romanticism. To go yet another step further, by weaving local Kootenay mountain legend into her story, Abdou emphasizes that the wealth of stories resides in their rootedness in place, and that place becomes rich in meaning through narrative. The local legend surrounding 'the Griz', a mythical figure who coaxes the snow from the sky and blesses the region with snowy abundance, enters Abdou's narrative as 'the Ull':

> Each November, the local ski crowd partied around a giant bonfire, burning old skis in sacrifice to the Ull in hopes he'd bless them with a winter of non-stop white stuff. (*CT* 70)

The Griz legend has penetrated local memory to such an extent that the community bases a winter festival on it and the hermit Heinz – "half man, half giant" (*CT* 70) – is frequently compared to the mythical creature.

One Fernie myth which outdoes "The Griz," and is comparable to "Frau Hitt," not only in its omnipresence in local mountain imaginary but also in the tale it tells, is the Ghostrider legend, on which Abdou indirectly bases the ending of her story. The Ghostrider legend is about the prospector William Fernie, the namesake of the ski resort, who promised to marry the Indian chief's daughter if he was shown the place where the tribe unearthed coal. When the natives showed him the sacred location of coal, Fernie broke the agreement, and the chief placed a curse on the Elk valley. The chief haunts the valley on his horse, a shadow on the face of Mt Hosmer, frequently besetting it with fires, floods, and mining disasters. *The Canterbury Trail* ends with a disaster that is bound to haunt the community and evokes the devastating effects on mountain business today, when an avalanche kills all those travellers who want to possess the mountain and are obscurely possessed by it. The only ones to survive are Janet and Heinz, who do not claim ownership but are understood as being "of nature now" (*CT* 2). Reading Abdou in the light of the alpine riches of local stories, one is tempted to see the avalanche as yet another strike of the curse brought down on to the community for their continuous exploitation of alpine riches. Abdou's tale about mountainous possessions ends with a snow desert stripped empty of the capitalizing mission, comparable to Frau Hitt's stone desert in Tyrol.

By remembering mountain myths like "The Griz" and "The Ghostrider" and by imaginatively placing beasts and gods back on mountaintops, Abdou and Jelinek offer a special kind of writing-back. In the language of ecocriticism, they write mountains back into the mythical world and contribute to a remembrance of a mythical wildness that does not mean an escape from present day obligations to history but invites instead a re-investigation of alpine riches and a reconsideration of one's own responsibilities towards the environment. In a postcolonial sense, Abdou and Jelinek put up resistance to the empire of alpine business by feeding subaltern mountain stories back into the present day. The riches that they return us to are different from those that capital (and empire) has led us to expect and desire.

Just as 'Alpenreich' plays out a double meaning in this essay, so, too. does the notion of writing back, since opposition primarily means returning to a mythical past. Jelinek and Abdou write back in a temporal sense as much as they do in the oppositional sense proposed by Ashcroft, Griffith, and Tiffin. They forge a reorientation towards a time in which the value of mountains lay not in how they can be wrung out to produce private riches, but in the intrinsic meaning that they carry. In other words, 'writing back' here means re-introducing older, more mountain-centric (as opposed to human-centric) stories into the historically embedded present, thereby undermining the dominant and domineering imperial narrative. This is why the ultimate narrator in *In den Alpen* and *The Canterbury Trail* is the mountain itself. A personified alpine environment in Jelinek and Abdou's stories clearly marks the re-orientation towards mountains, when Jelinek's Alps have had enough to eat, "the mountains are full,"[31] and spit their former consumers back like validated ski passes (*IDA* 23), and when Abdou has the personified mountain adopt the role of a narrator. In the eyes of Heinz, who "swears he hears the mountain sigh, a swooshing breath of utter contentment," the mountain prepares to tell its own story:

> All the world's a stage, he thinks, but not always in the way the Great Bard meant. More often than they think, humans are no more than a passive audience. The mountain, it appears, has called the final curtain on this performance. (*CT* 274)

---

[31] "Wir haben euch den Bergen vorgelegt, wir haben auch eine gute Zeit vorgelegt, aber die Berge waren schon satt und haben euch, allerdings unkenntlich gemacht und entwertet wie einen Schipaß vom vorherigen Jahr, wieder zurückgespuckt" (*IDA* 23).

The mountain breaks open, as if in divine retribution for the misuse of alpine riches, much like the one in "Frau Hitt" and the "Ghostrider," and takes charge of his stories. He "called the final curtain" (*CT* 274) and forces humans into the position of an audience.

By offering a postcolonial critique of mountain mass tourism, *The Canterbury Trail* and *In den Alpen* break the opposition of mystification and demystification, of centre and periphery, of past and present, and show that it is the stories of mountains that deserve attention. As the mountain takes care of its own representation, Jelinek's and Abdou's narratives, quite literally, teach us to read mountain regions Otherwise.

## Works Cited

Abdou, Angie. *The Canterbury Trail* (Victoria, BC: Brindle & Glass, 2011).

Akama, John. "Neocolonialism, Dependency and External Control of Africa's Tourism Industry," in *Tourism and Postcolonialism: Contested Discourses, Identities and Representation*, ed. Michael Hall & Hazel Tucker (London: Routledge, 2004): 140–51.

Ashcroft, Bill, Gareth Griffiths & Helen Tiffin. *Post-Colonial Studies: The Key Concepts* (London: Routledge, 2007).

Busk, R.H. *The Valleys of Tirol: Their Traditions and Customs and How to Visit Them* (London: Longmans, Green, 1874).

Carrigan, Anthony. *Postcolonial Tourism: Literature, Culture, and the Environment* (London: Routledge, 2011).

Conrad, Joseph. *Heart of Darkness & Other Stories* (1902; Hertfordshire: Wordsworth, 1995).

Cronon, William. "The Trouble with Wilderness: Or, Getting Back to the Wrong Nature," *Environmental History* 1.1 (1996): 7–28.

Degner, Ute. "Mythendekonstruktion," in *Jelinek-Handbuch*, ed. Pia Janke (Stuttgart: J.B. Metzler, 2013): 41–46.

Frost, Alan. "Old Colonisations and Modern Discontents: Legacies and Concerns," in *Proceedings of the Inaugural Conference of The Samuel Griffith Society, Hillton-on-the-Park, Melbourne*, 24–26 July 1992, http://www.samuelgriffith.org.au/papers/html/volume201/chap11.htm (accessed 15 February 2015).

Günther, Marie Alker von. *Tales and Legends of the Tyrol* (London: Chapman & Hall, 1874).

Jelinek, Elfriede. "In den Alpen," in Jelinek, *In Den Alpen: Drei Dramen* (Berlin: Berlin Verlag, 2002): 7–65.

Macfarlane, Robert. *Mountains of the Mind* (New York: Pantheon, 2003).

Ramsey–Kurz, Helga. "Dam Stories: When literature becomes concrete and concrete becomes literature," talk given at the University of Alberta, Edmonton, 16 October 2012).

Ramsey–Kurz, Helga. "Tokens or Totems? Eccentric Props in Postcolonial Re-Enactments of Colonial Consecration," *Literature and Theology* 21.3 (2007): 302–16.

Ribig, Rainer. *Tourismus in Zahlen: Österreichische und Internationale Tourismus- und Wirtschaftsdaten* (Vienna: Wirtschaftskammer Österreich, Statistik Austria, 2012).

Said, Edward W. *Culture and Imperialism* (New York: Vintage, 1994).

Shelley, Percy Bysshe. "Mont Blanc: Lines Written in the Vale of Chamouni" (1816), in *The Complete Poetic Works of Percy Bysshe Shelley*, ed. Thomas Hutchinson (Oxford: Oxford Wordsworth, 1914).

Slemon, Stephen. "The Brotherhood of the Rope: Commodification and Contradiction in the 'Mountaineering Community'," in *Renegotiating Community: Interdisciplinary Perspectives, Global Contexts*, ed. Diana Bryon & William D. Coleman (Vancouver: U of British Columbia P, 2008): 237–71.

Slemon, Stephen. "Tenzing Norgay's Four Flags," *Kunapipi* 34.2 (2012): 32–41.

Urry, John, & Jonas Larsen. *The Tourist Gaze 3.0* (London: Sage, 2011).

Wordsworth, William. *The Prelude, or Growth of a Poet's Mind: An Autobiographical Poem* (London: Edward Moxon, 1850).

❄

# How to Be Rich, Popular, and Have It All

## *Conflicted Attitudes to Wealth and Poverty in Postcolonial Fiction*

Melissa Kennedy

Sunjeev Sahota's Booker-listed novel *The Year of the Runaways* (2015)[1] relentlessly documents how characters confronting grinding poverty, failed upward mobility, and significant personal and familial sacrifices in India find no respite from squalor and blatant injustice as illegal immigrants in England. Damning in its portrayal of exploited informal labour gangs and the desperate competitive scrabble among illegals for limited work and living space in Britain today, Sahota's novel brings together the developing and the developed worlds to illuminate the structures of immiseration that exist in both. In its depiction of an almost textbook model of relative poverty,[2] the novel curtly dispels visions of the immigrant dream of a life of luxury in the developed West, and the common perception in rich nations that poverty only truly exists in undeveloped countries. In the novel's Epilogue, however, set ten years later, Sahota makes a surprising about-turn to depict the characters as having achieved extraordinary feats of upward mobility, to inexplicably become middle-class suburbanites. Randeep, whose attainment of comfort in the main story-line involves his rise from living rough under a bridge to the mitigated security of a temporary squat, has now become a white-collar office manager, and has provided a house in a new suburb for his parents to come from India and a studio flat for himself. Avtar, who renounced tertiary education for hand-to-mouth itinerant work, in which cleaning nightclub toilets was a step up from

---

1 Sunjeev Sahota, *The Year of the Runaways* (London: Picador, 2015).

2 Relative poverty identifies a national poverty line calculated at 60% of the median income. It is based on Amartya Sen's maxim that "*relative* deprivation in the space of *incomes* can yield *absolute* deprivation in the space of *capabilities*." See Sen, *Inequality Reexamined* (Cambridge MA: Harvard UP, 1992): 115 (italics in the original).

being locked in a shed with an illegal crew cleaning the city sewers, now lives on a sickness benefit, has brought his parents and siblings to Britain, and married his childhood sweetheart. The Dalit, Tochi, who, after a year's toil in two illegal jobs, left the UK empty-handed for equally illegal construction work in Spain, has overcome the prejudices against his caste to make a modest life for himself back in India, with wife, children, a flat, and a livelihood. In the novel's narrative logic, it is questionable that even these moderate success stories could have occurred at all, an inconsistency that Sahota deflects in the Epilogue by shifting his emphasis from materialist to psychological pressures, focusing on his characters' lingering dissatisfaction, unsettled belonging, and the sacrifices of displacement. While the body of the novel, through a social-realist mode that encourages its being read as a political work, condemns global inequality and its myriad local forms, this change of focus at the close drops poverty-politics in favour of identity-politics.

Sahota's is a recent example of a type of postcolonial fiction in which financial success tends to come by luck to deserving protagonists, with the unlikely economic trajectories and illogic of such plot-twists glossed over or happening outside the narrative frame. In other examples, Elvis in Chris Abani's *GraceLand* (2004)[3] escapes homelessness and begging in Lagos for a new start in the USA, with money and a fake passport acquired from unwittingly trading in organs to the Gulf States from sold or kidnapped children. Although Elvis's naivety saves him, and thus the sympathetic reader, from the moral guilt of complicity, Abani's happy ending, which abandons the narrative of immiseration to focus on Elvis's lucky break, suggests a reluctance to linger on the very real financial transactions that cause and maintain poverty: here, slum-clearance for luxury development and co-option of child soldiers to carry out cross-border human trafficking. In Vikas Swarup's *Q & A* (2005),[4] one of several Indian novels set in Mumbai's Dharavi slum, the entire story hinges on the 'luck' of an uneducated chai-wallah winning on the game show 'Who Wants to Be a Millionaire', while the backstories that lead to Ram's win are relentless and excoriating in their depiction of multiple forms of abuse and misuse committed against impoverished children, none of whom escapes the cycle of poverty, violence, and criminality. Like Sahota, Swarup ends the body of his narrative on a note of enduring marginalization, contradicted in an epilogue that portrays the entirely different life-world of the now-rich Ram, who recounts a life of luxury and philanthropy, and with the girl of his dreams.

---

3 Chris Abani, *GraceLand* (New York: Farrar, Straus & Giroux, 2004).

4 Vikas Swarup, *Q&A* (London: Black Swan, 2006).

Improbable leaps of fortune, such as in Sahota's, Abani's, and Swarup's novels, indicate a failure on the part of creative discourse – on the part of both writer and reader – to think a clear path through the economic motivations and steps required to move from developing-world illegal immigrant to developed-world middle-class mortgage-holder. This tendency to ignore the topic of money is not only a problem in literary fiction, but is also present in conflicting attitudes toward it that have become particularly evident in the contemporary environment of global neoliberal capitalism. The economist John Kenneth Galbraith, in his classic text *Money: Whence It Came, Where It Went* (1975), formulated the phenomenon by which people tend to think about money only when they don't have any: "When money is bad, people want to see it better. When it is good, they think of other things."[5] This sums up the concerns of the above-mentioned fiction, which explores the material mechanisms of poverty in close detail but swiftly drops the focus on finance in favour of other forms of marginalization and injustice when the basics of food and shelter are no longer so pressing.

Offering reasons for ambivalent attitudes to money, David Graeber, in his comprehensive history of debt, attributes the "moral confusion" surrounding money to the underlying fact that the exchange of currency is an abstraction of human interaction, a contact and contract between people in which debts and obligations mix messily with generosity and altruism, both reflecting and interrupting social life.[6] His wide-ranging study of five thousand years of documentation about money from archaeological, historical, literary, and anthropological sources reveals the multiple purposes, forms, beliefs, and moral codes surrounding financial exchange, a long-range perspective that contextualizes today's seemingly hegemonic global neoliberalism as by no means natural, logical, or unchangeable. His work encourages readers to conceptualize money and the social transaction it represents as both fact and fiction. On a functional level, it fulfils a simple purpose, but on a symbolic level it is imbued with an almost limitless number of imaginative projections, of varying degrees of realism and fancy. Against this background, the present essay explores conflicting attitudes to earning, possessing, and spending money in postcolonial literature, finding herein symptoms of moral and practical contradiction in capitalism.

---

5 John Kenneth Galbraith, *Money: Whence It Came, Where It Went* (Boston MA: Houghton Mifflin, 1975): 3.

6 David Graeber, "On the Experience of Moral Confusion," in Graeber, *Debt: The First 5,000 Years* (2011; London & New York: Melville House, 2014): 1–19.

Stories of upward mobility are the exception in recent postcolonial fiction concerned with the current conjuncture of global capitalism in developing-world spaces.[7] More commonly, fiction represents downward or lack of social mobility as well as abject poverty, with dramatic tension and the novels' pathos drawn from dashed hopes and thwarted dreams. Common narrative arcs include the downward mobility of the main characters in Rohinton Mistry's *A Fine Balance* (1996)[8] or very limited social movement, such as the slum setting of Zakes Mda's *Ways of Dying* (1995),[9] as well as tragedies based on the inability to rise from poverty and overcome discrimination, in Manil Suri's *The Death of Vishnu* (2001),[10] Valutha in *The God of Small Things* (1997),[11] and the homeless child, Azure, in K. Sello Duiker's *Thirteen Cents* (2000).[12] Many texts by well-known writers such as J.M. Coetzee, Nadine Gordimer, Chimamanda Ngozi Adichie, Vikram Seth, Hari Kunzru, Rohinton Mistry, and Amitav Ghosh portray and comment on poverty through sympathetic middle-class protagonists, whose perspectives are often difficult to separate from those of the educated writers who pen them. The liberal-humanist politics conveyed by such privileged narrator-writers, and likely shared by the middle-class Western reader, typically castigate the injustices of poverty without unduly challenging the structures of economic inequality that underpin the reader and writer's own superior material status. Although the reader tends to empathize with the protagonist, this connection to poverty is made within the safe confines of the story book, while real poverty happens elsewhere, usually out of sight.

By contrast, and as Helga Ramsey–Kurz argues in this collection, very little narrative space is given to wealthy characters. Two exceptions, Aravind Adiga's *The White Tiger* (2008)[13] and Mohsin Hamid's *How to Get Filthy Rich in Rising Asia* (2013),[14] are written in the satiric mode, using black comedy to portray stellar upward mobility from the slums to the wealthy and growing middle class. Reminiscent of earlier postcolonial satires on wealth and corruption in African

---

[7] My focus differs from the kind of middle-class concerns that previously dominated, particularly in fiction from Southern Africa and South Asia, as explored by Sandhya Shetty in this volume.

[8] Rohinton Mistry, *A Fine Balance* (London: Faber & Faber, 1996).

[9] Zakes Mda, *Ways of Dying* (New York: Picador, 1995).

[10] Manil Suri, *The Death of Vishnu* (London: Bloomsbury, 2001).

[11] Arundhati Roy, *The God of Small Things* (London: Flamingo, 1997).

[12] K. Sello Duiker, *Thirteen Cents* (Cape Town: David Philip, 2000).

[13] Aravind Adiga, *The White Tiger* (London & New York: Free Press, 2008).

[14] Mohsin Hamid, *How to Get Filthy Rich in Rising Asia* (London: Hamish Hamilton, 2013).

fiction, including Chinua Achebe's *A Man of the People* (1966)[15] and Ngũgĩ wa Thiong'o's *Devil on the Cross* (1980),[16] such texts indicate a squeamishness about wealth – an inability to write sympathetically of the well-off, or even to plot the road to riches, as Sahota's, Abani's, and Swarup's elliptical techniques also imply. Although both Adiga's and Hamid's novels begin with the familiar postcolonial trope of intergenerational chronic poverty, the dispassionate, clinical tone that captures the dirt and hunger of material immiseration, and the alcohol, violence, and physical and mental ill-health that are its social costs, mark a departure from the more usual empathetic voice of the reliable narrator. The stories describe a steady rise in fortune and fortunes for the narrators, who become rich through crimes of escalating severity, progressing from white lies, profit-skimming, and bribery to a climax of violence – Balram's murderous "act of entrepreneurship"[17] and Hamid's prosaic advice, apropos his hired thugs, that "becoming filthy rich requires a degree of unsqeamishness."[18] The plot-lines suggest that their account of the protagonists' financial successes take the stock, virtuously indignant postcolonial depiction of South Asian poverty and turns it on its head. The poor heroes join the rich villains, luxuriating in the comforts of ill-gotten wealth and, in neoliberal apostasy, denigrating as losers those who haven't made it – exactly those kinds of characters usually shown sympathetically in the literature. To judge from its over-emphasis on forms of poverty and under-representation of the wealth-creation and economic growth said to drive global capitalism, one can hardly say that postcolonial fiction captures in imaginative and logical detail either the leap from individual poverty to wealth or the mechanics of development necessary to bring the developing world into parity with the developed.

The economic sociologist Nigel Dodd begins *The Social Life of Money* (2014) with an epigraph from an Occupy Wall Street slogan: "I know no creative person can thrive in this economy. *You will lose us.* I am the 99%."[19] Dodd explains his own motivation, following the 2008 financial crisis, for researching the history of attitudes to money in order to stimulate public debate about

---

15 Chinua Achebe, *A Man of the People* (Oxford: Heinemann Educational, 1966).

16 Ngũgĩ wa Thiong'o, *Devil on the Cross* (Oxford: Heinemann, 1980).

17 Adiga, *The White Tiger*, 9.

18 Hamid, *How to Get Filthy Rich in Rising Asia*, 119.

19 Nigel Dodd, "Introduction" to Dodd, *The Social Life of Money* (Princeton NJ: Princeton UP, 2014): 1 (italics in the original).

> normative or utopian questions about the relationship between money as a social technology, and questions of inequality, financial exclusion, social justice, and social cohesion.
>
> In order to achieve this goal, we need to overcome the kind of disdain for money that has been displayed by so many modern social thinkers.[20]

Like the threat to creativity expressed unequivocally and with great urgency in the Occupy slogan, Dodd argues for the need to think outside the box of neoliberal capitalism that currently seeks to contain and control all aspects of social life.[21] The extent to which this dominant global frame has succeeded in blocking out alternative socio-economic models, and has, to a significant extent, fulfilled the prophecy of the Occupy poster that creativity *cannot* survive and *will* be lost, is registered in the inchoate gaps, unlikely economic trajectories, and general silence around wealth characteristic of postcolonial fiction. In the drive to financialize everything, founded on a fallacious belief that the free market both regulates and optimizes – what Dodd calls the translation of qualities into quantities[22] – the market has left little room for other forms of value: as the Occupy slogan implies, there is no space for unquantifiable values such as creativity. Writers[23] reluctant to focus on wealth in detail are here complicit in Dodd's perceived "disdain for money." Such literature, it thus appears, agrees with the Occupy slogan that it is an either–or equation, in which creativity and the economy cannot coexist, as if human and financial relations were independent of one another, and as if the social dimension were a more appropriate concern of fiction than economic aspects of life.

Contradicting the lack of postcolonial literature about money, studies of financial topics have appeared more frequently in mainstream popular culture since the 2008 financial crisis, in texts aimed at a more general readership, such as Graeber on debt and Dodd on money, as well as in documentaries, films, and

---

[20] Dodd, "Acknowledgements," in Dodds, *The Social Life of Money*, xvi.

[21] For Dodd, this takes the form of the restricted notion of money as national currencies used for financial transactions. He argues that the sub-prime, banking, and sovereign-debt crises show the failure of this monetary system, which fails to encompass multiple other kinds of social transactions.

[22] *The Social Life of Money*, 295.

[23] Literary criticism has been attentive to the co-option of the writer into the commodity market. See Pascale Casanova, *The World Republic of Letters*, tr. M.B. DeBevoise (*La République mondiale des lettres*, 1999; Cambridge MA & London: Harvard UP, 2004); Sarah Brouillette, *Postcolonial Writers in the Global Literary Marketplace* (London: Palgrave, 2007).

even post-Crash fiction, to which Adiga's[24] and Hamid's postcolonial exceptions belong. Capturing the contemporary mood, in which the world of entrepreneurism, finance, and even banking is suddenly trendy, the writer Lionel Shriver sardonically notes:

> Before the collapse of Lehman Brothers, I used the business section of the newspaper to clean my windows. So it was quite a surprise to find that economics had grown as nailbiting as the Bourne trilogy, as apocalyptic as *On the Beach*. Recent non-fiction titles, such as *Endgame* by John Mauldin and Jonathan Tepper and *Paper Money Collapse* by Detlev Schlichter, are every bit as horrifying as grim dystopian classics such as *Nineteen Eighty-Four*.[25]

Shriver, the author of a recent post-financial-crisis dystopian novel, identifies her new book, *The Mandibles* (2016), as part of a growing interest in narrativizing the 2008 financial crisis and its aftermath. In her editorial, Shriver claims:

> Financiers make ideal rogues. The easiest way to make characters unappealing is to make them rich – shorthand for spoiled, picky, superior, and cold-hearted.[26]

The same is true of money-lenders, who are condemned in literature as well as in many earlier texts of Western philosophy and the theology of all the major religions.[27] Shriver concludes that the motivation of greed and the competitive one-upmanship that equates winning with wealth mean that, for the super-rich, "the moral and cultural universe in which they circulate is therefore implicitly arid, sterile, and empty."[28] Certainly, the dearth of postcolonial fiction on wealth supports her claims that the topic of money is not worth writing about, with

---

[24] Although *The White Tiger* pre-dates the 2008 crisis, Adiga's career as a financial journalist and his public claim that the novel exposes the underside of capitalism that his journalism was unable to cover position this work as a critique of unregulated neoliberalism. See Sarah Brouillette, "On the Entrepreneurial Ethos in Aravind Adiga's *The White Tiger*," in *Reorientalism and South Asian Identity Politics: The Oriental Other Within*, ed. Lisa Lau & Ana Christina Mendes (London & New York: Routledge, 2011): 42.

[25] Lionel Shriver, "Is there any better villain than a banker?" *The Guardian* (13 May 2016), http://www.theguardian.com/books/2016/may/13/lionel-shriver-bankers-perfect-villains (accessed 1 August 2016).

[26] Shriver, "Is there any better villain than a banker?"

[27] See Graeber, *Debt: The First 5,000 Years*, and Tomáš Sedláček, *Economics of Good and Evil: The Quest for Economic Meaning from Gilgamesh to Wall Street* (Oxford & New York: Oxford UP, 2011).

[28] Shriver, "Is there any better villain than a banker?"

rich characters existing merely as the targets of satire or as agents of injustice, unfairness, and inequality.

Outside of fiction, however, discussions of wealth are both overt and often positive, with financial prowess and the luxuries it buys celebrated as desirable markers of success. Self-help books on career or investment strategies are likely to sit on the bookshelf alongside postcolonial Booker-Prize-listed novels, and consumers of books are also consumers of Hollywood films such as Martin Scorsese's *The Wolf of Wall Street* (2013) and Adam McKay's *The Big Short* (2015), television series such as the latest Danish hit, *Follow the Money* (2016), and reality shows like *The Real Housewives* and *The Apprentice*. Certainly, these books and media examples are Euro-American in origin, but the interest in money they represent is not contained in these spaces, usually known as the West, the developed world, or the Global North. *The Real Housewives* has franchised shows in cities in the USA, Canada, the UK, Australia, and New Zealand. *The Apprentice*, pioneered in the USA by Donald Trump in 2003, has spawned local versions in twenty-seven countries, in both the developed and the developing world, not least in Britain, where it is in its twelfth season in 2016, Switzerland, Turkey, Georgia, Russia, Brazil, Columbia, India, South Africa, Dubai, Indonesia, and Vietnam. For the economists George Akerlof and Robert Shiller, the show is indicative of the power of narrative in shaping socio-cultural attitudes to and ambitions for economic success and failure.[29] For postcolonialists intent on teasing out cultural specificity through which to encourage recognition and respect for under-represented world spaces, Akerlof and Shiller's claim that "the names and places change, but the stories are similar"[30] is counterintuitive. However, the global reach of capitalism – either chosen or enforced; either fully integrated into a political economy or held at a distance for specific purposes – tempers the possibility of protesting against their homogenizing claim. Certainly, the translatability of *The Apprentice* indicates commonalities of values by which people judge themselves and others according to salary, spending power, and possessions, and of motivations for financial success, in an individualistic, competitive environment where "Darwin beats Keynes."[31]

---

29 George Akerlof & Robert Shiller, "Preface" to Akerlof & Shiller, *Animal Spirits: How Human Psychology Drives the Economy, and Why It Matters for Global Capitalism* (Princeton NJ: Princeton UP, 2009): ix.

30 Akerlof & Shiller, "Preface" to *Animal Spirits*, ix.

31 Hans Schenk, "Urban Fringes in Asia: Markets versus Plans," in *Realigning Actors in an Urbanizing World: Governance and Institutions from a Development Perspective*, ed. I.S.A. Baud & Johan Post (Aldershot & Burlington VT: Ashgate, 2002): 131, quoted in Mike Davis, *Planet of Slums* (London & New York: Verso, 2006): 46.

In contrast to postcolonial fiction's concerted lack of interest in wealth, and in direct opposition to Shriver's claim of boring bankers and rich anti-heroes, popular culture shows great public interest in money-making and the lives of the rich and successful. In particular, the competitors and mentors in *The Apprentice*, Alan Sugar (UK) and Donald Trump (USA), are presented as modern-day urban heroes who fulfil the neoliberal meritocratic promise that street smarts, skill, hard work, and competitive entrepreneurism can result in dramatic upward mobility. For the show's annual winners, their triumph endorsed by the presence of their mentors and other members of the super-rich elite, including Richard Branson, Martha Stewart, Bill Gates, and Warren Buffett, the wealth ensuing from financial success has made them into public figures, their lives followed in the tabloids, their success decorated with national and even academic honours,[32] their investments charted in the *Financial Times*, and their philanthropy depended upon by many. Unlike postcolonial fiction, televised narratives of money-making, such as the entrepreneurism portrayed in *The Apprentice* or the stock-market trading in *The Wolf of Wall Street* and *The Big Short*, closely track the steps of upward mobility as well as the wealthy life-styles of those who have 'made it'. In Alan Sugar, a school dropout from an East London housing estate, and Jordan Belfort, Wall Street's "Wolf" and a failed door-to-door salesman, the average viewer can interpellate his or her own humble beginnings with the fond prospect of future wealth. Such stories fill the gaps that postcolonial fiction seems unable or unwilling to imagine. The type of story of money-making they tell, while quite unlike fiction's deserving poor and dastardly rich, are perhaps quite similar to the numerous self-help books on money-making that out-sell *literary* texts in bookshops around the world, including in postcolonial spaces.[33] While great wealth is confined to a statistical minority, captured in the concept of 'the one percent', the idea of wealth – how to get it and how to spend it – is amply represented in the media. Hollywood soap operas, films, and fiction such as that by Jackie Collins, Jilly Cooper, and much chick-lit, along with the advertising industry, encourage the consuming public

---

[32] Lord Sir Alan Sugar, MBE, received a Queen's Honour, and a peerage under Gordon Brown's government; Richard Branson, Bill Gates, and *The Apprentice* UK first series winner, Tim Campbell, were also knighted for services to entrepreneurship; Donald Trump is now US President; Warren Buffett received the highest US decoration, the Presidential Medal of Freedom, under the Obama administration.

[33] In a 2010 study of Zambian reading habits, Ranka Primovac found that the top-selling title in a Lusaka book shop was "Chibamba Kanyama's *Business Values for our Time* (2010), the first Zambian entrepreneurial manual"; Ranka Primorac, "Reasons for Reading in Postcolonial Zambia," *Journal of Postcolonial Writing* 48.5 (December 2012): 507.

to emulate the lives of the super-rich in luxury items and package holidays to cheap destinations, often bought with credit. While usurers make great villains in fiction, the mortgage brokers, credit-card companies, and hire-purchase deals that are their real-life counterparts are common in the contemporary world which, under free-market capitalism, is driven by debt.[34] In their focus on relative poverty and lack of upward mobility, postcolonial fiction portrays life-worlds at odds with those projected in Western mainstream media. Together, these narratives of money are antithetical to each other.

Fiction and media indicate that attitudes to money vacillate between desire to emulate the rich and moral unease with their profligacy, and views of the poor as alternately victims of circumstance and undeserving on account of their personal failures. Such conflicted judgments likely reflect the structural contradictions inherent in the capitalist economy[35] at the same time as they embody the ethical conundrums and hypocrisies of the socio-cultural connivances that work to uphold a world system founded on combined and uneven development.[36] A watershed moment in changing public discourse on local and global economic inequality, the 2008 financial crisis revealed these contradictions by highlighting discrepancies between myth and practice in such notions as the free market and its invisible hand, the rising tide lifting all boats, and the trickle-down effect of wealth. Certainly, critiques of the pervasiveness and power of money pre-date the most recent crisis. In particular, the idea that money is a force destroying human relations is integral to Karl Marx's critique of capitalism as well as to the work of Friedrich Nietzsche, Georg Simmel, Max Weber, Walter Benjamin, and Karl Polanyi. In the contemporary neoliberal context, Michael Sandel, in his book *What Money Can't Buy*,[37] illustrates the moral dilemma raised by contradictory ethical and financial values in the USA, such as the fact that prostitution is illegal but payment for surrogate mothers is not, and that the homeless can be moved on by police for loitering in public spaces but can be hired as line-standers to queue for public events. To his examples can be added

---

34 Graeber argues that the end of the Gold Standard in 1971 marks the most recent cyclical turn away from a bullion (money) economy to one of debt (*Debt*, 361).

35 See Ha-Joon Chang, *23 Things They Don't Tell You About Capitalism* (London: Penguin, 2012); Terry Eagleton, *Why Marx Was Right* (New Haven CT: Yale UP, 2011); David Harvey, *Seventeen Contradictions and the End of Capitalism* (Oxford: Oxford UP, 2014).

36 On the theories of the capitalist world system and combined and uneven development applied to literature, see the Warwick Research Collective, *Combined and Uneven Development: Towards a New Theory of World-Literature* (Liverpool: Liverpool UP, 2015).

37 Michael J. Sandel, *What Money Can't Buy: The Moral Limits of Markets* (London: Penguin, 2013).

the questionable ethical grounds on which the sub-prime lending crisis led to the eviction of homeowners for mortgage defaults but almost no prosecution of the financial engineers of the crisis, and the imposition of austerity policies on welfare recipients throughout Europe while taxpayer money was instead used to bail out and shore up bad banks.

Postcolonial fiction tends to reflect rather than to challenge or reconcile these contradictory attitudes towards money-making. Uncertainty over the position the developing world can take toward the global free market, expounded by developed nations and international monetary organizations, particularly the World Bank and the International Monetary Fund, is certainly understandable. The fact that developed nations did not themselves historically succeed by virtue of the very practices they now impose on developing economies,[38] and the very few clear examples around the world of increasing prosperity and wellbeing for each nation's majority through the lauded principles of growth, progress, and development, make whole-hearted belief in the current world order difficult.[39] Postcolonial fiction's inability to imagine or even to sympathetically represent upward mobility can thus be read as an accurate reflection of the very real gap between the theory and practice of neoliberal politics on the global scale, which Marxist commentators diagnose as constitutive of capitalism itself.[40] The following explores some of the ways in which authors' and characters' attitudes to poverty and wealth are not only contradictory, when set alongside each other, but may also conflict with reader expectations.

Novels of upward mobility out of the slums, such as *GraceLand*, *Q & A*, and *The Year of the Runaways*, rely on the sympathetic reader's willing suspension of disbelief, in which the desire for a happy ending appears synonymous with the reader's own investment in the possibility of upward mobility, even though it is unlikely in the narrated world – and increasingly improbable even in the Western world of the target reader. The ongoing popularity of *The Apprentice* (it still averages over seven million viewers) similarly indicates public belief in entrepreneurism as driver of the economy, creator of jobs and growth, and philosopher's stone of personal enrichment, despite post-Crash evidence of *declining*

---

[38] See Ha-Joon Chang, *Bad Samaritans: The Guilty Secrets of the Rich Nations and the Threat to Global Prosperity* (London: Random House, 2007).

[39] Even China, the model of success through its version of global capitalism, has seen such a radical increase in inequality between the rich and the poor that it is today the most unequal nation in the world, along with South Africa. See David Harvey, *Seventeen Contradictions and the End of Capitalism* (Oxford: Oxford UP, 2014): 169.

[40] See Eagleton, *Why Marx Was Right*, and David Harvey, *Seventeen Contradictions and the End of Capitalism*.

social mobility[41] due to the increasing price of education,[42] the importance of inter-generational family wealth,[43] and stagnating wages.[44] Recent attention to widening economic inequality around the world has exposed the factitiousness of the meritocratic ideal of equal opportunity that facilitates the stellar success-stories celebrated in the media. Nonetheless, the popularity of *The Apprentice* and stories such as *The Year of the Runaways*, which was positively reviewed for its hard-hitting realism, indicates reluctance on the part of writers and readers to give up on such stories or even to interpret them as fictitious.

The glamorous life-styles of the super-rich portrayed in visual and written media undo Shriver's claim that the desire for financial success is shallow and that such lives are "implicitly arid, sterile, and empty." Ram, in *Q & A*, enjoys his Mercedes–Benz car, in which his driver follows along behind when Ram goes for a walk along Mumbai's exclusive Marine Drive.[45] Adiga's Balram boasts "I love my start-up – this chandelier, and this silver laptop, and these twenty-six Toyota Qualises."[46] Abani concludes *GraceLand* with a lengthy description of Lagos's international airport, at which Elvis is already ensconced in the floor-to-ceiling glass ambience of the departure lounge, reading James Baldwin and drinking Coke in the café. Hamid's sarcastic tone throughout *How to Get Filthy Rich in Rising Asia* does not detract from the more empathetic tone of joy, wonder, and excitement expressed by the former slum-dwelling entrepreneur in dining for the first time at an expensive Western-style restaurant, in first contemplating the sea from a hotel penthouse room, and in his love for his son, growing up in health and comfort facilitated by attentive nanny, cook, housekeeper, driver, and tutors. Certainly, Balram's displaced affection for his chandeliers instead of his absent family, and Elvis's misplaced utopian view of the USA, are ripe for critique, and yet the lives these characters end up living, away from the hunger, beatings, and subjugation they formerly experienced, are qualitatively better. Anticipating and pre-empting the reader's suspicions that Balram's fight for financial supremacy must translate into a guilty conscience, Adiga's narrator mocks any such morality, which he says exists only in fiction. Whereas

---

41 See Thomas Piketty, *Capital in the Twenty-first Century*, tr. Arthur Goldhammer (*Le capital au XXI siècle*, 2013; Cambridge MA: Harvard UP/Belknap Press, 2014): 484–85.

42 See Phillip Brown, Hugh Lauder & David Ashton, *The Global Auction: The Broken Promises of Education, Jobs and Incomes* (Oxford: Oxford UP, 2011); Joseph Stiglitz, *The Great Divide: Unequal Societies and What We Can Do About Them* (New York: W.W. Norton, 2015).

43 See Joseph Stiglitz, *The Price of Inequality* (New York: Penguin, 2012).

44 See Robert Reich, *Beyond Outrage* (New York: Vintage, 2012).

45 Swarup, *Q&A*, 360.

46 Adiga, *The White Tiger*, 274.

in Hindi films and pulp-fiction murder mysteries the perpetrators are plagued by guilt or even haunted by moralistic ghosts, in real life, Balram claims,

> The real nightmare you get is the other kind. You toss about in the bed dreaming that you haven't done it – that you lost your nerve and let Mr Ashok get away – that you're still in Delhi, still the servant of another man, and then you wake up.
>
> The sweating stops. The heartbeat slows.
>
> *You did it! You killed him!*[47]

Through the critical function of satire, Adiga singles out the reader's contradictory desire for fiction to weigh in on the side of ethics over pragmatism. The novel thus asks questions about the role of fiction in perhaps filling or compensating for a moral universe that is disappearing from a world lacking the creativity to reconcile moral and financial values – a moral realm that is itself at odds with the global book market of publication and circulation.

*The White Tiger* and *How to Get Filthy Rich in Rising Asia* target the reader's unreconciled attitudes to money by subverting expected literary attitudes towards poverty and wealth, applauding neoliberal competitive individualism, and ridiculing the poor as failures in a free market providing boundless opportunity. Expressing a Darwinian attitude that equates money-making with survival, Balram ends his epistolary narrative by gloating that the world needs "masters like Mr Ashok – who, for all his numerous virtues, was not much of a master – to be weeded out, and exceptional servants like me to replace them."[48] Despite its depersonalizing narrative mode, Hamid's novel also works through the Darwinian model, running the full gamut of the individual's place in the capitalist society, the disenfranchised child rising to wealth and power before falling back into social and economic marginalization in his old age. Although the reader encourages these characters to *try* and succeed in their individualistic struggle against their impoverished milieux, and thereby to demonstrate positively connoted personal traits of ambition, self-sacrifice, and hard work, these same characters become instantly condemnable and contemptible as soon as they achieve success. Thus, these satires critique the neoliberal prioritizing of individual competitiveness over communal solidarity lauded without satire in *The Apprentice* and self-help books. They mock the postcolonial reader's trained instinct to root for the underdog, only to turn on him and his negative character traits if he or she 'makes it', preferring instead to empathize

---

47 Adiga, *The White Tiger*, 269 (italics in the original).

48 *The White Tiger*, 275.

with a character who remains a lovable failure. Siding with Shriver's identification of the nasty rich, which Hamid and Adiga mock but do not debunk, much postcolonial fiction implies that poor characters are morally superior to rich ones, as though it were better to be poor with integrity than better-off through callous methods. Adhering to the postcolonial credo of giving voice to the marginalized, such narratives ask the reader to respect lives lived in poverty, imagining, perhaps, that characters may be contented, or even happy, despite their dire material circumstances.

It is often possible for the reader to interpret characters in poverty positively, even in postcolonial novels that, unlike Abani's or Swarup's, do not explicitly offer a happy ending of upward social mobility. Not atypically, Alexis Wright's *Carpentaria* and Zakes Mda's *Ways of Dying* end on a note of cautious optimism, which may be interpreted as the triumph of marginalized characters. In *Carpentaria*, after a storm and flood that devastate their mining town, the Australian Aboriginal elder, Norm, and his grandchild walk empty-handed to the sound of nature reasserting itself. The frogs' "singing the country afresh"[49] encourages a positive interpretation of the primacy and continuity of the land. Mda's South African novel similarly ends on an upbeat yet lyrical tone in its depiction of Toloki and Noria's settlement shack on the night of New Year's Eve festivities:

> Somehow the shack seemed to glow in the light of the moon, as if the plastic colours are fluorescent. Crickets and other insects of the night are attracted by the glow.[50]

The idea of a new start to a new year is optimistic, and the lyrical voice implies that community cohesiveness, represented by Noria, has brought this peaceful warm glow to make up for the violence and death that have rocked the settlement throughout the arc of the story. The problem with such a reading is that it runs the risk of suggesting that poverty is acceptable or even somehow desirable, aestheticized in such passages as the above.

Dispelling the idea that poverty can ever be positively construed, Ngũgĩ wa Thiong'o argues, in his concept of poor theory, that it is important to grant dignity to the poor but not to poverty itself: "One does not want to give dignity to poverty by according it theory."[51] Walter Benn Michaels is more categorical in his condemnation of the way in which poverty has been co-opted as merely another form of difference deserving of respect, as if the rich and the poor –

---

[49] Alexis Wright, *Carpentaria* (2006; London: Constable, 2008): 438.

[50] Mda, *Ways of Dying*, 212.

[51] Ngũgĩ wa Thiong'o, *Globalectics: Theory and the Politics of Knowing* (New York: Columbia UP, 2012): 2.

once analysed in the now unfashionable term 'class' – were akin to race and culture. Classes, he pithily surmises,

> are not like races and cultures, and treating them as if they were – different but equal – is one of our strategies for managing inequality rather than minimizing or eliminating it. White is not better than black, but rich is definitely better than poor.[52]

Michaels's critique of the neoliberal Left's privileging of identity-politics over class, in order to avoid having to address economic inequality and lack of opportunity in the USA, is also pertinent to the biases of postcolonial literary critique that privileges the poor and ignores the rich. Jenny Lawn, summarizing the thrust of Michaels's argument in her recent study of the representation of neoliberalism in New Zealand literature, argues that materialist critique must

> [set] exploitation over discrimination, redistribution over recognition, needs over rights, equality over difference, and material oppression over symbolic marginalization.[53]

To re-read the endings of *Carpentaria* and *Ways of Dying* from her materialist perspective means to pay attention to the poverty that is unaffected by either the characters' positive racial and cultural identification or the texts' aesthetic. In *Carpentaria*, irrespective of the deep Aboriginal connection with the land recognized in animate nature, a materialist perspective sees that the land Norm is returning to is the space historically designated for Aboriginal settlement by white settlers, on the edge of the municipal rubbish dump, where he must rebuild his shack and his livelihood – now with a dependent child to care for. In Mda's novel, reading between the lines exposes a quite different reality from the depiction filtered through the narrator's rose-tinted spectacles, which lingers on the beautifully illuminated shack and describes Noria and Toloki's New Year as "a banquet in the oak dining room after taking a long walk in their garden,"[54] with party music and a bonfire. The narrator's language is merely hopeful euphemism. In the narrative action, Noria and Toloki share a frugal meal meant for two with hungry children in a furniture-less one-room mud-floored shack,[55]

---

52 Walter Benn Michaels, *The Trouble with Diversity: How We Learned to Love Identity and Ignore Inequality* (New York: Metropolitan, 2006): 10.

53 Jennifer Lawn, *Neoliberalism and Cultural Transition in New Zealand Literature, 1984–2008* (Lanham MD: Lexington, 2016): 5.

54 Mda, *Ways of Dying*, 211.

55 The shack is described on page 114: only the walls are covered with pictures of luxury furniture, "ideal gardens and houses and swimming pools, all from the *Home and Garden* magazines" (*Ways of Dying*, 111).

accompanied by car horns, clanging pots, and the smell of burning tyres – tyres used earlier in the novel by settlement youths to kill by 'necklacing' Noria's child.

The two quite opposite interpretative possibilities of these novels depend on whether the reader privileges symbolic human value or materialist financial value – whether, in Dodd's and Galbraith's terms, we disdain money to concentrate on something else instead. That the two forms of wealth have such diametric meanings – the former positive; the latter negative – exposes a contradictory attitude to wealth that reveals the discrepancy between forms of valuation based on a quantity/quality binary. Unlike the Occupy slogan, which cannot imagine creativity thriving under conditions of gross inequality, and which expresses fear of extinction or co-option into capital in the emphatic "you will lose us," these novels emphasize non-monetary forms of value. To imagine that Norm, Noria, and Toloki may be reconciled to their material immiseration buys into the widely held idea that 'money doesn't buy happiness' – a notion that imagines cultural fulfilment as independent of financial status. A materialist perspective, however, that finds the injustice of poverty morally offensive and, as Ngũgĩ urges, refuses to grant it dignity must be critical of this aphorism, exposing it as merely an emotional palliative (for the poor) or as justification (for the rich). Following Michaels, to accept wealth and happiness as unrelated is a technique for excusing rather than challenging structural inequality.

Analysis of the lack of attention to wealth in fiction reveals many of the contradictions – if not hypocrisies – of contemporary discourse on money, wealth, and success, and the corollaries of poverty, inequality, and morality. The mixed messages sent by the postcolonial fiction analysed in this essay suggest disparate attitudes to money operating in a variety of ways on the character, narrator, writer, and reader, with the gaps between these positions revealing and thus potentially challenging entrenched, hegemonic socio-economic and cultural values. Capturing the public unease with the latent but nevertheless blatant-enough contradictions of money exposed by the 2008 financial crisis, Shriver concludes her article thus:

> As a result of all this public education, we have a somewhat better grasp of what went wrong and why, if still quite a poor sense of how to keep it from happening again. [...] Because even economists seem to disagree on the crudest fundamentals, we've reached the disquieting conclusion that no one is in control.
>
> Better informed is not forearmed. We still feel helpless. Today, I'm more engrossed by a sphere that once seemed impenetrably dull, but I

> also feel far more anxious, and ever more incredulous that the international economy works at all.[56]

The register of Shriver's equivocal language – tenuous grasp, vague sense, disquiet, even helplessness – captures the difficulty of thinking and talking or writing about the world of money. Her evident fascination with the subject is nonetheless passive, with no desire to actively engage. The quasi-inability to challenge the current dominance of free-market liberalism by offering alternative options, I suggest, has to do with these contradictory attitudes to money-making or wealth-accumulation and with the lack of a language with which to imagine, let alone intellectualize, a different, better world.

## Works Cited


Abani, Chris. *GraceLand* (New York: Farrar, Straus & Giroux, 2004).

Achebe, Chinua. *A Man of the People* (Oxford: Heinemann, 1966).

Adiga, Aravind. *The White Tiger* (London: Free Press, 2008).

Akerlof, George, & Robert Shiller. *Animal Spirits: How Human Psychology Drives the Economy, and Why It Matters for Global Capitalism* (Princeton NJ: Princeton UP, 2009).

Brouillette, Sarah. "On the Entrepreneurial Ethos in Aravind Adiga's *The White Tiger*," in *Reorientalism and South Asian Identity Politics: The Oriental Other Within*, ed. Lisa Lau & Ana Christina Mendes (London: Routledge, 2011): 40–55.

Brouillette, Sarah. *Postcolonial Writers in the Global Literary Marketplace* (London: Palgrave, 2007).

Brown, Phillip, Hugh Lauder & David Ashton. *The Global Auction: The Broken Promises of Education, Jobs and Incomes* (Oxford: Oxford UP, 2011).

Casanova, Pascale. *The World Republic of Letters*, tr. M.B. DeBevoise (*La République mondiale des lettres*, 1999; Cambridge MA: Harvard UP, 2004).

Chang, Ha–Joon. *Bad Samaritans: The Guilty Secrets of the Rich Nations and the Threat to Global Prosperity* (London: Random House, 2007).

Chang, Ha–Joon. *23 Things They Don't Tell You About Capitalism* (London: Penguin, 2012).

Davis, Mike. *Planet of Slums* (London: Verso, 2006).

Dodd, Nigel. *The Social Life of Money* (Princeton NJ: Princeton UP, 2014).

Duiker, K. Sello. *Thirteen Cents* (Cape Town: David Philip, 2000).

Eagleton, Terry. *Why Marx Was Right* (New Haven CT: Yale UP, 2011).

Galbraith, John Kenneth. *Money: Whence It Came, Where It Went* (Boston MA: Houghton Mifflin, 1975).

Graeber, David. *Debt: The First 5,000 Years* (2011; London: Melville House, 2014).

Hamid, Mohsin. *How to Get Filthy Rich in Rising Asia* (London: Hamish Hamilton, 2013).


[56] Shriver, "Is there any better villain than a banker?"

Harvey, David. *Seventeen Contradictions and the End of Capitalism* (Oxford: Oxford UP, 2014).

Lawn, Jennifer. *Neoliberalism and Cultural Transition in New Zealand Literature, 1984–2008* (Lanham MD: Lexington, 2016).

Mda, Zakes. *Ways of Dying* (New York: Picador, 1995).

Michaels, Walter Benn. *The Trouble with Diversity: How We Learned to Love Identity and Ignore Inequality* (New York: Metropolitan, 2006).

Mistry, Rohinton. *A Fine Balance* (London: Faber & Faber, 1996).

Ngũgĩ wa Thiong'o. *Devil on the Cross* (Oxford: Heinemann, 1980).

Ngũgĩ wa Thiong'o. *Globalectics: Theory and the Politics of Knowing* (New York: Columbia UP, 2012).

Piketty, Thomas. *Capital in the Twenty-First Century*, tr. Arthur Goldhammer (*Le capital au XXI siècle*, 2013; Cambridge MA: Harvard UP/Belknap Press, 2014).

Primorac, Ranka. "Reasons for Reading in Postcolonial Zambia," *Journal of Postcolonial Writing* 48.5 (December 2012): 497–511.

Reich, Robert. *Beyond Outrage* (New York: Vintage, 2012).

Roy, Arundhati. *The God of Small Things* (London: Flamingo, 1997).

Sahota, Sunjeev. *The Year of the Runaways* (London: Picador, 2015).

Sandel, Michael J. *What Money Can't Buy: The Moral Limits of Markets* (London: Penguin, 2013).

Schenk, Hans. "Urban Fringes in Asia: Markets versus Plans," in *Realigning Actors in an Urbanizing World: Governance and Institutions from a Development Perspective*, ed. I.S.A. Baud & Johan Post (Aldershot & Burlington VT: Ashgate, 2002): 119–36.

Sedláček, Tomáš. *Economics of Good and Evil: The Quest for Economic Meaning from Gilgamesh to Wall Street* (Oxford & New York: Oxford UP, 2011).

Sen, Amartya. *Inequality Reexamined* (Cambridge MA: Harvard UP, 1992).

Shriver, Lionel. "Is there any better villain than a banker?" *The Guardian* (13 May 2016), http://www.theguardian.com/books/2016/may/13/lionel-shriver-bankers-perfect-villains (accessed 1 August 2016).

Stiglitz, Joseph. *The Great Divide: Unequal Societies and What We Can Do About Them* (New York: W.W. Norton, 2015).

Stiglitz, Joseph. *The Price of Inequality* (London: Penguin, 2012).

Suri, Manil. *The Death of Vishnu* (London: Bloomsbury, 2001).

Swarup, Vikas. *Q&A* (London: Black Swan, 2006).

Warwick Research Collective. *Combined and Uneven Development: Towards a New Theory of World-Literature* (Liverpool: Liverpool UP, 2015).

Wright, Alexis. *Carpentaria* (2006; London: Constable, 2008).


❄

## Notes on the Contributors and Editors

FRANCESCO CATTANI is a Tutor in Feminist Theory and Gender Studies at the University of Bologna and teaches English Literature at the Fondazione Scuole Civiche Milano. He is a member of the editorial board of *Between*, the journal of the Italian Association of Comparative Literature. His research covers the relationship between narration/construction of space and migration in black British literature and visual culture. He has written essays on postcolonial London, Ingrid Pollard and the British landscape, the Black Audio Film Collective, Aravind Adiga, and Ornela Vorpsi. His publications include *Questioning the European Identity/ies* (with Vita Fortunati, 2014).

SHEILA COLLINGWOOD–WHITTICK, formerly a Senior Lecturer in the Department of Anglophone Studies at the University of Grenoble III, is an independent researcher whose main interests are (post)colonial literatures and all aspects of indigenous Australians' experience of settler colonialism. Her publications include The Pain of Unbelonging: Alienation and Identity in Australasian Literature (2007) and *Biomapping Indigenous Peoples: Towards an Understanding of the Issues* (2012, ed. with Susanne Berthier Foglar and Sandrine Tolazzi), as well as numerous articles published in international journals such as *Commonwealth: Essays and Studies*, *World Literature Written in English*, and *Symbolism*. Some of the more recent books to which she has contributed chapters are: *Postcolonial Ghosts* (2009), *Science and Empire in the Nineteenth Century* (2010), *"We the Peoples": Critical Reflections on the United Nations Declaration on the Rights of Indigenous Peoples* (2012), *Remembering Place* (2013), and *Thinking and Practicing Reconciliation: Literary and Pedagogical Responses to Atrocity* (2014).

PAOLA DELLA VALLE completed her doctorate in English at the University of Turin, Italy, where she is currently working as a researcher. She specializes in New Zealand and Māori literature, postcolonial culture, and gender studies. Her articles have appeared in *English Studies*, the *Journal of Commonwealth Literature*, the *NZSA Bulletin of New Zealand Studies*, *Le Simplegadi*, *Il Castello di Elsinore*, and *Quaderni del '900*. She has published the monographs *From Silence to Voice: The Rise of Maori Literature* (2010), *Stevenson nel Pacifico: una lettura postcoloniale* (2013), and *Priestley e il tempo, il tempo di Priestley: Uno studio sul tempo nel teatro di J.B. Priestley* (2016). She has contributed to the volumes *Experiences of Freedom in Postcolonial Literatures and Cultures* (2011), *Contemporary Sites of Chaos in the Literatures and Arts of the Postcolonial World* (2013), and *L'immagine dell'Italia nelle letterature angloamericane e postcoloniali* (2014). She is a member of the International Advisory Board of the Journal of New Zealand and Pacific Studies.

SNEJA GUNEW (FRSC) B.A. (Melbourne), M.A. (Toronto), Ph.D. (Newcastle, NSW) has taught in England, Australia, and Canada. She has published widely on multicultural, postcolonial, and feminist critical theory and is Professor Emerita of English and Women's and Gender Studies at the University of British Columbia, Canada. She has edited and co-edited four anthologies of Australian women's and multicultural writings and in Australia compiled (with others) *A Bibliography of Australian Multicultural Writers* (the first such compilation in Australia) and co-edited *Striking Chords: Multicultural Literary Interpretations* (1992), the first collection of critical essay to deal with ethnic minority writings in the Australian context. Her books include *Framing Marginality: Multicultural Literary Studies* (1994) and *Haunted Nations: The Colonial Dimensions of Multiculturalisms* (2004). Based in Canada since 1993, she conducts her current work on comparative multiculturalisms and diasporic literatures and their intersections with national and global cultural formations. Her most recent book is *Post-Multicultural Writers as Neo-Cosmopolitan Mediators* (2017).

MELISSA KENNEDY lectures in literature and cultural studies at the universities of Vienna and Passau. She has published on New Zealand and Māori fiction, including chapters published in the MLA Approaches to Teaching series (2017) and the *Cambridge History of New Zealand Literature* (2016), and a monograph, *Striding Both Worlds: Witi Ihimaera and New Zealand's Literary Traditions* (2011). Her more recent work brings critiques of economic inequality to literary study, with essays published in *Reworking Postcolonialism: Globalization, Labour, Rights* (2016), the *Bloomsbury Handbook of Postcolonial Studies* (forthcoming, 2017), and a monograph, *Narratives of Inequality: Postcolonial Literary Economics* (2017).

NEIL LAZARUS is Professor of English and Comparative Literary Studies at Warwick University (UK). His research interests are postcolonial literatures and cultures, the world-literary system, postcolonial theory, imperialism, nationalism and anticolonial resistance, and globalization. Publications include: *Resistance in Postcolonial African Fiction* (1990), *Nationalism and Cultural Practice in the*

*Postcolonial World* (1999), *Marxism, Modernity and Postcolonial Studies* (2002), *The Cambridge Companion to Postcolonial Literary Studies* (2004), *The Postcolonial Unconscious* (2011), and, with the Warwick Research Collective, *Combined and Uneven Development: Towards a New Theory of World-Literature* (2015).

JOHN MCLEOD is Professor of Postcolonial and Diaspora Literatures at the University of Leeds (UK). His research interests include postcolonial literature, especially Caribbean and black British writing, and he has particular interests in theories and representations of diasporic and transcultural locations. Publications include: *Life Lines: Writing Transcultural Adoption* (2015), *Beginning Postcolonialism*(second edition, 2010), *Postcolonial London: Rewriting the Metropolis* (2004), *J.G. Farrell* (2007), and the edited volume *The Routledge Companion to Postcolonial Studies* (2007).

EVA–MARIA MÜLLER is a doctoral researcher and lecturer in the English department at the University of Giessen, Germany, where she is completing her doctoral project in postcolonial literature and mountain studies, funded by the Graduate Centre for the Study of Culture (GCSC) and the Mellon Foundation's Integrative Graduate Humanities Education and Research Training on indigeneity. She holds an MA from the University of Innsbruck, Austria, where she studied English, biology, and education. Her research is driven by a keen interest in alpine spaces, and currently focuses on postcolonial theory, travel writing, and mountain fiction. Müller also studied and researched at the University of Alberta, Canada.

HELGA RAMSEY–KURZ is an Associate Professor of English literature at the University of Innsbruck. Her research interests include migrant and refugee writing and postcolonial literatures and theory. At present she is working on a book provisionally titled 'Hidden Treasures: Ways of Not Seeing Wealth'. Her publications include *On the Move: The Journey of Refugees in New Literatures in English* and *Projections of Paradise: Ideal Elsewheres in Postcolonial Migrant Literature* (both with Geetha Ganapathy–Doré, 2012 and 2011), *Antipodean Childhoods: Growing Up in Australia and New Zealand* (with Ulla Ratheiser, 2010), and the monograph *The Non-Literate Other: Readings of Illiteracy in Twentieth-Century Novels in English* (2007).

GEOFF RODOREDA is a lecturer in the Department of New English Literature at the University of Stuttgart, Germany. He studied Social and Political Theory, Media Theory, and Journalism in Sydney, Australia, and was employed as a journalist at the Australian Broadcasting Corporation in Adelaide, Sydney, and Darwin before moving to Germany in 1996. In 2012, he gave up journalism work to concentrate on academic teaching and on writing his PhD, which examines the impact of the 1992 High Court Mabo decision on discourses of land and history in Australian fiction.

SANDHYA SHETTY is an Associate Professor of English at the University of New Hampshire, USA. Her research interests are in postcolonial studies, the British novel, and literature and medicine. She is completing a monograph on medicine, literature, and colonialism in South Asia. She has published on a variety of literary and theoretical subjects in journals such as *Contemporary Literature*, *Diacritics*, *differences*, the *Journal of Commonwealth Literature*, *Genders*, *LIT*, and the *Journal of Modern Literature*. Her essays have also appeared in edited collections. Her most recent publications include an essay on medicine and memory in Michael Ondaatje's *Anil's Ghost* (in *Biopolitics and Memory in Postcolonial Literature and Culture*). Her work on the making of Dr Anandibai Joshi, a high-caste Hindu lady doctor, in nineteenth-century America will appear in a forthcoming handbook of literature and medicine.

CHERYL STOBIE is an Associate Professor of English Studies at the University of KwaZulu–Natal, Pietermaritzburg campus. Her current research and teaching interests involve representations of gender, sexuality, race and nation in contemporary written and visual texts, mainly South/African. Some recent publications focus on African cinematic re-workings of the Carmen story, queer temporalities in film and fiction, and textual representations of Ubuntu. She combines an emphasis on cultural specificity with close textual analysis. She is a South African National Research Foundation-rated scholar, and is one of the editors of *Current Writing: Text and Reception in Southern Africa*.

HELEN TIFFIN is currently Adjunct Professor of English and Animal Studies at the University of Wollongong, Australia. She has published articles on post-colonial literatures and literary theory, and, with Gareth Griffiths and Bill Ashcroft, *The Empire Writes Back*, *Key Concepts in Post-Colonial Studies*, and *The Routledge Post-Colonial Studies Reader*. With Graham Huggan she is the co-author of *Postcolonial Ecocriticism: Animals, Environment and Postcolonial Literatures*. Her most recent publication is a joint work, with Robert Cribb and Helen Gilbert, on the cultural history of orangutans, *The Wild Man from Borneo*.

ALEX NELUNGO WANJALA is Senior Lecturer in the Department of Literature and the Sub-Department of French at the University of Nairobi. He earned his PhD in French Literatures and Civilizations from the Université Sorbonne-Nouvelle Paris 3 and also holds an MA (DEA) from the Université de Paris 13, Villetaneuse, and a BA from the University of Nairobi. His research interests include postcolonial theory, cultural studies, comparative literature, and African literature. Alex Wanjala is the editor for East Africa of the journal *Tydskrift vir*

*Letterkunde* and Chair of the East African branch of the Association for Commonwealth Literature and Language Studies (EAACLALS).

David Waterman is a Professeur des universités at the Université de La Rochelle, France, and a member of the research team CRHIA (Center for Research in International and Atlantic History) as well as Associate Director of the doctoral programme in the humanities. He is currently working on Pakistani history, culture, and literature in English and has served on the editorial team of *Pakistaniaat.* His most recent publication is *Where Worlds Collide: Pakistani Fiction in the New Millennium* (2015).

❄

# Index

www.ingramcontent.com/pod-product-compliance
Lightning Source LLC
LaVergne TN
LVHW021725021026
849161LV00004BA/688